Reading
Pop Culture

A Portable Anthology

JEFF OUSBORNE
Suffolk University

Bedford/St. Martin's   BOSTON ◆ NEW YORK

For Bedford/St. Martin's

Senior Executive Editor: Leasa Burton
Executive Editor: John E. Sullivan III
Production Editor: Annette Pagliaro Sweeney
Production Supervisor: Samuel Jones
Senior Marketing Manager: Molly Parke
Associate Editor: Alyssa Demirjian
Copy Editor: Hilly van Loon
Permissions Manager: Kalina K. Ingham
Senior Art Director: Anna Palchik
Text Design: Sandra Rigney and Janis Owens
Cover Design: Donna Lee Dennison
Cover Photo: Photograph by Ocean Photography. Courtesy of Veer, A Division of Corbis Corporation.
Composition: Jouve
Printing and Binding: RR Donnelley and Sons

President, Bedford/St. Martin's: Denise B. Wydra
Presidents, Macmillan Higher Education: Joan E. Feinberg and Tom Scotty
Editor in Chief: Karen S. Henry
Director of Marketing: Karen R. Soeltz
Production Director: Susan W. Brown
Associate Production Director: Elise S. Kaiser
Managing Editor: Elizabeth M. Schaaf

Library of Congress Control Number: 2012939212

Manufactured in the United States of America.

7 6 5 4 3
f e d c b

ISBN 978-1-4576-0602-1

Acknowledgments

Margaret Atwood. "Debtor's Prism." *Wall Street Journal*, September 20, 2008, p. W1. Reprinted by permission of the *Wall Street Journal*. Copyright © 2008, Dow Jones & Company, Inc. All rights reserved worldwide. License number 2761461149910.

Preface for Instructors

Those of us who have charted the changing nature of popular culture know that its increasing complexity makes it an excellent subject for the composition classroom. Pop culture artifacts are rhetorically and thematically rich, and so reward close analysis and sustained critical inquiry. Students, immersed in mass-mediated reality, are passionate about that immersion; yet, they often lack the ability to discern the contexts and implications of the popular culture that surrounds them.

Reading Pop Culture: A Portable Anthology taps into students' interest in pop culture while addressing their need for instruction in critical analysis. It uniquely combines currency, quality, brevity, and value in a collection of essays and images for first-year or themed writing courses. It presumes that learning to read effectively is crucial to learning to think and write critically. *Reading Pop Culture* is distinguished by its serious yet accessible investigation of key topics of popular culture and is intended to move students beyond enthusiasm, away from devotion, and toward reflection and deliberation, ultimately to critical distance and analysis, helping them write with skillful, focused creativity.

That can make for an engaging set of essays.

To sharpen those skills and foster student interest, *Reading Pop Culture* includes contemporary selections for students to analyze (such as Guillermo del Toro and Chuck Hogan's "Why Vampires Never Die" and Aymar Jean Christian's "The Problem of You-Tube") as well as several pieces that give students a framework from which to work—classics such as Roland Barthes's "Toys" and Susan Sontag's "The Imagination of Disaster." There are forty-three highly teachable essays covering a range of rhetorical styles, many never before published in a composition anthology. To foster a sense of inclusion and to represent the wide range of its subjects, *Reading Pop Culture* presents a variety of voices in terms of gender, sexuality, race, and culture, as well as in topics and time periods. The selections are of varied length and complexity, but all serve as sources of inspiration for students' own writing, providing excellent models of careful prose. More than thirty-five images throughout and a portfolio of ads in the advertising chapter provide additional rich material for analysis.

Reading Pop Culture is arranged in seven chapters, under themes that highlight the key areas of analysis for writing about pop culture: consumption, advertising, identity, technology, television, movies, and media dreams. Yet chapter themes range widely enough to hold student interest. Each chapter concludes with a set of paired readings for more focused connections.

Instructors who wish to teach the essays rhetorically can consult the supplemental table of contents found on pages xix–xxi. It identifies selections by their use of the modes: narration, description, exemplification, process, cause and effect, comparison and contrast, classification and division, definition, and argumentation.

Reading Pop Culture is not just a collection of great readings on timely topics; it is designed to encourage critical thinking and writing in the composition classroom. Unlike most popular culture readers, it presents a critical pedagogy. Strong writers are strong readers; these activities complement one another—reading helps students learn to write. Toward that end, *Reading Pop Culture* tasks students with careful reading and analysis, asking them to work by exploring, comparing, connecting, critiquing, and extending the ideas put forth in the selections.

This editorial apparatus allows instructors to shape the book to suit their needs. The general introduction provides advice for students on the key skills of active reading and writing, and includes an example of annotating and note taking. Headnotes for each selection provide a context that connects the reading selection to its writer and his or her place and time. Selective gloss notes augment this context for students by explaining unfamiliar cultural references. Several types of questions following the readings provide multiple avenues into the essays: questions that ask about the content of each selection allow students to develop habits of careful rereading; questions on the author's rhetorical strategy help students understand how to take context and audience into consideration when writing; questions that ask students to read one essay in light of another to facilitate connections among essays; and questions that encourage students to do research or to think about a selection in relation to their own experiences to connect the readings to issues in their lives and in the larger world.

YOU GET MORE DIGITAL CHOICES FOR *READING POP CULTURE*

Reading Pop Culture doesn't stop with a book. Online you'll find both free and affordable premium resources to help students get even more out of the book and your course. You'll also find convenient instructor resources, such as downloadable sample syllabi, classroom activities, and even a nationwide community of teachers. To learn more about or to order any of the products below, contact your Bedford/St. Martin's sales representative, e-mail sales support (sales_support@bfwpub.com), or visit the Web site at bedfordstmartins.com.

Student Resources

Send students to free and open resources, upgrade to an expanding collection of innovative digital content, or package a standalone CD-ROM for free with *Reading Pop Culture*.

Re:Writing, the best free collection of online resources for the writing class, offers clear advice on citing sources in *Research and Documentation Online* by Diana Hacker, 30 sample papers and designed documents, and over 9,000 writing and grammar exercises with immediate feedback and reporting in *Exercise Central*. Updated and redesigned, *Re:Writing* also features five free videos from *VideoCentral* and three new visual tutorials from our popular *ix visual exercises* by Cheryl Ball and Kristin Arola. *Re:Writing* is completely free and open (no codes required) to ensure access for all students. Visit bedfordstmartins.com/rewriting.

VideoCentral: English is a growing collection of videos for the writing class that captures real-world, academic, and student writers talking about how and why they write. Writer and teacher Peter Berkow interviewed hundreds of people—from Michael Moore to Cynthia Selfe—to produce 140 brief videos about topics such as revising and getting feedback. *VideoCentral* can be packaged with *Reading Pop Culture* at a significant discount. An activation code is required. To learn more, visit bedfordstmartins

.com/videocentral. To order *VideoCentral* packaged with the print book, use ISBN 978-1-4576-2975-4.

Re:Writing Plus gathers all of Bedford/St. Martin's premium digital content for composition into one online collection. It includes hundreds of model documents, the first-ever peer review game, and *VideoCentral*. *Re:Writing Plus* can be purchased separately or packaged with the print book at a significant discount. An activation code is required. To learn more, visit bedfordstmartins .com/rewriting. To order *Re:Writing Plus* packaged with the print book, use ISBN 978-1-4576-2974-7.

i-series on CD-ROM and online presents multimedia tutorials in a flexible format—because there are things you can't do in a book. To learn more, visit bedfordstmartins.com.

- *ix: visualizing composition* 2.0 (available online) introduces students to concepts that are fundamental to composing in any media. To order *ix: visualizing composition* packaged with the print book, use ISBN 978-1-4576-2973-0.
- *i-claim: visualizing argument* (available on CD-ROM) offers a new way to see argument—with 6 tutorials, an illustrated glossary, and over 70 multimedia arguments. To order *i-claim: visualizing argument* packaged with the print book, use ISBN 978-1-4576-2976-1.
- *i-cite: visualizing sources* (available online as part of *Re:Writing Plus*) brings research to life through an animated introduction, four tutorials, and hands-on source practice. To order *i-cite: visualizing sources* packaged with the print book, use ISBN 978-1-4576-2972-3.

Instructor Resources

You have a lot to do in your course. Bedford/St. Martin's wants to make it easy for you to find the support you need—and to get it quickly.

The ***Instructor's Manual for Reading Pop Culture*** is available in PDF format, which can be downloaded from bedfordstmartins .com/readingpopculture/catalog. In addition to chapter overviews and teaching tips, the *Instructor's Manual* includes sample syllabi and suggestions for classroom activities.

Teaching Central (bedfordstmartins.com/teachingcentral) offers the entire list of Bedford/St. Martin's print and online professional resources in one place. You'll find landmark reference works, sourcebooks on pedagogical issues, award-winning collections, and practical advice for the classroom—all free for instructors.

Bits (bedfordbits.com) collects creative ideas for teaching a range of composition topics in an easily searchable blog. A community of teachers—leading scholars, authors, and editors—discuss revision, research, grammar and style, technology, peer review, and much more. Take, use, adapt, and pass the ideas around. Then come back to the site to comment or share your own suggestions.

Free Bedford Coursepacks allow you to easily integrate our most popular content into your own course management systems. For details, visit bedfordstmartins.com/cms.

Acknowledgments

I am grateful for the suggestions from reviewers who provided feedback during the development of this project: Alex E. Blazer, Georgia College & State University; Jim Holte, East Carolina University; Thomas B. Pace, John Carroll University; Jennifer Richardson, SUNY Potsdam; Christopher Werry, San Diego State University; and Elise Ann Wormuth, San Francisco State University. I would also like to thank several reviewers who chose to remain anonymous.

I thank the people at Bedford/St. Martin's who made this book possible, particularly Joan Feinberg, Denise Wydra, Karen Henry, Leasa Burton, Steve Scipione, John Sullivan, Molly Parke, and Alyssa Demirjian. I am grateful for the help of Annette Pagliaro Sweeney, who guided the book through production; Hilly van Loon, for her careful copyediting; Donna Dennison, for the cover design; and Arthur Johnson and Susan Doheny, for obtaining permissions.

I am grateful to all of the writers included in this book for their vital, thoughtful, and provocative essays. I would like to thank my colleagues and students at Suffolk University, who teach me about teaching, writing, and so much else on a daily basis. Finally, I would like to thank my friends, my family, and, most of all, Kate, to whom this project is dedicated.

Contents

Preface for Instructors   iii

Rhetorical Table of Contents   xix

Introduction: Analyzing Popular Culture   1

     What Is Popular Culture?   1

     Thinking and Writing about Popular Culture   3

     Active, Mindful Reading   7

CHAPTER 1
Consumption   13

BENJAMIN BARBER, *Overselling Capitalism with Consumerism*   15

For a political theorist, the economic problems of the last several years illustrate the downside of consumerism: "The 'Protestant ethos' of hard work and deferred gratification has been replaced by an infantilist ethos of easy credit and impulsive consumption that puts democracy and the market system at risk."

SYLVIE KIM, *The End of Spam Shame: On Class, Colonialism, and Canned Meat*   19

A columnist writes of the cultural complexity surrounding Spam: "Both Asian Pacific Americans and Spam were the butt of a cruel joke: Please value what we deem subpar and make us money in the process. It's a terribly heavy load of symbolism to place on a pink block of meat."

ROLAND BARTHES, *Toys*   25

A semiotician shows how toys condition children to accept a ready-made and constructed world as natural and given. Toys "reveal the list of all the things the adult world does not find unusual: war, bureaucracy, ugliness . . ." and encourage children to identify as owners, not creators or inventors.

VIRGINIA POSTREL, *In Praise of Chain Stores*   30

Postrel refutes the conventional wisdom that chain stores make "everywhere look like everywhere else" in the United States: "Stores don't give places character. Terrain and weather and culture do."

MARGARET ATWOOD, *Debtor's Prism*   36

Atwood views our current preoccupation with debt (at both the personal and national level) as just the "latest chapter in a long cultural history" of an "ancient theme." In doing so, she writes about debt in terms of narrative, idea, metaphor, and even metaphysics.

PAIRED READINGS: Consuming Work   44

BARBARA EHRENREICH, *Selling in Minnesota*   44

Ehrenreich narrates her time working at a Wal-Mart, where the job pays low wages and degrades employees: "I have seen time move more swiftly during seven-hour airline delays."

ERIC SCHLOSSER, *Behind the Counter*   49

An investigative journalist examines the management and working conditions of people who prepare and serve food at a McDonald's. He also explores the fast-food industry as a whole: These businesses "employ about 3.7 million people worldwide, operate about 60,000 restaurants, and open a new fast-food restaurant every two hours."

CHAPTER 2
Advertising

CHAPTER 2
Advertising   60

WILLIAM LUTZ, *With These Words I Can Sell You Anything*   62

The former editor of the *Quarterly Review of Doublespeak* focuses on "weasel words" in dubious advertising: This language allows advertisers to appear to be making a claim for a product when "in fact they are making no claim at all."

DONNA WOOLFOLK CROSS, *Propaganda: How Not To Be Bamboozled*   71

A writer on language and media defines "propaganda" as a means of persuasion that can be used for "good or evil." It operates "by tricking us, by momentarily distracting the eye while the rabbit pops out from beneath the cloth."

JASON TANZ, *Selling Down: The Marketing of the Hip-Hop Nation*   87

"One of hip-hop's most powerful and elusive promises," writes the author of *Other People's Property: A Shadow History of Hip-Hop in White America*, "is that it will help us to come to terms with, understand, and maybe even participate in blackness. . . ." Yet marketers have "enlisted hip-hop to extend that promise to a mind-boggling array of products, reaching deep into the heart of mainstream America."

THE ECONOMIST, *The Ultimate Marketing Machine*   97

This essay examines the effects of the Internet on advertising. While consumers are "increasingly immune to the clichés" of advertising in older media, they may be more accepting of advertisements online.

PORTFOLIO OF ADVERTISEMENTS   107

Freerice.com   108
There Is No Easy Way In   109
Go Natural   110
You Can't Resist M and They Know It   111
Live Within Your Means. Dress Beyond Them.   112

PAIRED READINGS: Commercial Appeal   114

WINSTON FLETCHER, *Art or Puffery? A Defense of Advertising*   114

A former advertising executive surveys a range of arguments made about advertising and comes to a straightforward conclusion: "If consumers did not benefit from advertising, it would not work."

BILL BRYSON, *The Hard Sell: Advertising in America*   120

A versatile, best-selling author gives a historical perspective on the theory and practices of the modern advertising industry, especially as they pertain to the "identification and exploitation of the American consumer's Achilles' heel: anxiety."

CHAPTER 3
Identity   136

RAQUEL CEPEDA, *The N-Word Is Flourishing Among
Generation Hip-Hop Latinos: Why Should We
Care Now?*   138

A journalist, activist, and filmmaker looks at the use of the "n-word"
among young urban Latinos, whose vocabulary is "reaching an
almost caricaturist quality." The word has "found its way back into
hip-hop's critical zeitgeist: I'm interested in exploring, as a Dominican
New Yorker, how we as a community have propagated it."

HUA HSU, *The End of White America?*   144

A historian investigates the erosion of "whiteness"—demographically,
culturally—as a fundamental aspect of American identity: "At the
moment, we can call this the triumph of multiculturalism, or postracialism. But just as whiteness has no inherent meaning—it is a
vessel we fill with our hopes and anxieties—these terms may prove
equally empty in the long run."

ARIEL LEVY, *Women and the Rise of Raunch Culture*   158

In this excerpt from her book *Female Chauvinist Pigs: Women and
the Rise of Raunch Culture*, Ariel Levy considers the way "postfeminist" women participate in a "tawdry, tarty, cartoonlike version of
female sexuality." Yet, she notes, "'Raunchy' and 'liberated' are not
synonymous."

PAUL KIX, *Hip-Hop Is No Longer Cooler Than Me*   162

Recalling the intoxicating effect and cultural significance of early
hip-hop, Paul Kix illustrates how the music and culture have lost their
way: "A genre whirled out of the grist of urban pain and worn as a
low-slung hat and baggy jeans has somehow slipped on clown shoes
and taken up night classes in pantomime. Its dances are silly, its beats
infantile, its rhymes lazy. I am sorry to report this, but hip-hop is no
longer cooler than me."

PAIRED READINGS: Sporting Culture   168

ROB RUCK, *Where Have African-American Baseball
Players Gone?*   168

Ruck, a writer, filmmaker, and historian, begins his essay with a
remarkable fact: "More African-Americans were elected to Congress

as Republicans last November than appeared in the World Series." He
then charts the "staggering" decline of African Americans in baseball,
a trend significant enough to counter its "image as a democratic and
inclusive sport."

MALCOLM GLADWELL, *The Sports Taboo*   174

A best-selling author reflects on the connections between athletic
ability and racial identity: "Talking openly about the racial dimension
of sports in this way, of course, is considered unseemly. . . . What
you're not supposed to say is what we were saying in my track
days—that we were better because we were black, because of
something intrinsic to being black."

CHAPTER 4
Technology   186

NIKIL SAVAL, *Wall of Sound: The iPod Has Changed the Way
We Listen to Music*   188

Saval writes that the iPod "promises emancipation from questions of
taste. Differences in what people listen to, in a Shuffled world, may
have less and less to do with social class and purchasing power."

NEIL POSTMAN, *The Judgment of Thamus*   200

Using a story from Plato's *Phaedrus*, Postman, a media theorist and
educator, provides a revealing fable about progress and how we
should approach technology: "Every technology is both a burden and
a blessing; not either-or, but this-and-that."

AYMAR JEAN CHRISTIAN, *The Problem of YouTube*   216

YouTube has dominated Web video for the last five years; indeed, the
site is practically synonymous with Web video. Yet, says a communications scholar, "I've heard this time and again: YouTube puts the
focus on 'views,' not on building quality audiences for inventive and
'quality' forms of storytelling."

FARHAD MANJOO, *Is Facebook a Fad?*   222

A technology columnist for *Slate* says it is not: "Let me go out on a
limb and declare that Facebook isn't going to go away anytime
soon. . . . It's easy to go to a new search engine—just type *Bing*
instead of *Google*—and there's nothing stopping you from switching
your brand of computer or cellphone. You can't switch over to a new
social network, though, unless your friends do so as well."

PAIRED READINGS: Transformed by Technology   227

SHERRY TURKLE, *Can You Hear Me Now?*   227

For social science and technology professor Turkle, "we live a
contradiction: Insisting that our world is increasingly complex, we
nevertheless have created a communications culture that has
decreased the time available for us to sit and think, uninterrupted."
These changes affect not only our society and relationships, but the
very nature of the self.

CLAY SHIRKY, *Gin, Television, and Social Surplus*   236

New media thinker Shirky argues that our collective Internet
activities are evidence of a social and "cognitive surplus." He sees this
as a positive development, ultimately: "It's precisely when no one has
any idea how to deploy something that people have to start experimenting with it, in order for the surplus to get integrated, and the
course of that integration can transform society."

CHAPTER 5
Television   243

ROBERT KUBEY AND MIHALY CSIKSZENTMIHALYI, *Television
Addiction Is No Mere Metaphor*   245

Using biological and sociological evidence, the authors argue that
"the term 'TV addiction' is imprecise and laden with value judgments,
but it captures the essence of a very real phenomenon."

MARIE WINN, *Television: The Plug-In Drug*   256

Winn writes, "Television is not merely one of a number of important
influences upon today's child. Through the changes it has made in
family life, television emerges as *the* important influence in children's
lives today."

ERICA LIES, *Mary Tyler More*   266

Lies, an arts writer, places the sitcom *30 Rock* in the tradition of other
workplace comedies about smart, single women. According to Lies,
such shows have "played on the gender anxieties of its decade."

STEVEN JOHNSON, *Watching TV Makes You Smarter*   275

According to conventional wisdom, mass culture—television, video
games, and other forms of entertainment—steadily declines toward

low standards and the dumb, debased pleasures of the "masses."
Johnson disagrees: "The most debased forms of mass diversion . . .
turn out to be nutritional after all."

PAIRED READINGS: Watching Ourselves   289

GEORGE F. WILL, *Reality Television: Oxymoron*   289

A Pulitzer Prize–winning commentator sees reality television as
"televised degradation." For him, the popularity of such programs
highlights our unhealthy exhibitionism and our "increasingly
infantilized society."

MARK GREIF, *The Reality of Reality Television*   293

A cofounder of *n+1* offers a nuanced analysis of reality television's
appeal: "the cheapest and rawest reality TV offers you a chance to
judge people like you. . . . It is cheap, it is amoral, it has no veneer of
virtue, it is widely censured and a guilty pleasure, and it can be more
educational and truthful and American than most anything else, very
suitable for our great republic."

CHAPTER 6
Movies

CHAPTER 6
Movies   308

RITA KEMPLEY, *Mystical Black Characters Play Complex
Cinematic Role*   310

Kempley examines the archetype of the "magic negro," a stock figure
in American film dating back to the 1940s and 1950s: "It isn't that the
actors or the roles aren't likable, valuable or redemptive, but they are
without interior lives. For the most part, they materialize only to
rescue the better-drawn white characters."

SUSAN SONTAG, *The Imagination of Disaster*   316

Prominent critic Susan Sontag unpacks the components of science
fiction and disaster films, revealing the common devices that give
such movies their shape and their place in a long tradition: "A typical
science fiction film has a form as predictable as a Western, and is
made up of elements which are as classic as the saloon brawl, the
blonde schoolteacher from the East, and the gun duel on the deserted
main street."

LINDA SEGER, *Creating the Myth*   334

A Hollywood script consultant shows that a myth is the primal "story
beneath the story": "It's the universal pattern that shows us that
Gandhi's journey toward independence and Sir Edmund Hillary's
journey to the top of Mount Everest contain many of the same
dramatic beats. And these beats are the same beats . . . that Luke
Skywalker takes to defeat the Evil Empire."

ALONSO DURALDE, *Why Are So Many Films for Latinos Bad?*   346

With the Latino population in the United States growing as both an
economic and cultural force, a film critic ponders Hollywood's
tendency to make "dreadful movies for Latino audiences."

PAIRED READINGS: Tycoons and Working Stiffs   352

RICK GROEN, *Why Hollywood Hates Capitalism*   352

Groen, a film critic for the *Globe and Mail*, investigates a rich irony in
the American film industry: "Hollywood is a big business that, on the
screen at least, loathes and despises big business."

ROBERT NATHAN AND JO-ANN MORT, *Remembering*
Norma Rae   357

The authors reflect on 1979's *Norma Rae*, a politically charged movie
about organized labor. In the years since, Hollywood has distanced
itself from it—and from all movies about "working people fighting to
better their lives."

CHAPTER 7
Media Dreams   364

FRANK ROSE, *The Art of Immersion: Fear of Fiction*   366

From the printed novel to the motion picture to the Internet,
journalist Rose writes that every new technological medium has
"increased the transporting power of narrative" and has "aroused fear
and even hostility as a result."

GERARD JONES, *Violent Media Is Good for Kids*   372

A comic book author argues that allowing children to participate in
"creative violence" helps them overcome obstacles: "Through
immersion in imaginary combat and identification with a violent

protagonist, children engage the rage they've stifled, come to fear it less, and become more capable of utilizing it against life's challenges."

GUILLERMO DEL TORO AND CHUCK HOGAN, *Why Vampires Never Die*   378

In this essay, a filmmaker and a novelist trace the origins and the enduring appeal of the vampire and highlight how its popular constructions and reinventions reflect our cultural anxieties and preoccupations. "The current vampire pandemic serves to remind us that we have no true jurisdiction over our bodies, our climate or our very souls."

CHUCK KLOSTERMAN, *My Zombie, Myself: Why Modern Life Feels Rather Undead*   384

Zombies, says Klosterman, do not represent unconscious fears the way other monsters do. Rather, they provide an allegory for the contemporary world: "Zombies are like the Internet and the media and every conversation we don't want to have. All of it comes at us endlessly (and thoughtlessly), and—if we surrender—we will be overtaken and absorbed."

PAIRED READINGS: Avatars and Aesthetes   390

LANE WALLACE, *Can Video Games Teach Us How to Succeed in the Real World?*   390

Given the popularity and appeal of video games, some are trying to replicate the "attention, energy, focus, and potential addiction that video games inspire" for real-life activities. Yet Wallace is skeptical: "But there's still a difference between virtual reality and reality itself, and limits to how far the game analogy goes. . . . No virtual reward is as sweet as those that come from real experience, real risk, and real achievement."

KYLE CHAYKA, *Why Video Games Are Works of Art*   396

Chayka responds to film critic Roger Ebert, who claims that "video games can never be art." For Chayka, these games are not merely art, but a powerful fusion of image and music, poetry, and story.

Index of Authors and Titles   407

Rhetorical Contents

NARRATION

MARGARET ATWOOD, *Debtor's Prism*   36

BARBARA EHRENREICH, *Selling in Minnesota*   44

MALCOLM GLADWELL, *The Sports Taboo*   174

DESCRIPTION

ROLAND BARTHES, *Toys*   25

MARK GREIF, *The Reality of Reality Television*   293

SYLVIE KIM, *The End of Spam Shame: On Class,
Colonialism, and Canned Meat*   19

LANE WALLACE, *Can Video Games Teach Us How to Succeed
in the Real World?*   390

EXEMPLIFICATION

BILL BRYSON, *The Hard Sell: Advertising in America*   120

ALONSO DURALDE, *Why Are So Many Films for Latinos Bad?*   346

RICK GROEN, *Why Hollywood Hates Capitalism*   352

RITA KEMPLEY, *Mystical Black Characters Play Complex
Cinematic Role*   310

ERICA LIES, *Mary Tyler More*   266

PROCESS

BENJAMIN BARBER, *Overselling Capitalism with Consumerism*   15

THE ECONOMIST, *The Ultimate Marketing Machine*   97

ROBERT KUBEY AND MILHALY CSIKSZENTMIHALYI, *Television Addiction Is No Mere Metaphor*   245

ERIC SCHLOSSER, *Behind the Counter*   49

DONNA WOOLFOLK CROSS, *Propaganda: How Not To Be Bamboozled*   71

CAUSE AND EFFECT

HUA HSU, *The End of White America*   144

GERARD JONES, *Violent Media Is Good for Kids*   372

VIRGINIA POSTREL, *In Praise of Anywhere, USA*   30

ROB RUCK, *Where Have African-American Baseball Players Gone?*   168

JASON TANZ, *Selling Down: The Marketing of the Hip-Hop Nation*   87

SHERRY TURKLE, *Can You Hear Me Now?*   227

COMPARISON AND CONTRAST

AYMAR JEAN CHRISTIAN, *The Problem of YouTube*   216

MALCOLM GLADWELL, *The Sports Taboo*   174

STEVEN JOHNSON, *Watching TV Makes You Smarter*   275

PAUL KIX, *Hip-Hop Is No Longer Cooler Than Me*   162

CHUCK KLOSTERMAN, *My Zombie, Myself: Why Modern Life Feels Rather Undead*   384

NIKIL SAVAL, *Wall of Sound: The iPod Has Changed the Way We Listen to Music*   188

CLASSIFICATION AND DIVISION

GUILLERMO DEL TORO AND CHUCK HOGAN, *Why Vampires Never Die*   378

WILLIAM LUTZ, *With These Words I Can Sell You Anything*   62

LINDA SEGER, *Creating the Myth*   334

SUSAN SONTAG, *The Imagination of Disaster*   316

DEFINITION

RAQUEL CEPEDA, *The N-Word Is Flourishing Among Generation Hip-Hop Latinos*   138

KYLE CHAYKA, *Why Video Games Are Works of Art*   396

ARIEL LEVY, *Women and the Rise of Raunch Culture*   158

CLAY SHIRKY, *Gin, Television, and Social Surplus*   236

ARGUMENTATION

WINSTON FLETCHER, *Art or Puffery? A Defense of Advertising*   114

FARHAD MANJOO, *Is Facebook a Fad?*   222

NEIL POSTMAN, *The Judgment of Thamus*   200

GEORGE F. WILL, *Reality Television: Oxymoron*   289

MARIE WINN, *Television: The Plug-In Drug*   256

Introduction:
Analyzing Popular Culture

"This is our collective fear projection: that we will be consumed. Zombies are like the Internet and the media and every conversation we don't want to have. All of it comes at us endlessly (and thoughtlessly), and—if we surrender—we will be overtaken and absorbed."
—Chuck Klosterman, "My Zombie, Myself" (p. 384)

WHAT IS POPULAR CULTURE?

When we consider specific examples, we see popular culture everywhere. *Twilight* books and movies. Beyoncé. Facebook. *The Family Guy*. Chicken McNuggets. "The Wonderful World of Disney." Abercrombie and Fitch advertisements. Cats playing the piano on YouTube. Reality television shows. When we generalize about pop culture's relationship to "culture," however, we run into complications—especially in an academic context. In part, they result from the connotations of the word *culture*, which long ago calcified around Victorian critic Matthew Arnold's phrase "the best that has been thought and said." That means high culture with a capital "C": a legacy of art, music, and literature, with names like Michelangelo, Bach, and Shakespeare. Dressing up to hear the symphony (*Be quiet!*) or visit an art museum (*Don't touch!*)? Culture. Dressing up as Hermione Granger to see a Harry Potter movie? Pop culture.

We can also make a distinction within pop culture: the difference between *folk* culture and *mass* culture. Folk culture emerges from a particular place, community, or group: Appalachian folk music, Amish quilts, Southern cooking, the sea chanteys of working sailors, even the graffiti of street artists. Folk culture embodies

1

the *particular*. In contrast, mass culture products such as commercial television, retail chain stores, and fast-food restaurants are usually fashioned and distributed by corporations. Mass culture embodies the *standardized*: A McDonald's French fry is the same in Portland, Oregon, as it is in Portland, Maine. And that's the point of McDonald's food. The essays in this book address the mass culture that buzzes, pulses, and sizzles around us constantly; all the writers included here assume that it is worthy of consideration and analysis.

We should not take that assumption for granted. For much of the last century or so, critics and scholars put a higher value on both high culture *and* folk culture than on mass culture. Timeless, universal, leather-bound, museum-curated capital "C" culture ennobled and enriched us. To these critics and scholars, great books, art, and music were intrinsically valuable—the flowers of civilization. Likewise, genuine folk culture expressed worthy values like authenticity, spontaneity, and democracy. American critic Dwight MacDonald—an unrepentant highbrow snob—identified these virtues in his influential 1953 essay, "A Theory of Mass Culture." Folk culture "grew up from below" as a "spontaneous expression of the people, shaped by themselves . . . to suit their needs." He sharpened his point by contrasting endearing, democratic folk culture with its ugly, authoritarian twin, mass culture. The latter was "imposed from above . . . fabricated by technicians hired by businessmen." For MacDonald and many others, mass culture—say a film like *The Sound of Music*—was a con job imposed on passive consumers, a deceptive shell game that reduced all participation to the "choice between buying and not buying." According to this view, culture invariably becomes shoddy, formulaic, and manipulative when it is subjected to the economic marketplace. We can still find critics denouncing popular culture in similar terms today, as George F. Will does in "Reality Television: Oxymoron" (p. 289).

Yet stable categories like "high" and "low" culture tend to dissolve under historical scrutiny, as essays here demonstrate. In "The Art of Immersion: Fear of Fiction" (p. 366), Frank Rose shows that "classic" early novels were once popular entertainments, cultural products disparaged for their corrupting influence, much like video games are today. Popular culture has a way of transcending its low origins. After all, Shakespeare did not write his plays for the pleasure of English teachers or graduate students. He was a businessman as well as a dramatist and poet, a savvy entrepreneur whose plays pleased a popular audience with their trashy puns and sensational violence. The nineteenth-century English novelist Charles Dickens dominated the Victorian literary marketplace with mass-produced and serialized fictions; his novels were the equivalent of our cable television series or blockbuster movies. Now we study them as leather-bound "classics," culture with a capital "C." To take more recent American examples: In the early and mid-twentieth century, many culture critics disparaged popular jazz or ignored it altogether. But from our vantage point, jazz long ago put on a good suit and ascended to the concert hall, becoming culture with a capital "C." That process seems endless, as rap lyrics now appear regularly in academically sanctioned literary anthologies and hip-hop increasingly becomes a field for academic study.

If the border between "high" and "low" culture is often porous, so is the boundary separating mass culture and folk culture. Consider Bill Monroe, the father of American bluegrass music, a genre beloved for its roots in rural authenticity. Yet Monroe sold millions of records by pioneering a hybrid, fabricated musical style that was—almost from its conception—a mass media phenomenon. So where do we draw the line? Is local or regional folk culture inherently superior to standardized mass culture? When does folk culture become mass culture? Does it lose its value in the process? Several of the selections in this book explore these dichotomies, from Virginia Postrel's essay on the proliferation of retail chain stores to Jason Tanz's examination of hip-hop's place in contemporary marketing and advertising.

THINKING AND WRITING ABOUT POPULAR CULTURE

When we reflect on the value of writing about popular culture, we might heed words of poet and critic T. S. Eliot, the personification of elite cultural values and infamously "difficult" poetry: "It is just the literature that we read for amusement, or purely for pleasure, that may have the greatest and least suspected influence on us. . . . Hence, it is that the influence of popular novelists, and of popular playwrights of contemporary life, requires to be scrutinized most closely."[1] His point is still applicable: Mass-produced amusements and products suffuse our lives. Consequently, we should give them as much attention as we devote to the lofty artifacts of "high" culture. Literary history includes a long tradition of engagement with popular entertainment and consumer culture. In *The Tatler* and *Spectator*, eighteenth-century magazines long considered models of English criticism, Joseph Addison and Richard Steele wrote about commerce, fashion, and entertainment, as well as poetry and philosophy. Even Samuel Johnson, a writer central to the canon of English literature, turned his keen gaze to the proliferation of print advertising in his time (the 1700s), as well as to the tendency of readers to filter out these ads—over two centuries prior to TiVo: "Advertisements are now so numerous that they are very negligently perused, and it is therefore become necessary to gain attention by magnificent promises, and by eloquence sometimes sublime and sometimes pathetic."

But the academic study of popular culture grew from many disparate developments in twentieth-century scholarship and criticism—literary, sociological, linguistic, anthropological, political, and economic. In the 1920s and 1930s, American figures such as Vernon Parrington and F. O. Matthiesson developed the academic discipline now known as "American Studies," a field with a more holistic and inclusive notion of culture than the traditional study of literature. Influential German critics from the Frankfurt School argued that consumption deserved close scrutiny. Walter Benjamin's *Arcades Project*, for example, used shopping as the focus for a study of Paris. Many of these critics also thought mass culture deserved derision as an oppressive instrument of state and corporate capitalism. In their seminal essay, "The Culture Industry: Enlightenment as Mass Deception" (1944), Frankfurt School figures Theodor Adorno and Max Horkheimer dissected their subject with instruments from the Marxist tool kit: "The deception is not that the culture industry supplies amusement, but that it ruins the fun by allowing business considerations to involve it in the ideological clichés of a culture in the

---

[1]Indeed, Eliot's notoriously dense and allusive poem "The Waste Land" incorporates popular culture references into its matrix of allusions. It's also revealing that many years after Eliot's death, his book of verse *The Old Possum's Book of Practical Cats* became the basis for the musical *Cats*.

process of self-liquidation." When Adorno and Horkheimer looked behind pop culture phenomena like jazz, shiny cars, and the smiling face of Mickey Rooney on a movie screen, they saw the grim specter of fascism.

In the 1950s and 1960s, British cultural studies pioneers like Raymond Williams and Richard Hoggart expanded the scope of literary study from its focus on a select canon of masterpieces. For these critics, "culture" encompassed commerce, labor, technology, sports, leisure activities, and the practices of everyday life. So Hoggart's *The Uses of Literacy: Aspects of Working-Class Life* (1957), for example, investigated how emerging mass culture—movies, popular literature, magazines—destroyed and replaced traditional, local, and communal forms of popular culture. In their roles as professors, these critics moved away from training students to be comfortable connoisseurs and custodians of great art and literature. Instead, their pedagogy focused on the processes of culture itself, as well as on a political goal: radical social change.

The middle of the twentieth century saw many "serious" scholars and writers turning their attention to popular culture. Canadian literary critic and media theorist Marshall McLuhan analyzed advertisements in *The Mechanical Bride: Folklore of Industrial Man* (1951), teasing out their symbolism and revealing their cultural implications. For McLuhan, advertising was the "greatest art form of the twentieth century." French semiologist Roland Barthes deployed techniques from anthropology and linguistics to unravel the significance of popular amusements such as Marlon Brando movies, professional wrestling, and striptease shows in his *Mythologies* (1957). As McLuhan did, Barthes brought a sense of pleasure to his encounters with the "culture industry," even as he exposed the dishonesty of its claims. On the pages of American literary journals and general interest magazines of the 1960s, figures such as Susan Sontag and Tom Wolfe brought startling insight and sharp writing to subjects like "camp" culture, custom cars, and the city of Las Vegas.

Still, while fields like cultural studies became legitimate academic disciplines, many scholars remained skeptical of *popular* culture studies. When Ray Browne, an English professor at Bowling Green State University, founded the Center for Popular Culture Studies over forty years ago, many of his colleagues thought he was wasting time and (as he recalled) "disgracing the university in the eyes of the public and academics." Browne did not approach mass culture with the reflexive contempt displayed by so many earlier academic critics. He was intellectually engaged, but he also brought a sense of openness and idealism to the project: "Popular culture democratizes society and makes democracy truly democratic. It is the everyday world around us: the mass media, entertainments, and diversions. It is our heroes, icons, rituals, everyday actions, psychology, and religion—our total life picture. It is the way of living we inherit, practice, and modify as we please, and how we do it. It is the dreams we dream while asleep." These essays, and the spirit behind this book, share that expansive view, which is broad enough to include meditations on consumer debt, hip-hop, Spam, low-wage work, text-messaging, video games, and disaster movies.

But that broad perspective affects the style as well as the substance of many selections chosen here. Some earlier critics of mass culture wrote about it as condescending outsiders worried about getting their hands dirty. Adorno and Horkheimer had little interest in—or feel for—the formal qualities and pleasures of popular entertainment, for example, even as their ideas remain prescient (see Nikil Saval's "Wall of Sound" [p. 188] which is grounded in the work of Adorno). Several essays in this book, like William Lutz's classic "With These Words I Can Sell You Anything" (p. 62) are essentially how-to pieces for resisting the manipulations of mass culture. Even when encouraging resistance, however, almost all these authors bring a fluency and familiarity with their subjects: They write as insiders. For all its intellectual dexterity and critical detachment, Susan Sontag's "The Imagination of Disaster" (p. 316) suggests a genuine intimacy with popular science fiction films. Bill Bryson's "The Hard Sell: Advertising in America" (p. 120) encourages critical thinking about the advertising industry; yet, the essay is also a supple and closely argued formal analysis of advertisements by someone deeply familiar with Madison Avenue craft.

Writing about popular culture should be compatible with writing about "serious" academic subjects like literature or philosophy, not antagonistic or competitive. That is especially true in the context of composition classes. As writers like Roland Barthes and Rita Kempley illustrate, the critical skills that deconstruct children's playthings or identify clichéd tropes in contemporary films can be applied to poetry, literary theory, history, or any other discipline that requires critical thinking and writing. The habits and procedures are transferrable: reading closely, recognizing patterns, questioning assumptions, apprehending analogies, citing examples, making logical inferences and establishing connections. The selections in this book are excellent prompts for such intellectual investigation. In its own way, each essay functions as an important reminder: *Keep your brain turned on when you leave class and turn on your television set.* As Stephen Johnson writes in "Watching TV Makes You Smarter" (p. 275), "not having to think is boring." And this book accepts Johnson's premise that popular culture has become more sophisticated and more cognitively demanding over the last fifty years, not less so.

Furthermore we do not have to choose between high and low: between the work of Jean Jacques Rousseau and the TV show *Survivor* (Mark Greif analyzes both in "The Reality of Reality Television" [p. 293]); between reflecting on Bram Stoker's *Dracula* and considering the contemporary significance of the *Twilight* series (see Guillermo del Toro and Chuck Hogan's "Why Vampires Never Die" [p. 378]). The writers in this book also avoid glib, ahistorical views of culture and recognize important distinctions. The point is not that *Dracula* and *Twilight* are the same, or that there are no aesthetic differences between the works of Shakespeare and the works of George Lucas. Rather, the point is that the same skills used to discover mythic structures in *Star Wars* or to contextualize *30 Rock* can be turned to literature, sociology, or other disciplines.

But perhaps the epigraph at the start of this introduction provides the best reason to study popular culture: to avoid being overtaken, absorbed, and assimilated by zombies. Yet our zombification has less to do with the quality of popular culture and more to do with our reaction to the "Internet and the media and every conversation we don't want to have." Ultimately, mass culture is only mindless if we approach it mindlessly.

ACTIVE, MINDFUL READING

While much of our mass culture encourages passive consumption, good writing about mass culture should not. If we want to approach these essays and leave them as better writers, we need to read them thoughtfully and critically. That requires intellectual work, not forced labor. While selections in this book glow with memorable information, curious ideas, and lovely language, you should not be reading them to memorize data or acquire facts. You should be reading them actively. When you read actively, you respond to writing on every level—from the sound of the prose to the soundness of the logic, from the writer's underlying assumptions to the argument's place in a wider cultural context. Then you turn those responses into analysis and ideas of your own. So think of reading these essays as more like being part of a conversation, and less like listening to a series of lectures to pass an exam. This book can provide material for quizzes and tests, but they will be secondary to more important goals: becoming active readers and better writers.

Of course, the writers included here provide models of active reading as well as good writing. The two practices are inseparable. Consider Bill Bryson who, in his analysis of print advertising, discovers that product names "cluster around certain sounds," which often reveal a product's era (par. 20). Or observe as Steven Johnson takes a brief swatch of dialogue from the show *E.R.* and then uses it to illustrate "texture," "substance," and the architecture of television storytelling. Bryson and Johnson's sharp writing began with active and perceptive *reading*. In other words, they paid attention. Good writers notice things—and you can become a better "noticer" by slowing down when you read. That is not always easy, especially in a culture that values speed and immediacy. But to improve as a writer, you must give yourself time and space for active, reflective, deliberative, even playful reading. Here are some suggestions.

Read carefully and try to grasp the writer's thesis and main points, which will mean *re*reading.   That advice sounds obvious, but we sometimes approach texts hampered by our preconceptions and clichéd ideas. Then, we read selectively and use this cognitive shorthand to plaster over gaps in our comprehension. If the following essays were mere vessels for conventional wisdom or platitudes, they would be worthless in a composition class—or any other class. Likewise, when we impose bland clichés on writers or filter their arguments through our own unexamined assumptions about what we think teachers want to hear, we block the grace of good writing. For example, if we have some vague sense that racial diversity is "good," and then read Hua Hsu's "The End of White America" assuming he agrees and wants to provide us with evidence for what we already know, we miss most of what makes his essay provocative and powerful. If we approach Clay Shirky's "Gin, Television, and Social Surplus" (p. 236) assuming everyone already agrees that messing around on the Internet is a waste of time and that no professor would assign an essay that argued otherwise, we will probably miss Shirky's main point. So make sure to read the words that the author wrote and not what you *think* he or she wrote, or what you think your instructor wants you to say. You may find some familiar subjects and arguments in these essays, but you will also find provocations, challenges, and surprises. To that end, note what's confusing or unclear. It may turn out to be the most important part of the reading.

Talk back to the text.   Annotate, underline, make notes in the margins or elsewhere, and look up unfamiliar words. In his book *Here at The New Yorker*, the writer Brendan Gill recalls lending a copy of the novel *Moby Dick* to his cranky Uncle Arthur, who asked permission to annotate the book: "His weapon was a little stub of yellow pencil, with which he would indicate his disapproval of the contents of a book, writing in the margins, 'Bah!,' 'Nonsense!,' and the like. He never got through *Moby Dick*, but how savagely he fought with Melville throughout the first fifty or a hundred pages." Uncle Arthur was an active reader. So were Mark Twain, Susan Sontag, and David Foster Wallace—fine writers, all known for their sparkling marginal comments. Your responses should go beyond "Bah!" and "Nonsense!" of course, but gut reactions can provide openings for criticism, analysis, and counterarguments. Start with what you *notice*: what you like, what you do not like, where you agree with the writer and where you disagree—or even where the writer confuses you. Then figure out *why*. This habit will help you immeasurably with writing assignments. Your annotations, quibbles, and comments can form the basis for your own thesis questions, arguments, ideas, examples, counterexamples, and pathways for further research. Look for connections and tensions *between* these essays, as well. Record your responses and questions, and you will already have taken the key step in creating and shaping material for your own work. Think quality, not quantity: Highlighting every topic sentence in an essay is less useful than finding—and annotating—the passages that capture the essence of the writer's thesis, suggest the argument's widest implications, or even show the essay's *least convincing* logical leaps and blind spots.

Pay attention to form and structure. That is: Try to figure out *how* a piece of writing means, as well as *what* a piece of writing means. How do the essays begin? With a paradox, like Rick Groen's "Why Hollywood Hates Capitalism" (p. 352)? A curious fact, like Rob Ruck's "Where Have African-American Baseball Players Gone" (p. 168)? A quotation, like George Will's "Reality Television: Oxymoron" (p. 289)? How do different essays unfold and develop in different patterns? Some of these writers make their arguments in a linear way, moving directly from point to point; others set up oppositions and contrasts; still others use analogies. Many deploy all these techniques, and more. Look for the connective tissue between general assertions and specific examples. In the novel *A Prayer for Owen Meany*, the author John Irving writes, "Any good book is always in motion—from the general to the specific, from the particular to the whole, and back again. Good reading—and good writing about reading—moves in the same way." Notice how writers manage that motion and achieve that balance throughout their work. Consider the way essays end. For example, how do these writers avoid stock conclusions that begin, "All in all . . ." or "In sum . . ."? How do they avoid just reiterating their arguments and, instead, leave readers with an evocative thought or a clever turn—like a toy surprise in a cereal box?

Pay attention to style. Which voices hover off the page and stay with you—and why? All the authors here are competent, correct, and clear, but some of them are distinctive stylists, whose prose is as identifiable as their thumbprints. They compose with their ears tuned to sound, rhythm, and tone; such writers go beyond choosing language adequate for communication and instead choose the *best* words and phrases, which not only make their point, but shimmer on the page. Allow yourself to be influenced by your preferences. Which essayists here would you want to sound like, and why? T. S. Eliot once claimed that "immature poets imitate; mature poets steal; bad poets deface what they take, and good poets make it into something better." This is not a wholesale endorsement of theft or plagiarism, of course. Rather, Eliot's overstatement reminds us that good writing comes from absorbing *other good writing*, and from our attempts to take what we learn from the writers we admire and make it our own. So find writers that you like and then figure out what you like about them—the ways they manage introductions, incorporate evidence, choose examples, shape paragraphs, sustain a tone, achieve sentence variety, push readers beyond the obvious. Notice how they solve these and other writing problems because their problems are the same as yours, ultimately.

In order to show what active reading looks like, let's take a look at one student's annotation of paragraphs 19–20 from Hua Hsu's "The End of White America." (The full essay is on page 144.)

What does "mainstream" mean, exactly?

In this regard, Combs is both a product and a hero of the new cultural mainstream, which prizes diversity above all else, and whose ultimate goal is some vague notion of racial transcendence, rather than subversion or assimilation.

Is this a negative statement — "vague" notion?

Fame and money undercuts "street" authenticity?

Although Combs's vision is far from representative—not many hip-hop stars vacation in St. Tropez with a parasol-toting manservant shading their every step—his industry lies at the heart of this new mainstream. Over the past 30 years, few changes in American culture have been as significant as the rise of hip-hop. The genre has radically reshaped the way we listen to and consume music, first by opposing the pop mainstream and then by becoming it.

True? What about the Internet?

Why "antihero" and not just "hero"?

From its constant sampling of past styles and eras—old records, fashions, slang, anything—to its mythologization of the self-made black antihero, hip-hop is more than a musical genre: it's a philosophy, a political statement, a way of approaching and remaking culture. It's a lingua franca not just among kids in America, but also among young people worldwide. And its economic impact extends beyond the music industry, to fashion, advertising, and film. (Consider the producer Russell Simmons—the ur-Combs and a music, fashion, and television mogul—or the rapper 50 Cent, who has parlayed his rags-to-riches story line into extracurricular successes that include a clothing line; book, video-game, and film deals; and a startlingly lucrative partnership with the makers of Vitamin Water.)

Lingua franca?

"Rags to riches" — other hip-hop figures?

Symbolic of what?

"Suffered through" — negative.

Compare with Tanz and Kix essays: Is hip-hop still on its "own terms"?

But hip-hop's deepest impact is symbolic. <u>During popular music's rise in the 20th century, white artists and producers consistently "mainstreamed" African American innovations.</u> Hip-hop's ascension has been different. <u>Eminem notwithstanding, hip-hop never suffered through anything like an Elvis Presley moment, in which a white artist made a musical form safe for white America.</u> This is no dig at Elvis—the constrictive racial logic of the 1950s demanded the erasure of rock and roll's black roots, and if it hadn't been him, it would have been someone else. <u>But hip-hop—the sound of the post-civil-rights, post-soul generation—found a global audience on its own terms.</u>

With jazz, too.

"Constrictive racial logic" of an era. This essay is about today's "racial logic."

Notice how the student has underlined and highlighted important terms (such as "antihero") or ones he doesn't understand (such as "lingua franca"). These markings, particularly the marginal annotations, are an excellent way of preparing for class discussion. They are also extremely useful for beginning the process of responding to a piece of writing with an essay of your own.

CHAPTER 1

Consumption

"Capitalism's core virtue is that it marries altruism and self-interest," writes Benjamin Barber in an essay from this section. "In producing goods and services that answer real consumer needs, it secures a profit for producers." But what, exactly, are "real consumer needs"? From the stalls of the *agora*, which served as a marketplace in ancient Greece, to the endless aisles of a contemporary Wal-Mart, shopping has often meant more than just a simple financial transaction to satisfy bare human necessities. That is especially true in the United States. The French political philosopher Alexis de Tocqueville long ago noted the American propensity for consumer desire. Observing this country in the 1830s, he wrote that Americans "never stop thinking of the good things they have not got," even as they "hurry after some new delight."

If we associate consumerism in the United States with debt, excess, and self-indulgence, we also associate it with prosperity, liberty, and the egalitarian democracy of the market. After 9/11, shopping became patriotic, too, as public officials like New York Mayor Rudolph Giuliani urged Americans—the "best shoppers in the world"—to help New York recover by spending money. Some criticized these exhortations, but Giuliani had a point, at least in the short term: Seventy percent of the U.S. economy is based on consumption. If Americans changed their behavior en masse and became the best savers in the world rather than the best shoppers, the U.S. economy—and the global economy—would suffer. While U.S. consumer debt has fallen from its $14 trillion peak in 2008, Americans remain "overspent." And a high unemployment rate and contentious discussions of government budget deficits only reinforce anxieties about consumption and debt.

The essays in this section look at consumption, as well as our relationship to consumer products, debt, retail stores, and labor. In "Overselling Capitalism With Consumerism," Barber argues that consumerism ultimately perverts capitalism, as producers in search of buyers must "dumb down consumers" and "invent new needs." Writer Sylvie Kim looks at consumption literally in "The End of Spam Shame: On Class, Colonialism, and Canned Meat." For Kim, Spam—a product "synonymous" with "trashiness in American pop culture"—carries a "heavy load of symbolism" for America's enduring international presence. In "Toys," Roland Barthes shows how children's toys burst with significance, ideological and otherwise, when they are given a close reading. Virginia Postrel's "In Praise of Chain Stores" provides a bracing defense of retail chain stores, as the writer responds to snobby "cosmopolites" whose misguided "contempt for chains represents a brand-obsessed view of place." Novelist Margaret Atwood ("Debtor's Prism") sees debt through the literary prism of story arc and metaphor, touching on the enduring tales of Dickens's Scrooge and Marlowe's Faust in the process. In the paired essays, Barbara Ehrenreich and Eric Schlosser examine the world of work in two icons of mass consumer culture: Wal-Mart and fast-food restaurants, respectively.

BENJAMIN BARBER

Overselling Capitalism with Consumerism

Born in New York City in 1939, political theorist Benjamin Barber earned a Ph.D. in government at Harvard University. He has taught at the University of Maryland, Rutgers University, Princeton University, and several other colleges. Currently, he is a Distinguished Senior Fellow at Dēmos, a policy and research center, as well as president of Civ-World, the international program at Dēmos that encourages more democratic systems of government. Barber's work focuses on democracy, citizenship, civil society, education, and globalism. His books include Jihad vs. McWorld: How Globalism and Tribalism are Reshaping the World *(1995) and* Consumed: How Markets Corrupt Children, Infantilize Adults, and Swallow Citizens Whole *(2007). He writes for the* Huffington Post, *the* Nation, *the* Atlantic Monthly, *and other publications.*

In this Los Angeles Times *opinion column (April 15, 2007), Barber considers the economic problems of the last several years in the context of consumerism and the decline of an "ethos of hard work and deferred gratification." Why does this development threaten democracy as well as the economy?*

The crisis in subprime mortgages betrays a deeper predicament facing consumer capitalism triumphant: The "Protestant ethos" of hard work and deferred gratification has been replaced by an infantilist ethos of easy credit and impulsive consumption that puts democracy and the market system at risk.

Capitalism's core virtue is that it marries altruism and self-interest. In producing goods and services that answer real consumer needs, it secures a profit for producers. Doing good for others turns out to entail doing well for yourself.

Capitalism's success, however, has meant that core wants in

15

the developed world are now mostly met and that too many goods are chasing too few needs. Yet capitalism requires us to "need" all that it produces in order to survive. So it busies itself manufacturing needs for the wealthy while ignoring the wants of the truly needy. Global inequality means that while the wealthy have too few needs, the needy have too little wealth.

Capitalism is stymied, courting long-term disaster. We still work hard, but only so that we can pay and play. In order to turn reluctant consumers with few satisfied core needs into permanent shoppers, producers must dumb down consumers, shape their wants, take over their life worlds, encourage impulse buying, cultivate shopoholism and invent new needs.

At the same time, they empower kids as shoppers by legitimiz- 5 ing their unformed tastes and mercurial wants and detaching them from their gatekeeper mothers and fathers and teachers and pastors. The kids include toddlers who recognize brand logos before they can talk and commodity-minded baby Einsteins who learn to shop before they can walk.

Does the overextended American consumer have a leg left to stand on?

Consumerism needs this infantilist ethos because it favors lax-ity and leisure over discipline and denial, values childish impetu-osity and juvenile narcissism over adult order and enlightened self-interest, and prefers consumption-directed play to spontane-ous recreation. The ethos feeds a private-market logic ("What I want is what society needs!") and combats the public logic fash-ioned by democracy ("What society needs is what I want to want!").

This is capitalism's all-too-logical way of solving the problem of too many goods chasing too few needs. It makes consuming ubiquitous and omnipresent, turning shopping into an addiction facilitated by easy credit.

Compare any traditional town square with a modern suburban mall. In the square, you'll find a school, town hall, library, general store, park, movie house, church, art gallery and homes—a true neighborhood exhibiting our human diversity as beings who do more than simply consume. But our new town malls are all shop-ping, all the time.

When we see politics permeate every sector of life, we call it totalitarianism. When religion rules all, we call it theocracy. But when commerce dominates everything, we call it liberty. Can we redirect capitalism to its proper end: the satisfaction of real human needs? Well, why not?

The world teems with elemental wants and is peopled by bil- 10 lions who are needy. They do not need iPods, but they do need potable water, not colas but inexpensive medicines, not MTV but their ABCs. They need mortgages they can afford, not funny-money easy credit.

To serve such needs, however, capitalism must once again learn to defer profits and empower the needy as customers. Entre-preneurs wanted! With micro-credit, villagers can construct hand pumps and water filters from the clay under their feet.

Pharmaceutical companies ought to be thinking about how to sell inexpensive retro-virals to Africans with HIV instead of push-ing Botox to the "forever young" customers they are trying to manufacture here.

And parents can refuse to relinquish their gatekeeping roles and let marketers know they won't allow their kids to be targeted anymore.

To do this, we will require the assistance of democratic institu-tions and an adult ethos. Public citizens must be restored to their proper place as masters of their private choices. To sustain itself, capitalism once again will have to respond to real needs instead of trying to fabricate synthetic ones—or risk consuming itself.

For Discussion and Writing

1. According to Barber, what is the deep predicament that faces consumer capitalism?
2. The author refers to capitalism's "core virtue" (par. 2), and proposes that capitalism be redirected to its "proper end." How do you respond to these—and other—characterizations of our economic system in the essay? Do you agree with Barber's assumptions about the nature and function of capitalism?
3. **connections**   Barber writes about an "infantilist ethos" as it applies to consumerism (par. 6). Writing about television and entertainment, George F. Will refers to our "increasingly infantilized society" (par. 4) in "Reality Television: Oxymoron" (p. 289). How do their arguments overlap? Where do the writers differ?
4. Barber proposes an opposition between an "infantilist ethos" and an "adult ethos." How would you compare and contrast them? Use specific examples from your own life, society, and culture to illustrate the distinction.

SYLVIE KIM

The End of Spam Shame: On Class, Colonialism, and Canned Meat

Sylvie Kim is a blog editor and columnist for Hyphen, *an Asian American magazine that covers politics, culture, and the arts. Previously she served as the magazine's film editor. In "The End of Spam Shame," which originally appeared on* Hyphen's *blog, Kim writes about her affection for Spam, a precooked canned meat product made from pork and ham. Long a subject of jokes and an object of derision, Spam is entrenched in popular culture—from the 2004 musical comedy* Spam- alot *to the use of the term to denote unwanted e-mail messages. But Kim sees the canned meat as more than just a food or an easy punch- line. She ties Spam to immigration, assimilation, and the history of the American military's global presence. As you read, consider Kim's style, tone, and attitude toward her subject. How serious is she?*

I am quite familiar with processed meats. There's no punch line to that opener; I'm just being honest about what I know. And apparently, I'm not alone. A recent Hyphen Facebook post linking to the Multi-American blog's celebration of SPAM musubi brought all sorts of "likes" and "comments" to the virtual yard, signifying how ingrained the canned meat is to many Asian American lives and bellies.

My childhood was chock-full of nitrates, sodium, and an amal- gam of four-legged animals chopped and cured into uniform cuts of salty goodness that was inexpensive, easy to heat, and lasted for damn near forever—key to a family of five with immigrant par- ents who were struggling financially. Sliced hot dogs were thrown into kim bap and a delightful dish (whose name escapes me) which features potatoes, onions, soy sauce and sesame oil. Vienna sausages weren't my favorite, but they would do in a pinch despite their uncanny resemblance to amputated fingers. And then . . .

19

there was Spam. Sure, the pink sheen and sliminess found in every rectangular can was off-putting at first but our appetites always returned with a vengeance once the Spam was thrown onto a heat source: dipped in battered egg and fried in a pan, cubed and tossed into kimchee jjigae and kimchee fried rice, or nestled between toast and a fried egg.

Please, excuse the melodramatic overtones of my nostalgia about this particular processed meat, but I have an explanation. From roughly sixth grade to age 23, I had to eat my Spam in private.

I suffered from class-based Spam shame.

We grew up in the Midwest where Asian faces weren't in abun- 5 dance and our supposed weirdo Oriental ways in regards to language, customs, and food were already conspicuous enough. To throw in a hearty love for a meat that had become synonymous with poverty or "trashiness" in American pop culture would be making that bullseye even brighter on a young lass like me, who was preoccupied with cultural assimilation.

Articles have often remarked on the influence of Spam abroad, particularly in Asia and the Pacific Islands, often in contrast to how the luncheon meat is regarded as substandard or comedic fodder by the average American (or Briton, if you count Monty Python's legendary Spam sketch from which the term "spamming" for junk e-mail was born). Only in the recent economic downturn and rising food prices did the focus

"If you don't like Spam, there's something wrong with *you*."

shift to America's Spam consumption as a whole—rather than as kooky culinary statistics of foreign countries or ethnic groups— as sales for the oft-maligned meat surged. Others have touched on the stigma surrounding Spam, including guest blogger Dr. Sangyoub Park at Sociological Images, who argues that though Americans may perceive Spam's prestige in Korea (and, ostensibly, other parts of the world) to be weird, a Korean perspective finds that it is "perfectly sensible . . . and with boiled rice and kim-chi, totally delicious."

That deliciousness was something I would deny in my early years in my predominantly white, middle class suburb, where— in addition to self-imposing my own version of Don't Ask, Don't Tell policy on discussing my Korean heritage—you would have had to hold me at gunpoint for me to admit publicly that I (1) ate Spam and (2) really, fracking enjoyed eating Spam.

You could say that my yen for Spam was inherited. My mother, born in South Korea very shortly before the 1953 armistice which halted the hostilities of the Korean War, recalls Spam—along with cheese, M&M's, coffee and other food items brought to Korea to feed the US military—as delicacies for a nation whose land and economy had been razed during the war. American food was not imported for resale, so my mother's family and neighbors bought it illegally, typically through Korean women who had married and were living with American soldiers in town. A popular dish arose from the influx of western military cuisine: budae jjigae, or "army base stew," a hodgepodge of processed meats, vegetables, and whatever else happened to be available. (An urban legend floated around that cigarette butts were even added to the pot.)

Growing up in a war-torn, US-occupied country was no direct comparison to raising a family in 1980s Columbus, OH, but some commonalities existed: lack of income and resources, uneasy cultural interactions with Americans, and the often uncomfortable notions of what it meant to feel "at home." And waiting in our family pantry was always a can of Spam, a mainstay throughout the economic highs and lows in the Kim household. But the fact that Spam was cheap was simply a bonus. We would have eaten it, gladly, in any financial situation: it had become a part of our family's culinary culture.

In 2010's Asian American/Asian Research Institute (AAARI) 10 Summer Series, Robert Ji-song Ku, Visiting Professor in the

Department of Asian and Asian American Studies at SUNY Bing-hamton and self-professed lover of Spam, spoke of the meat and other foodstuffs in the context of his manuscript *Dubious Gastronomy: The Cultural Politics of Eating Asian in the USA.*

"Due to their long entangled history with the US military, these two places [South Korea and Hawaii] along with Guam lead the world in per capita consumption of the pink gelatinous pork. Immediately following World War II, the American GIs stationed in Asia and the Pacific curried favor with the impoverished natives by handing out such luxuries as chocolate, cigarettes and Spam which as part of the US Army's monotonous C-Ration was an object of scorn and mockery by most of the rank and file. Here in the US, Spam is widely regarded as vulgar, farcical and an affront to the very idea of real or whole food. To millions of devotees in and across the Pacific Ocean however, Spam is not only an essential part of the local indigenous cuisine, but a luxury commodity as well."

I didn't know it then, and perhaps it would have been futile to try to explain it to my peers, but my Spam consumption was largely the result of American military and political expansion abroad. I grew to love a food that was championed as a symbol of American ingenuity despite being denigrated by Americans themselves. I eat Spam and am judged for eating Spam because of America. Both Asian Pacific Americans and Spam were the butt of a cruel joke: Please value what we deem subpar and make us money in the process. It's a terribly heavy load of symbolism to place on a pink block of meat.

But Hormel Foods, the makers of Spam, pride themselves on their history of feeding the US military. In a press release promoting their scholarship fund for the children of military families, the company states: "Hormel Foods support of the military dates back to World War II, when more than 100 million pounds of SPAM® luncheon meat were shipped abroad to feed Allied troops. Canned meat became of particular importance during the war . . . its savory, salty-sweet flavor continues to be enjoyed today by the military as well as SPAM™ lovers around the world."

In a subsection of their company profile entitled "Going Global," Hormel states: "The changing economy of Eastern Europe and the advancement of Third World nations combined with exploding communications capabilities have driven our holding of minority interests in several entities operating in international markets," listing enterprises and joint ventures in Madrid, Manila, Okinawa, Shanghai, and Beijing.

Written between the lines of Hormel's history of military sup- 15 port and their broadening reach in a global market is the understanding that the former has allowed for the latter. There is no outward acknowledgement of the fact that the nations who cherish and consume Spam the most are also the ones who have been occupied and/or annexed by the US and are still home to American military bases today. From the corporation's standpoint, they just make one helluva meat product. The love of Spam—and the billions in profits from that love, to date—owes much to US imperialism and expansionism abroad. However, for many immigrants in the US and their brethren in their respective motherlands, Spam is Spam whether it's being given as a homecoming gift in the Philippines or stocked as currency in Tahiti.

For the generations of Asian Pacific Americans who descend from these folks, perhaps it is our job to assume a more critical perspective on the seemingly innocuous meat and connect the dots between it and its reverence in Asian, Pacific, and Asian Pacific American communities. That is not to say that we should be ashamed of our enjoyment of Spam. Nor can we re-write history to prevent or abate our love of Spam (would we want to?). But perhaps arming ourselves with some knowledge—as well as with our forks, spoons, chopsticks, or hands—before entering that global food discussion which is increasingly taking up a larger slice of the cultural/media pie (my sincerest apologies for the pie pun . . .), will help unearth the politics behind everyone's favorite life-sustaining activity.

And as Asian Pacific American and other ethnic cuisines continue to influence how the US eats—and as those cuisines are commodified by others—the steadfast stigma against Spam, pork rinds (mmm, chicarrones . . .) and other supposedly "untouchable" or "tacky" foods by American standards already seem to be weakening. Asian Pacific Americans may be left asking the question, "So, what, *now* everyone thinks it's cool to eat Spam?" But of course, the issue goes beyond what is and what is not culturally fashionable. As Ku states, "With every bite of Spam I consume layers of overlapping histories, migrations, and cultural transformations. With it I consume calamitous political turmoil, bloody military conflicts and other upheavals that shape much of the 21st century."

As for me, I gradually cast off the onerous chains of Spam shame throughout my early twenties. My tipping point came when I moved to the San Francisco bay area, one the largest concentrations of APAs in the country and where Spam musubi is rolled and devoured freely. Histrionics aside, food is a form of identity and to have that identity stifled in the name of racial, cultural or class assimiliation is pure bollocks. To paraphrase Dave Chappelle's classic stand-up bit on the racialized love connection between African Americans and fried chicken (a stereotype also fraught with history, born out of American slavery): "If you don't like Spam, then there's something wrong with *you.*"

For Discussion and Writing

1. Kim writes: "You could say that my yen for Spam was inherited" (par. 8). What does she mean by this?

2. The writer includes excerpts from a Hormel Foods press release about Spam. Why does she do this? How does her interpretation of the press release support her argument?

3. **connections**   Kim writes about an object of snobbery: a "vulgar" food product that is synonymous with "trashiness" and an "affront to the very idea of real or whole food" (pars. 5, 11). In "In Praise of Chain Stores" (p. 30), Virginia Postrel also defends oftenmaligned chain stores from the attacks of snobby, "bored cosmopolites" (par. 10). How are there arguments similar? How are they different? What role does irony play in each of the essays?

4. In the essay, Kim refers to her "family's culinary culture" (par. 9). Did you grow up with a family culinary culture of any kind? Kim has an attachment to Spam that is both personal and cultural. What food or foods hold a similar place in your life?

ROLAND BARTHES

Toys

Roland Barthes (1915–1980) was a literary theorist and semiotician born in the Normandy region of France. As a critic and essayist, his interests ranged from anthropology, existentialism, and Marxism to fashion and mass culture. While he deployed a variety of critical approaches, Barthes is probably best known for his interest in semiotics, a branch of linguistics that analyzes signs and symbols as elements of communication. Barthes used semiotics to analyze popular culture—perhaps most famously in Mythologies *(1957), a book that includes "Toys." By scrutinizing phenomena like toys, cars, and professional wrestling, Barthes revealed their hidden meanings. He also uncovered the unexamined assumptions, values, and myths of the society that consumes such products. The essays in* Mythologies *originally appeared in the literary magazine* Les Lettres Nouvelles *between 1954 and 1956. Barthes's other works include* Writing Degree Zero *(1953),* S/Z: An Essay *(1970), and* The Pleasure of the Text *(1973).*

While Barthes's style is witty and playful, he has a serious purpose in Mythologies: *"I resented seeing Nature and History confused at every turn, and I wanted to track down, in the decorative display of what-goes-without-saying, the ideological abuse which, in my view, is hidden there." As you read "Toys," notice how Barthes uncovers this meaningful "what-goes-without-saying" through keen observation and vivid description.*

French toys: one could not find a better illustration of the fact that the adult Frenchman sees the child as another self. All the toys one commonly sees are essentially a microcosm of the adult world; they are all reduced copies of human objects, as if in the eyes of the public the child was, all told, nothing but a smaller man, a homunculus to whom must be supplied objects of his own size.

"However, faced with this world of faithful and complicated objects, the child can only identify himself as owner, as user, never as creator; he does not invent the world, he uses it. . . ."

Invented forms are very rare: a few sets of blocks, which appeal to the spirit of do-it-yourself, are the only ones which offer dynamic forms. As for the others, French toys *always mean something*, and this something is always entirely socialized, constituted by the myths or the techniques of modern adult life: the Army, Broadcasting, the Post Office, Medicine (miniature instrument-cases, operating theatres for dolls), School, Hair-Styling (driers for permanent-waving), the Air Force (Parachutists), Transport (trains, Citroëns, Vedettes, Vespas, petrol-stations), Science (Martian toys).

The fact that French toys *literally* prefigure the world of adult functions obviously cannot but prepare the child to accept them all, by constituting for him, even before he can think about it, the alibi of a Nature which has at all times created soldiers, postmen and Vespas. Toys here reveal the list of all the things the adult does not find unusual: war, bureaucracy, ugliness, Martians, etc. It is not so much, in fact, the imitation which is the sign of an abdication, as its literalness: French toys are like a Jivaro head, in which one recognizes, shrunken to the size of an apple, the wrinkles and hair of an adult. There exist, for instance, dolls which urinate; they have an oesophagus, one gives them a bottle, they wet their nappies; soon, no doubt, milk will turn to water in their stomachs. This is meant to prepare the little girl for the causality of house-keeping, to "condition" her to her future role as mother. However, faced with this world of faithful and complicated objects, the child can only identify himself as owner, as user, never as creator; he does not invent the world, he uses it: there are, prepared for him, actions without adventure, without wonder, without joy. He is turned into a little stay-at-home householder who does not even have to invent the mainsprings of adult causality; they are supplied to him ready-made: he has only to help himself, he is never allowed to discover anything from start to finish. The merest set of blocks, provided it is not too refined, implies a very different learning of the world: then, the child does not in any way create meaningful objects, it matters little to him whether they have an adult name; the actions he performs are not those of a user but those of a demiurge. He creates forms which walk, which roll, he creates life, not property: objects now act by themselves, they are no longer an inert and complicated material in the palm of his hand. But such toys are rather rare: French toys are usually based on imitation, they are meant to produce children who are users, not creators.

The bourgeois status of toys can be recognized not only in their forms, which are all functional, but also in their substances. Current toys are made of a graceless material, the product of chemistry, not of nature. Many are now moulded from complicated mixtures; the plastic material of which they are made has an appearance at once gross and hygienic, it destroys all the pleasure, the sweetness, the humanity of touch. A sign which fills one with consternation is the gradual disappearance of wood, in spite of its being an ideal material because of its firmness and its softness, and the natural warmth of its touch. Wood removes, from all the forms which it supports, the wounding quality of angles which are too sharp, the chemical coldness of metal. When the child handles it and knocks it, it neither vibrates nor grates, it has a sound at once muffled and sharp. It is a familiar and poetic substance, which does not sever the child from close contact with the tree, the table, the floor. Wood does not wound or break down; it does not shatter, it wears out, it can last a long time, live with the child, alter little by little the relations between the object and the hand. If it dies, it is in dwindling, not in swelling out like those mechanical toys which disappear behind the hernia of a broken spring. Wood makes essential objects, objects for all time. Yet there hardly remain any of these wooden toys from the Vosges, these fretwork farms with their animals, which were only possible, it is true, in the days of the craftsman. Henceforth, toys are chemical in substance and colour; their very material introduces one to a coenaesthesis of use, not pleasure. These toys die in fact very quickly, and once dead, they have no posthumous life for the child.

For Discussion and Writing

1. Why does Barthes prefer wooden toys to toys made from plastic or metal?

2. According to Barthes, toys "*literally* prefigure the world of adult functions" (par. 3) and therefore "cannot but prepare the child to accept them all, by constituting for him, even before he can think about it, the alibi of a Nature . . ." (par. 3). What does he mean by the "alibi of a Nature"? Does he prove his claim persuasively throughout the essay? Why or why not?

3. **connections**   In "Why Video Games Are Works of Art" (p. 396), Kyle Chayka argues that video games provide deep, meaningful aesthetic experiences. How might you view video games using Barthes's framework? Do video games "socialize or "condition" players to accept certain "myths" or a certain view of the world? Are video game players like "owners" and "users," or are they more like "creators"?

4. Barthes writes that "French toys *always mean something*" (par. 2). Choose a toy, product, or common object and interpret its meaning as Barthes does in his essay. Focus on its function, material, and formal details: What do they suggest about its user's relationship to the world? How does the object reflect social values? What does the object "mean"?

VIRGINIA POSTREL

In Praise of Chain Stores

Critic Virginia Postrel (b. 1960) covers a broad swath of American politics, commerce, and culture—from fashion and design to healthcare and technology. The editor of Reason *magazine from 1989 to 2000, Postrel currently edits the blog DeepGlamour.net. Her columns and articles have appeared in the* New York Times, *the* Atlantic, *the* Wall Street Journal, Forbes, *and other publications. Postrel's books include* The Future and Its Enemies: The Growing Conflict Over Creativity, Enterprise, and Progress *(1998) and* The Substance of Style: How the Rise of Aesthetic Value Is Remaking Commerce, Culture, and Consciousness *(2003).*

"In Praise of Chain Stores," like much of Postrel's work, challenges conventional wisdom—in this case, received opinions about the geography and commerce in America. As you read the essay, note how the writer tries to overturn common perceptions of suburbs and chain stores. How effective is her approach?

Every well-travelled cosmopolite knows that the United States is mind-numbingly monotonous—"the most boring country to tour, because everywhere looks like everywhere else," as The *New York Times* columnist Thomas Friedman once told Charlie Rose. Boston has the same stores as Denver, which has the same stores as Charlotte or Seattle or Chicago. We live in a "Stepford world," says Rachel Dresbeck, the author of Insiders' Guide to Portland, Oregon. Even Boston's historic Faneuil Hall, she complains, is "dominated by the Gap, Anthropologie, Starbucks and all the other usual suspects. Why go anywhere? Every place looks the same."

This complaint is more than the old worry, dating back to the 1920s, that the big guys are putting Mom and Pop out of business. Today's critics focus less on what isn't there—Mom and

Pop—than on what is. Faneuil Hall actually has plenty of locally owned businesses, from the Geoclassics store selling minerals and jewelry, to Pizzeria Regina ("since 1926"). But you do find the same chains everywhere. The suburbs are the worst. Take Chandler, Ariz., just south of Phoenix. At Chandler Fashion Center, the area's big shopping mall, you'll find P. F. Chang's, California Pizza Kitchen, Chipotle Mexican Grill, and the Cheesecake Factory. Drive along Chandler's straight, flat boulevards, and you'll see Bed Bath & Beyond and Linens 'n Things; Barnes & Noble and Borders; PetSmart and Petco; Circuit City and Best Buy; Lowe's and Home Depot; CVS and Walgreens. Chandler has the Apple Store and Pottery Barn, the Gap and Ann Taylor, Banana Republic and DSW, and, of course, Target and Wal-Mart, Starbucks and McDonald's. For people allergic to brands, Chandler must be hell—even without the 110-degree days.

One of the fastest-growing cities in the country, Chandler is definitely the kind of place urbanists have in mind as they intone, "When every place looks the same, there is no such thing as place anymore." Like so many towns in the U.S., it has lost much of its historic character as a farming community. The annual Ostrich Festival still honors one traditional product, but these days Chandler raises more subdivisions and strip malls than ostrich plumes or cotton, another former staple. Yet it still refutes the common assertion that national chains are a blight on the landscape, that they've turned American towns into an indistinguishable "geography of nowhere."

The first thing you notice in Chandler is that, as a broad empirical claim, the cliché that "everywhere looks like everywhere else" is obvious nonsense. Chandler's land and air and foliage are peculiar to the desert Southwest. The people dress differently. Even the cookie-cutter housing developments, with their xeriscaping and washed-out desert palette, remind you where you are. Forget New England clapboard, Carolina columns or yellow Texas brick. In the intense sun of Chandler, the red-tile roofs common in California turn a pale, pale pink.

Stores don't give places their character. Terrain and weather and culture do. Familiar retailers may take some of the discovery out of travel—to the consternation of journalists looking for obvious local colour—but by holding some of the commercial

Because when you're *here*, you could be . . . *anywhere*.

background constant, chains make it easier to discern the real differences that define a place: the way, for instance, that people in Chandler come out to enjoy the summer twilight, when the sky glows purple and the dry air cools.

Besides, the idea that the U.S. was once filled with wildly varied business establishments is largely a myth. Big cities could, and still can, support more retail niches than small towns. And in a less competitive national market, there was certainly more variation in business efficiency—in prices, service and merchandise quality. But the range of retailing ideas in any given town was rarely that great. One deli or diner or lunch counter or cafeteria was pretty much like every other one. A hardware store was a hardware store, a pharmacy a pharmacy. Before it became a ubiquitous part of urban life, Starbucks was, in most American cities, a radically new idea.

Chains do more than bargain down prices from suppliers or divide fixed costs across a lot of units. They rapidly spread economic discovery—the scarce and costly knowledge of what retail concepts and operational innovations actually work. That knowledge can be gained only through the expensive and time-consuming process of trial and error. Expecting each town to independently invent every new business is a prescription for real monotony, at least for the locals. Chains make a large range of choices available in more places. They increase local variety, even as they reduce the differences from place to place. People who mostly stay put get to have experiences once available only to frequent travellers, and this loss of exclusivity is one reason why frequent travellers are the ones who complain. When Borders was a unique Ann Arbor, Mich., institution, people in places like Chandler—or, for that matter, Philadelphia and Los Angeles— didn't have much in the way of bookstores. Back in 1986, when California Pizza Kitchen was an innovative local restaurant about to open its second location, food writers at the L.A. Daily News declared it "the kind of place every neighbourhood should have." So what's wrong if the country has 158 neighbourhood CPKs instead of one or two?

The process of multiplication is particularly important for fast-growing towns like Chandler, where rollouts of established stores allow retail variety to expand as fast as the growing population can support new businesses. I heard the same refrain in Chandler that I've heard in similar boomburgs elsewhere, and for similar reasons. "It's got all the advantages of a small town, in terms of being friendly, but it's got all the things of a big town," says Scott Stephens, who moved from Manhattan Beach, Calif., in 1998 to work for Motorola. Chains let people in a city of 250,000 enjoy retail amenities once available only in a huge metropolitan center. At the same time, familiar establishments make it easier for people to make a home in a new place. When Nissan recently moved its headquarters from Southern California to Tennessee, an unusually high percentage of its Los Angeles–area employees accepted the transfer. "The fact that Starbucks are everywhere helps make moving a lot easier these days," a rueful Greg Whitney, vice-president of business development for the Los Angeles County Economic Development Corporation, told the Los Angeles Times reporter John O'Dell. Orth Hedrick, a Nissan product manager, decided he could stay with the job he loved when he turned off the interstate near Nashville and realized, "You could really be Anywhere, U.S.A. There's a great big regional shopping mall, and most of the stores and restaurants are the same ones we see in California. Yet a few miles away you're in downtown and there's lots of local color, too."

Contrary to the rhetoric of bored cosmopolites, most cities 10 don't exist primarily to please tourists. The children toddling through the Chandler mall hugging their soft Build-A-Bear animals are no less delighted because kids can also build a bear in Memphis or St. Louis. For them, this isn't tourism; it's life—the experiences that create the memories from which the meaning of a place arises over time. Among Chandler's most charming sights are the business-casual dads joining their wives and kids for lunch in the mall food court. The food isn't the point, let alone whether it's from Subway or Dairy Queen. The restaurants merely provide the props and setting for the family time. When those kids grow up, they'll remember the food court as happily as an older generation recalls the diners and motels of Route 66—not because of the businesses' innate appeal but because of the memories they evoke.

The contempt for chains represents a brand-obsessed view of place, as if store names were all that mattered to a city's character. For many critics, the name on the store really is all that matters. The planning consultant Robert Gibbs works with cities that want to revive their downtowns, and he also helps developers find space for retailers. To his frustration, he finds that many cities actually turn away national chains, preferring a moribund downtown that seems authentically local. But, he says, the same local activists who oppose chains "want specialty retail that sells exactly what the chains sell—the same price, the same fit, the same qualities, the same sizes, the same brands, even." You can show pictures of a Pottery Barn with nothing but the name changed, he says, and they'll love the store. So downtown stores stay empty, or sell low-value tourist items like candles and kites, while the chains open on the edge of town. In the name of urbanism, officials and activists in cities like Ann Arbor and Fort Collins, Colo., are driving business to the suburbs. "If people like shopping at the Banana Republic or the Gap, if that's your market—or Payless Shoes—why not?" says an exasperated Gibbs. "Why not sell the goods and services people want?"

For Discussion and Writing

1. According to the writer, the "idea that the U.S. was once filled with wildly varied business establishments is largely a myth" (par. 7). What other myths and misperceptions does she try to correct in this essay?

2. Postrel refers to "bored cosmopolites" and "urbanists." How does she characterize them? Why are they important to her overall purpose? Do you think they are her primary audience? Why or why not?

3. **connections** How is Postrel's argument similar to Steven Johnson's in "Watching TV Makes You Smarter" (p. 275)? What purposes, themes, and rhetorical strategies do the two writers share, despite their divergent subjects?

4. What are some of the benefits of chain stores, according to Postrel? List them in your own words. Do you agree? Why or why not? Use your responses to write an essay exploring your own view of retail and restaurant chains.

MARGARET ATWOOD

Debtor's Prism

*Born in Ottawa, Ontario, Canada, in 1939, Margaret Atwood is a pro-
lific novelist, literary critic, poet, essayist, and activist. She is best
known as a fiction writer across a variety of genres, including historical
fiction, science fiction, and children's literature. She has also taught
literature and writing at universities in the United States and Canada.
Atwood's novels include* Surfacing *(1972),* The Handmaid's Tale
(1985), and The Year of the Flood *(2009).*

"Debtor's Prism" was adapted from Atwood's 2008 nonfiction book
Payback: Debt and the Shadow Side of Wealth *and published in the*
Wall Street Journal. *For Atwood, indebtedness is inextricably bound to
narrative: "Without story, there is no debt." She writes in the wake of
contemporary financial and economic crises, even as she cites examples
from history and literature. As you read, notice how she frames debt
and indebtedness in terms of the stories we tell about ourselves and
about society as a whole.*

Without memory, there is no debt. Put another way: Without
story, there is no debt.

The story of debt reached a historic moment this week. An out-
sized bubble of interlocking debt burst, leading to the downfalls
of prominent companies. Loans by and to the government, financial institutions, and consumers collided on an epic scale. Still,
the idea of what we owe one another is an ancient theme, and this
is just the latest chapter in a long cultural history.

A story is a string of actions occurring over time—one damn
thing after another, as we glibly say in creative writing classes—
and debt happens as a result of actions occurring over time.
Therefore, any debt involves a plot line: how you got into debt,
what you did, said, and thought while you were in there, and
then—depending on whether the ending is to be happy or sad—

how you got out of debt, or else how you got further and further into it until you became overwhelmed by it and sank from view. The hidden metaphors are revealing: We get "into" debt, as if into a prison, swamp, or well, or possibly a bed; we get "out" of it, as if coming into the open air or climbing out of a hole. If we are "overwhelmed" by debt, the image is possibly that of a foundering ship, with the sea and the waves pouring inexorably in on top of us as we flail and choke. All of this sounds dramatic, with much physical activity: jumping in, leaping or clambering out, thrashing around, drowning. Metaphorically, the debt plot line is a far cry from the glum actuality, in which the debtor sits at a desk fiddling around with numbers on a screen, or shuffles past-due bills in the hope that they will go away, or paces the room wondering how he can possibly extricate himself from the fiscal molasses.

In our minds—as reflected in our language—debt is a mental ⁵ or spiritual non-place, like the Hell described by Christopher Marlowe's Mephistopheles when Faust asks him why he's not in Hell but right there in the same room as Faust. "Why, this is Hell, nor am I out of it," says Mephistopheles. He carries Hell around with him like a private climate: He's in it and it's in him. Substitute "debt" and you can see that, in the way we talk about it, debt is the same kind of placeless place. "Why, this is Debt, nor am I out of it," the beleaguered debtor might similarly declaim.

Which makes the whole idea of debt—especially massive and hopeless debt—sound brave and noble and interesting rather than merely squalid and gives it a larger-than-life tragic air. Could

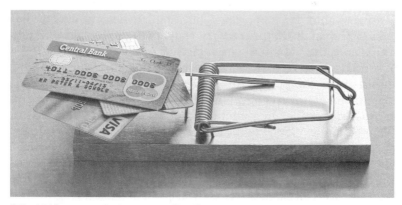

"The hidden metaphors are revealing."

it be that some people get into debt because, like speeding on a motorbike, it adds an adrenalin hit to their otherwise humdrum lives? When the bailiffs are knocking at the door and the lights go off because you didn't pay the water bill and the bank's threatening to foreclose, at least you can't complain of ennui.

Debt can constitute one such story-of-my-life. Eric Berne's 1964 bestselling book on transactional analysis, *Games People Play*, lists five "life games"—patterns of behavior that can occupy an individual's entire lifespan, often destructively, but with hidden psychological benefits or payoffs that keep the games going. Needless to say, each game requires more than one player—some players being consciously complicit, others being unwitting dupes. "Alcoholic," "Now I've Got You, You Son of a Bitch," "Kick Me," and "See What You Made Me Do" are Berne's titles for four of these life games. The fifth one is called "Debtor."

Mr. Berne says, "'Debtor' is more than a game. In America it tends to become a script, a plan for a whole lifetime, just as it does in some of the jungles of Africa and New Guinea. There the relatives of a young man buy him a bride at an enormous price, putting him in their debt for years to come." In North America, says Mr. Berne, "the big expense is not a bride but a house, and the enormous debt is a mortgage; the role of the relatives is taken by the bank. Paying off the mortgage gives the individual a purpose in life." Indeed, I can remember a time from my own childhood—was it the 1940s?—when it was considered cute to have a framed petit-point embroidered motto hanging in the bathroom that said "God Bless Our Mortgaged Home." During this period, people would have mortgage-burning parties at which they would, in fact, burn the mortgage papers in the barbecue or fireplace once they'd paid the mortgage off.

I pause here to add that "mortgage" means "dead pledge"—"mort" from the French for "dead," "gage" for "pledge," like the part in medieval romances where the knight throws down his glove, thus challenging another knight to a duel—the glove or gage being the pledge that the guy will actually show up on time to get his head bashed in, and the accepting of the gage being a reciprocal pledge. Which should make you think twice about engagement rings, since they too are a gage or pledge—what actually are you pledging when you present such a ring to your one true love?

So "paying off the mortgage" is what happens when people 10 play the life game of "Debtor" nicely. But what if they don't play nicely? Not-nice play involves cheating, as every child knows. But it's not always true that cheaters never prosper, and every child knows that, too: Sometimes they do prosper, in the playground and elsewhere.

Debt can have another kind of entertainment value when it becomes a motif, not in a real-life plot line, but in a fictional one. How this kind of debt plot unfolds and changes over time, as social conditions, class relations, financial climates, and literary fashions change; but debts themselves have been present in stories for a very long time.

I'd like to begin by interrogating a familiar character—a character so familiar that he's made it out of the fiction in which he stars into another kind of stardom: that of television and billboard advertising. That character is Ebenezer Scrooge, from Charles Dickens's *A Christmas Carol*. Even if you haven't read the book or seen the play or the several movies made about Scrooge, you'd probably recognize him if you met him on the street. "Give like Santa, save like Scrooge," as some ads have said, and we then have a lovable, twinkly old codger telling us about some great penny-pinching bargain or other.

But, wanting to have it both ways, the ads conflate two Scrooges: the reformed Scrooge, who signals the advent of grace and the salvation of his soul by going on a giant spend-o-rama, and the Scrooge we see at the beginning of the book—a miser so extreme that he doesn't even spend any of his money-hoard on himself—not on nice food, or heat, or warm outfits—not anything. Scrooge's abstemious gruel-eating lifestyle might have been applauded as a sign of godliness back in the days of the early bread-and-water saintly ascetic hermits, who lived in caves and said Bah! Humbug! to all comers. But this is not the case with mean old Ebenezer Scrooge, whose first name chimes with "squeezer" as well as with "geezer," whose last name is a combination of "screw" and "gouge," and whose author disapproves mightily of his ways:

Oh! But he was a tight-fisted hand at the grindstone, Scrooge! A squeezing, wrenching, grasping, scraping, clutching, covetous old sinner! Hard and sharp as flint, from which no steel had ever struck out generous fire; secret and self-contained and solitary as an oyster. The cold within him froze his old features, nipped his pointed nose, shrivelled his cheek, stiffened his gait; made his eyes red, his thin lips blue; and spoke out shrewdly in his grating voice.

That Scrooge has—consciously or not—made a pact with the 15 Devil is signaled to us more than once. Not only is he credited with the evil eye, that traditional mark of sold-to-the-Devil witches, but he's also accused of worshipping a golden idol; and when, during his night of visions, he skips forward to his own future, the only comment he can overhear being made about himself in his former place of business is ". . . old Scratch has got his own at last, hey?" Old Scratch is of course the Devil, and if Scrooge himself isn't fully aware of the pact he's made, his author most certainly is.

But it's an odd pact. The Devil may get Scrooge, but Scrooge himself gets nothing except money, and he does nothing with it except sit on it. Scrooge has some interesting literary ancestors. Pact-makers with the Devil didn't start out as misers—quite the reverse. Christopher Marlowe's late–16th-century Doctor Faustus sells his body and soul to Mephistopheles with a loan document signed in blood, collection due in 24 years, but he doesn't do it cheaply. He has a magnificent wish list, which contains just about everything you can read about today in luxury magazines for gentlemen. Faust wants to travel; he wants to be very, very rich; he wants knowledge; he wants power; he wants to get back at his enemies; and he wants sex with a facsimile of Helen of Troy.

Marlowe's Doctor Faustus isn't mean and grasping and covetous. He doesn't want money just to have it—he wants to dispense it on his other wishes. He's got friends who enjoy his company, he's a big spender who shares his wealth around, he likes food and drink and fun parties and playing practical jokes, and he uses his power to rescue at least one human being from death. In fact, he behaves like Scrooge, after Scrooge has been redeemed—the Scrooge who buys huge turkeys, giggles a lot, plays practical jokes on his poor clerk, Bob Cratchit, goes to his nephew's Christmas party and joins in the parlor games, and saves Bob's crippled offspring, Tiny Tim, leading us to wonder if Scrooge didn't inherit a latent gene for bon-vivantery from his distant ancestor Doctor Faustus—a gene that was just waiting to be epigenetically switched on.

The ghost of Scrooge's former business partner, Marley, displaying the principles of post-mortem-heart weighing worthy of the Ancient Egyptians and also of medieval Christianity, has to pay after death for Marley's sins during life. None of these sins involved a dalliance with Helen of Troy; all of them came from the relentless business practices typical both of Scrooge and of unbridled 19th-century capitalism. Marley totes a long chain made of "cash-boxes, keys, padlocks, ledgers, deeds, and heavy purses wrought in steel." He is fettered, he tells Scrooge, by the chain he forged in life—yet another example of the imagery of bondage and slavery so often associated with debt, except that now the chain is worn by the creditor. Indulging in grinding, usurious financial practices is a spiritual sin as well as a material one, for it requires a cold indifference to the needs and sufferings of others and imprisons the sinner within himself.

Scrooge is set free from his own heavy chain of cash boxes at the end of the book, when, instead of sitting on his pile of money, he begins to spend it. True, he spends it on others, thus displaying that most treasured of Dickensian body parts, an open heart; but the main point is that he does spend it. The saintly thing in earlier times would have been for him to have given the whole packet away, donned sackcloth, and taken up the begging bowl. But Dickens has nothing against Scrooge's being rich: in fact, there are quite a few delightful rich men in his work, beginning with Mr. Pickwick. It's not whether you have it; it's not even how you get it, exactly: the post-ghost Scrooge, for instance, doesn't give up his business, though whether it remained in part a money-lending business we aren't told. No, it's what you do with your riches that really counts.

Scrooge's big sin was to freeze his money; for money, as all 20 students of it recognize, is of use only when it's moving, since it derives its value entirely from whatever it can translate itself into. Thus the Scrooges of this world who refuse to change their money into anything else are gumming up the works: currency is called "currency" because it must flow. Scrooge's happy ending is therefore entirely in keeping with the cherished core beliefs of capitalism. His life pattern is worthy of Andrew Carnegie—make a bundle by squeezing and grinding, then go in for philanthropy. We love him in part because, true to the laws of wish-fulfillment, which always involve a free lunch or a get-out-of-jail-free card, he embodies both sides of the equation—the greedy getting and the gleeful spending—and comes out of it just fine.

But we don't have enough cash. Or so we keep telling ourselves. And that's why you lied to the charity worker at your door and said, "I gave at the office." You want it both ways. Just like Scrooge.

I began by talking about debt as a story-of-my-life plot line, which is the approach Eric Berne takes in describing the variants of the life game of "Debtor."

But debt also exists as a real game—an old English parlor game. In fact, it's one of the games witnessed by the invisible Scrooge at his nephew's Christmas party. By no accident on the part of Dickens—for everything Scrooge is shown by the spirits must have an application to his own wicked life—this game is "Forfeits."

"Forfeits" has many variants, but here are the rules for perhaps the oldest and most complete form of it that we know about. The players sit in a circle, and one of them is selected to be the judge. Each player—including the judge—contributes a personal article. Behind the judge's back, one of these articles is selected and held up. The following verse is recited:

Heavy, heavy hangs over thy head.   25
What shall I do to redeem thee?

The judge—not knowing whose article it is—names some stunt or other that the owner of the article then has to perform. Much merriment is had at the absurdities that follow.

There's nothing we human beings can imagine, including debt, that can't be turned into a game—something done for entertainment. And, in reverse, there are no games, however frivolous, that cannot also be played very seriously and sometimes very unpleasantly. You'll know this yourself if you've ever played social bridge with a gang of white-haired, ruthless ace-trumpers or watched any news items about cheerleaders' mothers trying to assassinate their daughters' rivals. Halfway between tiddlywinks and the Battle of Waterloo—between kids' games and war games—fall hockey and football and their ilk, in which the fans shouting "Kill!" are only partly joking. But when the play turns nasty in dead earnest, the game becomes what Eric Berne calls a "hard game." In hard games the stakes are high, the play is dirty, and the outcome may well be a puddle of gore on the floor.

For Discussion and Writing

1. What are the "hidden metaphors" (par. 4) of debt? What do they reveal about the meaning of indebtedness?

2. Atwood spends several paragraphs discussing Ebenezer Scrooge as both a literary character created by Charles Dickens and a long-standing pop culture image. She writes that Dickens had "nothing against Scrooge's being rich" (par. 19). Why is that important? As a cultural icon, what does Scrooge represent in the context of money and debt?

3. **connections**   Atwood refers to the "cherished core beliefs of capitalism" (par. 2). In "Overselling Capitalism with Consumerism" (p. 15), Benjamin Barber writes that capitalism's "core virtue is that it marries altruism and self-interest" (par. 2). Do you think Atwood would agree? How would you compare and contrast the two writers' views of capitalism and debt?

4. Atwood focuses on examples from history and literature to explore her topic. Using an example from popular culture, literature, or your own observations, write an essay that investigates and illustrates the nature and meaning of debt.

BARBARA EHRENREICH

Selling in Minnesota

While Barbara Ehrenreich (b. 1941) is known for her journalism and social activism, she originally studied chemistry and earned a Ph.D. in cellular biology from Rockefeller University. Rather than pursuing a career in science, however, she worked on women's health research and advocacy, a path that led to her writing career. Ehrenreich's criticism and social commentary have appeared regularly in the Atlantic Monthly, *the* Nation, *the* New Republic, Salon, *the* New York Times, TV Guide, *and many other publications over the last three decades. Ehrenreich has also written several books, including* Bait and Switch: The (Futile) Pursuit of the American Dream *(2005),* This Land Is Their Land: Reports from a Divided Nation *(2008), and* Bright-sided: How the Relentless Promotion of Positive Thinking Has Undermined America *(2009).*

Her 2001 bestseller Nickel and Dimed: On (Not) Getting By in America *recounted Ehrenreich's experiences working a variety of low-wage jobs. In the following selection, excerpted from that book, she recounts her employee orientation after being hired by Wal-Mart, the largest private employer in the world. The author practices experiential journalism: She is part of the story. As you read, however, note how Ehrenreich uses personal narrative to raise issues that go beyond her personal experience.*

For sheer grandeur, scale, and intimidation value, I doubt if any corporate orientation exceeds that of Wal-Mart. I have been told that the process will take eight hours, which will include two fifteen-minute breaks and one half-hour break for a meal, and will be paid for like a regular shift. When I arrive, dressed neatly in khakis and clean T-shirt, as befits a potential Wal-Mart "associate," I find there are ten new hires besides myself, mostly young and Caucasian, and a team of three, headed by Roberta, to do the "orientating." We sit around a long table in the same windowless room where I was interviewed, each with a thick folder of paperwork in front of us, and hear Roberta tell once again about raising six children, being a "people person," discovering that the three principles of Wal-Mart philosophy were the same as her own, and so on. We begin with a video, about fifteen minutes long, on the history and philosophy of Wal-Mart, or, as an anthropological observer might call it, the Cult of Sam. First young Sam Walton, in uniform, comes back from the war. He starts a store, a sort of five-and-dime; he marries and fathers four attractive children; he receives a Medal of Freedom from President Bush, after which he promptly dies, making way for the eulogies. But the company goes on, yes indeed. Here the arc of the story soars upward unstoppably, pausing only to mark some fresh milestone of corporate expansion. 1992: Wal-Mart becomes the largest retailer in the world. 1997: Sales top $100 billion. 1998: The number of Wal-Mart associates hits 825,000, making Wal-Mart the largest private employer in the nation. Each landmark date is accompanied by a clip showing throngs of shoppers, swarms of associates, or scenes of handsome new stores and their adjoining parking lots. Over and over we hear in voiceover or see in graphic display the "three principles," which are maddeningly, even defiantly, nonparallel: "respect for the individual, exceeding customers' expectations, strive for excellence."

"Respect for the individual" is where we, the associates, come in, because vast as Wal-Mart is, and tiny as we may be as individuals, everything depends on us. Sam always said, and is shown saying, that "the best ideas come from the associates"—for example, the idea of having a "people greeter," an elderly employee (excuse me, associate) who welcomes each customer as he or she enters the store. Three times during the orientation, which began at three and stretches to nearly eleven, we are reminded that this brainstorm originated in a mere associate, and who knows what revolutions in retailing each one of us may propose? Because our ideas are welcome, more than welcome, and we are to think of our managers not as bosses but as "servant leaders," serving us as well as the customers. Of course, all is not total harmony, in every instance, between associates and their servant-leaders. A video on "associate honesty" shows a cashier being caught on videotape as he pockets some bills from the cash register. Drums beat ominously as he is led away in handcuffs and sentenced to four years.

The theme of covert tensions, overcome by right thinking and positive attitude, continues in the twelve-minute video entitled *You've Picked a Great Place to Work*. Here various associates testify to the "essential feeling of family for which Wal-Mart is so well-known," leading up to the conclusion that we don't need a union. Once, long ago, unions had a place in American society, but they "no longer have much to offer workers," which is why people are leaving them "by the droves." Wal-Mart is booming; unions are declining: judge for yourself. But we are warned that "unions have been targeting Wal-Mart for years." Why? For the dues money of course. Think of what you would lose with a union: first, your dues money, which could be $20 a month "and sometimes much more." Second, you would lose "your voice" because the union would insist on doing your talking for you. Finally, you might lose even your wages and benefits because they would all be "at risk on the bargaining table." You have to wonder—and I imagine some of my teenage fellow orientees may be doing so— why such fiends as these union organizers, such outright extortionists, are allowed to roam free in the land.

One of nearly two million Wal-Mart workers worldwide greets shoppers at the entrance to a new store in Ohio.

There is more, much more than I could ever absorb, even if it were spread out over a semester-long course. On the reasonable assumption that none of us is planning to go home and curl up with the "Wal-Mart Associate Handbook," our trainers start reading it out loud to us, pausing every few paragraphs to ask, "Any questions?" There never are. Barry, the seventeen-year-old to my left, mutters that his "butt hurts." Sonya, the tiny African American woman across from me, seems frozen in terror. I have given up on looking perky and am fighting to keep my eyes open. No nose or other facial jewelry, we learn; earrings must be small and discreet, not dangling; no blue jeans except on Friday, and then you have to pay $1 for the privilege of wearing them. No "grazing," that is, eating from food packages that somehow become open; no "time theft." This last sends me drifting off in a sci-fi direction: *And as the time thieves headed back to the year 3420, loaded with weekends and days off looted from the twenty-first century* . . . Finally, a question. The old guy who is being hired as a people greeter wants to know, "What is time theft?" Answer: Doing anything other than working during company time, anything at all. Theft of *our* time is not, however, an issue. There are stretches amounting to many minutes when all three of our trainers wander off, leaving us to sit there in silence or take the opportunity to squirm. Or our junior trainers go through a section of the handbook, and then Roberta, returning from some other business, goes over the same section again. My eyelids droop and I consider walking out. I have seen time move more swiftly during seven-hour airline delays. In fact, I am getting nostalgic about seven-hour airline delays. At least you can read a book or get up and walk around, take a leak.

On breaks, I drink coffee purchased at the Radio Grill, as the   5 in-house fast-food place is called, the real stuff with caffeine, more because I'm concerned about being alert for the late-night drive home than out of any need to absorb all the Wal-Mart trivia coming my way. Now, here's a drug the drug warriors ought to take a little more interest in. Since I don't normally drink it at all—iced tea can usually be counted on for enough of a kick—the coffee has an effect like reagent-grade Dexedrine: my pulse races, my brain overheats, and the result in this instance is a kind of delirium. I find myself overly challenged by the little kindergarten-level tasks we are now given to do, such as affixing my personal bar code to my ID card, then sticking on the punch-out letters to spell my name. The letters keep curling up and sticking to my fingers, so I stop at "Barb," or more precisely, "BARB," drifting off to think of all the people I know who have gentrified their names in recent years—Patsy to Patricia, Dick to Richard, and so forth— while I am going in the other direction. Now we start taking turns going to the computers to begin our CBL, or Computer-Based Learning, and I become transfixed by the HIV-inspired module entitled "Bloodborne Pathogens," on what to do in the event that pools of human blood should show up on the sales floor. All right, you put warning cones around the puddles, don protective gloves, etc., but I can't stop trying to envision the circumstances in which these pools might arise: an associate uprising? a guest riot? I have gone through six modules, three more than we are supposed to do tonight—the rest are to be done in our spare moments over the next few weeks—when one of the trainers gently pries me away from the computer. We are allowed now to leave.

For Discussion and Writing

1. According to Ehrenreich's essay, what is Wal-Mart's attitude toward unions? How does the corporation communicate this message to its employees?

2. The Wal-Mart orientation emphasizes "respect for the individual" (par. 2). At the same time, prospective employees are discouraged from committing "time theft" (par. 4). How does Ehrenreich use these two phrases ironically? In what way do they support her main point?

3. **connections**   Both Ehrenreich in this essay and Eric Schlosser in "Behind the Counter" (p. 49) show how corporations seek—or encourage—certain values and attitudes in their employees. What are those attitudes and values? Would you like to have them? Do you see anything wrong with them, or are they necessary to standardization and productivity? How is the McDonald's approach to employees similar to Wal-Mart's approach?

4. For Ehrenreich, the orientation reveals Wal-Mart's view of itself as a corporation and its employees. Write about an experience you have had as an employee. How were you treated? Did your employer(s) try to shape your attitudes toward work? Was the experience rewarding or discouraging?

ERIC SCHLOSSER

Behind the Counter

Eric Schlosser (b. 1959) is an author and investigative journalist best known for his exposé of the United States fast food industry Fast Food Nation: The Dark Side of the All-American Meal *(2001). The controversial book, which examined a range of issues from the health and social costs of fast food to unsanitary meat-packing practices and the exploitation of immigrant labor, was made into a film by director Richard Linklater in 2006. Schlosser's other books include* Reefer Madness *(2003) and* Chew On This *(2006). He has also written for the* Atlantic Monthly, Rolling Stone, *the* New Yorker, *and the* Nation.

"Behind the Counter" is adapted from Fast Food Nation. *In this excerpt, Schlosser looks at the working conditions of fast food workers, as well as the employee management practices of companies like McDonald's and Burger King. Do you eat fast food? Have you ever wondered how these restaurants produce so many standardized meals with so much efficiency?*

Every Saturday Elisa Zamot gets up at 5:15 in the morning. It's a struggle, and her head feels groggy as she steps into the shower. Her little sisters, Cookie and Sabrina, are fast asleep in their beds. By 5:30, Elisa's showered, done her hair, and put on her McDonald's uniform. She's sixteen, bright-eyed and olive-skinned, pretty and petite, ready for another day of work. Elisa's mother usually drives her the half-mile or so to the restaurant, but sometimes Elisa walks, leaving home before the sun rises. Her family's modest townhouse sits beside a busy highway on the south side of Colorado Springs, in a largely poor and working-class neighborhood. Throughout the day, sounds of traffic fill the house, the steady whoosh of passing cars. But when Elisa heads for work, the streets are quiet, the sky's still dark, and the lights are out in the small houses and rental apartments along the road.

49

When Elisa arrives at McDonald's, the manager unlocks the door and lets her in. Sometimes the husband-and-wife cleaning crew are just finishing up. More often, it's just Elisa and the manager in the restaurant, surrounded by an empty parking lot. For the next hour or so, the two of them get everything ready. They turn on the ovens and grills. They go downstairs into the basement and get food and supplies for the morning shift. They get the paper cups, wrappers, cardboard containers, and packets of condiments. They step into the big freezer and get the frozen bacon, the frozen pancakes, and the frozen cinnamon rolls. They get the frozen hash browns, the frozen biscuits, the frozen McMuffins. They get the cartons of scrambled egg mix and orange juice mix. They bring the food upstairs and start preparing it before any customers appear, thawing some things in the microwave and cooking other things on the grill. They put the cooked food in special cabinets to keep it warm.

The restaurant opens for business at seven o'clock, and for the next hour or so, Elisa and the manager hold down the fort, handling all the orders. As the place starts to get busy, other employees arrive. Elisa works behind the counter. She takes orders and hands food to customers from breakfast through lunch. When she finally walks home, after seven hours of standing at a cash register, her feet hurt. She's wiped out. She comes through the front door, flops onto the living room couch, and turns on the TV. And the next morning she gets up at 5:15 again and starts the same routine.

Up and down Academy Boulevard, along South Nevada, Circle Drive, and Woodman Road, teenagers like Elisa run the fast food restaurants of Colorado Springs. Fast food kitchens often seem like a scene from *Bugsy Malone*, a film in which all the actors are children pretending to be adults. No other industry in the United States has a workforce so dominated by adolescents. About two-thirds of the nation's fast food workers are under the age of twenty. Teenagers open the fast food outlets in the morning, close them at night, and keep them going at all hours in between. Even the managers and assistant managers are sometimes in their late teens. Unlike Olympic gymnastics—an activity in which teenagers consistently perform at a higher level than adults—there's nothing about the work in a fast food kitchen that requires young employees. Instead of relying upon a small, stable, well-paid, and

"Throughput is all about increasing the speed of assembly, about doing things faster in order to make more."

well-trained workforce, the fast food industry seeks out part-time, unskilled workers who are willing to accept low pay. Teenagers have been the perfect candidates for these jobs, not only because they are less expensive to hire than adults, but also because their youthful inexperience makes them easier to control.

The labor practices of the fast food industry have their origins   5
in the assembly line systems adopted by American manufacturers in the early twentieth century. Business historian Alfred D. Chandler has argued that a high rate of "throughput" was the most important aspect of these mass production systems. A factory's throughput is the speed and volume of its flow—a much more crucial measurement, according to Chandler, than the number of workers it employs or the value of its machinery. With innovative technology and the proper organization, a small number of workers can produce an enormous amount of goods cheaply. Throughput is all about increasing the speed of assembly, about doing things faster in order to make more.

Although the McDonald brothers had never encountered the term "throughput" or studied "scientific management," they instinctively grasped the underlying principles and applied them in the Speedee Service System. The restaurant operating scheme they developed has been widely adopted and refined over the past half century. The ethos of the assembly line remains at its core. The fast food industry's obsession with throughput has altered the way millions of Americans work, turned commercial kitchens into small factories, and changed familiar foods into commodities that are manufactured.

At Burger King restaurants, frozen hamburger patties are placed on a conveyor belt and emerge from a broiler ninety seconds later fully cooked. The ovens at Pizza Hut and at Domino's also use conveyer belts to ensure standardized cooking times. The ovens at McDonald's look like commercial laundry presses, with big steel hoods that swing down and grill hamburgers on both sides at once. The burgers, chicken, french fries, and buns are all frozen when they arrive at McDonald's. The shakes and sodas begin as syrup. At Taco Bell restaurants the food is "assembled," not prepared. The guacamole isn't made by workers in the kitchen; it's made at a factory in Michoacán, Mexico, then frozen and shipped north. The chain's taco meat arrives frozen and precooked in vacuum-sealed plastic bags. The beans are dehydrated and look like brownish corn flakes. The cooking process is fairly simple. "Everything's add water," a Taco Bell employee told me. "Just add hot water."

Although Richard and Mac McDonald introduced the division of labor to the restaurant business, it was a McDonald's executive named Fred Turner who created a production system of unusual thoroughness and attention to detail. In 1958, Turner put together an operations and training manual for the company that was seventy-five pages long, specifying how almost everything should be done. Hamburgers were always to be placed on the grill in six neat rows; french fries had to be exactly 0.28 inches thick. The McDonald's operations manual today has ten times the number of pages and weighs about four pounds. Known within the company as "the Bible," it contains precise instructions on how various appliances should be used, how each item on the menu should look, and how employees should greet customers. Operators who disobey these rules can lose their franchises. Cooking instructions are not only printed in the manual, they are often

designed into the machines. A McDonald's kitchen is full of buzz-
ers and flashing lights that tell employees what to do.
At the front counter, computerized cash registers issue their
own commands. Once an order has been placed, buttons light up
and suggest other menu items that can be added. Workers at the
counter are told to increase the size of an order by recommending special promotions, pushing dessert, pointing out the financial logic behind the purchase of a larger drink. While doing so,
they are instructed to be upbeat and friendly. "Smile with a greeting and make a positive first impression," a Burger King training
manual suggests. "Show them you are GLAD TO SEE THEM. Include
eye contact with the cheerful greeting."

The strict regimentation at fast food restaurants creates stan-   10
dardized products. It increases the throughput. And it gives fast
food companies an enormous amount of power over their employees. "When management determines exactly how every task is to
be done . . . and can impose its own rules about pace, output,
quality, and technique," the sociologist Robin Leidner has noted,
"[it] makes workers increasingly interchangeable." The management no longer depends upon the talents or skills of its workers —
those things are built into the operating system and machines.
Jobs that have been "de-skilled" can be filled cheaply. The need to
retain any individual worker is greatly reduced by the ease with
which he or she can be replaced.

Teenagers have long provided the fast food industry with the
bulk of its workforce. The industry's rapid growth coincided with
the baby-boom expansion of that age group. Teenagers were in
many ways the ideal candidates for these low-paying jobs. Since
most teenagers still lived at home, they could afford to work for
wages too low to support an adult, and until recently, their limited skills attracted few other employers. A job at a fast food restaurant became an American rite of passage, a first job soon left
behind for better things. The flexible terms of employment in the
fast food industry also attracted housewives who needed extra
income. As the number of baby-boom teenagers declined, the fast
food chains began to hire other marginalized workers: recent
immigrants, the elderly, and the handicapped.

English is now the second language of at least one-sixth of the
nation's restaurant workers, and about one-third of that group

speaks no English at all. The proportion of fast food workers who cannot speak English is even higher. Many know only the names of the items on the menu; they speak "McDonald's English."

The fast food industry now employs some of the most disadvantaged members of American society. It often teaches basic job skills—such as getting to work on time—to people who can barely read, whose lives have been chaotic or shut off from the mainstream. Many individual franchisees are genuinely concerned about the well-being of their workers. But the stance of the fast food industry on issues involving employee training, the minimum wage, labor unions, and overtime pay strongly suggests that its motives in hiring the young, the poor, and the handicapped are hardly altruistic.

At a 1999 conference on foodservice equipment, top American executives from Burger King, McDonald's, and Tricon Global Restaurants, Inc. (the owner of Taco Bell, Pizza Hut, and KFC) appeared together on a panel to discuss labor shortages, employee training, computerization, and the latest kitchen technology. The three corporations now employ about 3.7 million people worldwide, operate about 60,000 restaurants, and open a new fast food restaurant every two hours. Putting aside their intense rivalry for customers, the executives had realized at a gathering the previous evening that when it came to labor issues, they were in complete agreement. "We've come to the conclusion that we're in support of each other," Dave Brewer, the vice president of engineering at KFC, explained. "We are aligned as a team to support this industry." One of the most important goals they held in common was the redesign of kitchen equipment so that less money needed to be spent training workers. "Make the equipment intuitive, make it so that the job is easier to do right than to do wrong," advised Jerry Sus, the leading equipment systems engineer at McDonald's. "The easier it is for him [the worker] to use, the easier it is for us not to have to train him." John Reckert—director of strategic operations and of research and development at Burger King—felt optimistic about the benefits that new technology would bring the industry. "We can develop equipment that only works one way," Reckert said. "There are many different ways today that employees can abuse our product, mess up the flow . . . If the equipment only allows one process, there's very little to train." Instead of giving written instructions to crew members, another panelist suggested, rely as much as possible on photographs of menu items, and "if there are instructions, make them very simple, write them at a fifth-grade level, and write them in Spanish and English." All of the executives agreed that "zero training" was the fast food industry's ideal, though it might not ever be attained.

While quietly spending enormous sums on research and tech-   15
nology to eliminate employee training, the fast food chains have accepted hundreds of millions of dollars in government subsidies for "training" their workers. Through federal programs such as the Targeted Jobs Tax Credit and its successor, the Work Opportunity Tax Credit, the chains have for years claimed tax credits of up to $2,400 for each new low-income worker they hired. In 1996 an investigation by the U.S. Department of Labor concluded that 92 percent of these workers would have been hired by the companies anyway—and that their new jobs were part-time, provided little training, and came with no benefits. These federal subsidy programs were created to reward American companies that gave job training to the poor.

Attempts to end these federal subsidies have been strenuously opposed by the National Council of Chain Restaurants and its allies in Congress. The Work Opportunity Tax Credit program was renewed in 1996. It offered as much as $385 million in subsidies the following year. Fast food restaurants had to employ a worker for only four hundred hours to receive the federal money—and then could get more money as soon as that worker quit and was replaced. American taxpayers have in effect subsidized the industry's high turnover rate, providing company tax breaks for workers who are employed for just a few months and receive no training. The industry front group formed to defend these government subsidies is called the "Committee for Employment Opportunities." Its chief lobbyist, Bill Signer, told the *Houston Chronicle* there was nothing wrong with the use of federal subsidies to create low-paying, low-skilled, short-term jobs for the poor. Trying to justify the minimal amount of training given to these workers, Signer said, "They've got to crawl before they can walk."

The employees whom the fast food industry expects to crawl are by far the biggest group of low-wage workers in the United

States today. The nation has about 1 million migrant farm workers and about 3.5 million fast food workers. Although picking strawberries is orders of magnitude more difficult than cooking hamburgers, both jobs are now filled by people who are generally young, unskilled, and willing to work long hours for low pay. Moreover, the turnover rates for both jobs are among the highest in the American economy. The annual turnover rate in the fast food industry is now about 300 to 400 percent. The typical fast food worker quits or is fired every three to four months.

The fast food industry pays the minimum wage to a higher proportion of its workers than any other American industry. Consequently, a low minimum wage has long been a crucial part of the fast food industry's business plan. Between 1968 and 1990, the years when the fast food chains expanded at their fastest rate, the real value of the U.S. minimum wage fell by almost 40 percent. In the late 1990s, the real value of the U.S. minimum wage still remained about 27 percent lower than it was in the late 1960s. Nevertheless, the National Restaurant Association (NRA) has vehemently opposed any rise in the minimum wage at the federal, state, or local level. About sixty large food-service companies—including Jack in the Box, Wendy's, Chevy's, and Red Lobster—have backed congressional legislation that would essentially eliminate the federal minimum wage by allowing states to disregard it. Pete Meersman, the president of the Colorado Restaurant Association, advocates creating a federal guest worker program to import low-wage food-service workers from overseas.

While the real value of the wages paid to restaurant workers has declined for the past three decades, the earnings of restaurant company executives have risen considerably. According to a 1997 survey in *Nation's Restaurant News*, the average corporate executive bonus was $131,000, an increase of 20 percent over the previous year. Increasing the federal minimum wage by a dollar would add about two cents to the cost of a fast food hamburger.

In 1938, at the height of the Great Depression, Congress passed 20 legislation to prevent employers from exploiting the nation's most vulnerable workers. The Fair Labor Standards Act established the first federal minimum wage. It also imposed limitations on child labor. And it mandated that employees who work more than forty hours a week be paid overtime wages for each additional hour.

The overtime wage was set at a minimum of one and a half times the regular wage.

Today few employees in the fast food industry qualify for overtime—and even fewer are paid it. Roughly 90 percent of the nation's fast food workers are paid an hourly wage, provided no benefits, and scheduled to work only as needed. Crew members are employed "at will." If the restaurant's busy, they're kept longer than usual. If business is slow, they're sent home early. Managers try to make sure that each worker is employed less than forty hours a week, thereby avoiding any overtime payments. A typical McDonald's or Burger King restaurant has about fifty crew members. They work an average of thirty hours a week. By hiring a large number of crew members for each restaurant, sending them home as soon as possible, and employing them for fewer than forty hours a week whenever possible, the chains keep their labor costs to a bare minimum.

A handful of fast food workers are paid regular salaries. A fast food restaurant that employs fifty crew members has four or five managers and assistant managers. They earn about $23,000 a year and usually receive medical benefits, as well as some form of bonus or profit sharing. They have an opportunity to rise up the corporate ladder. But they also work long hours without overtime—fifty, sixty, seventy hours a week. The turnover rate among assistant managers is extremely high. The job offers little opportunity for independent decision-making. Computer programs, training manuals, and the machines in the kitchen determine how just about everything must be done.

Fast food managers do have the power to hire, fire, and schedule workers. Much of their time is spent motivating their crew members. In the absence of good wages and secure employment, the chains try to inculcate "team spirit" in their young crews. Workers who fail to work hard, who arrive late, or who are reluctant to stay extra hours are made to feel that they're making life harder for everyone else, letting their friends and coworkers down. For years the McDonald's Corporation has provided its managers with training in "transactional analysis," a set of psychological techniques popularized in the book *I'm OK—You're OK* (1969). One of these techniques is called "stroking"—a form of positive reinforcement, deliberate praise, and recognition that many teenagers don't get at home. Stroking can make a worker feel that his or her contribution is sincerely valued. And it's much less expensive than raising wages or paying overtime.

The fast food chains often reward managers who keep their labor costs low, a practice that often leads to abuses. In 1997 a jury in Washington State found that Taco Bell had systematically coerced its crew members into working off the clock in order to avoid paying them overtime. The bonuses of Taco Bell restaurant managers were tied to their success at cutting labor costs. The managers had devised a number of creative ways to do so. Workers were forced to wait until things got busy at a restaurant before officially starting their shifts. They were forced to work without pay after their shifts ended. They were forced to clean restaurants on their own time. And they were sometimes compensated with food, not wages. Many of the workers involved were minors and recent immigrants. Before the penalty phase of the Washington lawsuit, the two sides reached a settlement; Taco Bell agreed to pay millions of dollars in back wages, but admitted no wrongdoing. As many as 16,000 current and former employees were owed money by the company. One employee, a high school dropout named Regina Jones, regularly worked seventy to eighty hours a week but was paid for only forty. In 2001, Taco Bell settled a class-action lawsuit in California, agreeing to pay $9 million in back wages for overtime and an Oregon jury found that Taco Bell managers had falsified the time cards of thousands of workers in order to get productivity bonuses.

For Discussion and Writing

1. According to Schlosser, about two-thirds of American fast food workers are under the age of twenty. Why are younger employees so appealing to the fast food industry, in his view?

2. Schlosser describes the elaborate instructions given to fast food employees. These guidelines regulate their actions on the job, as when cashiers take customer orders: "While doing so, they are instructed to be upbeat and friendly. 'Smile with a greeting and make a positive first impression,' a Burger King training manual suggests. 'Show them you are GLAD TO SEE THEM. Include eye contact with the cheerful greeting'" (par. 9). What is Schlosser's implied attitude about such instructions? How can you tell? Do you share his view? Why or why not?

3. **connections**   Both Schlosser and Barbara Ehrenreich in "Selling in Minnesota" (p. 44) write about the practices of large corporations

and their employees. But Schlosser writes in the third person, while Ehrenreich writes in the first person. How does this choice affect their essays? Which approach do you find more effective?

4. Schlosser's account of the fast food industry is almost entirely negative. Does it seem fair? Does his essay change your views of restaurants like McDonald's and Burger King? Will it affect your behavior in any way?

CHAPTER 2

Advertising

"The trade of advertising is now so near to perfection that it is not easy to propose any improvement." So wrote Samuel Johnson, the great English literary critic, in 1759. Although he lived long before the invention of pop-up Internet ads, electrified highway billboards, late-night television informercials, the Energizer bunny, *"Just Do It,"* and the Pepsi Generation, Johnson identified the essence of his subject: "Promise, large promise, is the soul of an advertisement." Over two and a half centuries later, advertising is still making those large promises.

While basic forms of advertising go back as least as far as ancient Egyptian papyrus posters, our familiar, modern form developed alongside print media. In the nineteenth century, newspapers began including paid advertisements in their pages, which lowered the price of publications. This model, which uses ad revenue to pay for editorial and entertainment "content," still drives our commercial print, radio, Internet, and television industries today. In the United States, manufacturing and productivity boomed in the late-nineteenth and early twentieth centuries—as did advertising, which became necessary to differentiate products in a competitive economy. Mass media made brands like Sears, Coca-Cola, and Kodak national phenomena by distributing their advertisements across the country.

At the beginning of the twentieth century, copywriter John E. Kennedy famously defined advertising as "salesmanship in print." But as the century progressed, commercial radio and television superseded print media in the proliferation of advertising. Consumers became more sophisticated, of course, but so did marketers and advertisers. Edward Bernays, political consultant and author of books such as *This Business of Propaganda* (1928), applied the psychological theories of his uncle, Sigmund Freud, to marketing, branding, and public relations. As the ad industry grew in size and influence, its legion of skeptics and detractors grew as well. For example, in 1957, journalist and social critic Vance Packard published *The Hidden Persuaders*, which exposed the manipulative tactics and psychological techniques used to influence consumers.

The essays in this section address advertising, marketing, and mass persuasion from a variety of angles. In "With These Words I Can Sell You Anything," William Lutz focuses on the specific language of marketers and advertisers; he also encourages consumers to view the claims of advertisers skeptically and "figure out exactly what each word is doing in an ad—what each word really means, not what the advertiser wants you to think it means." Similarly, Donna Woolfolk Cross's classic essay "Propaganda: How Not To Be Bamboozled" provides a concise primer on resisting informal fallacies and dishonest arguments. Jason Tanz looks at the use of hip-hop in marketing and advertising strategies that lure consumers with the promise of vicarious "blackness" ("Selling Down: The Marketing of the Hip-Hop Nation"). In "The Ultimate Marketing Machine," writers from the *Economist* magazine show how the Internet is changing the nature of marketing and advertising. In "Art or Puffery? A Defense of Advertising," the first of the paired readings, career ad man Winston Fletcher addresses the long-standing charge that manipulative advertising diverts people "towards inessential needs." Bill Bryson's witty "The Hard Sell: Advertising in America" gives historical perspective on the theory and practice of modern American advertising, especially the way advertisements identify and exploit the American consumer's anxiety.

WILLIAM LUTZ

With These Words
I Can Sell You Anything

William Lutz (b. 1940) taught English at Rutgers University from 1991 to 2006. He also edited the Quarterly Review of Doublespeak, *a publication that collected misleading language and euphemisms by politicians, advertisers, educators, and others. Lutz has worked with dozens of corporations and government agencies, consulting and conducting workshops on clear language. His books include* Doublespeak: From Revenue Enhancement to Terminal Living *(1989),* The New Doublespeak: No One Knows What Anyone's Saying Anymore *(1996), and* Doublespeak Defined *(1999).*

Lutz approaches the language of advertising in much the way a literary critic approaches a poem. He encourages his readers to use the same rigor: "Your job is to figure out exactly what each word is doing in the ad—what each word really means, not what the advertiser wants you to think it means." We often presume that the goal of language is clear and accurate communication. As you read his essay (adapted from the book Doublespeak: From Revenue Enhancement to Terminal Living*), notice how words can mask reality, or mislead us.*

One problem advertisers have when they try to convince you that the product they are pushing is really different from other, similar products is that their claims are subject to some laws. Not a lot of laws, but there are some designed to prevent fraudulent or untruthful claims in advertising. Generally speaking, advertisers have to be careful in what they say in their ads, in the claims they make for the products they advertise. Parity claims are safe because they are legal and supported by a number of court decisions. But beyond parity claims there are weasel words.

Advertisers use weasel words to appear to be making a claim for a product when in fact they are making no claim at all. Weasel words get their name from the way weasels eat the eggs they find in the nests of other animals. A weasel will make a small hole in the egg, suck out the insides, then place the egg back in the nest. Only when the egg is examined closely is it found to be hollow. That's the way it is with weasel words in advertising.

"HELP"—THE NUMBER ONE WEASEL WORD

The biggest weasel word used in advertising doublespeak is "help." Now "help" only means to aid or assist, nothing more. It does not mean to conquer, stop, eliminate, end, solve, heal, cure, or anything else. But once the ad says "help," it can say just about anything after that because "help" qualifies everything coming after it. The trick is that the claim that comes after the weasel word is usually so strong and so dramatic that you forget the word "help" and concentrate only on the dramatic claim. You read into the ad a message that the ad does not contain. More importantly, the advertiser is not responsible for the claim that you read into the ad, even though the advertiser wrote the ad so you would read that claim into it.

"Advertisers use weasel words to appear to be making a claim for a product when in fact they are making no claim at all."

The next time you see an ad for a cold medicine that promises that it "helps relieve cold symptoms fast," don't rush out to buy it. Ask yourself what this claim is really saying. Remember, "helps" means only that the medicine will aid or assist. What will it aid or assist in doing? Why, "relieve" your cold "symptoms." "Relieve" only means to ease, alleviate, or mitigate, not to stop, end, or cure. Nor does the claim say how much relieving this medicine will do. Nowhere does this ad claim it will cure anything. In fact, the ad doesn't even claim it will do anything at all. The ad only claims that it will aid in relieving (not curing) your cold symptoms, which are probably a runny nose, watery eyes, and a headache. In other words, this medicine probably contains a standard decongestant and some aspirin. By the way, what does "fast" mean? Ten minutes, one hour, one day? What is fast to one person can be very slow to another. Fast is another weasel word.

Look at ads in magazines and newspapers, listen to ads on   5
radio and television, and you'll find the word "help" in ads for all kinds of products. How often do you read or hear such phrases as "helps stop . . . ," "helps overcome . . . ," "helps eliminate . . . ," "helps you feel . . . ," or "helps you look . . ."? If you start looking for this weasel word in advertising, you'll be amazed at how often it occurs. Analyze the claims in the ads using "help," and you will discover that these ads are really saying nothing.

VIRTUALLY SPOTLESS

One of the most powerful weasel words is "virtually," a word so innocent that most people don't pay any attention to it when it is used in an advertising claim. But watch out. "Virtually" is used in advertising claims that appear to make specific, definite promises when there is no promise. After all, what does "virtually" mean? It means "in essence of effect, although not in fact." Look at that definition again. "Virtually" means not in fact. It does not mean "almost" or "just about the same as," or anything else.

The next time you see the ad that says that this dishwasher detergent "leaves dishes virtually spotless," just remember how advertisers twist the meaning of the weasel word "virtually." You can have lots of spots on your dishes after using this detergent and the ad claim will still be true, because what this claim really means is that this detergent does not in fact leave your dishes spotless. Whenever you see or hear an ad claim that uses the word "virtually," just translate that claim into its real meaning. So the television set that is "virtually trouble free" becomes the television set that is not in fact trouble free, the "virtually foolproof operation" of any appliance becomes an operation that is in fact not foolproof, and the product that "virtually never needs service" becomes the product that is not in fact service free.

NEW AND IMPROVED

If "new" is the most frequently used word on a product package, "improved" is the second most frequent. In fact, the two words are almost always used together. It seems just about everything sold these days is "new and improved." The next time you're in the supermarket, try counting the number of times you see these words on products.

Just what do these words mean? The use of the word "new" is restricted by regulations, so an advertiser can't just use the word on a product or in an ad without meeting certain requirements. For example, a product is considered new for about six months during a national advertising campaign. If the product is being advertised only in a limited test market area, the word can be used longer, and in some instances has been used for as long as two years.

What makes a product "new"? Some products have been 10 around for a long time, yet every once in a while you discover that they are being advertised as "new." Well, an advertiser can call a product new if there has been "a material functional change" in the product. What is "a material functional change," you ask? Good question. In fact it's such a good question it's being asked all the time. It's up to the manufacturer to prove that the product has undergone such a change. And if the manufacturer isn't challenged on the claim, then there's no one to stop it. Moreover, the change does not have to be an improvement in the product. One manufacturer added an artificial lemon scent to a cleaning product and called it "new and improved," even though the product did not clean any better than without the lemon scent. The manufacturer defended the use of the word "new" on the grounds that

ADVERTISING DOUBLESPEAK: QUICK QUIZ

Test your awareness of advertising doublespeak. The following is a list of statements from some recent ads. Your job is to figure out what each of these ads really says.

DOMINO'S PIZZA: "Because nobody delivers better."
SINUTAB: "It can stop the pain."
TUMS: "The stronger acid neutralizer."
LISTERMINT: "Making your mouth a cleaner place."
CASCADE: "For virtually spotless dishes."
NUPRIN: "Little. Yellow. Different. Better."
ANACIN: "Better relief."
ADVIL: "Advanced medicine for pain."
ALEVE COLD AND SINUS: "12 hours of relief."
PONDS COLD CREAM: "Ponds cleans like no soap can."
MILLER LITE BEER: "Tastes great. Less filling."
PHILLIPS MILK OF MAGNESIA: "Nobody treats you better than MOM."
BAYER: "The wonder drug that works wonders."
KNORR: "Where taste is everything."
ANUSOL: "Anusol is the word to remember for relief."
DIMETAPP: "It relieves kids as well as colds."
LIQUID DRĀNO: "The liquid strong enough to be called Drāno."
JOHNSON & JOHNSON BABY POWDER: "Like magic for your skin."
PURITAN: "Make it your oil for life."
PAM: "Pam, because how you cook is as important as what you cook."
TYLENOL GEL-CAPS: "It's not a capsule. It's better."
ALKA-SELTZER PLUS: "Breaks up your worst cold symptoms."

the artificial scent changed the chemical formula of the product and therefore constituted "a material functional change."

Which brings up the word "improved." When used in advertising, "improved" does not mean "made better." It only means "changed" or "different from before." So, if the detergent maker puts a plastic pour spout on the box of detergent, the product has been "improved," and away we go with a whole new advertising campaign. Or, if the cereal maker adds more fruit or a different kind of fruit to the cereal, there's an improved product. Now you know why manufacturers are constantly making little changes in their products. Whole new advertising campaigns, designed to convince you that the product has been changed for the better, are based on small changes in superficial aspects of a product. The next time you see an ad for an "improved" product, ask yourself what was wrong with the old one. Ask yourself just how "improved" the product is. Finally, you might check to see whether the "improved" version costs more than the unimproved one.

"New" is just too useful and powerful a word in advertising for advertisers to pass it up easily. So they use weasel words that say "new" without really saying it. One of their favorites is "introducing," as in, "Introducing improved Tide," or "Introducing the stain remover." The first is simply saying, here's our improved soap; the second, here's our new advertising campaign for our detergent. Another favorite is "now," as in, "Now there's Sinex," which simply means that Sinex is available. Then there are phrases like "Today's Chevrolet," "Presenting Dristan," and "A fresh way to start the day." The list is really endless because advertisers are always finding new ways to say "new" without really saying it.

ACTS FAST

"Acts" and "works" are two popular weasel words in advertising because they bring action to the product and to the advertising claim. When you see the ad for the cough syrup that "Acts on the cough control center," ask yourself what this cough syrup is claiming to do. Well, it's just claiming to "act," to do something, to perform an action. What is it that the cough syrup does? The ad doesn't say. It only claims to perform an action or do something on your "cough control center." By the way, what and where is your "cough control center"? I don't remember learning about that part of the body in human biology class.

Ads that use such phrases as "acts fast," "acts against," "acts to prevent," and the like are saying essentially nothing, because "act" is a word empty of any specific meaning. The ads are always careful not to specify exactly what "act" the product performs. Just because a brand of aspirin claims to "act fast" for headache relief doesn't mean this aspirin is any better than any other aspirin. What is the "act" that this aspirin performs? You're never told. Maybe it just dissolves quickly. Since aspirin is a parity product, all aspirin is the same and therefore functions the same.

WORKS LIKE ANYTHING ELSE

If you don't find the word "acts" in an ad, you will probably find 15 the weasel word "works." In fact, the two words are almost interchangeable in advertising. Watch out for ads that say a product "works against," "works like," "works for," or "works longer." As with "acts," "works" is the same meaningless verb used to make you think that this product really does something, and maybe even something special or unique. But "works," like "acts," is basically a word empty of any specific meaning.

LIKE MAGIC

Whenever advertisers want you to stop thinking about the product and to start thinking about something bigger, better, or more attractive than the product, they use that very popular weasel word, "like." The word "like" is the advertiser's equivalent of a magician's use of misdirection. "Like" gets you to ignore the product and concentrate on the claim the advertiser is making about it. "For skin like peaches and cream" claims the ad for a skin cream. What is that ad really claiming? It doesn't say this cream will give you peaches-and-cream skin. There is no verb in this claim, so it doesn't even mention using the product. How is skin ever like "peaches and cream"? The ad is making absolutely no promise or claim whatsoever for this skin cream. If you think this cream will give you soft, smooth, youthful-looking skin, you are the one who has read that meaning into the ad.

The wine that claims "It's like taking a trip to France" wants you to think about a romantic evening in Paris as you walk along the boulevard after a wonderful meal in an intimate little bistro. Of course, you don't really believe that a wine can take you to France, but the goal of the ad is to get you to think pleasant, romantic thoughts about France and not about how the wine tastes or how expensive it may be. That little word "like" has taken you away from crushed grapes into a world of your own imaginative making. Who knows, maybe the next time you buy wine, you'll think those pleasant thoughts when you see this brand of wine, and you'll buy it. Or, maybe you weren't even thinking about buying wine at all, but now you just might pick up a bottle the next time you're shopping. Ah, the power of "like" in advertising.

THE WORLD OF ADVERTISING

A study some years ago found the following words to be among the most popular used in U.S. television advertisements: "new," "improved," "better," "extra," "fresh," "clean," "beautiful," "free," "good," "great," and "light." At the same time, the following words were found to be among the most frequent on British television: "new," "good-better-best," "free," "fresh," "delicious," "full," "sure," "clean," "wonderful," and "special." While these words may occur most frequently in ads, and while ads may be filled with weasel words, you have to watch out for all the words used in advertising, not just the words mentioned here.

Every word in an ad is there for a reason; no word is wasted. Your job is to figure out exactly what each word is doing in an ad—what each word really means, not what the advertiser wants you to think it means. Remember, the ad is trying to get you to buy a product, so it will put the product in the best possible light, using any device, trick, or means legally allowed. Your only defense against advertising (besides taking up permanent residence on the moon) is to develop and use a strong critical reading, listening, and looking ability. Always ask yourself what the ad is really saying. When you see ads on television, don't be misled by the pictures, the visual images. What does the ad say about the product? What does the ad not say? What information is missing from the ad? Only by becoming an active, critical consumer of the doublespeak of advertising will you ever be able to cut through the doublespeak and discover what the ad is really saying.

For Discussion and Writing

1. According to Lutz, if " 'new' is the most frequently used word on a product package, 'improved' is the second most frequent" (par. 8).

What do these words mean in the context of packaging and advertising? What words do advertisers sometimes use in place of "new"?

2. Lutz addresses the reader as "you" throughout the essay. Why do you think he writes in the second person? How does this choice affect his main point and the essay's overall effectiveness?

3. **connections**   Compare Lutz's "weasel words" with the various techniques in Donna Woolfolk Cross's "Propaganda: How Not To Be Bamboozled" (p. 71). According to her, "propaganda works by tricking us, by momentarily distracting the eye while the rabbit pops out from beneath the cloth" (par. 2). Does the misleading language in Lutz's essay fit into any of Woolfolk Cross's categories? Evaluate "weasel words" as propaganda.

4. Lutz gives a quiz within his essay to test our awareness of tag lines, slogans, and doublespeak in advertising. Choose an advertisement—online, in a magazine, on television—and examine its language. Does it contain "weasel words"? What do they mean? Is the ad misleading or deliberately ambiguous? If the advertisement contains images, do they trick us, or redirect our attention from the product?

DONNA WOOLFOLK CROSS

Propaganda: How Not To Be Bamboozled

Born in 1947, Donna Woolfolk Cross graduated from the University of Pennsylvania and earned a master's degree in English from UCLA. She has written several nonfiction books, including Word Abuse: How the Words We Use Use Us *(1979) and* Mediaspeak: How Television Makes Up Your Mind *(1984). She is also the author of a novel,* Pope Joan *(1996).*

In "Propaganda: How Not To Be Bamboozled," Woolfolk Cross divides and classifies a variety of logical fallacies and propaganda techniques that "help shape our attitudes on a thousand subjects." She also pointedly reminds readers not to presume we are immune to propaganda. Indeed propagandists use these strategies because they work. According to the author, propaganda is a means of persuasion that can be put to good uses or bad ones. As you read, consider how you distinguish between "good" and "bad" propaganda. When does it seem justified or worthwhile?

Propaganda. If an opinion poll were taken tomorrow, we can be sure that nearly everyone would be against it because it *sounds* so bad. When we say, "Oh, that's just propaganda," it means, to most people, "That's a pack of lies." But really, propaganda is simply a means of persuasion and so it can be put to work for good causes as well as bad — to persuade people to give to charity, for example, or to love their neighbors, or to stop polluting the environment.

For good or evil, propaganda pervades our daily lives, helping to shape our attitudes on a thousand subjects. Propaganda probably determines the brand of toothpaste you use, the movies you see, the candidates you elect when you go to the polls. Propaganda works by tricking us, by momentarily distracting the eye while the rabbit pops out from beneath the cloth. Propaganda

71

works best with an uncritical audience. Joseph Goebbels, Propaganda Minister in Nazi Germany, once defined his work as "the conquest of the masses." The masses would not have been conquered, however, if they had known how to challenge and to question, how to make distinctions between propaganda and reasonable arguments.

People are bamboozled mainly because they don't recognize propaganda when they see it. They need to be informed about the various devices that can be used to mislead and deceive—about the propagandist's overflowing bag of tricks. The following, then, are some common pitfalls for the unwary.

1. NAME-CALLING

As its title suggests, this device consists of labeling people or ideas with words of bad connotation, literally, "calling them names." Here the propagandist tries to arouse our contempt so we will dismiss the "bad name" person or idea without examining its merits.

Bad names have played a tremendously important role in the   5
history of the world. They have ruined reputations and ended lives, sent people to prison and to war, and just generally made us mad at each other for centuries.

Name-calling can be used against policies, practices, beliefs and ideals, as well as against individuals, groups, races, nations. Name-calling is at work when we hear a candidate for office described as a "foolish idealist" or a "two-faced liar" or when an incumbent's policies are denounced as "reckless," "reactionary," or just plain "stupid." Some of the most effective names a public figure can be called are ones that may not denote anything specific: "Congresswoman Jane Doe is a *bleeding heart!*" (Did she vote for funds to help paraplegics?) or "The senator is a *tool of Washington!*" (Did he happen to agree with the president?) Senator Yakalot uses name-calling when he denounces his opponent's "radical policies" and calls them (and him) "socialist," "pinko," and part of a "heartless plot." He also uses it when he calls small cars "puddle-jumpers," "can openers," and "motorized baby buggies."

The point here is that when the propagandist uses name-calling, he doesn't want us to think—merely to react, blindly, unquestioningly. So the best defense against being taken in by name-calling

is to stop and ask, "Forgetting the bad name attached to it, what
are the merits of the idea itself? What does this name really mean,
anyway?"

2. GLITTERING GENERALITIES

Glittering generalities are really name-calling in reverse. Name-
calling uses words with bad connotations; glittering generalities
are words with good connotations—"virtue words," as the Institute for Propaganda Analysis has called them. The Institute
explains that while name-calling tries to get us to *reject* and *condemn* someone or something without examining the evidence,
glittering generalities try to get us to *accept* and *agree* without
examining the evidence.

We believe in, fight for, live by "virtue words" which we feel
deeply about: "justice," "motherhood," "the American way," "our
Constitutional rights," "our Christian heritage." These sound
good, but when we examine them closely, they turn out to have no
specific, definable meaning. They just make us feel good. Senator
Yakalot uses glittering generalities when he says, "I stand for all
that is good in America, for our American way and our American
birthright." But what exactly *is* "good for America"? How can we
define our "American birthright"? Just what part of the American
society and culture does "our American way" refer to?

We often make the mistake of assuming we are personally 10
unaffected by glittering generalities. The next time you find yourself assuming that, listen to a political candidate's speech on TV
and see how often the use of glittering generalities elicits cheers
and applause. That's the danger of propaganda; it *works*. Once
again, our defense against it is to ask questions: Forgetting the
virtue words attached to it, what are the merits of the idea itself?
What does "Americanism" (or "freedom" or "truth") really *mean*
here? . . .

Both name-calling and glittering generalities work by stirring
our emotions in the hope that this will cloud our thinking.
Another approach that propaganda uses is to create a distraction,
a "red herring," that will make people forget or ignore the real
issues. There are several kinds of "red herrings" that can be used
to distract attention.

3. PLAIN-FOLKS APPEAL

"Plain folks" is the device by which a speaker tries to win our confidence and support by appearing to be a person like ourselves—"just one of the plain folks." The plain-folks appeal is at work when candidates go around shaking hands with factory workers, kissing babies in supermarkets, and sampling pasta with Italians, fried chicken with Southerners, bagels and blintzes with Jews. "Now I'm a businessman like yourselves" is a plain-folks appeal, as is "I've been a farm boy all my life." Senator Yakalot tries the plain-folks appeal when he says, "I'm just a small-town boy like you fine people." The use of such expressions once prompted Lyndon Johnson to quip, "Whenever I hear someone say, 'I'm just an old country lawyer,' the first thing I reach for is my wallet to make sure it's still there."

The irrelevancy of the plain-folks appeal is obvious: even if the man *is* "one of us" (which may not be true at all), that doesn't mean that his ideas and programs are sound—or even that he honestly has our best interests at heart. As with glittering generalities, the danger here is that we may mistakenly assume we are immune to this appeal. But propagandists wouldn't use it unless it had been proved to work. You can protect yourself by asking, "Aside from his 'nice guy next door' image, what does this man stand for? Are his ideas and his past record really supportive of my best interests?"

4. *ARGUMENTUM AD POPULUM* (STROKING)

Argumentum ad populum means "argument to the people" or "telling the people what they want to hear." The colloquial term from the Watergate era is "stroking," which conjures up pictures of small animals or children being stroked or soothed with compliments until they come to like the person doing the complimenting—and, by extension, his or her ideas.

We all like to hear nice things about ourselves and the group 15 we belong to—we like to be liked—so it stands to reason that we will respond warmly to a person who tells us we are "hard-working taxpayers" or "the most generous, free-spirited nation in the world." Politicians tell farmers they are the "backbone of the American economy" and college students that they are the "leaders and

Presidential candidate Mitt Romney serves up some plain-folks appeal at the Iowa State Fair in August 2011.

Barack Obama makes the plain-folks appeal at a bowling alley in Altoona, Pennsylvania, while campaigning for President in 2008.

policy makers of tomorrow." Commercial advertisers use stroking more insidiously by asking a question which invites a flattering answer: "What kind of man reads *Playboy?*" (Does he really drive a Porsche and own $10,000 worth of sound equipment?) Senator Yakalot is stroking his audience when he calls them the "decent law-abiding citizens that are the great pulsing heart and the life blood of this, our beloved country," and when he repeatedly refers to them as "you fine people," "you wonderful folks." Obviously, the intent here is to sidetrack us from thinking critically about the man and his ideas. Our own good qualities have nothing to do with the issue at hand. Ask yourself, "Apart from the nice things he has to say about me (and my church, my nation, my ethnic group, my neighbors), what does the candidate stand for? Are his or her ideas in my best interests?"

5. ARGUMENTUM AD HOMINEM

Argumentum ad hominem means "argument to the man" and that's exactly what it is. When a propagandist uses *argumentum ad hominem*, he wants to distract our attention from the issue under consideration with personal attacks on the people involved. For example, when Lincoln issued the Emancipation Proclamation, some people responded by calling him the "baboon." But Lincoln's long arms and awkward carriage had nothing to do with the merits of the Proclamation or the question of whether or not slavery should be abolished.

Today *argumentum ad hominem* is still widely used and very effective. You may or may not support the Equal Rights Amendment,[1] but you should be sure your judgment is based on the merits of the idea itself, and not the result of someone's denunciation of the people who support the ERA as "fanatics" or "lesbians" or "frustrated old maids." Senator Yakalot is using *argumentum ad hominem* when he dismisses the idea of using smaller automobiles with a reference to the personal appearance of one of its supporters, Congresswoman Doris Schlepp. Refuse to be waylaid by *argumentum ad hominem* and ask, "Do the personal qualities

[1]*Equal Rights Amendment:* a proposed constitutional amendment designed to end gender discrimination which passed both the House and the Senate, but was never ratified. [Editor's note.]

of the person being discussed have anything to do with the issue at hand? Leaving him or her aside, how good is the idea itself?"

6. TRANSFER (GUILT OR GLORY BY ASSOCIATION)

In *argumentum ad hominem*, an attempt is made to associate negative aspects of a person's character or personal appearance with an issue or idea he supports. The transfer device uses this same process of association to make us accept or condemn a given person or idea.

A better name for the transfer device is guilt (or glory) by asso-   20 ciation. In glory by association, the propagandist tries to transfer the positive feelings of something we love and respect to the group or idea he wants us to accept. "This bill for a new dam is in the best tradition of this country, the land of Lincoln, Jefferson, and Washington," is glory by association at work. Lincoln, Jefferson, and Washington were great leaders that most of us revere and respect, but they have no logical connection to the proposal under consideration—the bill to build a new dam. Senator Yakalot uses glory by association when he says full-sized cars "have always been as American as Mom's apple pie or a Sunday drive in the country."

The process works equally well in reverse, when guilt by association is used to transfer our dislike or disapproval of one idea or group to some other idea or group that the propagandist wants us to reject and condemn. "John Doe says we need to make some changes in the way our government operates; well, that's exactly what the Ku Klux Klan has said, so there's a meeting of great minds!" That's guilt by association for you; there's no logical connection between John Doe and the Ku Klux Klan apart from the one the propagandist is trying to create in our minds. He wants to distract our attention from John Doe and get us thinking (and worrying) about the Ku Klux Klan and its politics of violence. (Of course, there are sometimes legitimate associations between the two things; if John Doe had been a *member* of the Ku Klux Klan, it would be reasonable and fair to draw a connection between the man and his group.) Senator Yakalot tries to trick his audience with guilt by association when he remarks that "the words 'community' and 'communism' look an awful lot alike!" He does it again when he mentions that Mr. Stu Pott "sports a Fidel Castro beard."

How can we learn to spot the transfer device and distinguish between the fair and unfair associations? We can teach ourselves to *suspend judgment* until we have answered these questions: "Is there any legitimate connection between the idea under discussion and the thing it is associated with? Leaving the transfer device out of the picture, what are the merits of the idea by itself?"

7. BANDWAGON

Ever hear of the small, ratlike animal called the lemming? Lemmings are arctic rodents with a very odd habit: periodically, for reasons no one entirely knows, they mass together in a large herd and commit suicide by rushing into deep water and drowning themselves. They all run in together, blindly, and not one of them ever seems to stop and ask, "*Why* am I doing this? Is this really what I want to do?" and thus save itself from destruction. Obviously, lemmings are driven to perform their strange mass suicide rites by common instinct. People choose to "follow the herd" for more complex reasons, yet we are still all too often the unwitting victims of the bandwagon appeal.

Essentially, the bandwagon urges us to support an action or an opinion because it is popular—because "everyone else is doing it." This call to "get on the bandwagon" appeals to the strong desire in most of us to be one of the crowd, not to be left out or alone. Advertising makes extensive use of the bandwagon appeal. ("join the Pepsi people"), but so do politicians ("Let us join together in this great cause"). Senator Yakalot uses the bandwagon appeal when he says that "More and more citizens are rallying to my cause every day," and asks his audience to "join them—and me—in our fight for America."

One of the ways we can see the bandwagon appeal at work is 25 in the overwhelming success of various fashions and trends which capture the interest (and the money) of thousands of people for a short time, then disappear suddenly and completely. For a year or two in the fifties, every child in North America wanted a coonskin cap so they could be like Davy Crockett; no one wanted to be left out. After that there was the hula-hoop craze that helped to dislocate the hips of thousands of Americans. [In the 1970s], what made millions of people rush out to buy their very own "pet rocks"?

The problem here is obvious: just because everyone's doing it doesn't mean that *we* should too. Group approval does not prove that something is true or is worth doing. Large numbers of people have supported actions we now condemn. [Within the last century], Hitler and Mussolini rose to absolute and catastrophically repressive rule in two of the most sophisticated and cultured countries in Europe. When they came into power they were welled up by massive popular support from millions of people who didn't want to be "left out" at a great historical moment.

Once the mass begins to move—on the bandwagon—it becomes harder and harder to perceive the leader *riding* the bandwagon. So don't be a lemming, rushing blindly on to destruction because "everyone is doing it." Stop and ask, "Where is this bandwagon headed? Never mind about everybody else, is this what is best for *me?*"

As we have seen, propaganda can appeal to us by arousing our emotions or distracting our attention from the real issues at hand. But there's a third way that propaganda can be put to work against us—by the use of faulty logic. This approach is really more insidious than the other two because it gives the appearance of reasonable, fair argument. It is only when we look more closely that the holes in the logical fiber show up. The following are some of the devices that make use of faulty logic to distort and mislead.

8. FAULTY CAUSE AND EFFECT

As the name suggests, this device sets up a cause-and-effect relationship that may not be true. The Latin name for this logical fallacy is *post hoc ergo propter hoc*, which means "after this, therefore because of this." But just because one thing happened after another doesn't mean that one *caused* the other.

An example of false cause-and-effect reasoning is offered by the story (probably invented) of the woman aboard the ship *Titanic*. She woke up from a nap and, feeling seasick, looked around for a call button to summon the steward to bring her some medication. She finally located a small button on one of the walls of her cabin and pushed it. A split second later, the *Titanic* grazed an iceberg in the terrible crash that was to send the entire ship to its destruction. The woman screamed and said, "Oh, God, what have I done? What have I done?" The humor of that anecdote comes from the absurdity of the woman's assumption that pushing the small red button resulted in the destruction of a ship weighing several hundred tons: "It happened after I pushed it, therefore it must be *because* I pushed it"—*post hoc ergo propter hoc* reasoning. There is, of course, no cause-and-effect relationship there.

The false cause-and-effect fallacy is used very often by political candidates. "After I came to office, the rate of inflation dropped to 6 percent." But did the person do anything to cause the lower rate of inflation or was it the result of other conditions? Would the rate of inflation have dropped anyway, even if he hadn't come to office? Senator Yakalot uses false cause and effect when he says "our forefathers who made this country great never had free hot meal handouts! And look what they did for our country!" He does it again when he concludes that "driving full-sized cars means a better car safety record on our American roads today."

False cause-and-effect reasoning is terribly persuasive because it seems so logical. Its appeal is apparently to experience. We swallowed X product—and the headache went away. We elected Y official and unemployment went down. Many people think, "There *must* be a connection." But causality is an immensely complex phenomenon; you need a good deal of evidence to prove that an event that follows another in time was "therefore" caused by the first event.

Don't be taken in by false cause and effect; be sure to ask, "Is there enough evidence to prove that this cause led to that effect? Could there have been any *other* causes?"

9. FALSE ANALOGY

An analogy is a comparison between two ideas, events, or things. But comparisons can be fairly made only when the things being compared are alike in significant ways. When they are not, false analogy is the result.

A famous example of this is the old proverb "Don't change 35 horses in the middle of a stream," often used as an analogy to convince voters not to change administrations in the middle of a war or other crisis. But the analogy is misleading because there are so many differences between the things compared. In what ways is a war or political crisis like a stream? Is the president or head of state really very much like a horse? And is a nation of millions of people comparable to a man trying to get across a stream? Analogy is false and unfair when it compares two things that have little in common and assumes that they are identical. Senator Yakalot tries to hoodwink his listeners with false analogy when he says, "Trying to take Americans out of the kind of cars they love is as undemocratic as trying to deprive them of the right to vote."

Of course, analogies can be drawn that are reasonable and fair. It would be reasonable, for example, to compare the results of busing in one small Southern city with the possible results in another, *if* the towns have the same kind of history, population, and school policy. We can decide for ourselves whether an analogy is false or fair by asking, "Are the things being compared truly alike in significant ways? Do the differences between them affect the comparison?"

10. BEGGING THE QUESTION

Actually, the name of this device is rather misleading, because it does not appear in the form of a question. Begging the question occurs when, in discussing a questionable or debatable point, a person assumes as already established the very point that he is trying to prove. For example, "No thinking citizen could approve such a completely unacceptable policy as this one." But isn't the question of whether or not the policy *is* acceptable the very point to be established? Senator Yakalot begs the question when he announces that his opponent's plan won't work "because it is unworkable."

We can protect ourselves against this kind of faulty logic by asking, "What is assumed in this statement? Is the assumption reasonable, or does it need more proof?"

11. THE TWO-EXTREMES FALLACY
(FALSE DILEMMA)

Linguists have long noted that the English language tends to view reality in sets of two extremes or polar opposites. In English, things are either black or white, tall or short, up or down, front or back, left or right, good or bad, guilty or not guilty. We can ask for a "straightforward yes-or-no answer" to a question, the understanding being that we will not accept or consider anything in between. In fact, reality cannot always be dissected along such strict lines. There may be (usually are) *more* than just two possibilities or extremes to consider. We are often told to "listen to both sides of the argument." But who's to say that every argument has only two sides? Can't there be a third—even a fourth or fifth—point of view?

The two-extremes fallacy is at work in this statement by Lenin, the great Marxist leader: "You cannot eliminate *one* basic assumption, one substantial part of this philosophy of Marxism (it is as if it were a block of steel), without abandoning truth, without falling into the arms of bourgeois-reactionary falsehood." In other words, if we don't agree 100 percent with every premise of Marxism, we must be placed at the opposite end of the political-economic spectrum—for Lenin, "bourgeois-reactionary falsehood." If we are not entirely *with* him, we must be against him; those are the only two possibilities open to us. Of course, this is a logical fallacy; in real life there are any number of political positions one can maintain *between* the two extremes of Marxism and capitalism. Senor Yakalot uses the two-extremes fallacy in the same way as Lenin when he tells his audience that "in this world a man's either for private enterprise or he's for socialism."

One of the most famous examples of the two-extremes fallacy in recent history is the slogan, "America: Love it or leave it," with its implicit suggestion that we either accept everything just as it is in America today without complaint—or get out. Again, it should be obvious that there is a whole range of action and belief between those two extremes.

Don't be duped; stop and ask, "Are those really the only two options I can choose from? Are there other alternatives not mentioned that deserve consideration?"

12. CARD STACKING

Some questions are so multifaceted and complex that no one can make an intelligent decision about them without considering a wide variety of evidence. One selection of facts could make us feel one way and another selection could make us feel just the opposite. Card stacking is a device of propaganda which selects only the facts that support the propagandist's point of view, and ignores all the others. For example, a candidate could be made to look like a legislative dynamo if you say, "Representative McNerd introduced more new bills than any other member of the Congress," and neglect to mention that most of them were so preposterous that they were laughed off the floor.

Senator Yakalot engages in card stacking when he talks about the proposal to use smaller cars. He talks only about jobs without mentioning the cost to the taxpayers or the very real—though still denied—threat of depletion of resources. He says he wants to help his countrymen keep their jobs, but doesn't mention that the corporations that offer the jobs will also make large profits. He praises the "American chrome industry," overlooking the fact that most chrome is imported. And so on.

The best protection against card stacking is to take the "Yes, but . . ." attitude. This device of propaganda is not untrue, but then again it is not the *whole* truth. So ask yourself, "Is this person leaving something out that I should know about? Is there some other information that should be brought to bear on this question?" 45

So far, we have considered three approaches that the propagandist can use to influence our thinking: appealing to our emotions, distracting our attention, and misleading us with logic that may appear to be reasonable but is in fact faulty and deceiving. But there is a fourth approach that is probably the most common propaganda trick of them all.

13. TESTIMONIAL

The testimonial device consists in having some loved or respected person give a statement of support (testimonial) for a given product or idea. The problem is that the person being quoted may *not* be an expert in the field; in fact, he may know nothing at all about it. Using the name of a man who is skilled and famous in one field to give a testimonial for something in another field is unfair and unreasonable.

Senator Yakalot tries to mislead his audience with testimonial when he tells them that "full-sized cars have been praised by great Americans like John Wayne and Jack Jones, as well as by leading experts on car safety and comfort."

Testimonial is used extensively in TV ads, where it often appears in such bizarre forms as Joe Namath's endorsement of a pantyhose brand. Here, of course, the "authority" giving the testimonial not only is no expert about pantyhose, but obviously stands to gain something (money!) by making the testimonial.

When celebrities endorse a political candidate, they may not 50 be making money by doing so, but we should still question whether they are in any better position to judge than we ourselves. Too often we are willing to let others we like or respect make our decisions *for us*, while we follow along acquiescently. And this is the purpose of testimonial—to get us to agree and accept *without* stopping to think. Be sure to ask, "Is there any reason to believe that this person (or organization or publication or whatever) has any more knowledge or information than I do on this subject? What does the idea amount to on its own merits, without the benefit of testimonial?"

The cornerstone of democratic society is reliance upon an informed and educated electorate. To be fully effective citizens we need to be able to challenge and to question wisely. A dangerous feeling of indifference toward our political processes exists today. We often abandon our right, our duty, to criticize and evaluate by dismissing *all* politicians as "crooked," *all* new bills and proposals as "just more government bureaucracy." But there are important distinctions to be made, and this kind of apathy can be fatal to democracy.

If we are to be led, let us not be led blindly, but critically, intelligently, with our eyes open. If we are to continue to be a government "by the people," let us become informed about the methods and purposes of propaganda, so we can be the masters, not the slaves of our destiny.

For Discussion and Writing

1. How would you define "begging the question" in your own words? Why does the author claim that the "name of this device is rather misleading" (par. 37)?

2. Woolfolk Cross uses many examples in her essay. What different kinds of examples does she use and how would you categorize them? In what way do they help to structure her argument? Which ones do you find the most or least effective? Why?

3. **connections**   In "The Ultimate Marketing Machine" from the *Economist* (p. 97), the writers suggest that even people who are increasingly immune to the techniques, clichés, and pitches of advertising on television and older media may be more accepting of advertising as it exists online. Do you think propaganda is affected by its medium? Are some propaganda techniques better suited to television or the Internet? How might different media forms make propaganda more difficult to recognize—and more effective?

4. Find an example of propaganda—an advertisement, a political speech, a film, an image, a public service campaign, an appeal to a cause, and so on, and analyze it through the lens of Woolfolk Cross's essay. What makes it propagandistic? What techniques does it use? How does it entice us not to think, but to "react, blindly, unquestioningly" (par. 7)? Your example might more subtle than Woolfolk Cross's, which tend to be obvious.

JASON TANZ

Selling Down: The Marketing of the Hip-Hop Nation

Jason Tanz (b. 1974) is a senior editor at Wired, *a magazine that covers technology and its effects on culture, politics, and the economy. He has written for the* New York Times, Esquire, Spin, *and other publications. Tanz is also the author of* Other People's Property: A Shadow History of Hip-Hop in White America *(2007), which examines the assimilation of hip-hop music and culture into the American mainstream. As you read "Selling Down: The Marketing of the Hip-Hop Nation" (adapted from Tanz's book), consider how once subversive or "edgy" subcultures become integrated into the mainstream. What specific aspects of hip-hop have led to its assimilation?*

> *Yo, Blood . . . You want fresh? Be a playa—first of your posse in da hood to have your tricked out wearin' dubs? If you want da bling, ya gotta have da juice. Talkin' cheddar here, boo . . . crisp Benjamins. Lots of 'em. Then your rims be kickin'.*
>
> *Yeah, if you wanna be da bomb . . . that's jiggy to you neophytes . . . the tire of choice for the ride of choice has become the color of cool: a big, black Pirelli. Bigger the better.*
>
> *At least, that's what Pirelli Tire North America Inc. execs are saying.*
>
> —Sigmund J. Mikolajczyk, "Hip-Hop Help?"
> Tire Business, *November 8, 2004*

I tend to grow paranoid when I think about advertising and marketing. Can you blame me? It is an industry that seems to thrive by tapping into our deepest fears, insecurities, anxieties, and

87

aspirations. Edward Bernays—Sigmund Freud's nephew, who is considered the father of modern public relations—drew on his uncle's theories of the subconscious to craft his marketing campaigns. In his 1928 book, *Propaganda*, he wrote that "the true ruling power of our country" belonged to those who could practice "the conscious and intelligent manipulation of the organized habits and opinions of the masses."[1] Almost thirty years later, in his 1957 book *The Hidden Persuaders*, Vance Packard argued that some advertisers were "systematically feeling out our hidden weaknesses and frailties in the hope that they can more efficiently influence our behavior."[2] Today, consultants promise marketers that they can use psychological techniques to uncover consumers' subliminal desires. One of the most successful marketing consultants, a former child psychiatrist named Clotaire Rapaille, told a reporter that his company excels at tapping into our "reptilian brain." "Most of the time, people have no idea why they're doing what they're doing," he said.[3] "It's fascinating to try to understand, to break the code."

But my paranoia reached new levels when I saw a recent television advertisement for T-Mobile, a cell-phone company, that seems to crack my own personal code and tap directly into my reptilian brain. The ad begins in a bowling alley, where a tall, attractive African American man is engaged in a cell-phone conversation. From the snippet that we can hear ("So, you want me to come over tonight? That's cool"), he sounds as if he has just secured some big-time sexual guarantee. Just then, with a samurai scream, a small Asian man wearing a powder-blue jumpsuit runs across the screen and wraps himself around the black man's thigh. He is, it turns out, a representative from Poser Mobile, the cell-phone company the black guy is using, and he's joined by six others, all of them nonblack (they appear to be white, Latino, and Asian), and all dressed in ridiculously oversized and out-of-date hip-hop fashions. "Poser Mobile says you're out of prepaid minutes, yo!" the Asian man announces, and when the black guy protests, he shouts back, "Fees, shorty! Fees!" But his obvious inauthenticity makes it hard to take him seriously, and the protagonist just grins and calls the gang "clowns." The Poser Mobile team

[1]Edward Bernays, *Propaganda* (Ig Publishing, 1928), 37.
[2]Vance Packard, *The Hidden Persuaders* (Pocket Books, 1957), 2.
[3]Barak Goodman and Rachel Dretzin, directors, "The Persuaders," *Frontline*, PBS, November 9, 2003.

stares silently for a second before breaking into a painfully cacophonous and arrhythmic bout of beatboxing. Eventually, the black man leaves to pick up a phone from T-Mobile To Go, which lets him avoid the hidden fees—and fake posturing—of Poser Mobile. "Straight up prepaid," the ad closes.

I suppose that I am meant to identify with the black guy, a cool customer under siege from clueless marketers hoping to tap into his preferred lifestyle in order to sell him products. But I don't. I identify with the Poser Mobile guys. They remind me of my own embarrassing attempts to prove myself as a full-fledged member of the hip-hop community. Whether T-Mobile's marketers intended to or not, they have brought up a long series of uncomfortable memories: the time I realized that everybody at the Third World Center at my college was laughing at my dancing; the time that the Digable Planets dismissively referred to me and my friends as "devils"; the time that guy laughed at my Malcolm X hat; the palpable anxiety and self-doubt I felt so many times when I had to interact with a black person and I couldn't help but think, *Is this working? Are they buying it? Am I a poser?* But apparently, all of that unease and despair wasn't the product of history or race or guilt or frustration or inequity. I just wasn't using the right cell-phone service.

One of hip-hop's most powerful and elusive promises is that it will help us come to terms with, understand, and maybe even participate in blackness. That we can change ourselves through our listening, make ourselves better and more comfortable and more accepting and accepted than we are. That through hip-hop, we can become down—completely and utterly comfortable with, and de facto members of, the black community. And because down is one of those unattainable states of grace that we can asymptotically approach but never actually achieve—like supreme self-confidence or utter peace or Zen-like enlightenment—we keep coming back over and over again.

We all know that marketers thrive by exploiting urges and   5
desires that can never be satisfied, and at long last it seems that, knowingly or not, they have stumbled upon our never-ending quest to be down. Hip-hop has always tossed up rapper-approved signifiers, commodities that promised to grant down status to anyone that consumes them—Adidas sneakers, Cross Colours sweatshirts, Cazal glasses, basketball jerseys, the music itself. Now marketers have enlisted hip-hop to extend that promise to a

"Is this working? Are they buying it? Am I a poser?"

mind-boggling array of products, reaching deep into the heart of mainstream America. White kids seeking a hip-hop stamp of approval are encouraged to buy slacks at JC Penney, which used Black Sheep's "The Choice Is Yours" to score a recent ad campaign. They can go back-to-school shopping at Target, which repurposed Sir Mix-A-Lot's "Baby Got Back," an infamous ode to the black female form, as "Baby Got Backpacks." Virtually any footwear white kids care to select can offer them a shot of hip-hop credibility; they can pick up Ludacris-endorsed Pumas, or Jay-Z-approved Reeboks, or "Hurricanes," sneakers designed by the gangsta-rap sensation The Game. If they don't feel like getting a T-Mobile phone, they can grab one from Boost Mobile, a Nextel brand with an ad campaign that features such luminaries as Fat Joe and Eve, and a tagline—"Where You At?"—that positively drips with hip-hop attitude. "For better or worse, for good or evil, hip-hop has become a weapon of choice for marketers," says Rob Schwartz, executive director of the Los Angeles office of TBWA\ Chiat\Day, an advertising agency.[4]

Of course, part of hip-hop's appeal is that it is impenetrable to exactly the kind of people who tend to run stodgy major corporations. Fortunately for the captains of industry, there are now dozens of boutique marketing, advertising, and public-relations firms dedicated to guiding big businesses through the sometimes forbidding landscape of the urban marketplace. In 2001, the performer then known as P. Diddy created Blue Flame Marketing + Advertising to help corporations tap into the next wave of tastemakers. Steve Stoute, a former manager of the acclaimed rapper Nas, formed Translation, an agency that has helped link brands such as Crest and Reebok to high-profile hip-hop stars. The Web site for Burrell Communications, an advertising firm, promises that it can "make your logo the next hot ankle tattoo," while describing the African American market as the firm's "specialty of the house." Morris L. Reid, the managing director of Westin Rinehart, a Washington, D.C., public affairs firm that works with multinational businesses and government agencies, describes the service that urban marketers provide thusly: "I'm the person that can tell you what's going on in the 'hood, and I can also come into your boardroom and not scare anyone."[5]

[4]Telephone interview with Rob Schwartz, November 7, 2005.
[5]Telephone interview with Morris L. Reid, November 14, 2005.

It is not hard to see why corporations would turn to hip-hop as a marketing platform. First and foremost it is overwhelmingly popular, the culture of teenage America, and this makes it the lingua franca that any lifestyle marketer must speak. Furthermore, compared to other social movements, hip-hop seems to lend itself particularly well to marketing messages. From its early days, it has blurred the distinction between art and advertising: graffiti writers splashed their tags across subway trains as a way of creating rolling billboards for themselves; the first MCs acted as pitchmen who existed solely to praise the DJ's skills and get the crowd riled up (today that role is played by the appropriately-named "hype man"); and rappers turned themselves into superhero icons, giving themselves new names, creating logos, and adopting certain verbal tics—for instance, the early-nineties rap duo Das EFX's fondness for dropping "iggidy" into the middle of words—to define themselves as entertainers. "More than anything else, hip-hop has been about marketing," Jameel Spencer, the president of Blue Flame Marketing + Advertising, told the *New York Times* in 2004,[6] "You're creating a brand for yourself." Nelson George has written that hip-hop arose as a way of "announcing one's existence to the world."[7] Could there be any better definition of the goals of marketing?

But if hip-hop rose to power as the voice of the streets, what does it mean that one of those streets is now Madison Avenue? In my crustier moments, it is easy for me to conclude that hip-hop has gone from black people's CNN to everybody's Home Shopping Network. And these moments have been coming faster and crustier. I have one almost every time I turn on MTV and find myself wondering whether the iPods and Sidekicks and Hummers that pop up in every hip-hop video are paid plugs. I have one when I log on to *Business Week*'s Web site and read about a conference put together by the youth-marketing division of McCann-Erickson, in which a group of rappers took the stage in front of fifty brand representatives of corporations including Wendy's, L'Oréal, and Verizon Wireless to tell them "what kind of sponsorships and marketing deals they would be interested in."[8] I had another one

[6]Nat Ives, "Hip-hop Admen: Walk This Way, Shop This Way," *New York Times*, August 9, 2004.
[7]Nelson George, *Hip Hop America* (Penguin, 1995), 14.
[8]David Kiley, "Hip Hop Gets Down with the Deals," businessweek.com, May 16, 2005.

when I learned about American Bandstand, a survey by a San Francisco marketing firm, Agenda Inc., that tracks the number of times that brand names are mentioned in the songs that make up the *Billboard* Top 20. Why does this bother me so much? Partly because I'm clinging to some pretty quaint notions of artistic purity. Blame the Romantics. They're the ones who, in the nineteenth century, came up with the idea that artists had a duty to oppose the compromises and corruptions of mainstream society. And that's been a hard attitude to shake. It led to the idea of the counterculture, which held that the only true enlightenment could come from living on society's margins. The counterculture has given us Giacomo Puccini's *La Bohème* and Ralph Waldo Emerson's and Henry David Thoreau's retreats back to nature. After World War II, the counterculture became a defining element of American life, underlying the promise of the beatnik, folk, hippie, rock, and punk movements. In fact, one of the great ironies of the counterculture is that its ideals of nonconformity and independence are so widespread that they have become integral parts of the mainstream society that the counterculture was created to counter. It was these ideals that drew me to hip-hop in the first place. Who could imagine that music so difficult, so aggressive, so *black*, would one day be used to sell backpacks?

If this makes me a curmudgeon, at least I am not alone. "I   10
think what made hip-hop compelling to white kids is that it seemed to exist outside the corporate-driven suburban monotony,"[9] says Douglas Rushkoff, a social theorist and writer of a *Frontline* documentary, "The Merchants of Cool," about youth marketing. "The function of hip-hop in the early days was to galvanize its audiences around certain kinds of values—of pride, of racial unity, of urban creativity. It was relatively hard to listen to 'The Message' and not go, 'Whoa. There's something happening here.' But now, when I listen to hip-hop, I think, 'Is this going to stay at number two? Is this going to be on a commercial? Are those diamonds in his teeth real?' That's a very different set of questions."

But hip-hoppers tend not to share my mistrust of corporate culture. Indeed, in hip-hop America, marketing is the sincerest

[9]Douglas Rushkoff, telephone interview, June 10, 2005.

form of flattery. Witness the response to Sprite's mid-1990s "Obey Your Thirst" advertising campaign, one of the most influential and successful of the decade. Between 1994 and 1997, Sprite produced television advertisements featuring some of hip-hop's most respected stars, including A Tribe Called Quest, Grand Puba, Large Professor, Pete Rock, C.L. Smooth, KRS-One, MC Shan, Nas, AZ, Eve, and Missy Elliott. By the end of the campaign Sprite, previously a distant second to 7-Up, held a dominating lead in the lemon-lime category. The campaign also proved that, unlike other musical movements that gestured toward ideological purity and authenticity, hip-hop's fans would not necessarily object to their culture's commercialization. Far from being shunned as an exploiter, which is how many Beatles fans responded to Nike when the company used the group's "Revolution" to score a sneaker ad, Sprite was enthusiastically welcomed as a full-fledged member of the hip-hop community.

"Back in 1994, hip-hop artists did not have big budgets with which to market themselves," Darryl Cobbin, one of the executives credited with creating the Sprite campaign, tells me.[10] "You did not have major companies platforming the culture. You had a couple of them that were dabbling in jingles, but not truly understanding the culture. We began to create a platform for those rappers that were most authentic and credible to talk about their culture, and to use 'Obey Your Thirst' as a vessel to fill with the creativity that is hip-hop. And that helped hip-hop. . . . This is what the best companies do. Find a way to help advance the culture and you will be rewarded."

"It sounds cartoonish that people were big-upping [praising] products for using hip-hop," Alan Light, the former editor in chief of *Vibe*, says.[11] "But at the time there was so much fear, so much resistance [to hip-hop from mainstream and corporate America], that it meant something."

It doesn't mean that much anymore. Now, almost every youth marketer recognizes the power and appeal of hip-hop. And while it would be nice to conclude that today's massive corporate investments are coming about as a result of a sincere desire to help spread the culture—or even a desire to sell product to the inner-

[10]Darryl Cobbin, telephone interview, December 1, 2005.
[11]In-person interview with Alan Light, January 30, 2006.

city black customers who constitute hip-hop's core audience—it's far more likely that big business sees hip-hop as a means to a more familiar end: the wallets of all those white kids out there. Black kids are what are known in the industry as "influencers," a group of consumers who have an inordinate impact on the tastes and behaviors of the rest of the country. As Ivan Juzang, the head of a Philadelphia firm that specializes in marketing to urban youth, told a reporter: "If you don't target the hard-core, you don't get the suburbs."[12] And so corporations go after the urban market because they've realized the truth of what the editor-in-chief of *Frontera* magazine triumphantly concluded in an opinion piece that ran in the *Daily News of Los Angeles* back in 1997: "Middle American teens and twentysomethings don't want to buy products pitched by suburban kids who look just like them."[13]

Not everybody views this as something to celebrate. Harvard University's Douglas Holt and Juliet B. Schor—marketing researchers who, it is safe to say, are no fans of hip-hop—have argued that the street image "has proven to be a potent commodity because its aesthetic offers an authentic threatening edginess that is very attractive both to white suburban kids who perpetually recreate radical youth culture in relation to their parents' conservative views about the ghetto, and to urban cultural elites for whom it becomes a form of cosmopolitan radical chic."[14]

But Darryl Cobbin, the creator of the Sprite campaign, who is African American and a lifelong hip-hop fan, sees different forces at work. He tells me that hip-hop succeeds as a marketing platform because it connotes values that people simply cannot help but respond to. "What's more honest than an MC describing what's happening in his neighborhood?" he says. "Who is more stylish than a b-boy rocking his block on a piece of cardboard? 'Obey Your Thirst' means trust your instinct, be true to yourself and others, and operate with confidence and swagger. That for us represented what hip-hop culture is all about." As he tells me this, I can't help but notice that all of these adjectives—honest, stylish,

[12]Marc Spiegler, "Marketing Street Culture," *American Demographics*, November 1996.

[13]Yvette C. Doss, "Locating 'Where It's At,'" *Daily News of Los Angeles*, January 24, 1997.

[14]Juliet B. Schor, *Born to Buy: The Commercialized Child and the New Consumer Culture* (Scribner, 2004), 48–49.

instinctive, true, confident, swaggering—pretty neatly describe all the characteristics that, in my younger days, in the deepest reaches of my subconscious, I always felt that I lacked and that I assumed those mysterious, authentic black folks possessed in abundance.

NOTE

My study of the nexus between commerce and culture was greatly aided by Thomas Frank's *Conquest of Cool* (University of Chicago Press, 1997) and by Joseph Heath and Andrew Potter's *Nation of Rebels* (HarperCollins, 2004). The PBS *Frontline* documentary "The Persuaders," directed by Barak Goodman and Rachel Dretzin, was also very helpful.

For Discussion and Writing

1. Tanz writes, "It is not hard to see why corporations would turn to hip-hop as a marketing platform" (par. 7). What reasons does he give for this?
2. What is the purpose of the discussion of nineteenth-century Romantics (par. 9) in the context of Tanz's main point? How does it support his argument?
3. **connections**   In "The End of White America" (p. 144) Hua Hsu argues that our society is experiencing a "triumph of multiculturalism, or postracialism" (par. 40), as "pop culture today rallies around an ethic of multicultural inclusion that seems to value every identity—except whiteness" (par. 25). Do you think Hsu's and Tanz's essays compliment one another, or complicate each other? How are the authors' arguments and conclusions similar? How are they different?
4. Tanz claims that hip-hop has always tied status and identity to brands, promoting "rapper-approved signifiers, commodities that promised to grant down status to anyone that consumes them—Adidas sneakers, Cross Colours sweatshirts, Cazal glasses, basketball jerseys, the music itself" (par. 5). Think about the brands in your own life, from the clothes you wear to the schools you have attended. Do you see them as a legitimate form of self-expression and group membership? What do your brands say about you?

The Ultimate Marketing Machine

Despite its name, the Economist *covers issues besides economics, including international politics, world news, science, education, and the arts. The London-based magazine, founded in 1843, is known for its elite readership, its global perspective, and its understated prose style. The* Economist *generally avoids giving bylines, striving instead for a unified editorial voice that some find wry and precise, while others find stuffy and pretentious. In this 2006 article, the magazine analyzes the present state—and future prospects—of marketing and advertising on the Internet. As you read, consider your own experiences as an online consumer. Do you find Internet advertising "relevant," "fun," or "useful"?*

In terms of efficiency, if not size, the advertising industry is only now starting to grow out of its century-long infancy, which might be called "the Wanamaker era." It was John Wanamaker, a devoutly Christian merchant from Philadelphia, who in the 1870s not only invented department stores and price tags (to eliminate haggling, since everybody should be equal before God and price), but also became the first modern advertiser when he bought space in newspapers to promote his stores. He went about it in a Christian way, neither advertising on Sundays nor fibbing (thus minting the concept of "truth in advertising"). And, with his precise business mind, he expounded a witticism that has ever since seemed like an economic law: "Half the money I spend on advertising is wasted," he said. "The trouble is, I don't know which half."

Wanamaker's wasted half is not entirely proverbial. The worldwide advertising industry is likely to be worth $428 billion in revenues this year, according to ZenithOptimedia, a market-research firm. Greg Stuart, the author of a forthcoming book on the industry and the boss of the Interactive Advertising Bureau, a trade association, estimates that advertisers waste—that is, they send messages that reach the wrong audience or none at all—$112 billion a year in America and $220 billion worldwide, or just over half of their total spending. Wanamaker was remarkably accurate. What Wanamaker could not have foreseen, however, was the Internet. A bevy of entrepreneurial firms—from Google, the world's most valuable online advertising agency disguised as a Web-search engine, to tiny Silicon Valley upstarts, many of them only months old—are now selling advertisers new tools to reduce waste. These come in many exotic forms, but they have one thing in common: a desire to replace the old approach to advertising, in which advertisers pay for the privilege of "exposing" a theoretical audience to their message, with one in which advertisers pay only for real and measurable actions by consumers, such as clicking on a Web link, sharing a video, placing a call, printing a coupon or buying something.

Rishad Tobaccowala, the "chief innovation officer" of Publicis, one of the world's biggest advertising groups, and boss of Denuo, a Chicago-based unit within Publicis with the job of probing the limits of new advertising models, likens traditional Wanamaker-era advertising to "an atom bomb dropped on a big city." The best example is the thirty-second spot on broadcast television. An independent firm (such as Nielsen, in America) estimates how many television sets are tuned to a given channel at a given time. Advertisers then pay a rate, called CPM (cost per thousand), for the right to expose the implied audience to their spot. If Nielsen estimates that, say, one million people ("the city") are watching a show, an advertiser paying a CPM of $20 would fork out $20,000 for his commercial ("the atom bomb").

GONE FOR A BREW

The problem is obvious. The television room may be empty. Its owners may have gone to the kitchen to make a cup of tea or to the toilet. They may have switched channels during the commercial break, be napping or talking on the telephone. The viewer may be a teenaged girl, even though the advertisement promotes Viagra. It might even be a TiVo or other such device that records the show so that the owner can watch it later and skip through the commercials. Parks Associates, a consumer-technology consultancy, estimates that ten million American households already have a digital video recorder.

"Segmentation," an advertising trend during the past two decades tied to fragmentation in the media, represents only a cosmetic change, thinks Mr. Tobaccowala. Advertisers airing a spot on a niche channel on cable television, for example, might be able to make more educated guesses about the audience (in their thirties, gay and affluent, say), but they are still paying a CPM rate in order blindly to cast a message in a general direction. Instead of atom bombs on cities, says Mr. Tobaccowala, segmentation is at best "dropping conventional bombs on villages." The collateral damage is still considerable.

By contrast, the new advertising models based on Internet technologies amount to innovation. Instead of bombs, says Mr. Tobaccowala, advertisers now "make lots of spearheads and then get people to impale themselves." The idea is based on consumers themselves taking the initiative by showing up voluntarily and interacting with what they find online.

In its simplest form, this involves querying a search engine with keywords ("used cars," say), then scanning the search results, as well as the sponsored links from advertisers, and then clicking on one such link. In effect, the consumer has expressed an intention twice (first with his query, then with his click). The average cost to an advertiser from one such combination is 50 cents, which corresponds to a CPM of $500; by contrast, the average CPM in traditional ("exposure") media is $20. A consumer's action, in other words, is twenty-five times as valuable as his exposure.

The person who deserves more credit than anybody else for this insight is Bill Gross, an Internet entrepreneur with a kinetic mind and frenetic speech who in 1996 started Idealab, a sort of factory for inventions. One of the companies to come out of his factory was GoTo.com, later renamed Overture, which pioneered the market for "paid search" or "pay-per-click" advertising. In 2001 Mr. Gross ran into Sergey Brin and Larry Page, the young co-founders of Google, a search engine that was just then becoming popular, but still had no way of making money. He offered them a partnership or merger, but Messrs. Brin and Page were purists at the time about not diluting the integrity of their search results with commercialism and they turned him down.

Within a year, however, Messrs. Brin and Page changed their 10 minds and came up with AdWords, a system based on Overture's idea of putting advertising links next to relevant search results and charging only for clicks (but with the added twist that advertisers could bid for keywords in an online auction). Google soon added AdSense, a system that goes beyond search-results pages and places "sponsored" (i.e., advertising) links on the Web pages of newspapers and other publishers that sign up to be part of Google's network. Like AdWords, these AdSense advertisements are "contextual"—relevant to the Web page's content—and the advertiser pays for them only when a Web surfer clicks. Together, AdWords and AdSense produced $6.1 billion in revenues for Google last year.

Because this advertising model is so lucrative, all Internet portals want to catch up with Google. In 2003 Yahoo!, the largest media property on the Web, bought Overture from Mr. Gross for $1.6 billion. Yahoo! then dropped the technology it had been licensing from Google. Then Microsoft, which owns MSN, another large Internet portal, built adCenter, its version of a "monetization engine," which has now replaced Yahoo! as the advertising system for searches on MSN. In addition, eBay, the largest auction site on the Web, has a version called AdContext. Pay-per-click advertising is not without its problems—especially "click fraud," the practice of generating bogus clicks for devious reasons, such as making a rival advertiser pay for nothing. Nonetheless, pay-per-click remains much more efficient than traditional marketing for many advertisers. It is the fastest-growing segment of the online advertising market.

Some companies are already exploring other methods of charging advertisers for consumers' actions. Mike Hogan, the boss of ZiXXo, a start-up near San Francisco, says that he is "disrupting the existing coupon system," dominated by companies such as Valpak and Valassis in America. Some 335 billion coupons were distributed in America last year—priced like other traditional media, in CPM—but only 4.5 billion were redeemed, which amounts to a "Wanamaker waste" of almost 99 percent. ZiXXo, by contrast, lets advertisers issue coupons online and places them on search results, online maps and other such places, but charges advertisers only when a consumer prints one out (50 cents per coupon from next year), thus expressing an intent to redeem it.

As ZiXXo is pioneering "pay-per-print" advertising, Ingenio, another San Francisco firm, is betting on "pay-per-call." Instead of coupons, it places toll-free telephone numbers on local-search pages—its biggest partner is AOL—and charges advertisers only when they receive a live call from a consumer. This is especially popular among accountants, lawyers, plumbers and other service providers who find it easier to close a deal on the telephone. EBay is planning to sell pay-per-call advertising on a larger scale, by placing little buttons from Skype, an Internet-telephony firm it bought last year, on its own Web pages and perhaps those of others, so that consumers can talk with a seller after just a single click.

Meanwhile, Mr. Gross, almost famous from his first innovation (and not at all bitter that Google got most of the credit), is once again busy pursuing what he considers the "Holy Grail" of advertising—the complete elimination of Wanamaker waste. He calls this cost-per-action, or CPA, although he means cost-per-sale, and says that it "just makes too much sense" not to catch on. His start-up this time is called Snap.com, a small search engine. An airline, say, that advertises on Snap's search results would pay not when a consumer clicks on its link but only when he buys a ticket. Google, which is researching almost all conceivable advertising methods, also has plans for CPA. Its new Google Checkout, an online payments system set up to rival eBay's PayPal, will allow Google to know more about how many users who click on one of its advertisements subsequently go on to complete a purchase.

BRANDED

If the Internet enables such snazzy performance-based advertis- 15 ing methods, it is also sparking a renaissance in branded advertising. Some products—such as mortgages—might conceivably be sold entirely through performance-based marketing one day, says Mr. Stuart at the Interactive Advertising Bureau, but many other products—such as cars, cosmetics and alcohol—will probably always require branding as well. Even when consumers start their shopping research on a search engine, they will see several competing sponsored links, and may be swayed by their previous brand exposure in deciding which one of these links to click on. And in the "offline" world, brands are still "the ultimate navigation device," says Mr. Tobaccowala at Denuo, and often determine which door a tired traveler far away from home walks through.

Brand advertising is inherently about leaving an impression on a consumer, and thus about some sort of exposure. On the Internet, however, an exposure can also be tied to an action by a consumer, and these actions can be counted, tracked and analyzed in ways that exposure in the established mass media cannot. Consumers also tend to be more alert on the Internet. Whereas people might watch a television show in a semi-comatose state of mind and at obtuse angles on their couches, consumers typically surf the Web leaning forward while "paying attention to the screen," says Mr. Stuart.

A good example is video games, which increasingly take place online and involve thousands or millions of other players. Companies such as Massive and Double Fusion are already placing two-dimensional brand advertisements into games. A player moving through the streets of New York to kill something or other might see a DHL truck or a billboard. "But the future is intelligent three-dimensional ads" and "ads with behavior," says Jonathan Epstein, Double Fusion's boss. For instance, his technology will soon allow Coca-Cola to place a Coke can into a game, where it fizzes when a player walks by and might give him certain powers if he picks it up. If a character uses a mobile phone inside a game, the technology can swap the brand and model of the phone depending on which country the player is in. But the most important aspect of the technology, says Mr. Epstein, is that it will track exactly how long the player uses the phone, thus leaving no doubt about whether an "impression" had indeed been made.

PROPAGATING THE MESSAGE

That same transparency is now coming to "viral" marketing. Kontraband, a firm in London, takes funny, bizarre, conspiratorial, or otherwise interesting video clips from its clients and places them on its own site and on popular video-sharing sites such as YouTube.com or Google Video. The hope in viral marketing is to create something that is so much fun that it will propagate by itself, as people e-mail it to each other or put the Web link on their blogs. This means that a pure "cost-per-feed" system is out of the question, says Richard Spalding, Kontraband's co-founder, since a successful viral campaign "that gets out of hand and is watched by millions would run the client out of business." So Kontraband charges a flat fee based on a hoped-for audience, leaving the client with the economic upside if the real audience turns out to be larger. The important point, says Mr. Spalding, is once again that the "sprites" (i.e., bits of software) inside the video let Kontraband track exactly how many times a video is viewed and where, so that clients can see neat pie charts that summarize their success.

Understandably, this strange and thrilling online world can be unsettling to the old hands of the advertising industry, whether they are marketing bosses for advertisers or intermediaries at the agencies. "All of us have been classically trained, and now we're in a jazz age," says Mr. Tobaccowala. Advertisers and their agents, he recalls, have already changed their minds about the Internet twice. During the technology boom of the late 1990s, he says, the general outcry was, "Oh my God, I need a dotcom unit." When the boom turned to bust at the beginning of this decade, he says, there was a sigh of relief ("See, the Internet is not for real."), and it suddenly seemed as though only those who did not "get it" still had jobs.

This was a mistake, says Mr. Tobaccowala, since the skeptics 20 confused the performance of the NASDAQ and the fate of individual dotcoms with genuine changes in consumer behavior. In the consumer-driven market for classified advertising, for instance, ordinary people instinctively grasped the efficiencies of online sites such as Craigslist, thus causing a drop in classified revenues at newspapers. The large advertisers stayed more conservative, however, which may explain why the Internet-advertising market is still disproportionately small. The Online Publishers Association, a trade group, estimates that all Web advertising in America came to about 6 percent of total advertising expenditures last year, even though consumers spent 23 percent of their media time online.

Now, however, chief executives are taking trips to Silicon Valley, often without their "chief marketing officers," to educate themselves. And what they hear impresses them. Tim Armstrong, Google's advertising boss in North America, preaches to his clients a "notion of asset management" for their products that "shocks" them. Traditionally, he says, most firms would advertise only 5 percent to 10 percent of their wares—the blockbusters—in the mass media to publicize their brand, hoping that it shines a halo on the remainder of their products. Now, however, "companies market each individual product in that big digital stream," says Mr. Armstrong, from the best seller to the tiniest toothbrush. This is called exploiting the economics of the "long tail."

They do this, first, because the Internet, in effect, eliminates scarcity in the medium. There are as many Web pages for advertisers as there are keywords that can be typed into a search engine, situations that game players might find themselves in, and so forth. Each one comes with its own context, and almost every context suits some product. The second reason is that if you can track the success of advertising, especially if you can follow sales leads, then marketing ceases to be just a cost-center, with an arbitrary budget allocated to it. Instead, advertising becomes a variable cost of production that measurably results in making more profit.

This often leads to more subtle changes in the way that advertisers think about their craft, says Mr. Armstrong. In the traditional media, he says, advertisers are always "trying to block the stream of information to the user" in order to "blast their message" to him. That quickly gets annoying and turns consumers off. In American prime-time television, advertising interruptions added up to eighteen minutes an hour last year, up from thirteen minutes an hour in 1992, according to Parks Associates. On the Internet, by contrast, advertisers have no choice but to "go with the user," says Mr. Armstrong, and "the information coming back from the user is more important than the messages going out."

For consumers this may turn out to be the biggest change. The kids in "Generation Y," "echo-boomers" and "millennials"—young people who tend to be adept at using media, constantly online and skeptical—are increasingly immune to the clichés of prime-time television and radio and mentally tune out these nuisances. Online, however, they may accept advertising if it is unobtrusive, relevant, and fun. Insofar as they took some action to invite the advertisement, they may even find it useful. And this, aptly enough, is a consumer reaction that John Wanamaker would have expected all along.

For Discussion and Writing

1. Ad executive Rishad Tobaccowala claims that new media advertisers must "make lots of spearheads and then get people to impale themselves" (par. 7). What process is he describing with this striking metaphor?

2. The writers refer to "'viral' marketing" (par. 18). What is viral marketing? How does it work? In what ways does it differ from more traditional models of marketing and advertising? Why is it significant for the Internet?

3. **connections**   In "Selling Down: The Marketing of the Hip-Hop Nation" (p. 87), Jason Tanz notes that advertising and marketing "thrive by tapping into our deepest fears, insecurities, anxieties, and aspirations" (par. 1). Tanz cites Edward Bernays, the "father of modern public relations," who wrote in 1928 that the true ruling power belonged to those who practiced the "conscious and intelligent manipulation of the organized habits and opinions of the masses" (par. 1). Do you believe such "manipulation" is necessary? Do you think that the Internet makes people more easy to manipulate, or less so? What role does marketing and advertising play in this context?

4. How would you respond to the writer's generalizations about "Generation Y" in his final paragraph? Do younger people generally accept participatory, online marketing and advertising if it's "relevant" and "fun"? Are they likely to think critically and skeptically about the "ultimate marketing machine"? How would you answer these questions regarding your own attitudes and online habits?

Portfolio of Advertisements

How can you help
fill this bowl?

FREE
Rice

www.freerice.com

The only online vocabulary
game feeding the world's hungry

WFP
World Food
Programme
wfp.org

Fighting Hunger Worldwide

THERE IS
NO EASY WAY IN.
THAT'S WHY THEY SEND IN THE MARINES.
THE MARINE CORPS IS OUR NATION'S PREMIERE EXPEDITIONARY FORCE, READY AT A MOMENT'S NOTICE TO PROTECT OUR NATION AND WAY OF LIFE. WHEN THERE IS NO EASY WAY IN, OUR NATION SENDS IN ITS MARINES.
MARINES.COM
MARINES
THE FEW. THE PROUD.

live within your means.
dress beyond them.
vintage rosette tank
just $32.99
jean capri
just $29.99
dressbarn
shop dressbarn.com

For Discussion and Writing

1. Advertisements for charities and hunger programs use a wide variety of appeals, depending on their goals and their audience. What demographic is the World Food Programme ad likely to appeal to and why?

2. How do the specific images and language in the Marine recruiting ad work together to create a dominant impression? What is that impression or message?

3. How does the word *natural* work in the context of the Kinky-Curly advertisement? What connotations does it have? Does the phrase "Go natural" have implications or associations beyond hair care?

4. Much like a piece of short fiction, the M&M'S® Brand Chocolate Candies advertisement seems to have both a plot and a theme. How would you describe the story in your own words? What is its theme or message? How do the specific elements—visual details, character, language—contribute to the theme?

5. What is the implied thesis of the Dress Barn advertisement? How would you restate it in your own words?

WINSTON FLETCHER

Art or Puffery?
A Defense of Advertising

Winston Fletcher (b. 1937) is the former director of DLKW, a British advertising agency. He currently chairs the Advertising Standards Board of Finance in England. He is also on the board of the Rationalist Association, which publishes the New Humanist *magazine. His book,* Powers of Persuasion: The Insider Story of British Advertising, *appeared in 2008.*

Although Fletcher writes in a British context, his essay is significant for American advertising as well. He addresses criticisms of advertising that have been common in the United States for decades—and standard in Britain since the nineteenth century, if not earlier. He also notes the disparity between public attitudes toward advertising and the opinions of intellectuals. Do you think such disparity exists in the United States?

At end of the 20th century British advertising creativity ruled the world. Brilliant campaigns—like those for Smash instant mashed potato (Martians); Heineken beer ("Refreshes The Parts Other Beers Cannot Reach"); Benson & Hedges cigarettes (Surrealist Posters); Levi's jeans ("Launderette"); the Health Education Council (Pregnant Man); John Smith's Bitter (Arkwright); Hovis bread (Boy on a Bike); Carlsberg beer (Dam Busters) and a galaxy of others garnered garlands galore at international creative festivals. In 1978 in Cannes, for example, Britain won the Grand Prix for both television and cinema—a rare occurrence—and snitched a massive 80 Gold, Silver, and Bronze Lions.

But none of this cut much ice with advertising's enemies back home. In the 1970s the advertising trade paper *Campaign* invited 21 influential opinion leaders to publish essays titled "What I Think About Advertising." The list included leftist Labor MP

114

Christopher Mayhew, economists Sir Roy Harrod and Joan Robinson, moral crusader Mary Whitehouse, television dramatist Ted Willis, academics John Cohen and Raymond Williams, and a newsroom full of top journalists including Richard Clements, Richard Ingrams, Brian Inglis, Peter Jenkins, Jill Tweedie and Peregrine Worsthorne. The series provoked outrage in the admen's favorite watering holes, from Soho pubs to St. James's clubs.

Nobody pretended the 21 were representative of the population at large. But they represented a fair slice of then current British intellectual opinion. And few of them liked advertising one iota. Twelve were extremely hostile, four were mildly hostile, four saw a few pros buried among countless cons—but only Peregrine Worsthorne was broadly enthusiastic about the contribution advertising makes to society.

The criticisms ranged from a fundamental disapproval of advertising as a phenomenon, to individual dislikes of certain of its characteristics. Christopher Mayhew contended that advertising had a wholly corrupting effect on society. Mary Whitehouse said it degraded women. *Tribune* editor Richard Clements believed it to be economically wasteful (echoing the views of the then Prime Minister, Harold Wilson). Many of the 21 insisted advertising encourages materialism. Christopher Mayhew—who in the 1950s had fought the launch of commercial television tooth and nail, supported by Tory as well as Labor leaders—argued:

"'Advertising introduces you to the good things of life.' Such   5
was the slogan plugged by the Advertising Association a few years ago. That is to say, the good things of life, according to the Advertising Association, are the things we see advertised, the things we can buy—not honesty, friendship, kindness, or good manners; not loyalty, respect for law or sense of duty; but cars, perfumes, chocolates, deodorants, aperients and aperitifs."

The other widespread criticism was that, as Professor John Cohen put it, advertisements only tell "half the truth." Almost all the contributors said they wanted advertisements to give more information, to be more factual, more honest.

When the series finished, *Campaign* magazine invited J. Walter Thompson chairman Dr. John Treasure, and me, to respond. In briefest summary, Treasure replied to Mayhew's argument, while I replied to Professor Cohen's. Treasure pointed out that nobody had ever claimed advertising promotes all the good things of life—there are numerous areas of life in which advertising is not involved—but for most people the good things in their lives include food, holidays, clothes, comfort and material possessions—and being able to choose between them. I argued that advertisements could not include all the facts about any product—the very notion is preposterous. So they select those positive facts in which advertisers believe consumers will be interested, and consumers are well aware advertisements are partial, biased in favour of the advertiser.

But their essays revealed how sharply the critics' opinions differed from those of the general population. Just about every market research study on the subject has shown—then as now—that around 80 per cent of the British public feel advertising to be a good thing. A survey at the time, Europe Today, showed 79 per cent of Britons believed advertising to be informative, while 70 per cent believed it to be essential. In Britain, during the last half-century surveys about advertising have been remarkably consistent, and remarkably favourable. (This is not true in all countries).

Intellectuals disagree with the public about many things, but the intellectuals are usually aware of the conflict. The Campaign articles made clear the critics felt their views to be so obviously correct that everyone in the country must surely agree with them. This was not so. But understandable.

Hostility to advertising among British intellectuals goes back a long way. In 1843 Thomas Carlyle dubbed it a "deafening blast of puffery," and at the end of that century the Society for Controlling the Abuses of Public Advertising (SCAPA) included among its members such notables as William Morris, Rudyard Kipling, Holman Hunt, Arthur Quiller-Couch and Sir John Millais—as well as Sydney Courtauld and the Fry chocolate family. But even then the public did not follow their leaders. Five hundred copies of SCAPA's polemical leaflet were printed. Only 30 were sold.

Still, the critics kept up their fire. Many of the attacks were well-worn retreads. But in 1980 Professor Raymond Williams took the arguments a stage further. Williams—an influential Marxist academic, social commentator, critic and novelist—published an essay called Advertising: The Magic System. Far from being too materialistic, Williams argued, modern advertising is not materialistic enough, because the images with which advertisements surround goods deliberately detract attention from the goods' material specifications: "If we were sensibly materialist we should find most advertising to be an insane irrelevance" he averred. In the 19th century he said, more or less accurately, advertising was generally factual and informative, except for fraudulent patent medicine and toiletry advertisements, which had already adopted the undesirable practices which later became commonplace. In other words Williams was not attacking all advertising, just most present day advertisements.

Why, he asked, do advertisements exploit "deep feelings of a personal and social kind"? His answer: because the concentration of economic power into ever larger units forces those units to make human beings consume more and more, in order for the units to stay operative. "The fundamental choice . . . set to us by modern industrial production, is between man as a consumer and man as a user." He argues that usage is continuous—today we might say sustainable—but consumption is inherently destructive. So the emphasis on consumers and consumption, rather than on users and usage, is inherently an emphasis on destruction. This emphasis occurs because destruction is necessary to keep the wheels of industry turning. (How we could use Liquorice Allsorts without consuming them Williams neglects to explain, but we'll let that pass.)

Like Christopher Mayhew (and J. K. Galbraith[1]), Williams contended that many laudable human needs—"hospitals, schools, quiet"—are out of phase with an industrialised society. So the industrialised society uses advertising to focus attention on its industrial output, and to detract humanity from its non-industrial aspirations. This, he says, is why modern advertisements usurp our sexual and emotional desires, attaching them to goods and services. It is akin to the voodoo of the primitive magic man— hence the essay's title: it diverts the tribe towards inessential needs.

At first glance this is a seductive argument. But it is wrong. While the usage of some goods—eye glasses, say, or paintings— does not destroy them, the usage of most goods—like Liquorice Allsorts—does destroy them. And this is perhaps fortunate, because the "the fundamental choice" is not, as Williams posits, "between man as consumer and man as user," but between man as consumer and man as producer (the male chauvinism is his,

---

[1]*J. K. Galbraith:* Canadian American economist John Kenneth Galbraith (1908–2006). [Editor's note.]

not mine). Williams correctly says advertising keeps the industrial wheels turning. But if the industrial wheels stopped turning there would be mass unemployment.

Above all, Williams is wrong because insofar as advertising   15
emphasises emotional and sexual desires—far less than he supposes—this is not merely because human beings inevitably have emotional relationships with material goods, but because most material goods have no intrinsic value: they are merely means to ends. His emphasis on the specifications of products misses the point: it is functionality which matters. Primitive man did not make spearheads because he needed spearheads: he made spearheads because he needed food and protection. People do not buy drills because they want drills, they buy drills because they want holes. Specifications are only important insofar as they deliver the required benefits. And the benefits may be material, or may be emotional.

Today few critics take issue with advertising as a phenomenon. Instead they focus on individual sectors—alcohol, fattening foods, financial credit, or whatever—where the issues are specific, and rather different. Today almost everyone who has examined the issues accepts that advertising does indeed help keep the wheels of industry turning, and hence keeps people in jobs. Today almost everyone accepts that by subsidizing the media, advertising helps keep them relatively inexpensive and relatively free from government control. (This, too, is not true in all countries.)

The area where contention still rages is how advertising benefits consumers (if at all). But the great French essayist Montaigne hit the spot in his 1595 essay "Of a Defect in our Policies." How, he asked, can sellers and buyers successfully communicate with each other? And like many other early commentators he believed the principal loser from the lack of communication to be the buyer. Unless buyers know about all the goods offered, they miss out. And nobody since Montaigne (since ancient Athens come to that) has devised a better way than advertising to bridge this knowledge gap. If consumers did not benefit from advertising, it would not work.

Happily, in Britain we get two-for-the-price-of-one: an economic service—with added creativity (which, again, is not true in all countries). And maybe the creativity is catalysed by the criticisms.

For Discussion and Writing

1. According to Fletcher, what are the benefits of advertising?

2. The writer spends much of the article summarizing—and responding to—the arguments of advertising's critics. How would you characterize his style and tone toward these critics? Does he respond to them effectively? Why or why not?

3. **connections**   In both his opening and his conclusion, Fletcher emphasizes the "creativity" of advertising. Would Bill Bryson agree with this assessment ("The Hard Sell: Advertising in America" [p. 120])? How does Bryson view advertising's creativity in his essay?

4. Fletcher writes: "Just about every market research study on the subject has shown . . . that around 80 per cent of the British public feel advertising to be a good thing" (par. 8). What is your opinion? Do you think advertising is, generally, a "good thing"? Explain your point of view.

BILL BRYSON

The Hard Sell:
Advertising in America

A versatile American author of several books on travel, science, and literature, Bill Bryson (b. 1951) has spent much of his career working and living in Britain. From 2005 to 2011, he served as chancellor of Durham University in England; in 2006 he was awarded the Order of the British Empire, an honorary order of chivalry granted by Queen Elizabeth II. His books include Notes from a Small Island *(1995),* A Short History of Nearly Everything *(2003),* Shakespeare: The World as Stage *(2007), and* At Home: A Short History of Private Life *(2010).*

"The Hard Sell" is excerpted from Bryson's 1994 book Made in America: An Informal History of the English Language in the United States. *As he traces the evolution of the advertising industry, Bryson also highlights the comical aspects of branding and advertisements. How does Bryson achieve comic effects?*

In 1885, a young man named George Eastman formed the Eastman Dry Plate and Film Company in Rochester, New York. It was rather a bold thing to do. Aged just 31, Eastman was a junior clerk in a bank on a comfortable but modest salary of $15 a week. He had no background in business. But he was passionately devoted to photography and had become increasingly gripped with the conviction that anyone who could develop a simple, untechnical camera, as opposed to the cumbersome, outsized, fussily complex contrivances then on the market, stood to make a fortune.

Eastman worked tirelessly for three years to perfect his invention, supporting himself in the meantime by making dry plates for commercial photographers, and in June 1888 produced a camera that was positively dazzling in its simplicity: a plain black box just six and a half inches long by three and a quarter inches wide, with a button on the side and a key for advancing the film. Eastman called his device the *Detective Camera*. Detectives were all the thing—Sherlock Holmes was just taking off with American readers—and the name implied that it was so small and simple that it could be used unnoticed, as a detective might. The camera had no viewfinder and no way of focusing. The *photographer* or *photographist* (it took a while for the first word to become the established one) simply held the camera in front of him, pressed a button on the side, and hoped for the best. Each roll held a hundred pictures. When a roll was fully exposed, the anxious owner sent the entire camera to Rochester for developing. Eventually he received the camera back, freshly loaded with film, and—assuming all had gone well—one hundred small circular pictures, two and a half inches in diameter. . . .

In September 1888, Eastman changed the name of the camera to *Kodak*—an odd choice, since it was meaningless, and in 1888 no one gave meaningless names to products, especially successful products. Since British patent applications at the time demanded full explanation of trade and brand names, we know how Eastman arrived at his inspired name. He crisply summarized his reasoning in his patent application: "First. It is short. Second. It is not capable of mispronunciation. Third. It does not resemble anything in the art and cannot be associated with anything in the art except the Kodak." Four years later the whole enterprise was renamed the Eastman Kodak Company.

Despite the considerable expense involved—a Kodak camera sold for $25, and each roll of film cost $10, including developing—by 1895, over 100,000 Kodaks had been sold and Eastman was a seriously wealthy man. A lifelong bachelor, he lived with his mother in a thirty-seven-room mansion with twelve bathrooms. Soon people everywhere were talking about snapshots, originally a British shooting term for a hastily executed shot. Its photographic sense was coined by the English astronomer Sir John Herschel, who also gave the world the terms *positive* and *negative* in their photographic senses.

From the outset, Eastman developed three crucial strategies that have been the hallmarks of virtually every successful consumer goods company since. First, he went for the mass market, reasoning that it was better to make a little money each from a lot of people rather than a lot of money from a few. He also showed

5

a tireless, obsessive dedication to making his products better and cheaper. In the 1890s, such an approach was widely perceived as insane. If you had a successful product you milked it for all it was worth. If competitors came along with something better, you bought them out or tried to squash them with lengthy patent fights or other bullying tactics. What you certainly did not do was create new products that made your existing lines obsolescent. Eastman did. Throughout the late 1890s, Kodak introduced a series of increasingly cheaper, niftier cameras—the Bull's Eye model of 1896, which cost just $12, and the famous slimline Folding Pocket Kodak of 1898, before finally in 1900 producing his eureka model: the little box Brownie, priced at just $1 and with film at 15 cents a reel (though with only six exposures per reel).

Above all, what set Eastman apart was the breathtaking lavishness of his advertising. In 1899 alone, he spent $750,000, an unheard-of sum, on advertising. Moreover, it was *good* advertising: crisp, catchy, reassuringly trustworthy. "You press a button— we do the rest" ran the company's first slogan, thus making a virtue of its shortcomings. Never mind that you couldn't load or unload the film yourself. Kodak would do it for you. In 1905, it followed with another classic slogan: "If It Isn't an Eastman, It Isn't a Kodak."

Kodak's success did not escape other businessmen, who also began to see virtue in the idea of steady product refinement and improvement. AT&T and Westinghouse, among others, set up research laboratories with the idea of creating a stream of new products, even at the risk of displacing old ones. Above all, everyone everywhere began to advertise.

Advertising was already a well-established phenomenon by the turn of the twentieth century. Newspapers had begun carrying ads as far back as the early 1700s, and magazines soon followed. (Benjamin Franklin has the distinction of having run the first magazine ad seeking the whereabouts of a runaway slave, in 1741.) By 1850, the country had its first *advertising agency*, the American Newspaper Advertising Agency, though its function was to buy advertising space rather than come up with creative campaigns. The first advertising agency in the modern sense was N. W. Ayer & Sons of Philadelphia, established in 1869. To *advertise* originally carried the sense of to broadcast or disseminate news. Thus a nineteenth-century newspaper that called itself the

An 1889 advertisement for an early Kodak camera.

Advertiser meant that it had lots of news, not lots of ads. By the early 1800s the term had been stretched to accommodate the idea of spreading the news of the availability of certain goods or services. A newspaper notice that read "Jos. Parker, Hatter" was essentially announcing that if anyone was in the market for hats, Jos. Parker had them. In the sense of persuading members of the public to acquire items they might not otherwise think of buying—items they didn't know they needed—advertising is a phenomenon of the modern age.

By the 1890s, advertising was appearing everywhere—in news- 10 papers and magazines, on *billboards* (an Americanism dating from 1850), on the sides of buildings, on passing streetcars, on paper bags, even on matchbooks, which were invented in 1892 and were being extensively used as an advertising medium within three years.

Very early on, advertisers discovered the importance of a good slogan. Many of our more venerable slogans are older than you might think. Ivory Soap's "99 44/100 percent pure" dates from 1879. Schlitz has been calling itself "the beer that made Milwaukee famous" since 1895, and Heinz's "57 varieties" followed a year later. Morton Salt's "When it rains, it pours" dates from 1911, the American Florist Association's "Say it with flowers" was first used in 1912, and the "good to the last drop" of Maxwell House coffee, named for the Maxwell House Hotel in Nashville, where it was first served, has been with us since 1907. (The slogan is said to have originated with Teddy Roosevelt, who pronounced the coffee "good to the last drop," prompting one wit to ask, "So what's wrong with the last drop?")

Sometimes slogans took a little working on. Coca-Cola described itself as "the drink that makes a pause refreshing" before realizing, in 1929, that "the pause that refreshes" was rather more succinct and memorable. A slogan could make all the difference to a product's success. After advertising its soap as an efficacious way of dealing with "conspicuous nose pores," Woodbury's Facial Soap came up with the slogan "The skin you love to touch" and won the hearts of millions. The great thing about a slogan was that it didn't have to be accurate to be effective. Heinz never actually had exactly "57 varieties" of anything. The catchphrase arose simply because H. J. Heinz, the company's founder, decided he liked the sound of the number. Undeterred by considerations of verity, he had the slogan slapped on every one of the products he produced, already in 1896 far more than fifty-seven. For a time the company tried to arrange its products into fifty-seven arbitrary clusters, but in 1969 it gave up the ruse altogether and abandoned the slogan.

Early in the 1900s, advertisers discovered another perennial feature of marketing—the *giveaway*, as it was called almost from the start. Consumers soon became acquainted with the irresistibly tempting notion that if they bought a particular product they could expect a reward—the chance to receive a prize, a free book (almost always ostensibly dedicated to the general improvement of one's well-being but invariably a thinly disguised plug for the manufacturer's range of products), a free sample, or a rebate in the form of a shiny dime, or be otherwise endowed with some gratifying bagatelle. Typical of the genre was a turn-of-the-century tome called *The Vital Question Cook Book*, which was promoted as an aid to livelier meals, but which proved upon receipt to contain 112 pages of recipes all involving the use of Shredded Wheat. Many of these had a certain air of desperation about them, notably the "Shredded Wheat Biscuit Jellied Apple Sandwich" and the "Creamed Spinach on Shredded Wheat Biscuit Toast." Almost all involved nothing more than spooning some everyday food on a piece of shredded wheat and giving it an inflated name. Nonetheless the company distributed no fewer than four million copies of *The Vital Question Cook Book* to eager consumers.

The great breakthrough in twentieth-century advertising, however, came with the identification and exploitation of the American consumer's Achilles' heel: anxiety. One of the first to master the form was King Gillette, inventor of the first safety razor and one of the most relentless advertisers of the early 1900s. Most of the early ads featured Gillette himself, who with his fussy toothbrush mustache and well-oiled hair looked more like a caricature of a Parisian waiter than a captain of industry. After starting with a few jaunty words about the ease and convenience of the safety razor—"Compact? Rather!"—he plunged the reader into the heart of the matter: "When you use my razor you are exempt from the dangers that men often encounter who allow their faces to come in contact with brush, soap, and barbershop accessories used on other people."

Here was an entirely new approach to selling goods. Gillette's 15 ads were in effect telling you that not only did there exist a product that you never previously suspected you needed, but if you *didn't* use it you would very possibly attract a crop of facial diseases you never knew existed. The combination proved irresistible. Though the Gillette razor retailed for a hefty $5—half the average workingman's weekly pay—it sold by the millions, and King Gillette became a very wealthy man. (Though only for a time, alas. Like many others of his era, he grew obsessed with the idea of the perfectibility of mankind and expended so much of his energies writing books of convoluted philosophy with titles like *The Human Drift* that he eventually lost control of his company and most of his fortune.)

By the 1920s, advertisers had so refined the art that a consumer could scarcely pick up a magazine without being bombarded with unsettling questions: "Do You Make These Mistakes in English?"; "Will Your Hair Stand Close Inspection?"; "When Your Guests Are Gone—Are You Sorry You Ever Invited Them?" (because, that is, you lack social polish); "Did Nature fail to put roses in your cheeks?"; "Will There be a Victrola in Your Home This Christmas?"[1] The 1920s truly were the Age of Anxiety. One ad pictured a former golf champion, "now only a wistful onlooker,"

---

[1]The most famous 1920s ad of them all didn't pose a question, but it did play on the reader's anxiety: "They Laughed When I Sat Down, but When I Started to Play. . . ." It was originated by the U.S. School of Music in 1925.

whose career had gone sour because he had neglected his teeth. Scott Tissues mounted a campaign showing a forlorn-looking businessman sitting on a park bench beneath the bold caption "A Serious Business Handicap—These Troubles That Come from Harsh Toilet Tissue." Below the picture the text explained: "65% of all men and women over 40 are suffering from some form of rectal trouble, estimates a prominent specialist connected with one of New York's largest hospitals. 'And one of the contributing causes,' he states, 'is inferior toilet tissue.'" There was almost nothing that one couldn't become uneasy about. One ad even asked: "Can You Buy a Radio Safely?" Distressed bowels were the most frequent target. The makers of Sal Hepatica warned: "We rush to meetings, we dash to parties. We are on the go all day long. We exercise too little, and we eat too much. And, in consequence, we impair our bodily functions—often we retain food within us too long. And when that occurs, poisons are set up— *Auto-Intoxication begins.*"

In addition to the dread of auto-intoxication, the American consumer faced a gauntlet of other newly minted maladies— *pyorrhea, halitosis* (coined as a medical term in 1874, but popularized by Listerine beginning in 1922 with the slogan "Even your best friend won't tell you"), *athlete's foot* (a term invented by the makers of Absorbine Jr. in 1928), *dead cuticles, scabby toes, iron-poor blood, vitamin deficiency* (*vitamins* had been coined in 1912, but the word didn't enter the general vocabulary until the 1920s, when advertisers realized it sounded worryingly scientific), *fallen stomach, tobacco breath,* and *psoriasis,* though Americans would have to wait until the next decade for the scientific identification of the gravest of personal disorders—*body odor,* a term invented in 1933 by the makers of Lifebuoy soap and so terrifying in its social consequences that it was soon abbreviated to a whispered *B.O.*

The white-coated technicians of American laboratories had not only identified these new conditions, but—miraculously, it seemed—simultaneously come up with cures for them. Among the products that were invented or rose to greatness in this busy, neurotic decade were *Cutex* (for those deceased cuticles), *Vick's VapoRub, Geritol, Serutan* ("Natures spelled backwards," as the voiceover always said with somewhat bewildering reassurance, as if spelling a product's name backward conferred some medicinal benefit), *Noxzema* (for which read: "knocks eczema"), *Preparation H*, *Murine* eyedrops, and *Dr. Scholl's Foot Aids*.[2] It truly was an age of miracles—one in which you could even cure a smoker's cough by smoking, so long as it was Old Golds you smoked, because as the slogan proudly if somewhat untruthfully boasted, they contained "Not a cough in a carload." (As late as 1943, L&M cigarettes were advertised as "just what the doctor ordered!")

By 1927, advertising was a $1.5-billion-a-year industry in the United States and advertising people were held in such awe that they were asked not only to mastermind campaigns but even to name products. An ad man named Henry N. McKinney, for instance, named *Keds* shoes, *Karo* syrup, *Meadow Gold* butter, and *Uneeda Biscuits*.

Product names tend to cluster around certain sounds. Break- 20 fast cereals often ended in *ies (Wheaties, Rice Krispies, Frosties)*; washing powders and detergents tended to be gravely monosyllabic *(Lux, Fab, Tide, Duz)*. It is often possible to tell the era of a product's development by its termination. Thus products dating from the 1920s and early 1930s often ended in *-ex (Pyrex, Cutex, Kleenex, Windex)*, while those ending in *-master (Mixmaster, Toastmaster)* generally betray a late-1930s or early-1940s genesis. The development of *Glo-Coat* floor wax in 1932 also heralded the beginning of American business's strange and long-standing infatuation with illiterate spellings, a trend that continued with *ReaLemon* juice in 1935, *Reddi-Wip* whipped cream in 1947, and many hundreds of others since, from *Tastee-Freez* drive-ins to *Toys 'Я' Us*, along with countless others with a *Kwik*, *E-Z* or *U* (as in *While-U-Wait*) embedded in their titles. The late 1940s saw the birth of a brief vogue for endings in *-matic*, so that car manufacturers offered vehicles with *Seat-O-Matic* levers and *Cruise-O-Matic* transmissions, and even fitted sheets came with *Ezy-Matic* corners. Some companies became associated with certain types of names. DuPont, for instance, had a special fondness for words ending in *-on*. The practice began with *nylon*—a name that was concocted out of thin air and owes nothing to its chemical

---

[2]And yes, there really was a Dr. Scholl. His name was William Scholl, he was a real doctor, genuinely dedicated to the well-being of feet, and they are still very proud of him in his hometown of LaPorte, Indiana.

properties—and was followed with *Rayon, Dacron, Orlon,* and *Teflon,* among many others. In recent years the company has moved on to what might be called its *Star Trek* phase with such compounds as *Tyvek, Kevlar, Sontara, Cordura, Nomex,* and *Zemorain.* Such names have more than passing importance to their owners. If American business has given us a large dose of anxiety in its ceaseless quest for a healthier *bottom line* (a term dating from the 1930s, though not part of mainstream English until the 1970s), we may draw some comfort from the thought that business has suffered a great deal of collective anxiety over protecting the names of its products.

A certain cruel paradox prevails in the matter of preserving brand names. Every business naturally wants to create a product that will dominate its market. But if that product so dominates the market that the brand name becomes indistinguishable in the public mind from the product itself—when people begin to ask for a *thermos* rather than a "Thermos brand vacuum flask"— then the term has become generic and the owner faces loss of its trademark protection. That is why advertisements and labels so often carry faintly paranoid-sounding lines like "Tabasco is the registered trademark for the brand of pepper sauce made by McIlhenny Co." and why companies like Coca-Cola suffer palpatations when they see a passage like this (from John Steinbeck's *The Wayward Bus*):

> "Got any coke?" another character asked.
> "No," said the proprietor. "Few bottles of Pepsi-Cola. Haven't had any coke for a month. . . . It's the same stuff. You can't tell them apart."

An understandable measure of confusion exists concerning the distinction between patents and trademarks and between trademarks and trade names. A *patent* protects the name of the product and its method of manufacture for seventeen years. Thus from 1895 to 1912, no one but the Shredded Wheat Company could make shredded wheat. But because patents require manufacturers to divulge the secrets of their products—and thus make them available to rivals to copy when the patent runs out—companies sometimes choose not to seek their protection. *Coca-Cola,* for one, has never been patented. A *trademark* is effectively the name of a product, its *brand name.* A *trade name* is the name of the manufacturer. So *Ford* is a trade name, *Taurus* a trademark. Trademarks apply not just to names, but also to logos, drawings, and other symbols and depictions. The MGM lion, for instance, is a trademark. Unlike patents, trademark protection goes on forever, or at least as long as the manufacturer can protect it. For a long time, it was felt that this permanence gave the holder an unfair advantage. In consequence, America did not enact its first trademark law until 1870, almost a century after Britain, and then it was declared unconstitutional by the Supreme Court. Lasting trademark protection did not begin for American companies until 1881. Today, more than a million trademarks have been issued in the United States and the number is rising by about thirty thousand a year.

A good trademark is almost incalculably valuable. Invincible- 25
seeming brand names do occasionally falter and fade. *Pepsodent,* *Rinso, Chase & Sanborn, Sal Hepatica, Vitalis, Brylcreem,* and *Burma-Shave* all once stood on the commanding heights of consumer recognition but are now defunct or have sunk to the status of what the trade calls "ghost brands"—products that are still produced but little promoted and largely forgotten. For the most part, however, once a product establishes a dominant position in a market, it is exceedingly difficult to depose it. In nineteen of twenty-two product categories, the company that owned the leading American brand in 1925 still has it today—*Nabisco* in cookies, *Kellogg's* in breakfast cereals. *Kodak* in film, *Sherwin Williams* in paint, *Del Monte* in canned fruit, *Wrigley's* in chewing gum, *Singer* in sewing machines, *Ivory* in soap, *Campbell's* in soup, *Gillette* in razors. Few really successful brand names of today were not just as familiar to your grandparents or even great-grandparents, and a well-established brand name has a sort of self-perpetuating power. As *The Economist* has noted: "In the category of food blenders, consumers were still ranking General Electric second twenty years after the company had stopped making them."

An established brand name is so valuable that only about 5 percent of the sixteen thousand or so new products introduced in America each year bear all-new brand names. The others are variants on an existing product—*Tide with Bleach, Tropicana Twister Light Fruit Juices,* and so on. Among some types of product a certain glut is evident. At last count there were 220 types of branded breakfast cereal in America. In 1993, according to an international business survey, the world's most valuable brand was *Marlboro*, with a value estimated at $40 billion, slightly ahead of *Coca-Cola*. Among the other top ten brands were *Intel*, *Kellogg's*, *Budweiser*, *Pepsi*, *Gillette*, and *Pampers*, *Nescafé* and *Bacardi* were the only foreign brands to make the top ten, underlining American dominance.

Huge amounts of effort go into choosing brand names. General Foods reviewed 2,800 names before deciding on *Dreamwhip*. (To put this in proportion, try to think of just ten names for an artificial whipped cream.) Ford considered more than twenty thousand possible car names before finally settling on *Edsel* (which proves that such care doesn't always pay), and Standard Oil a similar number of names before it opted for *Exxon*. Sometimes, however, the most successful names are the result of a moment's whimsy. *Betty Crocker* came in a flash to an executive of the Washburn Crosby Company (later absorbed by General Mills), who chose *Betty* because he thought it sounded wholesome and sincere and *Crocker* in memory of a beloved fellow executive who had recently died. At first the name was used only to sign letters responding to customers' requests for advice or information, but by the 1950s, Betty Crocker's smiling, confident face was appearing on more than fifty types of food product, and her loyal followers could buy her recipe books and even visit her "kitchen" at the General Foods headquarters.

Great efforts also go into finding out why people buy the brands they do. Advertisers and market researchers bandy about terms like *conjoint analysis technique*, *personal drive patterns*, *Gaussian distributions*, *fractals*, and other such arcana in their quest to winnow out every subliminal quirk in our buying habits. They know, for instance, that 40 percent of all people who move to a new address will also change their brand of toothpaste, that the average supermarket shopper makes fourteen impulse decisions in each visit, that 62 percent of shoppers will pay a premium for mayonnaise even when they think a cheaper brand is just as good, but that only 24 percent will show the same largely irrational loyalty to frozen vegetables.

To preserve a brand name involves a certain fussy attention to linguistic and orthographic details. To begin with, the name is normally expected to be treated not as a noun but as a proper adjective—that is, the names should be followed by an explanation of what it does: *Kleenex facial tissues, Q-Tip cotton swabs, Jell-O brand gelatin dessert, Sanka brand decaffeinated coffee.* Some types of products—notably cars—are granted an exemption, which explains why General Motors does not have to advertise *Cadillac self-propelled automobiles* or the like. In all cases, the name may not explicitly describe the product's function though it may hint at what it does. Thus *Coppertone* is acceptable; *Coppertan* would not be.

The situation is more than a little bizarre. Having done all they 30 can to make their products household words, manufacturers must then in their advertisements do all in their power to imply that they aren't. Before trademark law was clarified, advertisers positively encouraged the public to treat their products as generics. Kodak invited consumers to "Kodak as you go," turning the brand name into a dangerously ambiguous verb. It would never do that now. The American Thermos Product Company went so far as to boast, "Thermos is a household word," to its considerable cost. Donald F. Duncan, Inc., the original manufacturer of the *Yo-Yo*, lost its trademark protection partly because it was amazingly casual about capitalization in its own promotional literature. "In case you don't know what a yo-yo is . . ." one of its advertisements went, suggesting that in commercial terms Duncan didn't. Duncan also made the elemental error of declaring, "If It Isn't a Duncan, It Isn't a Yo-Yo," which on the face of it would seem a reasonable claim, but was in fact held by the courts to be inviting the reader to consider the product generic. Kodak had long since stopped saying "If it isn't an Eastman, it isn't a Kodak."

Because of the confusion, and occasional lack of fastidiousness on the part of their owners, many dozens of products have lost their trademark protection, among them *aspirin, linoleum, yo-yo, thermos, cellophane, milk of magnesia, mimeograph, lanolin, celluloid, dry ice, escalator, shredded wheat, kerosene*, and *zipper*. All were once proudly capitalized and worth a fortune.

On July 1, 1941, the New York television station WNBT-TV interrupted its normal viewing to show, without comment, a Bulova watch ticking. For sixty seconds the watch ticked away mysteriously, then the picture faded and the normal programming resumed. It wasn't much, but it was the first television *commercial*.

Both the word and the idea were already well established. The first commercial—the term was used from the very beginning—had been broadcast by radio station WEAF in New York on August 28, 1922. It lasted for either ten or fifteen minutes, depending on which source you credit. Commercial radio was not an immediate hit. In its first two months, WEAF sold only $550 worth of airtime. But by the mid-1920s, sponsors were not only flocking to buy airtime but naming their programs after their products—*The Lucky Strike Hour, The A&P Gypsies, The Lux Radio Theater*, and so on. Such was the obsequiousness of the radio networks that by the early 1930s, many were allowing the sponsors to take complete artistic and production control for the programs. Many of the most popular shows were actually written by the advertising agencies, and the agencies naturally seldom missed an opportunity to work a favorable mention of the sponsor's products into the scripts.

With the rise of television in the 1950s, the practices of the radio era were effortlessly transferred to the new medium. Advertisers inserted their names into the program title—*Texaco Star Theater, Gillette Cavalcade of Sports, Chesterfield Sound-Off Time, The U.S. Steel Hour, Kraft Television Theater, The Chevy Show, The Alcoa Hour, The Ford Star Revue, Dick Clark's Beechnut Show*, and the arresting hybrid *The Lux-Schlitz Playhouse*, which seemed to suggest a cozy symbiosis between soapflakes and beer. The commercial dominance of program titles reached a kind of hysterical peak with a program officially called *Your Kaiser Dealer Presents Kaiser-Frazer "Adventures in Mystery" Starring Betty Furness in "Byline."* Sponsors didn't write the programs any longer, but they did impose a firm control on the contents, most notoriously during a 1959 *Playhouse 90* broadcast of *Judgment at Nuremberg*, when the sponsor, the American Gas Association, managed to have all references to gas ovens and the gassing of Jews removed from the script.

Where commercial products of the late 1940s had scientific-sounding names, those of the 1950s relied increasingly on secret ingredients. Gleem toothpaste contained a mysterious piece of alchemy called *GL-70*.[3] There was never the slightest hint of what

[3]For purposes of research, I wrote to Procter & Gamble, Gleem's manufacturer, asking what GL-70 was, but the public relations department evidently thought it eccentric of me to wonder what I had been putting in my mouth all through childhood and declined to reply.

GL-70 was, but it would, according to the advertising, not only rout odor-causing bacteria but "wipe out their enzymes"!

A kind of creeping illiteracy invaded advertising, too, to the dismay of many. When Winston began advertising its cigarettes with the slogan "Winston tastes good like a cigarette should," nationally syndicated columnists like Sydney J. Harris wrote anguished essays on what the world was coming to—every educated person knew it should be "as a cigarette should"—but the die was cast. By 1958, Ford was advertising that you could "travel smooth" in a Thunderbird Sunliner and the maker of Ace Combs was urging buyers to "comb it handsome"—a trend that continues today with "pantihose that fits you real comfortable" and other grammatical manglings too numerous and dispiriting to dwell on.

We may smile at the advertising ruses of the 1920s—frightening people with the threat of "fallen stomach" and "scabby toes"—but in fact such creative manipulation still goes on, albeit at a slightly more sophisticated level. *The New York Times Magazine* reported in 1990 how an advertising copywriter had been told to come up with some impressive labels for a putative hand cream. She invented the arresting and healthful-sounding term *oxygenating moisturizers* and wrote accompanying copy with reference to "tiny bubbles of oxygen that release moisture into your skin." This done, the advertising was turned over to the company's research and development department, which was instructed to come up with a product that matched the copy.

If we fall for such commercial manipulation, we have no one to blame but ourselves. When Kentucky Fried Chicken introduced "Extra Crispy" chicken to sell alongside its "Original" chicken, and sold it at the same price, sales were disappointing. But when its advertising agency persuaded it to promote "Extra Crispy" as a premium brand and to put the price up, sales soared. Much of the same sort of verbal hypnosis was put to work for the benefit of the fur industry. Dyed muskrat makes a perfectly good fur, for those who enjoy cladding themselves in dead animals, but the name clearly lacks stylishness. The solution was to change the name to *Hudson seal*. Never mind that the material contained not a strand of seal fur. It sounded good, and sales skyrocketed.

Truth has seldom been a particularly visible feature of American advertising. In the early 1970s, Chevrolet ran a series of ads for the Chevelle boasting that the car had "109 advantages to keep

it from becoming old before its time." When looked into, it turned
out that these 109 vaunted features included such items as rear-
view mirrors, backup lights, balanced wheels, and many other
components that were considered pretty well basic to any car.
Never mind; sales soared. At about the same time, Ford, not to be
outdone, introduced a "limited edition" Mercury Monarch at
$250 below the normal list price. It achieved this, it turned out, by
taking $250 worth of equipment off the standard Monarch.

And has all this deviousness led to a tightening of the rules   40
concerning what is allowable in advertising? Hardly. In 1986, as
William Lutz relates in *Doublespeak*, the insurance company
John Hancock launched an ad campaign in which "real people
in real situations" discussed their financial predicaments with
remarkable candor. When a journalist asked to speak to these real
people, a company spokesman conceded that they were actors
and "in that sense they are not real people."

During the 1984 presidential campaign, the Republican
National Committee ran a television advertisement praising President Reagan for providing cost-of-living pay increases to federal
workers "in spite of those sticks-in-the-mud who tried to keep
him from doing what we elected him to do." When it was pointed
out that the increases had in fact been mandated by law since
1975 and that Reagan had in any case three times tried to block
them, a Republican official responded: "Since when is a commercial supposed to be accurate?" Quite.

In linguistic terms, perhaps the most interesting challenge facing advertisers today is that of selling products in an increasingly
multicultural society. Spanish is a particular problem, not just
because it is spoken over such a widely scattered area but also
because it is spoken in so many different forms. Brown sugar is
azucar negra in New York, *azucar prieta* in Miami, *azucar morena*
in much of Texas, and *azucar pardo* pretty much everywhere
else—and that's just one word. Much the same bewildering mul-
tiplicity applies to many others. In consequence, embarrassments
are all but inevitable.

In mainstream Spanish, *bichos* means *insects*, but in Puerto
Rico it means *testicles*, so when a pesticide maker promised to
bring death to the *bichos*, Puerto Rican consumers were at least
bemused, if not alarmed. Much the same happened when a maker
of bread referred to its product as *un bollo de pan* and discovered

that to Spanish-speaking Miamians of Cuban extraction that means a woman's private parts. And when Perdue Chickens translated its slogan "It takes a tough man to make a tender chicken" into Spanish, it came out as the slightly less macho "It takes a sexually excited man to make a chick sensual."

Never mind. Sales soared.

For Discussion and Writing

1. Bryson begins his essay with a narrative account of George Eastman and the development of the Kodak camera. Why do you think the writer chose to start with this story? What purpose does it serve? How is it tied to the main point? How else might he have begun his essay?

2. What is the "cruel paradox" (par. 23) of brand names, particularly for popular products that come to dominate a market?

3. **connections**   According to Bryson, the "great breakthrough in twentieth-century advertising . . . came with the identification and exploitation of the American consumer's Achilles' heel: anxiety" (par. 14). How might Winston Fletcher respond to this claim ("Art or Puffery? A Defense of Advertising" [p. 114])?

4. Bryson writes: "Great efforts also go into finding out why people buy the brands they do" (par. 28). Consider your own brand preferences and loyalties. Why are you attached to a particular brand? Are brands connected with your sense of personal, social, or professional identity? Bryson spends much of his essay closely reading the language of branding and advertising. In your own reflection on these questions, pay similar attention to words, sounds, and images. How are they connected to the brand's meaning and associations?

CHAPTER 3

Identity

In 1909, the English writer Israel Zangwill staged *The Melting Pot* in the United States for the first time. The play follows the fortunes of a Russian-Jewish immigrant, David Quixano, who comes to America, reinvents himself as a composer, and marries a gentile. For Quixano, America is "God's crucible," a place where "all races and nations come to labor and look forward." Zangwill was not the first person to use the "melting pot" metaphor for national and ethnic assimilation. But the play's thesis resonated with President Theodore Roosevelt, who attended the show that evening. "That's a great play, Mr. Zangwill, that's a great play," Roosevelt shouted from his box. Indeed, the melting pot still seems like a perfect evocation of an American ideal: *E pluribus unum:* "Out of many, one."

In the years since, however, many people have contested the melting pot, both as a practice and as an ideal. While the United States has often embraced the "tired, . . . poor, and . . . huddled masses yearning to breathe free," American history includes its share of xenophobia and anxiety about immigration. Similarly, the country has always struggled with race and racial assimilation, from the colonial period and the Civil War, up through the civil rights era and into the "post-racial" presidency (as some had dreamed) of Barack Obama, who is biracial. Questions about race, ethnicity, and culture are public and social. Do we want a melting pot that creates homogeneous "Americans"? Do we want a multicultural salad bowl? An ethnic stew? These issues are matters of personal identity, too. What does it mean for any individual to be white or black, Asian, Latino, or post-racial in a hyperconnected, multicultural world? Do we define ourselves primarily by race and nationality, ethnicity and gender? What are the private and public consequences of these definitions?

The selections in this section look at these public and private questions through the lens of popular culture. Raquel Cepeda's "The N-Word Is Flourishing Among Generation Hip-Hop Latinos: Why Should We Care Now?" explores the revival and meaning of a taboo racial term in a particular ethnic subculture. In "The End of White America?" Hua Hsu looks at the past, present, and future of "the real America" and "whiteness," moving fluidly from discussions of *The Great Gatsby* to reflections on rapper Sean Combs. Ariel Levy ("Women and the Rise of Raunch Culture") writes about social and cultural pressures that encourage supposedly "liberated" women to embrace a "tawdry, tarty, cartoonlike version of female sexuality." For Paul Kix, hip-hop once carried a powerful, race-inflected message of "urban pain"; now, as he writes in "Hip-Hop Is No Longer Cooler Than Me," the genre has "somehow slipped on clown shoes and taken up night classes in pantomime." In paired readings "Where Have African-American Baseball Players Gone?" and "The Sports Taboo," writers Rob Ruck and Malcolm Gladwell focus on the provocative intersections of race and sports.

RAQUEL CEPEDA

The N-Word Is Flourishing Among Generation Hip-Hop Latinos: Why Should We Care Now?

Raquel Cepeda is a cultural activist, award-winning journalist, and documentary filmmaker whose interests include race in America, international hip-hop culture, and Latino American issues. Her work has appeared in the Village Voice, People, *and other publications. Cepeda edited* And It Don't Stop: The Best American Hip-Hop Journalism of the Last 25 Years *(2004). She is the author of the forthcoming* i, Latina? My Year Trippin' Through My Ancestral DNA, Running the Fuku Down, and Making Peace with Dad Along the Way, *as well as the director and coproducer of* Bling: A Planet Rock *(2010), a documentary film about the intersection of hip-hop and the diamond trade in Sierra Leone.*

In the following essay from the Village Voice *(2008), she examines the use of the "n-word" among Afro-Latinos in New York City: "I'm interested in exploring, as a Dominican New Yorker, how we as a community have propagated it." But her essay raises more general issues as well, such as the status of taboo words and the role that language plays in defining cultural and ethnic membership. How does Cepeda use the n-word to enter into a dialogue about broader issues of race in her community?*

"Yo, my nigga, that nigga's crazy," declares a young Dominican guy in his late teens, early twenties. "Yeah, my nigga, that nigga was buggin' last night, my nigga," responds another hermano. Chatter like this floated in the air like the whiff of days-old garbage smoldering in the heat while I took my frequent summer jaunts along Vermilyea Avenue way uptown in Inwood, with my 11-year-old daughter in tow.

Initially, you'd find mostly Caribbean Latinos dropping n-bombs into rap lyrics—"Pigs," off Cypress Hill's classic self-titled 1991 debut, is just one example—but nearly two decades later, the profusion of the word into the New York City Latino vocabulary is reaching an almost caricaturist quality. In Spanish Harlem, el Bronx, and the Lower East Side, it's enthusiastically deployed in an almost faddish manner, as if it's going out of style literally tomorrow. With Nas threatening to name his latest album Nigga (he relented, eventually, but most fans still call it that anyway) a few months ago, and iconic Latino artists from the authentic urban native Fat Joe[1] to one of my favorite internationalists, Immortal Technique,[2] still flinging it about freely, the word, its meaning, and our sense of who can and cannot use it still dominates public conversation. The palpable racial tension that's been rearing its head this historic presidential election, the subject of race and who is truly considered black or white in this black-and-white race, is something Latinos need to pay attention to. For many of us, especially those of Caribbean descent who make up a sizable chunk of New York Latinos, race should matter, and so should that one particular word.

Personal feelings, premonitions, and politics aside, I took the two young boys' exchange as an interesting opportunity, an exercise in thinking about Afro-Latino identity in an unlikely way: through a hip-hop lens. Aside from the fact that we're in the thick of a predominantly Dominican enclave (for now) in our beloved Uptown Manhattan, and the first guy I'd overheard wore an oversized white T-shirt emblazoned with our motherland's flag, homeboy could've passed for an African-American man on any other stretch of blocks stateside. By comparison, his comrade looked more like Fat Joe's skinnier brother, with light eyes and pale skin. Was it OK, or more OK, for the darker-skinned kid to use the term?

As many times as I've heard it yelled across the streets and in playgrounds lately, it doesn't take away the sting. But it's naive to think Puerto Rican, Dominican, and Cuban kids in New York City aren't calling each other and themselves the n-word, especially in

[1]Fat Joe: stage name for Bronx-born rapper Joseph Antonio Cartagena. [Editor's note.]

[2]Immortal Technique: stage name for Peruvian-born rapper Felipe Andres Coronel. [Editor's note.]

2008. (It's a global phenomenon, too: In West African cities like
Freetown and Accra, heads that find out you're from the States
and part of the hip-hop community will find creative ways to work
the word into a conversation.) For us, the word usually surfaces
in the same context that arises among young African-Americans:
as a term of inclusion and solidarity. "It's just a code of communication to us, a 'hood word people throw around frequently," says
half-African-American, half-Dominican rapper AZ, who released
his "rap thesis" on the subject, titled N.4.L. (Niggaz 4 Life), last
month. "I guess people want to use it now for press and all that; I
don't understand what's all the big fuss about."

Somehow, the n-word has found its way back into hip-hop's   5
critical zeitgeist: I'm interested in exploring, as a Dominican New
Yorker, how we as a community have propagated it. Recently, due
to the mounting criticism of Boricua rapper Fat Joe's use of the
term eight albums deep into his career (including his latest, The
Elephant in the Room), Latinos are being challenged to intro-
spect. But I can see why an impulse to laser-focus on the issue
now would bewilder a veteran rapper like Joe; he's used the word
consistently since emerging in 1993, as have the Beatnuts,[3] Hur-
ricane G,[4] and his late Puerto Rican cohort Big Pun, to name a
few. In an interview with Chicago-based WGCI radio personality
Leon Rogers, Joe said that while he didn't know exactly when
Latinos started using the n-word, he felt that "somehow it became
a way to embrace each other." He added: "Crazy shit is, my man
Reverend Al Sharpton,[5] whenever I see him, he'll be like, 'Wassup
Joe, my nigga,' and he's the dude that protests 'my nigga.' He's my
friend, so he says it to me as a term of endearment."

"It draws the racial differentiations into the Latino community,
which I agree with," says New York University Professor of Social
and Cultural Analysis, Juan Flores, who regularly teaches courses
on Afro-Latino identity here and abroad. "It's just an opportunity
to check the power that Black Latinos reflect off each other and

[3]The Beatnuts: hip-hop group and production company based in Queens, New
York. [Editor's note.]
[4]Hurricane G: stage name for Brooklyn-born rapper Gloria Rodríguez. [Editor's
note.]
[5]Al Sharpton: American minister, civil rights activist, and talk show host. [Editor's
note.]

the Latino population." In other words, Latino artists use the n-word as a reminder that they too have been oppressed and are products of the transatlantic slave trade.

There may be a reason for the lack of attention: Many Caribbean Latinos are, to Americans at least, ethnically ambiguous products of miscegenation. Regardless of what we've learned in grade school, our history extends past Columbus and our Spanish conquistadores. "The European Spaniards have left a legacy of self-hatred and racism among the Latino population; without acknowledging that, we will not evolve past our own inequity," says Immortal Technique, an Afro-Peruvian hip-hop artist who also uses the n-word. "Racism in America, as horrible and ugly as it may be, still isn't as bad as what it is in Latin America, and the sad part is that we are being racist against ourselves."

Maybe, in a way, that's the statement Dania Ramirez intended to make when, as part of Nas's Grammy-night entourage earlier this year, the dark-brown Dominican actress sported a black T-shirt emblazoned with the n-word. Many folks in our parents' generation have rejected their blackness—I have older Latino neighbors who won't vote for Barack Obama simply because he's black—but those generations more informed by hip-hop are embracing their Afro-Latino identity and evolving past our own self-hatred. Perhaps. "One fallacy is that [the n-word is] blasé, like, 'Ah well, everyone can use it now that it has a different meaning,' because it's not completely meaningless," says Professor Flores. "The other extreme, though, is the absolutist who thinks no one can use it because it's taboo, under any circumstances. That's a problem, too, because every expression has the potential for ulterior meanings, depending on the circumstances of the person."

Crystal, a 13-year-old fair-skinned Dominican girl attending eighth grade in an Inwood public school, remembers first hearing the n-word in a song while hanging out with her aunt. "So then, we got on the computer and we looked it up, and it had the meaning and everything," she recalls. "I was like, 'Why would you say it in a song?' From there, you started hearing everybody on the street saying it, and then everybody started getting used to it." To be fair, parents aren't always able to interfere because they speak little to no English; those reared by hip-hop culture in the last two decades often use it themselves.

The similar term *cocolo*—most popularly used as an insult 10
against Haitians by Dominicans, and by Puerto Ricans against
Dominican immigrants who look Haitian—is another word
gradually being assigned a new meaning here among Latinos.
Other words that translate to mean "black" among Caribbean
Latinos are moreno/a and negrito/a, almost always used as terms
of endearment. However, because none of these words have had
the fraternal stamp of hip-hop approval, they have yet to receive
their proverbial ghetto passes; speaking of which, Jennifer Lopez
might've surrendered hers when she left the Bronx eons ago.
While it's a fact that men in the hip-hop industry can get away
with murder, women are held to impossibly high standards, and
the question of authenticity played a role in how negatively the
public reacted to J. Lo's use of the n-word on the remix for her
2001 single "I'm Real."

"I think that with that, it was really based more upon class
than anything else," Immortal Technique says. "Many people saw
Fat Joe as technically black even though he was a light-skinned
Puerto Rican, and he had affiliations with the streets that Jennifer
Lopez probably lost on the way to Hollywood."

With few exceptions within our community—Raquel Rivera's
2003 book *New York Ricans From the Hip Hop Zone* devoted
prime real estate to the discussion of Latino identity in hip-hop—
this is a conversation we've failed to have, whatever our personal
feelings. "It really don't matter if you're white, you're black, you're
brown, or from the Boogie Down—it irks me to death," says
Alain "KET" Maridueña, 37, an entrepreneur and artist. "Latinos
in our neighborhood use it a lot—like every other word—and I'm
trying to check people because I find that we're suffering, we're
going through our thing, times are hard, there aren't enough
opportunities out there, and I want us to rise up." But we won't
rise up if we can't talk about the reasons why we haven't quite gotten there yet, and the words that've risen in prominence as a result.

For Discussion and Writing

1. According to the article, why did some people so react negatively to
   Jennifer Lopez's use of the "n-word" in her 2001 song "I'm Real,"
   even if the same people do not mind when rappers such as Fat Joe
   or Immortal Technique use the term?

2. What do the words "authentic" (par. 2) and "authenticity" (par. 10) mean in the context of this essay? Why are they important? How do notions of authenticity shape perceptions of racial, ethnic, and cultural identity?

3. **connections**   In "Selling Down: The Marketing of the Hip-Hop Nation" (p. 87), Jason Tanz claims that hip-hop has "always tossed up rapper-approved signifiers, commodities that promised to grant down status to anyone that consumes them—Adidas sneakers, Cross Colours sweatshirts, Cazal glasses, basketball jerseys, the music itself" (par. 5). Similarly, Cepeda suggests that the n-word has the "fraternal stamp of hip-hop approval" (par. 10). Is the word just another "rapper-approved signifier"? How is it different from Adidas sneakers and other commodities? Should the word be appropriated for marketing or advertising purposes, as it nearly was in the case of rapper Nas's album?

4. In Cepeda's article, Professor Juan Flores claims: "One fallacy is that the [n-word] is blasé, like 'Ah, well, everyone can use it now that it has a different meaning,' because it's not completely meaningless. . . . The other extreme, though, is the absolutist who thinks no one can use it because it's taboo, under any circumstances. That's a problem, too, because every expression has the potential for ulterior meanings, depending on the circumstances of the person" (par. 8). How do you understand the significance of this "taboo" word? Is its use ever acceptable? Does its meaning change, depending on the identity of the person using it? If so, why? Do certain people have a right to use this word, while others do not?

HUA HSU

The End of White America?

Hua Hsu (b. 1977) earned a Ph.D. from the History of American Civilization program at Harvard University and now teaches English at Vassar College. His scholarly interests include cultural studies, arts criticism, and American intellectual history. Hsu also writes for publications such as the Atlantic Monthly, Slate, *and the* New York Times.

In "The End of White America?" which originally appeared in the Atlantic Monthly, *Hsu investigates the decline of "whiteness"—demographically and culturally—as a fundamental aspect of American identity. As you read, consider how our notions of race and ethnicity are changing as the United States population changes. Hsu refers to the "triumph of multiculturalism" and "postracialism." Do you see our society in those terms? Why or why not?*

"Civilization's going to pieces," he remarks. He is in polite company, gathered with friends around a bottle of wine in the late-afternoon sun, chatting and gossiping. "I've gotten to be a terrible pessimist about things. Have you read *The Rise of the Colored Empires* by this man Goddard?" They hadn't. "Well, it's a fine book, and everybody ought to read it. The idea is if we don't look out the white race will be—will be utterly submerged. It's all scientific stuff; it's been proved.

He is Tom Buchanan, a character in F. Scott Fitzgerald's *The Great Gatsby*, a book that nearly everyone who passes through the American education system is compelled to read at least once. Although Gatsby doesn't gloss as a book on racial anxiety—it's too busy exploring a different set of anxieties entirely—Buchanan was hardly alone in feeling besieged. The book by "this man Goddard" had a real-world analogue: Lothrop Stoddard's *The Rising Tide of Color Against White World-Supremacy*, published in 1920, five years before *Gatsby*. Nine decades later, Stoddard's

144

polemic remains oddly engrossing. He refers to World War I as the "White Civil War" and laments the "cycle of ruin" that may result if the "white world" continues its infighting. The book features a series of foldout maps depicting the distribution of "color" throughout the world and warns, "Colored migration is a universal peril, menacing every part of the white world."

As briefs for racial supremacy go, *The Rising Tide of Color* is eerily serene. Its tone is scholarly and gentlemanly, its hatred rationalized and, in Buchanan's term, "scientific." And the book was hardly a fringe phenomenon. It was published by Scribner, also Fitzgerald's publisher, and Stoddard, who received a doctorate in history from Harvard, was a member of many professional academic associations. It was precisely the kind of book that a 1920s man of Buchanan's profile—wealthy, Ivy League–educated, at once pretentious and intellectually insecure—might have been expected to bring up in casual conversation.

As white men of comfort and privilege living in an age of limited social mobility, of course, Stoddard and the Buchanans in his audience had nothing literal to fear. Their sense of dread hovered somewhere above the concerns of everyday life. It was linked less to any immediate danger to their class's political and cultural power than to the perceived fraying of the fixed, monolithic identity of whiteness that sewed together the fortunes of the fair-skinned.

From the hysteria over Eastern European immigration to the   5
vibrant cultural miscegenation of the Harlem Renaissance,[1] it is easy to see how this imagined worldwide white kinship might have seemed imperiled in the 1920s. There's no better example of the era's insecurities than the 1923 Supreme Court case *United States v. Bhagat Singh Thind*, in which an Indian-American veteran of World War I sought to become a naturalized citizen by proving that he was Caucasian. The Court considered new anthropological studies that expanded the definition of the Caucasian race to include Indians, and the justices even agreed that traces of "Aryan blood" coursed through Thind's body. But these technicalities availed him little. The Court determined that Thind was not white "in accordance with the understanding of the common

[1]Harlem Renaissance: a Harlem-based cultural movement of African American literature, music, and art during the 1920s and 1930s. [Editor's note.]

man" and therefore could be excluded from the "statutory category" of whiteness. Put another way: Thind was white, in that he was Caucasian and even Aryan. But he was not white in the way Stoddard or Buchanan were white.

The '20s debate over the definition of whiteness—a legal category? a commonsense understanding? a worldwide civilization?—took place in a society gripped by an acute sense of racial paranoia, and it is easy to regard these episodes as evidence of how far we have come. But consider that these anxieties surfaced when whiteness was synonymous with the American mainstream, when threats to its status were largely imaginary. What happens once this is no longer the case—when the fears of Lothrop Stoddard and Tom Buchanan are realized, and white people actually become an American minority?

Whether you describe it as the dawning of a post-racial age or just the end of white America, we're approaching a profound demographic tipping point. According to an August 2008 report by the U.S. Census Bureau, those groups currently categorized as racial minorities—blacks and Hispanics, East Asians and South Asians—will account for a majority of the U.S. population by the year 2042. Among Americans under the age of 18, this shift is projected to take place in 2023, which means that every child born in the United States from here on out will belong to the first post-white generation.

Obviously, steadily ascending rates of interracial marriage complicate this picture, pointing toward what Michael Lind has described as the "beiging" of America. And it's possible that "beige Americans" will self-identify as "white" in sufficient numbers to push the tipping point further into the future than the Census Bureau projects. But even if they do, whiteness will be a label adopted out of convenience and even indifference, rather than aspiration and necessity. For an earlier generation of minorities and immigrants, to be recognized as a "white American," whether you were an Italian or a Pole or a Hungarian, was to enter the mainstream of American life; to be recognized as something else, as the Thind case suggests, was to be permanently excluded. As Bill Imada, head of the IW Group, a prominent Asian American communications and marketing company, puts it: "I think in the 1920s, 1930s, and 1940s, [for] anyone who immigrated, the aspiration was to blend in and be as American as possible so that white America wouldn't be intimidated by them. They wanted to imitate white America as much as possible: learn English, go to church, go to the same schools."

Today, the picture is far more complex. To take the most obvious example, whiteness is no longer a precondition for entry into the highest levels of public office. The son of Indian immigrants doesn't have to become "white" in order to be elected governor of Louisiana. A half-Kenyan, half-Kansan politician can self-identify as black and be elected president of the United States.

As a purely demographic matter, then, the "white America" 10 that Lothrop Stoddard believed in so fervently may cease to exist in 2040, 2050, or 2060, or later still. But where the culture is concerned, it's already all but finished. Instead of the long-standing model of assimilation toward a common center, the culture is being remade in the image of white America's multiethnic, multicolored heirs.

For some, the disappearance of this centrifugal core heralds a future rich with promise. In 1998, President Bill Clinton, in a now-famous address to students at Portland State University, remarked:

> Today, largely because of immigration, there is no majority race in Hawaii or Houston or New York City. Within five years, there will be no majority race in our largest state, California. In a little more than 50 years, there will be no majority race in the United States. No other nation in history has gone through demographic change of this magnitude in so short a time . . . [These immigrants] are energizing our culture and broadening our vision of the world. They are renewing our most basic values and reminding us all of what it truly means to be American.

Not everyone was so enthused. Clinton's remarks caught the attention of another anxious Buchanan—Pat Buchanan, the conservative thinker. Revisiting the president's speech in his 2001 book, *The Death of the West*, Buchanan wrote: "Mr. Clinton assured us that it will be a better America when we are all minorities and realize true 'diversity.' Well, those students [at Portland State] are going to find out, for they will spend their golden years in a Third World America."

Today, the arrival of what Buchanan derided as "Third World America" is all but inevitable. What will the new mainstream of America look like, and what ideas or values might it rally around?

What will it mean to be white after "whiteness" no longer defines the mainstream? Will anyone mourn the end of white America? Will anyone try to preserve it?

Another moment from *The Great Gatsby*: as Fitzgerald's narrator and Gatsby drive across the Queensboro Bridge into Manhattan, a car passes them, and Nick Carraway notices that it is a limousine "driven by a white chauffeur, in which sat three modish negroes, two bucks and a girl." The novelty of this topsy-turvy arrangement inspires Carraway to laugh aloud and think to himself, "Anything can happen now that we've slid over this bridge, anything at all. . . ." 15

For a contemporary embodiment of the upheaval that this scene portended, consider Sean Combs, a hip-hop mogul and one of the most famous African Americans on the planet. Combs grew up during hip-hop's late-1970s rise, and he belongs to the first generation that could safely make a living working in the industry—as a plucky young promoter and record-label intern in the late 1980s and early 1990s, and as a fashion designer, artist, and music executive worth hundreds of millions of dollars a brief decade later.

In the late 1990s, Combs made a fascinating gesture toward New York's high society. He announced his arrival into the circles of the rich and powerful not by crashing their parties, but by inviting them into his own spectacularly over-the-top world. Combs began to stage elaborate annual parties in the Hamptons, not far from where Fitzgerald's novel takes place. These "white parties"—attendees are required to wear white—quickly became legendary for their opulence (in 2004, Combs showcased a 1776 copy of the Declaration of Independence) as well as for the cultures-colliding quality of Hamptons elites paying their respects to someone so comfortably nouveau riche. Prospective business partners angled to get close to him and praised him as a guru of the lucrative "urban" market, while grateful partygoers hailed him as a modern-day Gatsby.

"Have I read *The Great Gatsby*?" Combs said to a London newspaper in 2001. "I am the Great Gatsby."

Yet whereas Gatsby felt pressure to hide his status as an arriviste, Combs celebrated his position as an outsider-insider—someone who appropriates elements of the culture he seeks to join without attempting to assimilate outright. In a sense, Combs

"Combs is both a product and a hero of the new cultural mainstream, which prizes diversity above all else, and whose ultimate goal is some vague notion of racial transcendence, rather than subversion or assimilation."

was imitating the old WASP establishment; in another sense, he was subtly provoking it, by over-enunciating its formality and never letting his guests forget that there was something slightly off about his presence. There's a silent power to throwing parties where the best-dressed man in the room is also the one whose public profile once consisted primarily of dancing in the background of Biggie Smalls videos. ("No one would ever expect a young black man to be coming to a party with the Declaration of Independence, but I got it, and it's coming with me," Combs joked at his 2004 party, as he made the rounds with the document, promising not to spill champagne on it.)

In this regard, Combs is both a product and a hero of the new 20 cultural mainstream, which prizes diversity above all else, and whose ultimate goal is some vague notion of racial transcendence, rather than subversion or assimilation. Although Combs's vision is far from representative—not many hip-hop stars vacation in St. Tropez with a parasol-toting manservant shading their every step—his industry lies at the heart of this new mainstream. Over the past 30 years, few changes in American culture have been as significant as the rise of hip-hop. The genre has radically reshaped the way we listen to and consume music, first by opposing the pop mainstream and then by becoming it. From its constant sampling of past styles and eras—old records, fashions, slang, anything—to its mythologization of the self-made black antihero, hip-hop is more than a musical genre: it's a philosophy, a political statement, a way of approaching and remaking culture. It's a lingua franca[2] not just among kids in America, but also among young people worldwide. And its economic impact extends beyond the music industry, to fashion, advertising, and film. (Consider the producer Russell Simmons—the ur-Combs and a music, fashion, and television mogul—or the rapper 50 Cent, who has parlayed his rags-to-riches story line into extracurricular successes that include a clothing line; book, video game, and film deals; and a startlingly lucrative partnership with the makers of Vitamin Water.)

But hip-hop's deepest impact is symbolic. During popular music's rise in the 20th century, white artists and producers consistently "mainstreamed" African American innovations. Hip-hop's ascension has been different. Eminem notwithstanding, hip-hop never suffered through anything like an Elvis Presley moment, in which a white artist made a musical form safe for white America. This is no dig at Elvis—the constrictive racial logic of the 1950s demanded the erasure of rock and roll's black roots, and if it hadn't been him, it would have been someone else. But hip-hop—the sound of the post–civil-rights, post-soul generation—found a global audience on its own terms.

Today, hip-hop's colonization of the global imagination, from fashion runways in Europe to dance competitions in Asia, is Disneyesque. This transformation has bred an unprecedented cultural confidence in its black originators. Whiteness is no longer a threat or an ideal: it's kitsch[3] to be appropriated, whether with gestures like Combs's "white parties" or the trickle-down epidemic of collared shirts and cuff links currently afflicting rappers. And an expansive multiculturalism is replacing the us-against-the-world

[2]lingua franca: any language that is widely used as a means of communication among speakers of other languages. [Editor's note.]
[3]kitsch: any entertainment or artifact with enormous popular appeal, but usually associated with bad taste, like sensationalism and sentimentality. [Editor's note.]

bunker mentality that lent a thrilling edge to hip-hop's mid-1990s rise.

Peter Rosenberg, a self-proclaimed "nerdy Jewish kid" and radio personality on New York's Hot 97 FM—and a living example of how hip-hop has created new identities for its listeners that don't fall neatly along lines of black and white—shares another example: "I interviewed [the St. Louis rapper] Nelly this morning, and he said it's now very cool and in to have multicultural friends. Like you're not really considered hip or 'you've made it' if you're rolling with all the same people."

Just as Tiger Woods forever changed the country-club culture of golf, and Will Smith confounded stereotypes about the ideal Hollywood leading man, hip-hop's rise is helping redefine the American mainstream, which no longer aspires toward a single iconic image of style or class. Successful network-television shows like *Lost*, *Heroes*, and *Grey's Anatomy* feature wildly diverse casts, and an entire genre of half-hour comedy, from *The Colbert Report* to *The Office*, seems dedicated to having fun with the persona of the clueless white male. The youth market is following the same pattern: consider the Cheetah Girls, a multicultural, multi-platinum, multiplatform trio of teenyboppers who recently starred in their third movie, or Dora the Explorer, the precocious, bilingual 7-year-old Latina adventurer who is arguably the most successful animated character on children's television today. In a recent address to the Association of Hispanic Advertising Agencies, Brown Johnson, the Nickelodeon executive who has overseen Dora's rise, explained the importance of creating a character who does not conform to "the white, middle-class mold." When Johnson pointed out that Dora's wares were outselling Barbie's in France, the crowd hooted in delight.

Pop culture today rallies around an ethic of multicultural 25 inclusion that seems to value every identity—except whiteness. "It's become harder for the blond-haired, blue-eyed commercial actor," remarks Rochelle Newman-Carrasco, of the Hispanic marketing firm Enlace. "You read casting notices, and they like to cast people with brown hair because they could be Hispanic. The language of casting notices is pretty shocking because it's so specific: 'Brown hair, brown eyes, could look Hispanic.' Or, as one notice put it: 'Ethnically ambiguous.'"

"I think white people feel like they're under siege right now—

like it's not okay to be white right now, especially if you're a white male," laughs Bill Imada, of the IW Group. Imada and Newman-Carrasco are part of a movement within advertising, marketing, and communications firms to reimagine the profile of the typical American consumer. (Tellingly, every person I spoke with from these industries knew the Census Bureau's projections by heart.)

"There's a lot of fear and a lot of resentment," Newman-Carrasco observes, describing the flak she caught after writing an article for a trade publication on the need for more-diverse hiring practices. "I got a response from a friend—he's, like, a 60-something white male, and he's been involved with multicultural recruiting," she recalls. "And he said, 'I really feel like the hunted. It's a hard time to be a white man in America right now, because I feel like I'm being lumped in with all white males in America, and I've tried to do stuff, but it's a tough time.'"

"I always tell the white men in the room, 'We need you,'" Imada says. "We cannot talk about diversity and inclusion and engagement without you at the table. It's okay to be white!

"But people are stressed out about it. 'We used to be in control! We're losing control!'"

If they're right—if white America is indeed "losing control," 30 and if the future will belong to people who can successfully navigate a postracial, multicultural landscape—then it's no surprise that many white Americans are eager to divest themselves of their whiteness entirely.

"I get it: as a straight white male, I'm the worst thing on Earth," Christian Lander says. Lander is a Canadian-born, Los Angeles–based satirist who in January 2008 started a blog called "Stuff White People Like" (stuffwhitepeoplelike.com), which pokes fun at the manners and mores of a specific species of young, hip, upwardly mobile whites. (He has written more than 100 entries about whites' passion for things like bottled water, "the idea of soccer," and "being the only white person around.") At its best, Lander's site—which formed the basis for a recently published book of the same name (reviewed in the October 2008 *Atlantic*)— is a cunningly precise distillation of the identity crisis plaguing well-meaning, well-off white kids in a post-white world.

Lander's "white people" are products of a very specific historical moment, raised by well-meaning Baby Boomers to reject the old ideal of white American gentility and to embrace diversity and fluidity instead. ("It's strange that we are the kids of Baby Boomers, right? How the hell do you rebel against that? Like, your parents will march against the World Trade Organization next to you. They'll have bigger white dreadlocks than you. What do you do?") But his lighthearted anthropology suggests that the multicultural harmony they were raised to worship has bred a kind of self-denial.

Matt Wray, a sociologist at Temple University who is a fan of Lander's humor, has observed that many of his white students are plagued by a racial-identity crisis: "They don't care about socioeconomics; they care about culture. And to be white is to be culturally broke. The classic thing white students say when you ask them to talk about who they are is, 'I don't have a culture.' They might be privileged, they might be loaded socioeconomically, but they feel bankrupt when it comes to culture. . . . They feel disadvantaged, and they feel marginalized. They don't have a culture that's cool or oppositional." Wray says that this feeling of being culturally bereft often prevents students from recognizing what it means to be a child of privilege—a strange irony that the first wave of whiteness-studies scholars, in the 1990s, failed to anticipate.

"The best defense is to be constantly pulling the rug out from underneath yourself," Wray remarks, describing the way self-aware whites contend with their complicated identity. "Beat people to the punch. You're forced as a white person into a sense of ironic detachment. Irony is what fuels a lot of white subcultures. You also see things like Burning Man, when a lot of white people are going into the desert and trying to invent something that is entirely new and not a form of racial mimicry. That's its own kind of flight from whiteness. We're going through a period where whites are really trying to figure out: Who are we?"

The "flight from whiteness" of urban, college-educated, liberal whites isn't the only attempt to answer this question. You can flee into whiteness as well. This can mean pursuing the authenticity of an imagined past: think of the deliberately white-bread world of Mormon America, where the '50s never ended, or the anachronistic WASP entitlement flaunted in books like last year's *A Privileged Life: Celebrating WASP Style*, a handsome coffee-table book compiled by Susanna Salk, depicting a world of seersucker blazers, whale pants, and deck shoes. (What the book celebrates is the "inability to be outdone," and the "self-confidence and security that comes with it," Salk tells me. "That's why I call it 'privilege.' It's this privilege of time, of heritage, of being in a place longer than anybody else.") But these enclaves of preserved-in-amber whiteness are likely to be less important to the American future than the construction of whiteness as a somewhat pissed-off minority culture.

As with the unexpected success of the apocalyptic *Left Behind* novels, or the Jeff Foxworthy–organized Blue Collar Comedy Tour, the rise of country music and auto racing took place well off the American elite's radar screen. (None of Christian Lander's white people would be caught dead at a NASCAR race.) These phenomena reflected a growing sense of cultural solidarity among lower-middle-class whites—a solidarity defined by a yearning for American "authenticity," a folksy realness that rejects the global, the urban, and the effete in favor of nostalgia for "the way things used to be."

Like other forms of identity politics, white solidarity comes complete with its own folk heroes, conspiracy theories (Barack Obama is a secret Muslim! The U.S. is going to merge with Canada and Mexico!), and laundry lists of injustices. The targets and scapegoats vary—from multiculturalism and affirmative action to a loss of moral values, from immigration to an economy that no longer guarantees the American worker a fair chance—and so do the political programs they inspire. But the core grievance, in each case, has to do with cultural and socioeconomic dislocation—the sense that the system that used to guarantee the white working class some stability has gone off-kilter.

Wray is one of the founders of what has been called "white-trash studies," a field conceived as a response to the perceived elite-liberal marginalization of the white working class. He argues that the economic downturn of the 1970s was the precondition for the formation of an "oppositional" and "defiant" white-working-class sensibility—think of the rugged, anti-everything individualism of 1977's *Smokey and the Bandit*. But those anxieties took their shape from the aftershocks of the identity-based movements of the 1960s. "I think that the political space that the civil-rights movement opens up in the mid-1950s and '60s is the transformative thing," Wray observes. "Following the black-power movement, all of the other minority groups that followed took up various forms of activism, including brown power and yellow power and red power. Of course the problem is, if you try and have a 'white power' movement, it doesn't sound good."

The result is a racial pride that dares not speak its name, and that defines itself through cultural cues instead—a suspicion of intellectual elites and city dwellers, a preference for folksiness and plainness of speech (whether real or feigned), and the association of a working-class white minority with "the real America." (In the Scots-Irish belt that runs from Arkansas up through West Virginia, the most common ethnic label offered to census takers is "American.") Arguably, this white identity politics helped swing the 2000 and 2004 elections, serving as the powerful counterpunch to urban white liberals, and the McCain–Palin campaign relied on it almost to the point of absurdity (as when a McCain surrogate dismissed Northern Virginia as somehow not part of "the real Virginia") as a bulwark against the threatening multiculturalism of Barack Obama. Their strategy failed, of course, but it's possible to imagine white identity politics growing more potent and more forthright in its racial identifications in the future, as "the real America" becomes an ever-smaller portion of, well, the real America, and as the soon-to-be white minority's sense of being besieged and disdained by a multicultural majority grows apace.

At the moment, we can call this the triumph of multicultural- 40 ism, or postracialism. But just as whiteness has no inherent meaning—it is a vessel we fill with our hopes and anxieties— these terms may prove equally empty in the long run. Does being postracial mean that we are past race completely, or merely that race is no longer essential to how we identify ourselves? Karl Carter, of Atlanta's youth-oriented GTM, Inc. (Guerrilla Tactics Media), suggests that marketers and advertisers would be better off focusing on matrices like "lifestyle" or "culture" rather than race or ethnicity. "You'll have crazy in-depth studies of the white consumer or the Latino consumer," he complains. "But how do skaters feel? How do hip-hoppers feel?"

The logic of online social networking points in a similar direction. The New York University sociologist Dalton Conley has written of a "network nation," in which applications like Facebook and MySpace create "crosscutting social groups" and new, flexible identities that only vaguely overlap with racial identities.

Perhaps this is where the future of identity after whiteness lies—in a dramatic departure from the racial logic that has defined American culture from the very beginning. What Conley, Carter, and others are describing isn't merely the displacement of whiteness from our cultural center; they're describing a social structure that treats race as just one of a seemingly infinite number of possible self-identifications.

The problem of the 20th century, W. E. B. Du Bois famously predicted, would be the problem of the color line. Will this continue to be the case in the 21st century, when a black president will govern a country whose social networks increasingly cut across every conceivable line of identification? The ruling of *United States v. Bhagat Singh Thind* no longer holds weight, but its echoes have been inescapable: we aspire to be postracial, but we still live within the structures of privilege, injustice, and racial categorization that we inherited from an older order. We can talk about defining ourselves by lifestyle rather than skin color, but our lifestyle choices are still racially coded. We know, more or less, that race is a fiction that often does more harm than good, and yet it is something we cling to without fully understanding why—as a social and legal fact, a vague sense of belonging and place that we make solid through culture and speech.

But maybe this is merely how it used to be—maybe this is already an outdated way of looking at things. "You have a lot of young adults going into a more diverse world," Carter remarks. For the young Americans born in the 1980s and 1990s, culture is something to be taken apart and remade in their own image. "We came along in a generation that didn't have to follow that path of race," he goes on. "We saw something different." This moment was not the end of white America; it was not the end of anything. It was a bridge, and we crossed it.

For Discussion and Writing

1. According to Hsu, how is "whiteness" or the "white American" identity viewed by minorities and immigrants in America? How is this perspective different from that of earlier generations of minorities and immigrants?

2. Hsu quotes sociologist Matt Wray, who describes the "racial-identity crisis" of his white students: "They don't care about socioeconomics; they care about culture. And to be white is to be culturally broke"

(par. 33). What does this mean? Why would the distinction between socioeconomics and culture be important? How can someone be "broke" culturally?

3. **connections**   Hsu describes "hip-hop's colonization of the global imagination" as "Disneyesque": "This transformation has bred an unprecedented cultural confidence in its black originators. Whiteness is no longer a threat or an ideal: it's kitsch to be appropriated" (par. 22). How would you view Hsu's claims in the context of Jason Tanz's "Selling Down: The Marketing of the Hip-Hop Nation" (p. 87)? For example, has hip-hop itself become another form of kitsch to be appropriated by marketers and advertisers? Tanz asserts that "one of hip-hop's most powerful and elusive promises is that it will help us come to terms with, understand, and maybe even participate in blackness" (par. 4). What role does this "promise" play in changing people's views of race and ethnicity, "blackness" and "whiteness"?

4. Hsu writes of the "new cultural mainstream, which prizes diversity above all else, and whose ultimate goal is some vague notion of racial transcendence, rather than subversion or assimilation" (par. 20). Do you agree with this characterization of the "mainstream" and its assumptions and aims? Why or why not? Hsu uses many examples from American culture to support his points. Choose your examples to make your case. You might also consider this question in light of the contrasting attitudes of Bill Clinton and Pat Buchanan (pars. 11–14).

ARIEL LEVY

Women and the Rise of Raunch Culture

A staff writer for the New Yorker *magazine since 2008, Ariel Levy (b. 1974) is perhaps best known for her book* Female Chauvinist Pigs: Women and the Rise of Raunch Culture *(2005). She has also written for the* Washington Post, Vogue, Slate, *and other publications. In this excerpt from* Female Chauvinist Pigs, *Levy considers the way "post-feminist" women participate in a "tawdry, tarty, cartoonlike version of female sexuality." But as she notes, "'Raunchy' and 'liberated' are not synonymous." Do you agree with Levy? How does she use examples to support her main point?*

I first noticed it several years ago. I would turn on the television and find strippers in pasties explaining how best to lap dance a man to orgasm. I would flip the channel and see babes in tight, tiny uniforms bouncing up and down on trampolines. Britney Spears was becoming increasingly popular and increasingly unclothed, and her undulating body ultimately became so familiar to me I felt like we used to go out.

Charlie's Angels, the film remake of the quintessential jiggle show, opened at number one in 2000 and made $125 million in theaters nationally, reinvigorating the interest of men and women alike in leggy crime fighting. Its stars, who kept talking about "strong women" and "empowerment," were dressed in alternating soft-porn styles—as massage parlor geishas, dominatrixes, yodeling Heidis in alpine bustiers. (The summer sequel in 2003—in which the Angels' perilous mission required them to perform stripteases—pulled in another $100 million domestically.) In my own industry, magazines, a porny new genre called the Lad Mag, which included titles like *Maxim*, *FHM*, and *Stuff*, was hitting the stands and becoming a huge success by delivering what *Playboy*

158

had only occasionally managed to capture: greased celebrities in little scraps of fabric humping the floor. This didn't end when I switched off the radio or the television or closed the magazines. I'd walk down the street and see teens and young women—and the occasional wild fifty-year-old—wearing jeans cut so low they exposed what came to be known as butt cleavage paired with miniature tops that showed off breast implants and pierced navels alike. Sometimes, in case the overall message of the outfit was too subtle, the shirts would be emblazoned with the Playboy bunny or say PORN STAR across the chest.

Some odd things were happening in my social life, too. People I knew (female people) liked going to strip clubs (female strippers). It was sexy and fun, they explained; it was liberating and rebellious. My best friend from college, who used to go to Take Back the Night marches on campus, had become captivated by porn stars. She would point them out to me in music videos and watch their (topless) interviews on *Howard Stern*. As for me, I wasn't going to strip clubs or buying *Hustler* T-shirts, but I was starting to show signs of impact all the same. It had only been a few years since I'd graduated from Wesleyan University, a place where you could pretty much get expelled for saying "girl" instead of "woman," but somewhere along the line I'd started saying "chick." And, like most chicks I knew, I'd taken to wearing thongs.

What was going on? My mother, a shiatsu masseuse who   5 attended weekly women's consciousness-raising groups for twenty-four years, didn't own makeup. My father, whom she met as a student radical at the University of Wisconsin, Madison, in the sixties was a consultant for Planned Parenthood, NARAL, and NOW. Only thirty years (my lifetime) ago, our mothers were "burning their bras" and picketing Playboy, and suddenly we were getting implants and wearing the bunny logo as supposed symbols of our liberation. How had the culture shifted so drastically in such a short period of time?

What was almost more surprising than the change itself were the responses I got when I started interviewing the men and—often—women who edit magazines like *Maxim* and make programs like *The Man Show* and *Girls Gone Wild*. This new raunch culture didn't mark the death of feminism, they told me; it was evidence that the feminist project had already been achieved. We'd *earned* the right to look at *Playboy*; we were *empowered* enough to get Brazilian bikini waxes. Women had come so far, I learned, we no longer needed to worry about objectification or misogyny. Instead, it was time for us to join the frat party of pop culture, where men had been enjoying themselves all along. If Male Chauvinist Pigs were men who regarded women as pieces of meat, we would outdo them and be Female Chauvinist Pigs: women who make sex objects of other women and of ourselves.

When I asked female viewers and readers what they got out of raunch culture, I heard similar things about empowering miniskirts and feminist strippers, and so on, but I also heard something else. They wanted to be "one of the guys"; they hoped to be experienced "like a man." Going to strip clubs or talking about porn stars was a way of showing themselves and the men around them that they weren't "prissy little women" or "girly-girls." Besides, they told me, it was all in fun, all tongue-in-cheek, and for me to regard this bacchanal as problematic would be old-school and uncool.

I tried to get with the program, but I could never make the argument add up in my head. How is resurrecting every stereotype of female sexuality that feminism endeavored to banish *good* for women? Why is laboring to look like Pamela Anderson empowering? And how is imitating a stripper or a porn star—a woman whose *job* is to imitate arousal in the first place—going to render us sexually liberated?

Despite the rising power of Evangelical Christianity and the political right in the United States, this trend has only grown more extreme and more pervasive in the years that have passed since I first became aware of it. A tawdry, tarty, cartoonlike version of female sexuality has become so ubiquitous, it no longer seems particular. What we once regarded as a *kind* of sexual expression we now view *as* sexuality. As former adult film star Traci Lords put it to a reporter a few days before her memoir hit the bestseller list in 2003, "When I was in porn, it was like a back-alley thing. Now it's everywhere." Spectacles of naked ladies have moved from seedy side streets to center stage, where everyone—men and women—can watch them in broad daylight. *Playboy* and its ilk are being "embraced by young women in a curious way in a postfeminist world," to borrow the words of Hugh Hefner.

But just because we are post doesn't automatically mean we are feminists. There is a widespread assumption that simply 10 because my generation of women has the good fortune to live in a world touched by the feminist movement, that means everything we do is magically imbued with its agenda. It doesn't work that way. "Raunchy" and "liberated" are not synonyms. It is worth asking ourselves if this bawdy world of boobs and gams we have resurrected reflects how far we've come, or how far we have left to go.

For Discussion and Writing

1. Levy uses anecdotal evidence and examples to support her argument, including some "odd things" that were happening in her social life (par. 4). What odd things did she notice?

2. In writing about a shift in popular culture and attitudes about women, Levy writes: "What we once regarded as a *kind* of sexual expression we now view *as* sexuality" (par. 9). What does she mean by this?

3. **connections** In "Mary Tyler More" (p. 266), Erica Lies writes about Liz Lemon, Tina Fey's character on *30 Rock*, as well as other female characters from situation comedies: "Perhaps audiences love Fey-as-Lemon because of Fey's embrace of her brain and her relative disinterest in her sex appeal" (par. 15). Do you think Lies would agree with Levy's thesis in "Women and the Rise of Raunch Culture"? Why or why not? Does *30 Rock* seem like a counterweight to "raunch culture," or an extension of it?

4. Levy interviews women who claim that the "new raunch culture" was evidence that the "feminist project had already been achieved" (par. 6). Levy disagrees. What is your position on this issue? Can raunchiness be "empowering" (par. 7)? Levy asserts that "'raunchy' and 'liberated' are not synonyms" (par. 10). Are they mutually exclusive?

PAUL KIX

Hip-Hop Is No Longer Cooler Than Me

A graduate of Iowa State University, Paul Kix (b. 1981) is a general editor at ESPN: The Magazine *and was former senior editor at* Boston *magazine. He has also written for* New York, Salon, Men's Journal, *and other publications. In this essay, which originally appeared in* Salon *in 2008, Kix attempts to "chronicle hip-hop's decline." But instead of being confused, annoyed, or angry about the "problem with hip-hop today," the writer is embarrassed: "Since when did young black men, heretofore the arbiters of pop culture, become so lame?" As you read, consider the role that race plays in Kix's argument.*

I must have been 8 when I heard N.W.A.'s "Fuck tha Police." That seems about right, because us Iowa farm kids heard everything of cultural significance a year or two after it was important, and I remember being in third grade (this was 1989) when my life changed for the better. I was on the bus, with an older fat kid everyone called Speed sitting the row in front of me. Speed and I had a special bond: We were perhaps the only kids in central Iowa to love rap. "Listen to this," he said, discreetly sliding me his cassette player and mix tape. It wasn't just the swear words, though at first that was a big part of N.W.A.'s appeal. It was Ice Cube's anger, and Eazy-E's bemused inventiveness, and Dr. Dre's beats. As I grew up, N.W.A. led me to Snoop Dogg's "Doggystyle," which led to the oeuvre of Biggie, and the life and times of one Shawn Carter. But what I loved about hip-hop—what I still love about it—is its brashness. The uncouth bravura of Wildean[1] M.C.s is intoxicating.

[1]Wildean: resembling the witty, clever, punning literary style of Irish playwright, poet, and critic Oscar Wilde (1854–1900). [Editor's note.]

This brings us, inevitably, to the problem with hip-hop today. A genre whirled out of the grist of urban pain and worn as a low-slung hat and baggy jeans has somehow slipped on clown shoes and taken up night classes in pantomime. Its dances are silly, its beats infantile, its rhymes lazy. I am sorry to report this, but hip-hop is no longer cooler than me. I've known it to be true for some time but dared not acknowledge it—until I saw Bo Ryan do the "Soulja Boy." Bo Ryan is the men's basketball coach at the University of Wisconsin. He is old, he's white, and he should have nothing to do with pop-cultural relevance. And yet there he is, online, dancing the Soulja Boy, an ongoing craze among young aficionados based on the song "(Crank Dat) Soulja Boy" by an artist of the same name. Soulja Boy's Internet sales of his 2007 self-titled album have exceeded 3.3 million copies, the most ever on the Web.

The problem isn't that Ryan fails inexorably in his attempt at the Soulja Boy. It's that he nails it. The slight bend of the knees and cross step, the rednecky hop and flip of the wrist, the goofy Superman in flight—it's all, alas, straight-up Soulja Boy. In fact, if you compare Ryan's rendition with the original, you, too, might find yourself preferring the subtlety of Ryan's moves. (His cross steps aren't as aggrandized, for one.) Are these not trying days when a 60-year-old Wisconsinite improves "the game," when even Democratic presidential candidate Mike Gravel tries his hand at the Soulja boy?

We are witnessing nothing less than the Macarena-zation of a genre. Because of Soulja Boy's success, industry execs now demand that new artists have dances at the ready to accompany their albums. The dances help drive up sales, that fast-disappearing commodity. And so the airwaves and Interwebs are still filthy with song-and-dance numbers, like Pop It Off Boyz' "Crank Dat Batman" and last year's "Chicken Noodle Soup" song, which accomplishes the impossible by being dumber than it sounds but remains great fun for 50-year-olds in middle management.

Hip-hop hasn't always had the most discerning taste; witness   5
the electric slide and M.C. Hammer. But the music's coolness used to be matched by the culture it inspired: break dancers working to DJ Grandmaster Flash; horny kids grinding to 'Pac and Dre; poor kids krumping as a way out, every move informed by the street and its music. The problem today is that the newest dances are informed by nothing more than their potential profit

Definitely not cooler than you.

margins. And in that grab for accessibility, the songs lose their credibility.

Or at least that's one popular theory. But I think this theory is ludicrous. Hip-hop has sought commercial viability since the mid-'90s. Jay-Z has built an entire career out of finding listeners like me, and you'd be hard-pressed to say his music suffers because of his pandering. I think, instead, today's young M.C.s are given too much credit, as if they're choosing to dumb it down. The problem with the dances of hip-hop—and with the genre as a whole—is that these artists are in fact choosing to do what they're capable of. This is their *best*, people. And I say that because the only thing more insipid than the dances are the songs themselves.

It's an amorphous thing, to chronicle hip-hop's decline, but I trace its genesis to the sound every fan loved: Atlanta at the turn of the century, repelling what New York and Los Angeles did, finding its own way with krunked-out beats and slurred lyrics. Atlanta (Outkast and Ludacris mostly) begat the Cash Money Millionaires of New Orleans (think Juvenile and "Back That Ass Up"). The music then evolved, except that T.I. and his ilk in Atlanta and Lil Wayne and his in N'Awlins were neither as clever with the rhymes as Ludacris nor as adept in the production as Outkast. A sound that was already simpler than what Dre out west or Puffy out east would have allowed became lazy, less crisp, and the lyrics were all that much harder to decipher, hiding behind drawls and weighed down by bling. Then the music shifted again in, roughly, 2006. Things got so dire that Nas, one of the great New York rappers, released an album called "Hip-Hop Is Dead." The new sound's beats were as simple as the rhymes were unnecessary. And into this void, exemplifying it, stepped Soulja Boy. His hit is a three-note wonder seemingly played on a xylophone. Now, Dr. Dre used to spend up to 100 hours perfecting a beat. Soulja Boy? He sees what's hot at the nearest elementary school and calls it his own.

In his defense, Soulja Boy operates in the "snap music" subgenre of hip-hop, which will never be accused of musical complexity. Snap music is big because radio stations tired of the sluggish tempos coming out of Houston last year. (A shame. I love the Houston stuff.) The difference here is that the Houston guys— Slim Thug, Paul Wall, Mike Jones et al.—could rap; the near stasis of the backdrop only brightened the glare of the M.C.'s spotlight.

Here's Paul Wall, from his 2005 hit, "Grillz," an ode to the diamond or gold mouthpieces rappers love(d) to wear: "I got da wrist wear and neck wear dats captivatin' / but it's my smile dat's got these onlookers spectatin' / My mouth piece simply certified a total package / Open up my mouth and you see mo carrots than a salad / My teeth are mind blowin, givin everybody chillz / Call me George Foreman cuz I'm selling everybody grillz."

Now that's funny. It just is. And it's an example of hip-hop going light but not going easy on the lyrics. That took Paul Wall some time to think up. By contrast, here is "(Crank Dat) Soulja Boy"; "I'm bouncin' on my toe / watch me take to Areab / And he gonna take it up for sho / Haterz want to be me / Soulja Boy, I'm the man / They be looking at my neck / Sayin' is them rubber bands man?" No. 1: He's not trying to be funny. It just sounds that way. No. 2, and this is kind of obvious: He's not really trying at all. I mean, listen to the song and it actually sounds like he's a first-time freestyler, the rhythm is so off. It's as if even he can't wait to get back to the chorus. And the chorus! My God, the chorus. "Superman dat ho" is a sexual euphemism that's not really all that illicit, as most sexual euphemisms go. It's just . . . infantile.

The most depressing part is that Soulja Boy is not alone in 10 lacking creativity. Webbie, Lil' Phat and Lil Boosie sometimes don't know what else to say, so they literally start spelling words. Lil Wayne, under the influence of a talk box,[2] has made a hit out of saying "lollypop" over and over. And Fat Joe's latest, "I Won't Tell," succeeds only because J. Holiday has a good voice—which is still better than Fat Joe's 2004 hit "Lean Back," a dance song for people who don't dance, who just, you guessed it, lean back. These three tracks—Webbie's, Lil Wayne's and Fat Joe's—currently reside on Billboard's Top 50 hip-hop list, and Lil Wayne's song is No. 1.

Look, I'm not confused or annoyed by hip-hop, like older rock fans are by, say, Fall Out Boy. More than anything I'm embarrassed. Since when did young black men, heretofore the arbiters of pop culture, become so lame? And since when did the citizens of that culture not know the difference? One Saturday not long ago, my wife called me into the living room. MTV had on some

---

[2]talk box: a device that allows musicians and singers to make speech sounds using musical instruments. [Editor's note.]

dance competition show, and an earnest group from Philly did the Soulja Boy. My wife and I watched, stunned, as the crowd and apparently all of America cheered on the group's shuffles. Iterations were involved, but it was a largely faithful piece. The kids in the crowd had to be quieted. I wish I could have been there, a cassette player and a 20-year-old mix tape in my clenched fist. I would have handed it over to any kid who looked like he needed it, much as Speed once passed it to me. And I would have said, simply, "Here. Let this guide you."

For Discussion and Writing

1. What has happened to hip-hop, according to Kix? How has it changed in the last ten years?

2. In the essay, Kix gives one common theory about the decline of hip-hop, but then claims that "this theory is ludicrous" (par. 6). What is the "theory"? Why does he find it ludicrous? Do you agree?

3. **connections**   Kix writes that hip-hop is increasingly "lame" (par. 11): "A genre whirled out of the grist of urban pain and worn as a low-slung hat and baggy jeans has somehow slipped on clown shoes and taken up night classes in pantomime" (par. 2). Compare Kix's examples and arguments with those in Jason Tanz's "Selling Down: The Marketing of Hip-Hop Nation" (p. 87). Tanz believes that hip-hop is becoming just another mainstream marketing platform. Is Tanz's term "down" the same as Kix's notion of "cool"? Are these words synonyms? What contributes to music or culture becoming less "cool"?

4. Kix begins his essay by recalling an experience of "cultural significance" that shaped his identity and his sensibility—both as a child and now (par. 1). Write about an experience with culture in your own life—music, a book, a film, a piece of art—that influenced you in some way. Kix says that he immediately liked hip-hop for its "brashness" and "uncouth bravura" (par. 1). What did you like about your example?

ROB RUCK

Where Have African-American Baseball Players Gone?

Rob Ruck (b. 1950) is a writer and documentary filmmaker, as well as a senior lecturer in the history department at the University of Pittsburgh. His books include Sandlot Seasons: Sport in Black Pittsburgh *(1993),* The Tropic of Baseball: Baseball in the Dominican Republic *(1999), and* Raceball: How the Major Leagues Colonized the Black and Latin Game *(2011). Ruck's documentary* Kings on the Hill: Baseball's Forgotten Men *(1993) won an Emmy for cultural programming.*

The following essay originally appeared in Salon.com *in 2011. Like much of Ruck's work, it explores the intersections of race, ethnicity, sports, and American history. The writer is especially interested in baseball's place in American culture and race relations, as he charts the "meteoric rise and decline" of African Americans in the game. As you read, consider the meaning of baseball and "its image as a democratic and inclusive sport." What does it mean to say that a sport is "democratic"?*

It's come to this: More African-Americans were elected to Congress as Republicans last November than appeared in the World Series. Texas Rangers reliever Darren Oliver was the sole African-American on the field. And while the number of black Republicans in Congress—two—is unlikely to grow any time soon, neither are the ranks of African-American major leaguers.

The meteoric rise and decline in African-American baseball has been staggering. Dark-skinned players, of course, were everywhere in the Series. They made up 40 percent of the players, but most came from the Caribbean or were Hispanic Americans. Few were U.S.-born blacks.

That's a stunning reversal. African-Americans changed baseball after Jackie Robinson, Willie Mays, Henry Aaron and other men schooled in the Negro Leagues brought a revelatory combination of speed and power to the majors. Eight Negro Leaguers who entered the major leagues became Hall-of-Famers. So did another nine African-Americans born before Robinson integrated the Dodgers but who were too young to play black baseball. By 1975, African-Americans constituted over a quarter of all players and were over-represented among the game's elite. More important, they made baseball, once an obstacle to social change, a catalyst for it.

In 1962 when San Francisco first appeared in the Series, the Giants had more black and Latino players than any major league squad to date. Led by Mays, Juan Marichal, Orlando Cepeda, Willie McCovey and Felipe Alou, they came within inches of beating the Yankees, one of baseball's whitest and most native-born teams. Marichal et al.—among the first Latino major leaguers after Jackie Robinson opened the door to players of color in 1947— have watched their progeny multiply ever since. Latinos currently constitute 27 percent of all major leaguers and about half of those in the minors. African-Americans, no longer so prominent, now make up less than a tenth of big league rosters.

Why?   5

Before integration, African-American boys learned baseball on the other side of the racial boundary demarcating American sport. They played for sandlot and Negro League teams organized and managed by African-Americans. When that sporting infrastructure crumbled after integration, no alternative black-controlled institutions emerged. Black youth were left with fewer ways to learn the muscle memory, intricacies and lore of the game.

Basketball and football, meanwhile, became more popular during the 1950s. As schools began admitting African-Americans, these sports offered scholarships that could be more rewarding than brief careers in professional sport. Prospective college players, moreover, could develop their talents in high school or the AAU network. Baseball, though, remained an afterthought at most high schools, in part because it's a summer game.

Making matters worse, growing inequality meant that few African-American boys could afford to cultivate baseball skills.

Jackie Robinson returns to the clubhouse after the Brooklyn Dodgers beat the New York Yankees in Game 6 of the 1956 World Series.

These days, aspiring ballplayers hone their game on travel teams that are expensive to join. Boys in fatherless households are unlikely to grow up with a love for the game or the bucks to participate.

Meanwhile, college baseball became the chief source of native-born professional talent. In 2005, major league organizations chose twice as many collegiate as high school players in their annual draft. But few African-Americans were playing college baseball—just 4.5 percent of NCAA baseball players in 2003–04—because baseball scholarships are partial grants-in-aid (11.7 are awarded per team and split among 20–30 players). Instead, athletically talented African-Americans sought the full ride that basketball and football offered and secured 42 percent of NCAA basketball and 32.3 percent of football scholarships in 2003–04.

Finally, the NBA and NFL have destroyed MLB's pretension 10 that it's the national pastime; among African-Americans, they are far more popular than baseball. In a 2005 Harris Poll, 47 percent of African-Americans named pro football their favorite sport; only 6 percent chose baseball. Baseball has become an afterthought in black America.

So what?

African-Americans hardly lack sporting opportunities. If anything, sport holds too much sway among black youth and diverts attention from academic and vocational alternatives. Nor does the black community still rely on baseball to gain the cohesion and collective self-esteem that the Negro Leagues offered it during segregation or the energy that Robinson's triumph generated. It suffers little from a low profile in the game.

Major League Baseball has more at stake, including its image as a democratic and inclusive sport. Its capacity to peddle nostalgia has helped it overcome enormous competitive imbalances among big and small markets and a head-in-the-sand approach to performance-enhancing drugs. Baseball regularly salutes the Negro Leagues as a marketing ploy and hails Robinson as its greatest hero. Unlike the 1940s, when many owners feared that Robinson would attract black fans and scare away white ones, they would welcome more black stars and patrons today. They're worried about their fan base.

MLB was thrilled when C.C. Sabathia threw the first pitch of the 2009 World Series to Jimmy Rollins—only the second time a Series began with an African-American on the mound and another at bat. Both had played for RBI (Reviving Baseball in Inner Cities), a program rebuilding baseball's infrastructure in hard-pressed areas. MLB, which backs RBI and promoted it relentlessly during the postseason, has committed to building an urban academy modeled after its Compton, Calif., facility in each of its franchise cities. One measure of this effort's success will be how many boys eventually sign professionally; another would be whether it helps repair the fabric of neighborhoods that MLB has long shunned. To do that, groups like the Josh Gibson Foundation in Pittsburgh need to lead the way. Sean Gibson, the Foundation's executive director and Josh's great-grandson, wants an academy built on the Hill, the historic heart of Pittsburgh's black community. "We are part of this community," Gibson explained. "We want its needs served first and foremost. Baseball can help bring it back, but the community needs to lead the way." Even with community buy-in and ongoing MLB support, the African-American contingent is not likely to return to its historic highs of the 1970s.

And baseball will be poorer for it. "All cultures bring some-   15 thing different to the game," Mets outfielder Gary Matthews Jr. told the Times' David Waldstein last spring as baseball celebrated Jackie Robinson Day. "The African American player, there is a charisma that he brings from his culture . . . a little spice. . . . That little spice is missing when we're not participating." Matthews, the lone African-American on the Mets that day, was released later that summer.

Baseball's tortured past was inextricably linked to its exclusion of African-Americans. Their subsequent entry into baseball was the game's finest moment. But its future most likely lies elsewhere, in the Caribbean and the nation's growing Latino communities.

For Discussion and Writing

1. Ruck focuses primarily on race in this essay, but in his view, economics also influence who plays baseball. How do money and class affect the sport's demographics?

2. Racial segregation is generally viewed in a bad light. Does Ruck see any benefits to Negro League baseball? What were they? Do you find his characterization persuasive?

3. **connections**   Malcolm Gladwell also explores race and sports in "The Sports Taboo" (p. 174). He writes about the "taboo" of openly discussing the "racial dimension of sports" (par. 3) in terms of biological and genetic differences. Do you think Ruck breaks this taboo or avoids it? Gladwell dismisses another writer on the social significance of race and sports: "Please. . . . Sometimes a baseball player is just a baseball player, and sometimes an observation about

racial difference is just an observation about racial difference" (par. 5). How do you think Gladwell would respond to Ruck's essay?

4. According to Ruck, the "NBA and NFL have destroyed MLB's pretension that it's the national pastime" (par. 10). Do you agree? What makes any given sport or activity a "national pastime"? Write an essay defending baseball as the national pastime, or arguing that another sport or activity has superseded baseball in that role.

MALCOLM GLADWELL

The Sports Taboo

A staff writer for the New Yorker, *Canadian journalist Malcolm Gladwell (b. 1963) writes about complex subjects—social psychology, statistics, economics, epidemiology—in a lively, accessible style. Before joining the* New Yorker, *Gladwell worked for the* American Spectator, Insight on the News, *and the* Washington Post. *He is the author of* The Tipping Point: How Little Things Can Make a Big Difference *(2000),* Blink: The Power of Thinking Without Thinking *(2005),* Outliers: The Story of Success *(2008), and* What the Dog Saw: And Other Adventures *(2009).*

Gladwell's work often upends common assumptions. In "The Sports Taboo" those assumptions include unspoken rules about discussing the racial dimensions of athleticism and the genetic differences between black and white athletes: "There is nothing particularly scary about this fact, and certainly nothing to warrant the kind of gag order on talk of racial differences which is now in place." Do you agree with Gladwell that "There is a point at which it becomes foolish to deny the fact of black athletic prowess" in many cases? Are there any problems with framing discussions of race in this way?

1.

The education of any athlete begins, in part, with an education in the racial taxonomy of his chosen sport—in the subtle, unwritten rules about what whites are supposed to be good at and what blacks are supposed to be good at. In football, whites play quarterback and blacks play running back; in baseball whites pitch and blacks play the outfield. I grew up in Canada, where my brother Geoffrey and I ran high-school track, and in Canada the rule of running was that anything under the quarter-mile belonged to the West Indies. This didn't mean that white people didn't run the sprints. But the expectation was that they would never win, and, sure enough, they rarely did. There was just a handful of West Indian immigrants in Ontario at that point—clustered in and around Toronto—but they owned Canadian sprinting, setting up under the stands at every major championship, cranking up the reggae on their boom boxes, and then humiliating everyone else on the track. My brother and I weren't from Toronto, so we weren't part of that scene. But our West Indian heritage meant that we got to share in the swagger. Geoffrey was a magnificent runner, with powerful legs and a barrel chest, and when he was warming up he used to do that exaggerated, slow-motion jog that the white guys would try to do and never quite pull off. I was a miler, which was a little outside the West Indian range. But, the way I figured it, the rules meant that no one should ever outkick me over the final two hundred meters of any race. And in the golden summer of my fourteenth year, when my running career prematurely peaked, no one ever did.

When I started running, there was a quarter-miler just a few years older than I was by the name of Arnold Stotz. He was a bulldog of a runner, hugely talented, and each year that he moved through the sprinting ranks he invariably broke the existing four-hundred-meter record in his age class. Stotz was white, though, and every time I saw the results of a big track meet I'd keep an eye out for his name, because I was convinced that he could not keep winning. It was as if I saw his whiteness as a degenerative disease, which would eventually claim and cripple him. I never asked him whether he felt the same anxiety, but I can't imagine that he didn't. There was only so long that anyone could defy the rules. One day, at the provincial championships, I looked up at the results board and Stotz was gone.

Talking openly about the racial dimension of sports in this way, of course, is considered unseemly. It's all right to say that blacks dominate sports because they lack opportunities elsewhere. That's the "Hoop Dreams" line, which says whites are allowed to acknowledge black athletic success as long as they feel guilty about it. What you're not supposed to say is what we were saying in my track days—that we were better because we were black, because of something intrinsic to being black. Nobody said anything like that publicly last month when Tiger Woods won the Masters or when, a week later, African men claimed thirteen out of the top twenty places in the Boston Marathon. Nor is it likely to come up this month, when African-Americans will make up eighty per cent of the players on the floor for the N.B.A. playoffs. When the popular television sports commentator Jimmy (the Greek) Snyder did break this taboo, in 1988—infamously ruminating on the size and significance of black thighs—one prominent N.A.A.C.P. official said that his remarks "could set race relations back a hundred years." The assumption is that the whole project of trying to get us to treat each other the same will be undermined if we don't all agree that under the skin we actually are the same.

The point of this, presumably, is to put our discussion of sports on a par with legal notions of racial equality, which would be a fine idea except that civil-rights law governs matters like housing and employment and the sports taboo covers matters like what can be said about someone's jump shot. In his much heralded book *Darwin's Athletes*, the University of Texas scholar John Hoberman tries to argue that these two things are the same, that it's impossible to speak of black physical superiority without implying intellectual inferiority. But it isn't long before the argument starts to get ridiculous. "The spectacle of black athleticism," he writes, inevitably turns into "a highly public image of black retardation." Oh, really? What, exactly, about Tiger Woods's victory in the Masters resembled "a highly public image of black retardation"? Today's black athletes are multimillion-dollar corporate pitchmen, with talk shows and sneaker deals and publicity machines and almost daily media opportunities to share their thoughts with the world, and it's very hard to see how all this contrives to make them look stupid. Hoberman spends a lot of time trying to inflate the significance of sports, arguing that how we talk about events on the baseball diamond or the track has grave consequences for how we talk about race in general. Here he is, for example, on Jackie Robinson:

> The sheer volume of sentimental and intellectual energy that has been invested in the mythic saga of Jackie Robinson has discouraged further thinking about what his career did and did not accomplish. . . . Black America has paid a high and largely unacknowledged price for the extraordinary prominence given the black athlete rather than other black men of action (such as military pilots and astronauts), who represent modern aptitudes in ways that athletes cannot.

Please. Black America has paid a high and largely unacknowl- 5
edged price for a long list of things, and having great athletes is

far from the top of the list. Sometimes a baseball player is just a baseball player, and sometimes an observation about racial difference is just an observation about racial difference. Few object when medical scientists talk about the significant epidemiological differences between blacks and whites—the fact that blacks have a higher incidence of hypertension than whites and twice as many black males die of diabetes and prostate cancer as white males, that breast tumors appear to grow faster in black women than in white women, that black girls show signs of puberty sooner than white girls. So why aren't we allowed to say that there might be athletically significant differences between blacks and whites?

According to the medical evidence, African-Americans seem to have, on the average, greater bone mass than do white Americans—a difference that suggests greater muscle mass. Black men have slightly higher circulating levels of testosterone and human-growth hormone than their white counterparts, and blacks overall tend to have proportionally slimmer hips, wider shoulders, and longer legs. In one study, the Swedish physiologist Bengt Saltin compared a group of Kenyan distance runners with a group of Swedish distance runners and found interesting differences in muscle composition: Saltin reported that the Africans appeared to have more blood-carrying capillaries and more mitochondria (the body's cellular power plant) in the fibres of their quadriceps. Another study found that, while black South African distance runners ran at the same speed as white South African runners, they were able to use more oxygen—eighty-nine per cent versus eighty-one per cent—over extended periods: somehow, they were able to exert themselves more. Such evidence suggested that there were physical differences in black athletes which have a bearing on activities like running and jumping, which should hardly come as a surprise to anyone who follows competitive sports.

To use track as an example—since track is probably the purest measure of athletic ability—Africans recorded fifteen out of the twenty fastest times last year in the men's ten thousand-meter event. In the five thousand meters, eighteen out of the twenty fastest times were recorded by Africans. In the fifteen hundred meters, thirteen out of the twenty fastest times were African, and in the sprints, in the men's hundred meters, you have to go all the way down to the twenty-third place in the world rankings—to

Geir Moen, of Norway—before you find a white face. There is a point at which it becomes foolish to deny the fact of black athletic prowess, and even more foolish to banish speculation on the topic. Clearly, something is going on. The question is what.

2.

If we are to decide what to make of the differences between blacks and whites, we first have to decide what to make of the word "difference," which can mean any number of things. A useful case study is to compare the ability of men and women in math. If you give a large, representative sample of male and female students a standardized math test, their mean scores will come out pretty much the same. But if you look at the margins, at the very best and the very worst students, sharp differences emerge. In the math portion of an achievement test conducted by Project Talent—a nationwide survey of fifteen-year-olds—there were 1.3 boys for every girl in the top ten per cent, 1.5 boys for every girl in the top five per cent, and seven boys for every girl in the top one per cent. In the fifty-six-year history of the Putnam Mathematical Competition, which has been described as the Olympics of college math, all but one of the winners have been male. Conversely, if you look at people with the very lowest math ability, you'll find more boys than girls there, too. In other words, although the average math ability of boys and girls is the same, the distribution isn't: there are more males than females at the bottom of the pile, more males than females at the top of the pile, and fewer males than females in the middle. Statisticians refer to this as a difference in variability.

This pattern, as it turns out, is repeated in almost every conceivable area of gender difference. Boys are more variable than girls on the College Board entrance exam and in routine elementary-school spelling tests. Male mortality patterns are more variable than female patterns; that is, many more men die in early and middle age than women, who tend to die in more of a concentrated clump toward the end of life. The problem is that variability differences are regularly confused with average differences. If men had higher average math scores than women, you could say they were better at the subject. But because they are only more variable the word "better" seems inappropriate.

The same holds true for differences between the races. A racist 10 stereotype is the assertion of average difference—it's the claim that the typical white is superior to the typical black. It allows a white man to assume that the black man he passes on the street is stupider than he is. By contrast, if what racists believed was that black intelligence was simply more variable than white intelligence, then it would be impossible for them to construct a stereotype about black intelligence at all. They wouldn't be able to generalize. If they wanted to believe that there were a lot of blacks dumber than whites, they would also have to believe that there were a lot of blacks smarter than they were. This distinction is critical to understanding the relation between race and athletic performance. What are we seeing when we remark black domination of elite sporting events—an average difference between the races or merely a difference in variability?

This question has been explored by geneticists and physical anthropologists, and some of the most notable work has been conducted over the past few years by Kenneth Kidd, at Yale. Kidd and his colleagues have been taking DNA samples from two African Pygmy tribes in Zaire and the Central African Republic and comparing them with DNA samples taken from populations all over the world. What they have been looking for is variants— subtle differences between the DNA of one person and another— and what they have found is fascinating. "I would say, without a doubt, that in almost any single African population—a tribe or however you want to define it—there is more genetic variation than in all the rest of the world put together," Kidd told me. In a sample of fifty Pygmies, for example, you might find nine variants in one stretch of DNA. In a sample of hundreds of people from around the rest of the world, you might find only a total of six variants in that same stretch of DNA—and probably every one of those six variants would also be found in the Pygmies. If everyone in the world was wiped out except Africans, in other words, almost all the human genetic diversity would be preserved.

The likelihood is that these results reflect Africa's status as the homeland of Homo sapiens: since every human population outside Africa is essentially a subset of the original African population, it makes sense that everyone in such a population would be a genetic subset of Africans, too. So you can expect groups of Africans to be more variable in respect to almost anything that has a genetic component. If, for example, your genes control how you react to aspirin, you'd expect to see more Africans than whites for whom one aspirin stops a bad headache, more for whom no amount of aspirin works, more who are allergic to aspirin, and more who need to take, say, four aspirin at a time to get any benefit—but far fewer Africans for whom the standard two-aspirin dose would work well. And to the extent that running is influenced by genetic factors you would expect to see more really fast blacks—and more really slow blacks—than whites but far fewer Africans of merely average speed. Blacks are like boys. Whites are like girls.

There is nothing particularly scary about this fact, and certainly nothing to warrant the kind of gag order on talk of racial differences which is now in place. What it means is that comparing elite athletes of different races tells you very little about the races themselves. A few years ago, for example, a prominent scientist argued for black athletic supremacy by pointing out that there had never been a white Michael Jordan. True. But, as the Yale anthropologist Jonathan Marks has noted, until recently there was no black Michael Jordan, either. Michael Jordan, like Tiger Woods or Wayne Gretzky or Cal Ripken, is one of the best players in his sport not because he's like the other members of his own ethnic group but precisely because he's not like them—or like anyone else, for that matter. Elite athletes are elite athletes because, in some sense, they are on the fringes of genetic variability. As it happens, African populations seem to create more of these genetic outliers than white populations do, and this is what underpins the claim that blacks are better athletes than whites. But that's all the claim amounts to. It doesn't say anything at all about the rest of us, of all races, muddling around in the genetic middle.

3.

There is a second consideration to keep in mind when we compare blacks and whites. Take the men's hundred-meter final at the Atlanta Olympics. Every runner in that race was of either Western African or Southern African descent, as you would expect if

Africans had some genetic affinity for sprinting. But suppose we forget about skin color and look just at country of origin. The eight-man final was made up of two African-Americans, two Africans (one from Namibia and one from Nigeria), a Trinidadian, a Canadian of Jamaican descent, an Englishman of Jamaican descent, and a Jamaican. The race was won by the Jamaican-Canadian, in world-record time, with the Namibian coming in second and the Trinidadian third. The sprint relay—the 4 × 100— was won by a team from Canada, consisting of the Jamaican-Canadian from the final, a Haitian-Canadian, a Trinidadian-Canadian, and another Jamaican-Canadian. Now it appears that African heritage is important as an initial determinant of sprinting ability, but also that the most important advantage of all is some kind of cultural or environmental factor associated with the Caribbean.

Or consider, in a completely different realm, the problem of hypertension. Black Americans have a higher incidence of hypertension than white Americans, even after you control for every conceivable variable, including income, diet, and weight, so it's tempting to conclude that there is something about being of African descent that makes blacks prone to hypertension. But it turns out that although some Caribbean countries have a problem with hypertension, others—Jamaica, St. Kitts, and the Bahamas— don't. It also turns out that people in Liberia and Nigeria—two countries where many New World slaves came from—have similar and perhaps even lower blood-pressure rates than white North Americans, while studies of Zulus, Indians, and whites in Durban, South Africa, showed that urban white males had the highest hypertension rates and urban white females had the lowest. So it's likely that the disease has nothing at all to do with Africanness.

The same is true for the distinctive muscle characteristic observed when Kenyans were compared with Swedes. Saltin, the Swedish physiologist, subsequently found many of the same characteristics in Nordic skiers who train at high altitudes and Nordic runners who train in very hilly regions—conditions, in other words, that resemble the mountainous regions of Kenya's Rift Valley, where so many of the country's distance runners come from. The key factor seems to be Kenya, not genes.

Lots of things that seem to be genetic in origin, then, actually aren't. Similarly, lots of things that we wouldn't normally think might affect athletic ability actually do. Once again, the social-science literature on male and female math achievement is instructive. Psychologists argue that when it comes to subjects like math, boys tend to engage in what's known as ability attribution. A boy who is doing well will attribute his success to the fact that he's good at math, and if he's doing badly he'll blame his teacher or his own lack of motivation—anything but his ability. That makes it easy for him to bounce back from failure or disappointment, and gives him a lot of confidence in the face of a tough new challenge. After all, if you think you do well in math because you're good at math, what's stopping you from being good at, say, algebra, or advanced calculus? On the other hand, if you ask a girl why she is doing well in math she will say, more often than not, that she succeeds because she works hard. If she's doing poorly, she'll say she isn't smart enough. This, as should be obvious, is a self-defeating attitude. Psychologists call it "learned helplessness"—the state in which failure is perceived as insurmountable. Girls who engage in effort attribution learn helplessness because in the face of a more difficult task like algebra or advanced calculus they can conceive of no solution. They're convinced that they can't work harder, because they think they're working as hard as they can, and that they can't rely on their intelligence, because they never thought they were that smart to begin with. In fact, one of the fascinating findings of attribution research is that the smarter girls are, the more likely they are to fall into this trap. High achievers are sometimes the most helpless. Here, surely, is part of the explanation for greater math variability among males. The female math whizzes, the ones who should be competing in the top one and two per cent with their male counterparts, are the ones most often paralyzed by a lack of confidence in their own aptitude. They think they belong only in the intellectual middle.

The striking thing about these descriptions of male and female stereotyping in math, though, is how similar they are to black and white stereotyping in athletics—to the unwritten rules holding that blacks achieve through natural ability and whites through effort. Here's how *Sports Illustrated* described, in a recent article, the white basketball player Steve Kerr, who plays alongside Michael Jordan for the Chicago Bulls. According to the magazine, Kerr is a "hard-working overachiever," distinguished by his "work ethic and heady play" and by a shooting style "born of a million practice shots." Bear in mind that Kerr is one of the best shooters in basketball today, and a key player on what is arguably one of the finest basketball teams in history. Bear in mind, too, that there is no evidence that Kerr works any harder than his teammates, least of all Jordan himself, whose work habits are legendary. But you'd never guess that from the article. It concludes, "All over America, whenever quicker, stronger gym rats see Kerr in action, they must wonder, How can that guy be out there instead of me?"

There are real consequences to this stereotyping. As the psychologists Carol Dweck and Barbara Licht write of high-achieving schoolgirls, "[They] may view themselves as so motivated and well disciplined that they cannot entertain the possibility that they did poorly on an academic task because of insufficient effort. Since blaming the teacher would also be out of character, blaming their abilities when they confront difficulty may seem like the most reasonable option." If you substitute the words "white athletes" for "girls" and "coach" for "teacher," I think you have part of the reason that so many white athletes are underrepresented at the highest levels of professional sports. Whites have been saddled with the athletic equivalent of learned helplessness—the idea that it is all but fruitless to try and compete at the highest levels, because they have only effort on their side. The causes of athletic and gender discrimination may be diverse, but its effects are not. Once again, blacks are like boys, and whites are like girls.

4.

When I was in college, I once met an old acquaintance from my 20 high-school running days. Both of us had long since quit track, and we talked about a recurrent fantasy we found we'd both had for getting back into shape. It was that we would go away somewhere remote for a year and do nothing but train, so that when the year was up we might finally know how good we were. Neither of us had any intention of doing this, though, which is why it was a fantasy. In adolescence, athletic excess has a certain appeal—during high school, I happily spent Sunday afternoons running up and down snow-covered sandhills—but with most of us that obsessiveness soon begins to fade. Athletic success depends on having the right genes and on a self-reinforcing belief in one's own ability. But it also depends on a rare form of tunnel vision. To be a great athlete, you have to care, and what was obvious to us both was that neither of us cared anymore. This is the last piece of the puzzle about what we mean when we say one group is better at something than another: sometimes different groups care about different things. Of the seven hundred men who play major-league baseball, for example, eighty-six come from either the Dominican Republic or Puerto Rico, even though those two islands have a combined population of only eleven million. But then baseball is something that Dominicans and Puerto Ricans care about—and you can say the same thing about African-Americans and basketball, West Indians and sprinting, Canadians and hockey, and Russians and chess. Desire is the great intangible in performance, and unlike genes or psychological affect we can't measure it and trace its implications. This is the problem, in the end, with the question of whether blacks are better at sports than whites. It's not that it's offensive, or that it leads to discrimination. It's that, in some sense, it's not a terribly interesting question; "better" promises a tidier explanation than can ever be provided.

I quit competitive running when I was sixteen—just after the summer I had qualified for the Ontario track team in my age class. Late that August, we had travelled to St. John's, Newfoundland, for the Canadian championships. In those days, I was whippet-thin, as milers often are, five feet six and not more than a hundred pounds, and I could skim along the ground so lightly that I barely needed to catch my breath. I had two white friends on that team, both distance runners, too, and both, improbably, even smaller and lighter than I was. Every morning, the three of us would run through the streets of St. John's, charging up the hills and flying down the other side. One of these friends went on to have a distinguished college running career, the other became a world-class miler; that summer, I myself was the Canadian record holder in the fifteen hundred metres for my age class. We were almost terrifyingly competitive, without a shred of doubt in our ability, and as we raced along we never stopped talking and joking, just to prove how absurdly easy we found running to be. I thought of us all as equals. Then, on the last day of our stay in

St. John's, we ran to the bottom of Signal Hill, which is the town's principal geographical landmark—an abrupt outcrop as steep as anything in San Francisco. We stopped at the base, and the two of them turned to me and announced that we were all going to run straight up Signal Hill backward. I don't know whether I had more running ability than those two or whether my Africanness gave me any genetic advantage over their whiteness. What I do know is that such questions were irrelevant, because, as I realized, they were willing to go to far greater lengths to develop their talent. They ran up the hill backward. I ran home.

For Writing and Discussion

1. Gladwell writes that, as a younger runner, he always tracked the progress of an older "quarter miler" who "moved through the sprinting ranks" (par. 2). Why did Gladwell keep an eye on this runner? How does this anecdote support his main point?

2. For Gladwell, racial and genetic dispositions toward athletic talent are similar to racial dispositions toward diabetes and hypertension. Do you find this analogy persuasive? Why or why not?

3. **connections**   In "Where Have African-American Baseball Players Gone?" (p. 168), Rob Ruck charts the "staggering" (par. 2) decline of African Americans in professional baseball. Can Gladwell's essay give any insight into this trend? How might Gladwell answer Ruck's question?

4. According to Gladwell, "there are real consequences to . . . stereotyping" (par. 19). He explores a variety of stereotypes, including perceptions based on gender. Have you ever been stereotyped, either positively or negatively? What was the basis for the stereotype? Did it have consequences for you?

CHAPTER 4

Technology

In "The Judgment of Thamus" (included in this section), media critic Neil Postman provides a pointed and sobering appraisal of technological advancement. He argues that every technology is "both a burden and a blessing; not either-or, but this-and-that." For Postman, such innovations are never merely additions or points along a linear course of "progress." Instead, technologies such as the book, the steam engine, and the computer are transformative. They redefine "'freedom,' 'truth,' 'intelligence,' 'fact,' 'wisdom,' 'memory,' 'history'—all the words we live by."

Americans tend to be optimistic about technology and progress: We are more likely to quote the oracular pronouncements of Facebook's Mark Zuckerberg than remember the cautionary words of a critic like Postman. That idealism shapes contemporary life in innumerable ways, from the convenience of our consumer products and the limitless information of our Internet search engines, to our relationships with friends, money, education, jobs, and culture. Increasingly our lives are mediated through technology. Even America's sense of national identity is shaped by technological achievement—and a perpetual anxiety that the rest of the world is catching up. In his 2011 State of the Union address, President Barack Obama said, "In a single generation, revolutions in technology have transformed the way we live, work and do business. . . . Meanwhile, nations like China and India realized that with some changes of their own, they could compete in this new world."

In "Wall of Sound: The iPod Has Changed the Way We Listen to Music," Nikil Saval draws on the history of listening and the work of theorist Theodor Adorno to illuminate the meaning of music in a "Shuffled world." Postman encourages us to view that "new world" with open eyes: Technological innovations giveth, but they also taketh away. All of the essays here wrestle with similar tensions, as well as other questions: What does technology mean? *How* does it mean? In what ways does it alter human psychology, social relationships, culture, and entertainment? Aymar Jean Christian looks at the dominance of YouTube ("The Problem of YouTube"), as well as the prospect of other sites that might promote "inventive and 'quality' forms of storytelling." Farhad Manjoo speculates about the future of Facebook in "Is Facebook a Fad?" and disagrees with those who dismiss the site as a momentary trend. Sherry Turkle's "Can You Hear Me Now?" sounds an anxious note about technology's effects on the "self," while Clay Shirky's "Gin, Television, and Social Surplus" provides a (mostly) optimistic view of a society stumbling through the process of technological transformation.

NIKIL SAVAL

Wall of Sound: The iPod Has Changed the Way We Listen to Music

Nikil Saval (b. 1982) is an assistant editor at the literary magazine n+1 *and a Ph.D. candidate in English at Stanford University. His writing has appeared in the* London Review of Books, *the* New York Times, *the* New Statesman, *and other publications. In this essay, which was adapted from a longer* n+1 *article and published in* Slate, *Saval considers how the iPod has changed the way we listen to—and consume— music. He draws on the history of Western music, from Beethoven, jazz, and Jimi Hendrix to countless subgenres of hip-hop and heavy metal. He also frames his argument using the opposing theories of German-born philosopher Theodor Adorno (1903–1969) and the French sociologist Pierre Bourdieu (1930–2002). In the process, Saval highlights the various ways that we use music, whether we are hearing it in the background of our shopping or relying on it to help us "swallow an unpalatable life." As you read, think about the ways you listen to music and your reasons for doing so. Do you agree with Saval that we live in a dystopian "counterfeit heaven where music plays all the time"?*

Two years ago, at the nadir of the financial crisis, the urban sociologist Sudhir Venkatesh wondered aloud in the *New York Times* why no mass protests had arisen against what was clearly a criminal coup by the banks. Where were the pitchforks, the tar, the feathers? Where, more importantly, were the crowds? Venkatesh's answer was the iPod: "In public spaces, serendipitous interaction is needed to create the 'mob mentality,' Most iPod-like devices separate citizens from one another; you can't join someone in a movement if you can't hear the participants. Congrats Mr. Jobs for impeding social change." Venkatesh's suggestion was glib, tossed off—yet it was also a rare reminder, from the quasi-left, of how urban life has been changed by recording technologies.

The concern that recorded music promotes solipsism and isolation isn't new. Before the invention of the record and the gramophone (1887), the only form of listening people knew was social; the closest thing to a private musical experience was playing an instrument for yourself, or silently looking over a score. More often, if you had the means, you got to sit in the panopticon of the concert hall, seeing and being seen to the accompaniment of Verdi—an experience most fully described by Edith Wharton in the opening scene of *The Age of Innocence* (1920), just as it was going out of style. With mechanical reproduction came the hitherto unimaginable phenomenon of listening to multi-instrumental music by *yourself*. How, a contributor to *Gramophone* magazine asked in 1923, would you react if you stumbled upon somebody in the midst of this private rapture? It would be "as if you had discovered your friend sniffing cocaine, emptying a bottle of whisky, or plaiting straws in his hair. People, we think, should not do things 'to themselves,' however much they may enjoy doing them in company."

But it wasn't only solitary hyper-listening that recording facilitated. By 1960, recorded popular music had begun, in mysterious ways, to promote new social movements. Former Black Panther[1] Bobby Seale recounts in his memoir how Huey Newton developed an elaborate reading of Dylan's "Ballad of a Thin Man" as an allegory of race: "This song Bobby Dylan was singing became a very big part of that whole publishing operation of the Black Panther paper. And in the background, while we were putting this paper out, this record came up and I guess a number of papers were published, and many times we would play that record." The song wasn't overtly political but its mood of stately menace seems to have insinuated itself into the politics of the Panthers.

The '60s were a decade of both mass protests and mass concerts, and this was more than a coincidence. Barbara Ehrenreich has suggested that the roots of second-wave feminism could be found in the tens of thousands of shrieking girls who filled arenas and ballparks at the Beatles' American stops, from the Hollywood Bowl to Shea. These girls, unladylike, insistent, were going to scream for what they wanted. Social change drove musical experimentation, and—more remarkably—vice versa.

[1]Black Panthers: A revolutionary leftist and black nationalist organization founded in the 1960s. [Editor's note.]

The music of this era was—it's worth repeating—an incite-   5
ment to social change. It was the sound of not going reflexively to
war, of mingling across class and racial lines, of thinking it might
be all right to sleep around a little, of wanting to work a job that
didn't suck.
Of course the radical hopes of the '60s collapsed. The highest-
rated YouTube comment on a video of Joan Baez singing "We
Shall Overcome" manages to be both smug and glum: "Though
we obviously failed, I am so glad that I am of a generation that
believed we could make a difference." By the early '70s, popular
music had more or less forfeited its capacity to promote social
movements. From then on its different varieties would be associated with defining lifestyle niches, consumer habits, and subcul-
tural affiliations. In this way the make-it-new modernist impera-
tive, which seized pop music several decades late, came to seem
little different from the program of advertisers launching fresh
product lines. Jadedness swept pop music enthusiasts, many of
whom, heartbroken by their brief glimpse of collective life, would
discount the whole era of the '60s as history's cunning preparation for a descent into hellish consumerism. Welcome to dystopia, a counterfeit heaven where music plays all the time.

The first to ring the alarm about the omnipresence of recorded
music were classical music snobs who, as part of their contracted
duties as university professors, had to spend time on college cam-
puses. "This is being written in a study in a college of one of the
great American universities," wrote George Steiner[2] in 1974. "The
walls are throbbing gently to the beat of music coming from one
near and several more distant amplifiers. The walls quiver to the
ear or to the touch roughly eighteen hours per day, sometimes
twenty-four." Allan Bloom[3] picked up the beat in *The Closing of
the American Mind* (1987): "Though students do not have books,
they most emphatically do have music. . . . Nothing is more singular about this generation than its addiction to music." Steiner:
"It matters little whether it is that of pop, folk or rock. What
counts is the all-pervasive pulsation, morning to night and into the
night, made indiscriminate by the cool burn of electronic timbre."

[2]George Steiner (b. 1929): French-born literary critic, philosopher, and novelist.
[Editor's note.]
[3]Allan Bloom (1930–1992): American philosopher and classicist. [Editor's note.]

The Apple doesn't fall far from the tree.

The only historical analogy Bloom could think of was to the Wagner cult of the late 19th century. Yet even world-conquering Wagner appealed to a limited class, who could only hear his works in opera houses. By contrast the music of the late-20th-century world was truly ubiquitous. Steiner: "When a young man walks down a street in Vladivostok or Cincinnati with his transistor blaring, when a car passes with its radio on at full blast, the resulting sound-capsule encloses the individual." Bloom: "There is the stereo in the home, in the car; there are concerts; there are music videos, with special channels devoted to them, on the air, nonstop; there are the Walkmans so that no place—not public transportation, not the library—prevents students from communing with the Muse, even while studying." Steiner: "What tissues of sensibility are being numbed or exacerbated?"

Yadda, yadda. Yet Bloom and Steiner were right! In fact they had no idea how right they would become. If the spread of home stereo equipment in the 1970s, followed by that of portable devices (the boom box, the Walkman, briefly the Discman), brought music to the masses in a new way, digitization and the iPod have made recorded music even more plentiful and ubiquitous. The fears in Bloom's time that cassette tapes would bring down the music industry are quaint now, in the face of trillions of bytes of music traded brazenly over the Internet every minute. So, too, does the disc mania of record collectors pale in the face of digital collections measured in weeks of music. A DJ's crate of 100 LPs amounts to about three days of straight listening; your standard 60-gigabyte iPod, 50 days. Has anyone these days listened to all of their music, even once through?

Nobody knows how much music we listen to, since so often we're not even listening. The American Time Use Survey, performed every year by the Bureau of Labor Statistics, throws up its hands. Does music playing in the background at a café count? Music in a film? Music played to drown out other music? Music played while reading, writing, cleaning, exercising, eating, sleeping—all of this has to count in some way. Stumbling into a college dorm now to ask the kids to turn it down, Steiner would find them all earmuffed with headphones as they stare at their computers, each listening to his own private playlist while something else plays on the stereo loud enough for a communal spirit to be maintained. And this is true not only of colleges but the world at large.

If it's easier than ever to listen to other people's music, it's also 10 more tempting than ever to do so all alone. Walkman listening never lost the stigma of the juvenile; the sophistication—and expense—of the iPod have made adulthood safe for solipsism as never before. What does it mean for us, on the listening end, as we pad around the world with our iPods, trying to keep those shitty white earbuds from falling out of our ears? Public music criticism—a wasteland—isn't much help. It mainly focuses on individual works or single performances, when it isn't giving us drooling profiles of artists. This has nothing to do with our current mode of listening, which only rarely obsesses on particular works or genres, let alone worships particular figures. In light of the epoch-making iPod, we need a way to find out what all this music listening is doing to us, or what we're doing with it.

In the 20th century, the two most considered attempts to connect music and society were those of the philosopher Theodor Adorno and the sociologist Pierre Bourdieu.

Among the main philosophers of Western music—Schopenhauer, Nietzsche, Kierkegaard—Adorno knew the most about music and worked hardest to figure out its relationship to history. For Adorno, it wasn't just that historical forces circumscribed the production and reception of musical works; it was that historical conflicts appeared in music in mediated form. Thus a seemingly autonomous, nonrepresentational, and nonlinguistic art transfigured the world and returned it to the listener in a way that oriented him ideologically. The huge melodic conflicts animating Beethoven's symphonies and the brassy, thumping triumphs with which they concluded announced the era of bourgeois ascendancy after the French Revolution. The "emancipation of dissonance" in the atonal works of Schoenberg suggested a crisis of the bourgeoisie in which the self-evidence of tonality, like that of human progress, began to crack up.

Infamously, when society began to produce new forms of music that accompanied unrest by workers and students, the old Marxist turned a deaf ear. His essays on jazz and pop music are notorious classics of "bad" Adorno. The syncopations of bebop were only a mirage of liberty, and the relentless repetitiveness of rock and roll a virtual embodiment of a reified, historyless, mythological consciousness. The problem here was not exactly snobbism or even unconscious racism. It's that Adorno seemed only to understand and accept a model of listening in which music solicits and rewards the listener's whole attention. This is a musical sociology of the concert hall and the study, not the street, store, workplace, block party, or demonstration. From its standpoint, contemporary music of less-than-Schoenbergian melodic complexity can only seem simple, in the sense of dumb.

Bourdieu was a kind of anti-Adorno, his sociology a negation of the traditional aesthetics Adorno had mastered. Bourdieu practiced a deliberate and heroic philistinism. He seemed to know virtually nothing about music; it's not even clear he liked it. "Music is the 'pure' art par excellence," he wrote in *Distinction*. "It says nothing and it has *nothing to say*." Adorno would have recognized this ostensibly timeless aperçu as a historically specific statement, the product of a whole century (the 19th) of debate over precisely this question: What and how does music communicate? Yet out of this falsehood Bourdieu came to a startling conclusion, the truth of which we've all had to concede: "Nothing more clearly affirms one's 'class,' nothing more infallibly classifies, than tastes in music." In the mid-1960s, he conducted a giant survey of French musical tastes, and what do you know? The haute bourgeoisie loved *The Well-Tempered Clavier*; the upwardly mobile got high on "jazzy" classics like "Rhapsody in Blue"; while the working class dug what the higher reaches thought of as schmaltzy trash, the "Blue Danube" waltz and Petula Clark.[4] Bourdieu drew the conclusion that judgments of taste reinforce forms of social inequality, as individuals imagine themselves to possess superior or inferior spirit and perceptiveness, when really they just like what their class inheritance has taught them to. *Distinction* appeared in English in 1984, cresting the high tide of the culture wars about to hit the universities. Adorno had felt that advanced art-music was doing the work of revolution. *Are you kidding, Herr Professor?* might have been Bourdieu's response. And thus was Adorno dethroned, all his passionate arguments

[4]Petula Clark (b. 1932): British singer of many popular songs in the 1960s. [Editor's note.]

about history as expressed in musical form recast as moves in the game of taste, while his dismissal of jazz became practically the most famous cultural mistake of the 20th century.

In Adorno and Bourdieu we have two radically different perspec- 15 tives, inhabiting each other's blind spots, with a convergence in both authors' political sympathy with socialism. We can agree with Adorno that music has immanent, formal properties that are connected, somehow, to large-scale historical forces. And we can agree with Bourdieu that musical taste is an instrument in the legitimation of class hierarchies.

So Bourdieu is helpful when we ask what the iPod has wrought in the realm of musical classification. The social world of opera-going may be headed the way of polar bears and ice caps, but *society* hasn't disappeared. A hierarchical social world has managed to absorb the omnipresence of music pretty effortlessly. You can see this in the violent intragenre squabbling that animates indie rock circles, and in the savage takedowns of avant-garde opera performances in art-music magazines. Meanwhile the proliferation of genre names represents an ever finer process of social differentiation, each genre's acolytes determining (as Serge Gainsbourg[5] put it) *qui est* "in," *qui est* "out." The rise of generic distinctions has lately reached a climax of absurdity, such that we can name off the top of our heads: house, witch house, dub, dub-step, hardstep, dancehall, dance-floor, punk, post-punk, noise, "Noise," new wave, nu wave, No Wave, emo, post-emo, hip-hop, conscious hip-hop, alternative hip-hop, jazz hip-hop, hardcore hip-hop, nerd-core hip-hop, Christian hip-hop, crunk, crunkcore, metal, doom metal, black metal, speed metal, thrash metal, death metal, Christian death metal, and, of course, shoe-gazing, among others. (Meanwhile, 1,000 years of European art music is filed under "classical.") Some people listen to some of these; others, to only one; and others still, to nearly all. And this accomplishes a lot of handy social sorting, especially among the young, whenever music is talked about or played so that more than one person can hear it.

At the same time, modes of listening seem to be moving toward

---

[5]Serge Gainsbourg (1928–1991): Popular French singer, songwriter, actor, and director. [Editor's note.]

the (apparent) opposite of micro-differentiation: a total pluralism of taste. This has become the most celebrated feature of the
iPod era. "I have seen the future," Alex Ross, music critic of *The
New Yorker*, wrote in 2004, "and it is called the Shuffle—the setting on the iPod that skips randomly from one track to another."
Here the iPod, or the digitization of musical life it represents,
promises emancipation from questions of taste. Differences in
what people listen to, in a Shuffled world, may have less and less
to do with social class and purchasing power. Or, better yet, taste
won't correlate to class distinction: The absence of taste will.
As certain foodies score points by having eaten everything—
blowfish, yak milk tea, haggis, hot dogs—so the person who
knows and likes all music achieves a curious sophistication-
through-indiscriminateness.

   Adorno would be more at home analyzing the uses to which
the omnipresence of music has been put in the service of "the
administered life"—the background Musak and easy listening,
the somehow consolingly melancholy shopping pop, that we hear
in malls and supermarkets almost without noticing. "I do love a
new purchase!" says the Gang of Four outright—while all the
other songs merely insinuate it. Around the holidays, Banana
Republic will alternate familiar hits like George Michael's "Last
Christmas" with pounding C-grade techno, lulling you into a state
of sickly nostalgia before ramping up your heart rate—a perfect
way to goose you into an impulse buy. So, too, as Adorno would
have been unsurprised to find out, has music become a common
way for people to get through the workday. Your local café's
barista may literally depend on Bon Iver's reedy lugubriousness
to palliate a dreary job as you depend on coffee.

   On the other hand, Adorno's prejudice against empirical
research—as Brecht[6] said, Adorno "never took a trip in order to
see"—meant that he never understood how music could be used
for different purposes by the very people it was supposed to manage and administer. People not only use music to help them swallow an unpalatable life, but to enhance and enlarge their capaci-
ties for action. If a bass line of a standard 12-bar blues, repeating
with machinelike regularity, keeps you clicking through the data

[6]Bertolt Brecht (1898–1956): German playwright and poet. [Editor's note.]

entry sheet, a sharp post-punk squall can move you to sabotage and revolt, and vice versa. Of course music can also move you in less obviously political ways, filling you with romantic enthusiasm or unshakable sorrow. Then there are all the uses of music that are beneath good and evil, that neither shore up nor undermine the system. In utopia, as under late capitalism, there will still be a lot of cooking and cleaning to do, as well as long drives to take in our electric cars. These slightly boring parts of life are made less so by listening to slightly boring music.

If Adorno, in his emphasis on the immanent unfolding of musi- 20 cal works as cognition, didn't understand the mixed uses of distracted listening, Bourdieu missed something even more important. His empiricism blinded him to the utopian potential in music. You would never guess, to read his books, that they were published *after* the '60s, an extraordinary period that demonstrated the capacity of musical taste to break down as well as reinforce social boundaries. Shoveled at us now as commodities played ad nauseam on Clear Channel, the "classic rock" of the '60s no longer discloses its role in the social movements of that time. And yet—Hendrix, Joplin; Coltrane, Davis, Coleman; the Stones, the Beatles; and Riley, Young, Reich—even if they didn't sing a single revolutionary word, even if they chastised you for "carrying pictures of Chairman Mao," they were all either directly involved with social movements or deeply implicated in them.

The great 1990s magazine the *Baffler* spent its first half-decade analyzing how the culture industry managed, with increasing success, to recognize new musical trends and package them and sell them back at a markup to the people who'd pioneered them. The *Baffler* looked back to the punk scene of the early '80s for inspiration; it spoke up for small labels that sold music to local constituencies. If you couldn't get what you wanted on the radio, you would have to find it left of the dial—and keep looking over your shoulder for the man.

The danger now is different. The man no longer needs a monopoly on musical taste. He just wants a few cents on the dollar of every song you download, he doesn't care what that song says. Other times he doesn't even care if you pay that dollar, as long as you listen to your stolen music on his portable MP3 player, store it on his Apple computer, send it to your friends through his Verizon network. To paraphrase Yeltsin's[7] famous offer to the Chechens, take as much free music as you can stomach. We'll see where it gets you.

If recording and mechanical reproduction opened up the world of musical pluralism—of listening to other people's music until you and they became other people yourselves—digital reproduction expanded that pluralism to the point where it reversed itself. You have all the world's music on your iPod, in your earphones. Now it's "other people's music"—which should be very exciting to encounter—as played in cafés and stores that is the problem. In any public setting, it acquires a coercive aspect. The iPod is the thing you have to buy in order not to be defenseless against the increasingly sucky music played to make you buy things.

One radical option remains: abnegation—some "Great Refusal" to obey the obscure social injunction that condemns us to a lifetime of listening. *Silence*: The word suggests the torture of enforced isolation, or a particularly monkish kind of social death. But it was the tremendously congenial avant-garde gadabout John Cage[8] who showed, just as the avalanche of recorded music was starting to bury us, how there was "no such thing as silence," that listening to an absence of listener-directed sounds represented a profounder and far more heroic submission than the regular attitude adopted in concert halls—a willingness to "let sounds be," as he put it. Such were Cage's restrictions that he needed to herd everyone into their seats in order to make his point—an authoritarian gesture toward an anarchic result. But now in conditions of relative freedom we can listen to 4'33" on record, or on our iPods, and the change in attention it demands is exactly the opposite of our endless contemporary communing with music, our neurotic search for the right sound, the exact note that never comes. What if we tried to listen to nothing? Silence is the feature of our buzzing sound-world we enjoy least, whose very existence we threaten to pave over track by track. Silence is the most endangered musical experience in our time.

---

[7]Boris Yeltsin (1931–2007): First president of the Russian Federation (1991–1999) after the fall of the Soviet Union. [Editor's note.]
[8]John Cage (1912–1992): American composer, music theorist, and artist. [Editor's note.]

Turning it up, we might figure out what all our music listening is meant to drown out, the thing we can't bear to hear.

For Writing and Discussion

1. According to Saval, what was the big difference between American popular music in the 1960s and American popular music in the 1970s?

2. While Saval writes broadly about contemporary music and musical history, including many references to specific composers and artists, he offers no real close analysis of specific songs, performers, or genres. Why do you think he avoids doing so? Would his essay be stronger if he included more attention to particular songs and individual artists? Why or why not?

3. **connections**   In "The Art of Immersion: Fear of Fiction" (p. 366), Frank Rose writes about "weirdly immersive" (par. 2) entertainment, which (some argue) can be addictive and can cut us off from authenticity, reality, and real human connections. He traces this anxiety back to early novels such as *Don Quixote* and up through the early years of film and television, as "every new medium has aroused fear and even hostility" (par. 4). Rose focuses on the "new and dangerously immersive" Internet (par. 22), as well as the latest generation of 3-D movies. Is his analysis applicable to Saval's "Wall of Sound"? Can music be "weirdly immersive"? How do you think Rose would respond to Saval's essay? Are Saval's anxieties about the omnipresence of music—even as it isolates listeners—unfounded or overstated? Why or why not?

4. Pierre Bourdieu argues that "nothing more clearly affirms one's 'class,' nothing more infallibly classifies, than tastes in music" (par. 14). Saval concurs, writing that musical choices "accomplis[h] a lot of handy social sorting, especially among the young" (par. 16). How do your musical preferences indicate or affirm your identity—socioeconomically, culturally, ethnically, or otherwise? Do you use music for "social sorting," or for establishing relationships and communities?

NEIL POSTMAN

The Judgment of Thamus

Neil Postman (1931–2003) was an American media theorist, cultural critic, and educator. He also founded the graduate program in Media Ecology at New York University's Steinhart School of Education, where he taught for many years. Postman is best known for his sharp and witty criticism of technology and the media. His books include Teaching as a Subversive Activity *(1969), cowritten with Charles Weingartner;* Amusing Ourselves to Death: Public Discourse in the Age of Show Business *(1985); and* The End of Education: Redefining the Value of School *(1995).*

The following essay, Chapter 1 from his 1992 book Technopoly: The Surrender of Culture to Technology, *brings together several of Postman's recurrent themes and preoccupations, especially the meaning of technological progress: "Every technology is both a burden and a blessing; not either-or, but this-and-that. . . ." He grounds his argument in Plato's dialogue* Phaedrus: *an ancient story that proves prescient and relevant to contemporary debates about technology. "The Judgment of Thamus" was published twenty years ago. As you read, consider technological "progress" during the last two decades. How have developments like the Internet, smartphones, and iPods affected our culture and society in light of Postman's analysis? Do his questions and concerns still seem relevant?*

You will find in Plato's *Phaedrus* a story about Thamus, the king of a great city of Upper Egypt. For people such as ourselves, who are inclined (in Thoreau's phrase) to be tools of our tools, few legends are more instructive than his. The story, as Socrates tells it to his friend Phaedrus, unfolds in the following way: Thamus once entertained the god Theuth, who was the inventor of many things, including number, calculation, geometry, astronomy, and writing. Theuth exhibited his inventions to King Thamus, claiming that they should be made widely known and available to Egyptians. Socrates continues:

> Thamus inquired into the use of each of them, and as Theuth went through them expressed approval or disapproval, according as he judged Theuth's claims to be well or ill founded. It would take too long to go through all that Thamus is reported to have said for and against each of Theuth's inventions. But when it came to writing, Theuth declared, "Here is an accomplishment, my lord the King, which will improve both the wisdom and the memory of the Egyptians. I have discovered a sure receipt for memory and wisdom." To this, Thamus replied, "Theuth, my paragon of inventors, the discoverer of an art is not the best judge of the good or harm which will accrue to those who practice it. So it is in this; you, who are the father of writing, have out of fondness for your off-spring attributed to it quite the opposite of its real function. Those who acquire it will cease to exercise their memory and become forgetful; they will rely on writing to bring things to their remembrance by external signs instead of by their own internal resources. What you have discovered is a receipt for recollection, not for memory. And as for wisdom, your pupils will have the reputation for it without the reality: they will receive a quantity of information without proper instruction, and in consequence be thought very knowledgeable when they are for the most part quite ignorant. And because they are filled with the conceit of wisdom instead of real wisdom they will be a burden to society."[1]

I begin . . . with this legend because in Thamus' response there are several sound principles from which we may begin to learn how to think with wise circumspection about a technological society. In fact, there is even one error in the judgment of Thamus, from which we may also learn something of importance. The error is not in his claim that writing will damage memory and create false wisdom. It is demonstrable that writing has had such an effect. Thamus' error is in his believing that writing will be a burden to society and *nothing but a burden*. For all his wisdom, he fails to imagine what writing's benefits might be, which, as we know, have been considerable. We may learn from this that it is a mistake to suppose that any technological innovation has a one-sided effect. Every technology is both a burden and a blessing; not either-or, but this-and-that.

Nothing could be more obvious, of course, especially to those

[1]Plato, *Phaedrus and Letters VII and VIII* (New York: Penguin Classics, 1973), p. 96.

who have given more than two minutes of thought to the matter. Nonetheless, we are currently surrounded by throngs of zealous Theuths, one-eyed prophets who see only what new technologies can do and are incapable of imagining what they will *undo*. We might call such people Technophiles. They gaze on technology as a lover does on his beloved, seeing it as without blemish and entertaining no apprehension for the future. They are therefore dangerous and are to be approached cautiously. On the other hand, some one-eyed prophets, such as I (or so I am accused), are inclined to speak only of burdens (in the manner of Thamus) and are silent about the opportunities that new technologies make possible. The Technophiles must speak for themselves, and do so all over the place. My defense is that a dissenting voice is sometimes needed to moderate the din made by the enthusiastic multitudes. If one is to err, it is better to err on the side of Thamusian skepticism. But it is an error nonetheless. And I might note that, with the exception of his judgment on writing, Thamus does not repeat this error. You might notice on rereading the legend that he gives arguments *for* and *against* each of Theuth's inventions. For it is inescapable that every culture must negotiate with technology, whether it does so intelligently or not. A bargain is struck in which technology giveth and technology taketh away. The wise know this well, and are rarely impressed by dramatic technological changes, and never overjoyed. Here, for example, is Freud on the matter, from his doleful *Civilization and Its Discontents*:

> One would like to ask: is there, then, no positive gain in pleasure, no unequivocal increase in my feeling of happiness, if I can, as often as I please, hear the voice of a child of mine who is living hundreds of miles away or if I can learn in the shortest possible time after a friend has reached his destination that he has come through the long and difficult voyage unharmed? Does it mean nothing that medicine has succeeded in enormously reducing infant mortality and the danger of infection for women in childbirth, and, indeed, in considerably lengthening the average life of a civilized man?

Freud knew full well that technical and scientific advances are not to be taken lightly, which is why he begins this passage by acknowledging them. But he ends it by reminding us of what they have undone:

If there had been no railway to conquer distances, my child would never have left his native town and I should need no telephone to hear his voice; if traveling across the ocean by ship had not been introduced, my friend would not have embarked on his sea-voyage and I should not need a cable to relieve my anxiety about him. What is the use of reducing infantile mortality when it is precisely that reduction which imposes the greatest restraint on us in the begetting of children, so that, taken all round, we nevertheless rear no more children than in the days before the reign of hygiene, while at the same time we have created difficult conditions for our sexual life in marriage. . . . And, finally, what good to us is a long life if it is difficult and barren of joys, and if it is so full of misery that we can only welcome death as a deliverer?[2]

In tabulating the cost of technological progress, Freud takes a   5 rather depressing line, that of a man who agrees with Thoreau's remark that our inventions are but improved means to an unimproved end. The Technophile would surely answer Freud by saying that life has always been barren of joys and full of misery but that the telephone, ocean liners, and especially the reign of hygiene have not only lengthened life but made it a more agreeable proposition. That is certainly an argument I would make (thus proving I am no one-eyed Technophobe), but it is not necessary at this point to pursue it. I have brought Freud into the conversation only to show that a wise man—even one of such a woeful countenance—must begin his critique of technology by acknowledging its successes. Had King Thamus been as wise as reputed, he would not have forgotten to include in his judgment a prophecy about the powers that writing would enlarge. There is a calculus of technological change that requires a measure of even-handedness.

So much for Thamus' error of omission. There is another omission worthy of note, but it is no error. Thamus simply takes for granted—and therefore does not feel it necessary to say—that writing is not a neutral technology whose good or harm depends on the uses made of it. He knows that the uses made of any technology are largely determined by the structure of the technology itself—that is, that its functions follow from its form. This is why Thamus is concerned not with *what* people will write; he is

[2]Sigmund Freud, *Civilization and Its Discontents* (New York: W. W. Norton, 1961), pp. 38–39.

concerned *that* people will write. It is absurd to imagine Thamus advising, in the manner of today's standard-brand Technophiles, that, if only writing would be used for the production of certain kinds of texts and not others (let us say, for dramatic literature but not for history or philosophy), its disruptions could be minimized. He would regard such a counsel as extreme naïveté. He would allow, I imagine, that a technology may be barred entry to a culture. But we may learn from Thamus the following: once a technology is admitted, it plays out its hand; it does what it is designed to do. Our task is to understand what that design is— that is to say, when we admit a new technology to the culture, we must do so with our eyes wide open.

All of this we may infer from Thamus' silence. But we may learn even more from what he does say than from what he doesn't. He points out, for example, that writing will change what is meant by the words "memory" and "wisdom." He fears that memory will be confused with what he disdainfully calls "recollection," and he worries that wisdom will become indistinguishable from mere knowledge. This judgment we must take to heart, for it is a certainty that radical technologies create new definitions of old terms, and that this process takes place without our being fully conscious of it. Thus, it is insidious and dangerous, quite different from the process whereby new technologies introduce new terms to the language. In our own time, we have consciously added to our language thousands of new words and phrases having to do with new technologies—"VCR," "binary digit," "software," "front-wheel drive," "window of opportunity," "Walkman," etc. We are not taken by surprise at this. New things require new words. But new things also modify old words, words that have deep-rooted meanings. The telegraph and the penny press changed what we once meant by "information." Television changes what we once meant by the terms "political debate," "news," and "public opinion." The computer changes "information" once again. Writing changed what we once meant by "truth" and "law"; printing changed them again, and now television and the computer change them once more. Such changes occur quickly, surely, and, in a sense, silently. Lexicographers hold no plebiscites on the matter. No manuals are written to explain what is happening, and the schools are oblivious to it. The old words

Tomorrow's technology, yesterday.

still look the same, are still used in the same kinds of sentences. But they do not have the same meanings; in some cases, they have opposite meanings. And this is what Thamus wishes to teach us—that technology imperiously commandeers our most important terminology. It redefines "freedom," "truth," "intelligence," "fact," "wisdom," "memory," "history"—all the words we live by. And it does not pause to tell us. And we do not pause to ask.

... There are several more principles to be mined from the judgment of Thamus that require mentioning because they presage all I will write about. For instance, Thamus warns that the pupils of Theuth will develop an undeserved reputation for wisdom. He means to say that those who cultivate competence in the use of a new technology become an elite group that are granted undeserved authority and prestige by those who have no such competence. There are different ways of expressing the interesting implications of this fact. Harold Innis, the father of modern communication studies, repeatedly spoke of the "knowledge monopolies" created by important technologies. He meant precisely what Thamus had in mind: those who have control over the workings of a particular technology accumulate power and inevitably form a kind of conspiracy against those who have no access to the specialized knowledge made available by the technology. In his book *The Bias of Communication*, Innis provides many historical examples of how a new technology "busted up" a traditional knowledge monopoly and created a new one presided over by a different group. Another way of saying this is that the benefits and deficits of a new technology are not distributed equally. There are, as it were, winners and losers. It is both puzzling and poignant that on many occasions the losers, out of ignorance, have actually cheered the winners, and some still do.

Let us take as an example the case of television. In the United States, where television has taken hold more deeply than anywhere else, many people find it a blessing, not least those who have achieved high-paying, gratifying careers in television as executives, technicians, newscasters, and entertainers. It should surprise no one that such people, forming as they do a new knowledge monopoly, should cheer themselves and defend and promote television technology. On the other hand and in the long run, television may bring a gradual end to the careers of schoolteachers, since school was an invention of the printing press and must stand or fall on the issue of how much importance the printed word has. For four hundred years, schoolteachers have been part of the knowledge monopoly created by printing, and they are now witnessing the breakup of that monopoly. It appears as if they can do little to prevent that breakup, but surely there is something perverse about schoolteachers being enthusiastic about what is happening. Such enthusiasm always calls to my mind an image of some turn-of-the-century blacksmith who not only sings the praises of the automobile but also believes that his business will be enhanced by it. We know now that his business was not enhanced by it; it was rendered obsolete by it, as perhaps the clearheaded blacksmiths knew. What could they have done? Weep, if nothing else.

We have a similar situation in the development and spread of computer technology, for here too there are winners and losers. There can be no disputing that the computer has increased the power of large-scale organizations like the armed forces, or airline companies or banks or tax-collecting agencies. And it is equally clear that the computer is now indispensable to high-level researchers in physics and other natural sciences. But to what extent has computer technology been an advantage to the masses of people? To steelworkers, vegetable-store owners, teachers, garage mechanics, musicians, bricklayers, dentists, and most of the rest into whose lives the computer now intrudes? Their private matters have been made more accessible to powerful institutions. They are more easily tracked and controlled; are subjected to more examinations; are increasingly mystified by the decisions made about them; are often reduced to mere numerical objects. They are inundated by junk mail. They are easy targets for advertising agencies and political organizations. The schools teach their children to operate computerized systems instead of teaching things that are more valuable to children. In a word, almost nothing that they need happens to the losers. Which is why they are losers.

It is to be expected that the winners will encourage the losers to be enthusiastic about computer technology. That is the way of winners, and so they sometimes tell the losers that with personal computers the average person can balance a checkbook more neatly, keep better track of recipes, and make more logical shopping lists. They also tell them that their lives will be conducted more efficiently. But discreetly they neglect to say from whose point of view the efficiency is warranted or what might be its costs. Should the losers grow skeptical, the winners dazzle them with the wondrous feats of computers, almost all of which have only marginal relevance to the quality of the losers' lives but which are nonetheless impressive. Eventually, the losers succumb, in part because they believe, as Thamus prophesied, that the specialized knowledge of the masters of a new technology is a form of wisdom. The masters come to believe this as well, as Thamus also prophesied. The result is that certain questions do not arise. For example, to whom will the technology give greater power and freedom? And whose power and freedom will be reduced by it?

I have perhaps made all of this sound like a well-planned conspiracy, as if the winners know all too well what is being won and what lost. But this is not quite how it happens. For one thing, in cultures that have a democratic ethos, relatively weak traditions, and a high receptivity to new technologies, everyone is inclined to be enthusiastic about technological change, believing that its benefits will eventually spread evenly among the entire population. Especially in the United States, where the lust for what is new has no bounds, do we find this childlike conviction most widely held. Indeed, in America, social change of any kind is rarely seen as resulting in winners and losers, a condition that stems in part from Americans' much-documented optimism. As for change brought on by technology, this native optimism is exploited by entrepreneurs, who work hard to infuse the population with a unity of improbable hope, for they know that it is economically unwise to reveal the price to be paid for technological change. One might say, then, that, if there is a conspiracy of any kind, it is that of a culture conspiring against itself.

In addition to this, and more important, it is not always clear, at least in the early stages of a technology's intrusion into a culture, who will gain most by it and who will lose most. This is because the changes wrought by technology are subtle if not downright mysterious, one might even say wildly unpredictable. Among the most unpredictable are those that might be labeled ideological. This is the sort of change Thamus had in mind when he warned that writers will come to rely on external signs instead of their own internal resources, and that they will receive quantities of information without proper instruction. He meant that new technologies change what we mean by "knowing" and "truth"; they alter those deeply embedded habits of thought which give to a culture its sense of what the world is like—a sense of what is the natural order of things, of what is reasonable, of what is necessary, of what is inevitable, of what is real. Since such changes are expressed in changed meanings of old words, I will hold off . . . discussing the massive ideological transformation now occurring in the United States. Here, I should like to give only one example of how technology creates new conceptions of what is real and, in the process, undermines older conceptions. I refer to the seemingly harmless practice of assigning marks or grades to the answers students give on examinations. This procedure seems so natural to most of us that we are hardly aware of its significance. We may even find it difficult to imagine that the number or letter is a tool or, if you will, a technology; still less that, when we use such a technology to judge someone's behavior, we have done something peculiar. In point of fact, the first instance of grading students' papers occurred at Cambridge University in 1792 at the suggestion of a tutor named William Farish.[3] No one knows much about William Farish; not more than a handful have ever heard of him. And yet his idea that a quantitative value should be assigned to human thoughts was a major step toward constructing a mathematical concept of reality. If a number can be given to the quality of a thought, then a number can be given to the qualities of mercy, love, hate, beauty, creativity, intelligence, even sanity itself. When Galileo said that the language of nature is written in mathematics, he did not mean to include human feeling or accomplishment or insight. But most of us are now inclined to make these inclusions. Our psychologists, sociologists, and educators find it quite impossible to do their work without numbers. They believe that without numbers they cannot acquire or express authentic knowledge.

I shall not argue here that this is a stupid or dangerous idea, only that it is peculiar. What is even more peculiar is that so many of us do not find the idea peculiar. To say that someone should be doing better work because he has an IQ of 134, or that someone is a 7.2 on a sensitivity scale, or that this man's essay on the rise of capitalism is an A—and that man's is a C+ would have sounded like gibberish to Galileo or Shakespeare or Thomas Jefferson. If it makes sense to us, that is because our minds have been conditioned by the technology of numbers so that we see the world differently than they did. Our understanding of what is real is different. Which is another way of saying that embedded in every tool is an ideological bias, a predisposition to construct the world as one thing rather than another, to value one thing over another, to amplify one sense or skill or attitude more loudly than another.

[3] This fact is documented in Keith Hoskin's "The Examination, Disciplinary Power and Rational Schooling," in *History of Education*, vol. VIII, no. 2 (1979), pp. 135–46. Professor Hoskin provides the following story about Farish: Farish was a professor of engineering at Cambridge and designed and installed a movable partition wall in his Cambridge home. The wall moved on pulleys between downstairs and upstairs. One night, while working late downstairs and feeling cold, Farish pulled down the partition. This is not much of a story, and history fails to disclose what happened next. All of which shows how little is known of William Farish.

This is what Marshall McLuhan[4] meant by his famous apho-   15
rism "The medium is the message." This is what Marx meant
when he said, "Technology discloses man's mode of dealing with
nature" and creates the "conditions of intercourse" by which we
relate to each other. It is what Wittgenstein meant when, in refer-
ring to our most fundamental technology, he said that language is
not merely a vehicle of thought but also the driver. And it is what
Thamus wished the inventor Theuth to see. This is, in short, an
ancient and persistent piece of wisdom, perhaps most simply
expressed in the old adage that, to a man with a hammer, everything looks like a nail. Without being too literal, we may extend
the truism: To a man with a pencil, everything looks like a list. To
a man with a camera, everything looks like an image. To a man
with a computer, everything looks like data. And to a man with a
grade sheet, everything looks like a number.

But such prejudices are not always apparent at the start of a
technology's journey, which is why no one can safely conspire to
be a winner in technological change. Who would have imagined,
for example, whose interests and what world-view would be ultimately advanced by the invention of the mechanical clock? The
clock had its origins in the Benedictine monasteries of the twelfth
and thirteenth centuries. The impetus behind the invention was
to provide a more or less precise regularity to the routines of the
monasteries, which required, among other things, seven periods
of devotion during the course of the day. The bells of the monastery were to be rung to signal the canonical hours; the mechanical clock was the technology that could provide precision to these
rituals of devotion. And indeed it did. But what the monks did not
foresee was that the clock is a means not merely of keeping track
of the hours but also of synchronizing and controlling the actions
of men. And thus, by the middle of the fourteenth century, the
clock had moved outside the walls of the monastery, and brought
a new and precise regularity to the life of the workman and the
merchant. "The mechanical clock," as Lewis Mumford wrote,
"made possible the idea of regular production, regular working
hours and a standardized product." In short, without the clock,

[4]Marshall McLuhan (1911–1980): Canadian communications theorist and literary
and media critic. [Editor's note.]

capitalism would have been quite impossible.[5] The paradox, the surprise, and the wonder are that the clock was invented by men who wanted to devote themselves more rigorously to God; it ended as the technology of greatest use to men who wished to devote themselves to the accumulation of money. In the eternal struggle between God and Mammon, the clock quite unpredictably favored the latter.

Unforeseen consequences stand in the way of all those who think they see clearly the direction in which a new technology will take us. Not even those who invent a technology can be assumed to be reliable prophets, as Thamus warned. Gutenberg, for example, was by all accounts a devout Catholic who would have been horrified to hear that accursed heretic Luther describe printing as "God's highest act of grace, whereby the business of the Gospel is driven forward." Luther understood, as Gutenberg did not, that the mass-produced book, by placing the Word of God on every kitchen table, makes each Christian his own theologian—one might even say his own priest, or, better, from Luther's point of view, his own pope. In the struggle between unity and diversity of religious belief, the press favored the latter, and we can assume that this possibility never occurred to Gutenberg.

Thamus understood well the limitations of inventors in grasping the social and psychological—that is, ideological—bias of their own inventions. We can imagine him addressing Gutenberg in the following way: "Gutenberg, my paragon of inventors, the discoverer of an art is not the best judge of the good or harm which will accrue to those who practice it. So it is in this; you, who are the father of printing, have out of fondness for your offspring come to believe it will advance the cause of the Holy Roman See, whereas in fact it will sow discord among believers; it will destroy the authenticity of your beloved Church and destroy its monopoly."

We can imagine that Thamus would also have pointed out to Gutenberg, as he did to Theuth, that the new invention would create a vast population of readers who "will receive a quantity of information without proper instruction . . . [who will be] filled

---

[5]For a detailed exposition of Mumford's position on the impact of the mechanical clock, see his *Technics and Civilization* (New York: Harcourt Brace, 1934).

with the conceit of wisdom instead of real wisdom"; that reading, in other words, will compete with older forms of learning. This is yet another principle of technological change we may infer from the judgment of Thamus: new technologies compete with old ones—for time, for attention, for money, for prestige, but mostly for dominance of their world-view. This competition is implicit once we acknowledge that a medium contains an ideological bias. And it is a fierce competition, as only ideological competitions can be. It is not merely a matter of tool against tool—the alphabet attacking ideographic writing, the printing press attacking the illuminated manuscript, the photograph attacking the art of painting, television attacking the printed word. When media make war against each other, it is a case of world-views in collision.

In the United States, we can see such collisions everywhere—   20
in politics, in religion, in commerce—but we see them most clearly in the schools, where two great technologies confront each other in uncompromising aspect for the control of students' minds. On the one hand, there is the world of the printed word with its emphasis on logic, sequence, history, exposition, objectivity, detachment, and discipline. On the other, there is the world of television with its emphasis on imagery, narrative, presentness, simultaneity, intimacy, immediate gratification, and quick emotional response. Children come to school having been deeply conditioned by the biases of television. There, they encounter the world of the printed word. A sort of psychic battle takes place, and there are many casualties—children who can't learn to read or won't, children who cannot organize their thought into logical structure even in a simple paragraph, children who cannot attend to lectures or oral explanations for more than a few minutes at a time. They are failures, but not because they are stupid. They are failures because there is a media war going on, and they are on the wrong side—at least for the moment. Who knows what schools will be like twenty-five years from now? Or fifty? In time, the type of student who is currently a failure may be considered a success. The type who is now successful may be regarded as a handicapped learner—slow to respond, far too detached, lacking in emotion, inadequate in creating mental pictures of reality. Consider: What Thamus called the "conceit of wisdom"—the unreal knowledge acquired through the written word—eventually became the pre-eminent form of knowledge valued by the schools.

There is no reason to suppose that such a form of knowledge must always remain so highly valued.

To take another example: In introducing the personal computer to the classroom, we shall be breaking a four-hundred-year-old truce between the gregariousness and openness fostered by orality and the introspection and isolation fostered by the printed word. Orality stresses group learning, cooperation, and a sense of social responsibility, which is the context within which Thamus believed proper instruction and real knowledge must be communicated. Print stresses individualized learning, competition, and personal autonomy. Over four centuries, teachers, while emphasizing print, have allowed orality its place in the classroom, and have therefore achieved a kind of pedagogical peace between these two forms of learning, so that what is valuable in each can be maximized. Now comes the computer, carrying anew the banner of private learning and individual problem-solving. Will the widespread use of computers in the classroom defeat once and for all the claims of communal speech? Will the computer raise egocentrism to the status of a virtue?

These are the kinds of questions that technological change brings to mind when one grasps, as Thamus did, that technological competition ignites total war, which means it is not possible to contain the effects of a new technology to a limited sphere of human activity. If this metaphor puts the matter too brutally, we may try a gentler, kinder one: Technological change is neither additive nor subtractive. It is ecological. I mean "ecological" in the same sense as the word is used by environmental scientists. One significant change generates total change. If you remove the caterpillars from a given habitat, you are not left with the same environment minus caterpillars: You have a new environment, and you have reconstituted the conditions of survival; the same is true if you add caterpillars to an environment that has had none. This is how the ecology of media works as well. A new technology does not add or subtract something. It changes everything. In the year 1500, fifty years after the printing press was invented, we did not have old Europe plus the printing press. We had a different Europe. After television, the United States was not America plus television; television gave a new coloration to every political campaign, to every home, to every school, to every church, to every industry. And that is why the competition among media is so fierce. Surrounding every technology are institutions whose orga-nization—not to mention their reason for being—reflects the world-view promoted by the technology. Therefore, when an old technology is assaulted by a new one, institutions are threatened. When institutions are threatened, a culture finds itself in crisis. This is serious business, which is why we learn nothing when educators ask, Will students learn mathematics better by com-puters than by textbooks? Or when businessmen ask, Through which medium can we sell more products? Or when preachers ask, Can we reach more people through television than through radio? Or when politicians ask, How effective are messages sent through different media? Such questions have an immediate, practical value to those who ask them, but they are diversionary. They direct our attention away from the serious social, intellec-tual, and institutional crises that new media foster.

Perhaps an analogy here will help to underline the point. In speaking of the meaning of a poem, T. S. Eliot[6] remarked that the chief use of the overt content of poetry is "to satisfy one habit of the reader, to keep his mind diverted and quiet, while the poem does its work upon him: much as the imaginary burglar is always provided with a bit of nice meat for the house-dog." In other words, in asking their practical questions, educators, entrepre-neurs, preachers, and politicians are like the house-dog munch-ing peacefully on the meat while the house is looted. Perhaps some of them know this and do not especially care. After all, a nice piece of meat, offered graciously, does take care of the prob-lem of where the next meal will come from. But for the rest of us, it cannot be acceptable to have the house invaded without protest or at least awareness.

What we need to consider about the computer has nothing to do with its efficiency as a teaching tool. We need to know in what ways it is altering our conception of learning, and how, in con-junction with television, it undermines the old idea of school. Who cares how many boxes of cereal can be sold via television? We need to know if television changes our conception of reality, the relationship of the rich to the poor, the idea of happiness itself. A preacher who confines himself to considering how a

---

[6]T. S. Eliot (1888–1965): American and British poet, literary critic, and playwright. [Editor's note.]

medium can increase his audience will miss the significant question: In what sense do new media alter what is meant by religion, by church, even by God? And if the politician cannot think beyond the next election, then *we* must wonder about what new media do to the idea of political organization and to the conception of citizenship.

To help us do this, we have the judgment of Thamus, who, in 25 the way of legends, teaches us what Harold Innis, in his way, tried to. New technologies alter the structure of our interests: the things we think *about*. They alter the character of our symbols: the things we think *with*. And they alter the nature of community: the arena in which thoughts develop. As Thamus spoke to Innis across the centuries, it is essential that we listen to their conversation, join in it, revitalize it. For something has happened in America that is strange and dangerous, and there is only a dull and even stupid awareness of what it is—in part because it has no name. I call it Technopoly.

For Discussion and Writing

1. While Postman believes that Thamus's judgment contains "several sound principles" (par. 2), he also argues that the king's response to Theuth also contains an instructive error. What is the error? How is the mistake related to Postman's main point?

2. Although Postman concedes the value of technological progress, he proposes that in judging technology, "it is better to err on the side of Thamusian skepticism" (par. 3) than on the side of the "Technophiles." Do you agree with this principle? Why or why not?

3. **connections**   For Postman, every technology is both a blessing and a curse; moreover, every technology brings some form of "ideological bias" (par. 14). Compare his point of view with Sherry Turkle's in "Can You Hear Me Now?" (p. 227). Do Turkle's arguments support or align with Postman's? How? Where do the author's differ?

4. Writing before the popularity of the Internet, Postman asks skeptically: "But to what extent has computer technology been an advantage to the masses of people?" (par. 10). How would you answer that question now? For example, what effect has the Internet had on "knowledge monopolies" (par. 8)? Has it changed our ideas of "knowing" and "truth" (par. 13)?

AYMAR JEAN CHRISTIAN

The Problem of YouTube

Aymar Jean Christian (b. 1984) is a doctoral student at the Annenberg School for Communications at the University of Pennsylvania. His research focuses on new media, especially film and Web video. In addition to his scholarly work and presentations, Christian's writing has appeared in the Wall Street Journal, Newsweek, *the* Washington Post, *and* FlowTV, *an online journal covering television and new media.*

In this essay from FlowTV, *he discusses YouTube as a platform for filmmakers. YouTube represents the freedom and chaos of the Web, as well as an opportunity for amateurs to publicize their work. Yet for Christian, the site seems to benefit only a small group of users, as it fails to build "quality audiences for inventive and 'quality' forms of storytelling." As you read, consider your own experience with sites like YouTube. Why do you visit them? Why do you return to them? What do you expect them to provide?*

Few people have heard of Strike TV. The web video network, started in 2008 by Hollywood professionals protesting during the writer's strike, was an act of revolt against the industry. But it was also a protest against the industry's antithesis: YouTube. Caught in the middle, between an industry trying to control the web and the user-generated Internet, filmmakers, writers and directors decided to strike out on their own. "There wasn't an outlet online for us," founder and CEO Peter Hyoguchi told me. "There's not a lot of incentive for a Hollywood professional to put something on YouTube when it's going to be shoulder to shoulder with a cat jumping on a piano." Strike TV started its own website, while still cross-distributing on YouTube, to showcase independent films and web series made by professionals working outside the industry system: content intended to have crisper writing and cinematography than YouTube's most popular videos.

After five years of domination, YouTube is synonymous with

web video. Yet almost since its early years, the site has had strong detractors and competitors, mostly from corporations seeking more control over content and more advertiser-friendly spaces. The problem of YouTube has always been about control over the growing market for web video. Over the last few years a new group of YouTube detractors has emerged: independent and professional filmmakers and entrepreneurs like those who populate Strike TV. The complaint is about control, again, but also highlights broader qualms about the digital economy. Plainly, YouTube has come to represent the chaos of the web itself, the chaotic home to amateurs churning out low quality content to rack up views from low ad rates.[1] What YouTube's critics seek is a more sustainable and less "viral" way to fund non-corporate content: a sustainable industry for independent web video.

A late-summer imbroglio reveals the tension. In what has become its own genre of reporting, *The Business Insider* published a list of "the richest independent YouTube stars," all of which earned more than six figures.[2] The top YouTubers are personalities who vlog, with a handful but growing number of independent filmmakers making comedic shorts. *Business Insider*'s list set off a debate in the "other" web video community: filmmakers who are professionally oriented making more expensive-to-produce episodic programs: web series, primarily. Tubefilter, the community's main site, called it an "identity crisis."[3] YouTubers are great at building audiences[4] but not the market necessary to fund a larger number of independent professionals, they claim. It has been good to several dozen personalities who have built up viewers, but it hasn't created anything like television: advertiser-friendly, capable of bringing in new professionals, stressing quality (production) along with quantity ("views").

The core of the argument against YouTube is simple: the site is "viral." Few people beyond the small, relatively stable group of YouTubers have been able to replicate their skill at getting millions to tune in consistently. Advertisers, save Old Spice, are growing disillusioned.[5] In interviews with independent producers, I've heard this time and again: YouTube puts the focus on "views" not on building quality audiences for inventive and "quality" forms of storytelling. Simplicity aside, they have a point. To be sure, YouTube is a complex site, easily misunderstood.[6] YouTube is both a place for "amateurs"—the best of which are no longer amateurs and get lucrative product placement and TV deals[7]—and corporations distributing content like music videos. It's a social networking site and a broadcasting one. It's a complex organism with its own internal tensions.[8]

But talk to filmmakers, many of whom spend thousands of dol-   5 lars creating often complex and lush narratives (music videos, sitcoms, dramas, docu-series) and they lament how difficult it is to break through the sea of content. The past couple of years have seen growing disenchantment with the "long tail," the idea that the web has created viable markets for those beyond the elite few.[9] Matthew Hindman argues, somewhat persuasively, the Internet actually creates large inequalities. A few sites dominate traffic, overshadowing a large number of sites without many views at all and a noticeable "missing middle."[10] In the world of web video, the missing middle consists of sites who get more views and traffic than the unseen masses, but not enough to generate revenue and mass visibility: the recently profitable *Huffington Post* is at the top, the blogger in his basement at the bottom, and few blogs can survive in between, the theory goes. Independent filmmakers, like the ones Strike TV wooed, are in the latter category. YouTube seems to be replicating this dynamic, long thought to apply only to corporate sites (Google, CNN) and the minor blogs and user-generated content that can't compete. The top YouTubers are the tip of the site's iceberg, and they are the only ones making six figures.

Web video entrepreneurs and companies have been fleeing. First went the mainstream media and its stars, who created comedy sites as anti-YouTubes: NBC, TBS, and HBO count among the few serious efforts, all of which eventually shuttered, except a few, like FunnyOrDie or Viacom's Atom. Sony has developed Crackle as space for high quality web series and films, working with brands for product placement and branded entertainment. Of course Hulu is the most visible "YouTube killer," its ideological antithesis, the corporate grandpa to YouTube's youngsters.[11] None of these sites has matched YouTube's dominance in revenue, video views or unique viewers, but they do make money, in part because they curate their content. As opposed to the vast sea, they give advertisers a small pond, clean and closed.

Seeing Hulu's success, a handful of independent entrepreneurs are now trying to replicate its walled-garden model. Banking on low-cost, high-definition videos, they offer a chance for filmmakers to reach niche audiences and match them with advertisers so they can make money: a place for semi-skilled artists rather than, say, upstart personalities, to crudely caricature YouTube's stars. Strike TV was among the first. Many, like MyDamnChannel and Babelgum, focus on comedy, while others, like Koldcast or Strike, are omnibus sites focused on producers with interesting ideas. Over the last year, sites targeting minorities have debuted, trying to connect black, gay, Latino and women-produced shows with hard-to-reach audiences: RowdyOrbit, GLO TV Network, Digital Chick TV, VisionTube, BetterBlackTV, among others.[12] YouTube, while diverse, is a tough space for minorities to break out.

"I've been on YouTube but there's a limit to how much you can get out of it," VisionTube's creator and mainstream media veteran Charles Williams told me in an interview. He started the site for multicultural web series and films after hearing the troubles of black filmmakers. "We would love to take our stuff off of You-Tube," they told him. "We actually professionally thought about this [their work], cast it and produced it."

The debate over YouTube is hardly surprising. New media, from radio to television, often create new opportunities for a diverse group of players: amateurs, professionally oriented independents and corporations. When opportunities arise, people rush in and tussle over the future of the market and the meaning of the medium.[13] What the web adds is the greater potential for a "middle" ground between amateurs and corporations. With low barriers to distribution, independents—film school graduates, skilled amateurs and corporate refugees—have access to advertising and viewers.

But creating a sustainable market for independent video is 10 hard. A lot of puzzle pieces need to come together. Independent video networks and filmmakers need to learn from YouTubers' skill at getting buzz and views. The press needs to shower as much attention on the middle-market as they do television (Hulu) and user-generated content (YouTube). Policymakers need to safeguard net neutrality. Video measurement needs to be streamlined. Advertising rates and targeting strategies need to mature. Instead of searching for "YouTube killers," web video creators would do well to work towards a diversified market, like that for cinema, a place where Hollywood, independents and industry outsiders focus on separate markets, ultimately profiting and benefiting from each other.

Notes

1. The parallel debate in the world of web publishing is over "content farms." See MacManus, Richard. 2009. Content Farms: Why Media, Blogs & Google Should Be Worried. ReadWriteWeb, 13 December, http://www.readwriteweb.com/archives/content_farms_impact.php.

2. Wei, William. 2010. Meet The YouTube Stars Making $100,000 Plus Per Year. *Business Insider.* 19 August, http://www.businessinsider.com/meet-the-richest-independent-youtube-stars-2010-8.

3. Hustvedt, Marc. 2010. The Web Series Identity Crisis. *Tubefilter.* 3 September, http://news.tubefilter.tv/2010/09/03/the-web-series-identity-crisis.

4. Miller, Liz Shannon. 2010. The Lessons YouTubers Teach Us. *NewTeeVee.* 30 August, http://newteevee.com/2010/08/30/the-lessons-youtubers-teach-us.

5. Louderback, Jim. 2010. There, I Said It: Screw Viral Videos. *Advertising Age.* 30 August.

6. Green, Joshua. 2008. "MisUnderstanding YouTube." *Flow.* 8 August.

7. YouTube's Lucas Cruikshank is the site's most successful crossover to TV, see Cohen, Joshua. (2010). 'Fred: The Movie' Draws 7.6 Million Viewers. *Tubefilter.* September 20, http://news.tubefilter.tv/2010/09/20/fred-the-movie-draws-7-6-million-viewers. For examples of how brands use YouTubers, see Slutsky, Irina. (2010), Meet YouTube's Most In-Demand Brand Stars. *Advertising Age*, 13 September, http://adage.com/digital/article?article_id=145844.

8. See Burgess, Jean and Green, Joshua. *YouTube: Online Video and Participatory Culture.* Cambridge: Polity Press, 2009, and Jarrett, K. 2008. Beyond Broadcast Yourself: The future of YouTube. *Media International Australia,* 126, February, pp. 132–144.

9. Anderson, Chris. *The Long Tail: Why the Future of Business Is Selling Less of More.* New York: Hyperion, 2008.

10. Hindman, Matthew S. *The Myth of Digital Democracy.* Princeton: Princeton University Press, 2009.

11. Christian, Aymar Jean. 2010. Is Hulu Winning the Web Video Wars? Televisual. 29 July, http://blog.ajchristian.org/2010/07/29/has-hulu-won.

12. Christian, Aymar Jean. 2010. Rise of the Black Network? Online and On-Air, Growing Alternatives to YouTube and BET. *Black Web 2.0.* 15 October, http://www.blackweb20.com/2010/10/15/rise-of-the-black-network-online-and-on-air-growing-alternatives-to-youtube-and-bet.

13. Radio is a classic example. As Susan Douglas noted in her history of early radio: "amateur operators constructed their sets of meanings around radio, meanings with which large institutions had to come to terms." Douglas, Susan. *Inventing American Broadcasting, 1899–1922.* Baltimore: Johns Hopkins University Press, 1987, xxvii. For a broader perspective on the cycle of

new media, see also Wu, Tim. *The Master Switch: The Rise and Fall of Information Empires*. New York: Knopf, 2010.

For Discussion and Writing

1. What do YouTube's main critics seek, according to Christian?
2. In the article, Strike TV founder Peter Hyoguchi claims, "There's not a lot of incentive for a Hollywood professional to put something on YouTube when it's going to be shoulder to shoulder with a cat jumping on a piano" (par. 1). What point is he highlighting? How do you compare the value of popular amateur online videos with the work of professional filmmakers, writers, and directors?
3. **connections** According to Steven Johnson in "Watching TV Makes You Smarter" (p. 275), people mistakenly assume that "mass culture follows a path declining steadily toward lowest-common-denominator standards, presumably because the 'masses' want dumb, simple pleasures" (par. 3), when in fact, mass culture is "getting more cognitively demanding, not less" (par. 3). Could Johnson's argument apply to YouTube and other Web video sites, where people can create and distribute their own work? Do you think Web videos will get "more cognitively demanding" in the future? Why or why not?
4. Christian notes that YouTube is a "chaotic home to amateurs churning out low quality content to rack up views from low ad rates" (par. 2). What qualities make an amateur video go "viral"? Can you isolate specific characteristics common to the most popular or memorable videos that you have seen from the site? How might you generalize about YouTube's aesthetic? Do you agree with Christian that the content is mostly "low quality"?

FARHAD MANJOO

Is Facebook a Fad?

A graduate of Cornell University, Farhad Manjoo (b. 1978) now writes a regular technology column for Slate *and contributes frequently to* National Public Radio. *Before working for* Slate, *Manjoo wrote for* Salon.com *and* Wired News. *He is also the author of* True Enough: Learning to Live in a Post-Fact Society *(2008). First published in* Slate, *"Is Facebook a Fad?" was part of Manjoo's series on the future of mobile gadgets, the Internet, and home entertainment. Do you use Facebook and other online social networking sites? How many of your relationships—personal, commercial, professional—are already conducted online? As you read Manjoo's essay, reflect on how social networking sites may evolve in the future.*

On Wednesday, to no one's surprise, Google launched yet another effort to take on Facebook. The new service is called +1, and it works just like the Facebook Like buttons you now see all over the Web. When you come across a link in Google's search results that you want to share with your friends, you can click the +1 button. When your friends do a similar search, they'll see your recommendation. For now, the +1 button appears only on Google's search pages, but the company will soon allow publishers to place them on other sites, too. This might sound superfluous—don't we already have enough ways to tell people what we like online? With Facebook, Twitter, Reddit, the nearly departed Digg, and good old email, it sometimes seems like the Internet is overflowing with suggestions. How much more recommending do Web companies think we can stand? Will this ever stop?

Nope. Not soon anyway. Over the last few weeks I've been writing a series on the future of technology. In this last piece, I'm looking at one of the most volatile, exciting, and unpredictable parts of the Web—social networking. The proliferation of social sites hit its peak a few years ago, when every start-up and Web giant seemed to be releasing its own network. Now the fight seems relatively settled: Facebook, with its more than 600 million "active users," has trounced everyone else, and with the Like button and the rest of its plugins, it has managed to co-opt the rest of the Web, too.

Despite this success, I often hear from readers who suggest that Facebook might be a fad. Someday soon something new will come along, they argue, and we'll all switch over to that. The larger complaint is that social networking isn't an important tech trend—that it's something we'll get over, and that what really determines the future of tech are the chips, algorithms, and other stuff computer scientists work on. These comments, it seems to me, reflect a deep concern about what all our friending, Liking, and sharing amount to. Readers often complain that Facebook in particular, and social networking in general, detracts from real-life relationships. We're worried not just that it's going to change the Web, but our offline lives as well.

Let me go out on limb and declare that Facebook isn't going to go away anytime soon. The site is more entrenched than just about any other technology we use. It's easy to go to a new search engine—just type *Bing* instead of *Google*—and there's nothing stopping you from switching your brand of computer or cellphone. You can't switch over to a new social network, though, unless your friends do so as well. Sure, this could happen—fashions change, of course, and the inherent stickiness of social networks didn't save all the ones that came before Facebook. But Facebook seems to have hit a critical mass. Not only does it have a huge number of users (more than any previous social network), but its audience is spread across every demographic (which wasn't true of MySpace), and they're ferociously committed to the site (nearly half log in every day). It also shows no signs of slowing its growth—and the bigger Facebook gets, the harder it becomes to switch to a new platform. If a storm of criticism surrounding its privacy practices and its frequent, confusing redesigns haven't done anything to stem its growth (and those controversies haven't), I'm not sure what could push Facebook off the main stage in the near term.

The big question for the future of social networking isn't whether Facebook will be the largest and most influential site five 5 years from now. It's whether it will be the only one. Will Facebook be the exclusive catalog of our interests and relationships, or will it coexist with several others?

This is what I meant when I said that the future of social networking was unpredictable. There are huge swaths of the Web that aren't under Facebook's sway: When you email someone a link, share photos on Flickr, or review a restaurant on Yelp, you're engaging in "social" activity outside of Facebook's purview. Sources at Google have told me that even though the search company doesn't have a successful social network of its own (Orkut doesn't count), Google believes it can build a realistic picture of your social life by mining all this other activity. That seems to be what it's doing now: With your permission, Google indexes some or all of your activity on Twitter, Flickr, and Quora. It also keeps track of social networks you're building in Google's own products (people in your Gmail chat list, your Google Contacts, or people you follow on Google Reader). Add all this together and Google has a pretty robust picture of your social connections—and because it's constantly crawling the Web to build its search engine, it can easily pick up what you do on any brand-new network that comes along. This suggests a long-term counterweight to Facebook's power: As long as people keep commenting and voting and writing on sites other than Facebook, Google will be able to build a social network of its own.

On the other hand, Google doesn't have access to the mother-lode of your social activity: stuff you post on Facebook itself, data that is closed off to mining from most other companies online. Every time you press the Like button or use one of Facebook's plugins to post a comment, you're telling Facebook something about yourself and your friends. What's more, Facebook's reach keeps extending. Today, many people connect their activity on a host of sites—including Twitter, Flickr, Quora, Amazon, and Yelp—with their Facebook accounts. They do so because it makes intuitive sense to keep one social network—maintaining separate networks on different sites is too much work. If we're sticking to one network, it makes sense to stay where all our friends are—and that's Facebook.

This will be especially true if Facebook adds better tools for maintaining discrete groups within our larger friend network (which it already does quite well). In other words, hey, maybe

Facebook already has this social-networking thing all wrapped up. We don't know what the site will look like by 2016; it's possible that, with all the ways it's infiltrating the wider Web, Facebook.com will be just one small part of the Facebook empire. You may be using Facebook wherever you are online—and no other network will matter.

Why is any of this important—why do these Web giants want to catalog your interests and relationships? There's an obvious answer—because doing so allows them to sell ads targeted to you—and a less obvious one: Social signals are becoming the primary organizing structure of the Web. Today most of the links you see online are determined by editors or algorithms—that is, by people who create sites manually, or by Google, which uses computers to guess what you might be interested in. But both these methods are imperfect. The people who create *Slate*'s home page every day are just guessing what you'd like to read. Google, meanwhile, serves up thousands of links in response to your query, and even though it's often right, it's far from perfect. Web companies see social data as the solution to this problem: That trail of Likes you're leaving around the Web forms a picture of your deepest desires. With this picture, sites of all kinds— news sites, shopping sites, travel sites—can tailor themselves to your interests. In five years' time, you and your dad may visit the Huffington Post and not see any stories that overlap. The site will know, based on your social network, exactly what you want to read.

This isn't really a novel idea. "Link analysis" was at the heart of 10 PageRank, the breakthrough algorithm that powered Google's revolutionary search engine. When one site linked to another, PageRank saw the link as a recommendation; the more inbound links a site garnered, the higher it tended to appear in Google. But what's a link? It's one human being's decision to tell other human beings that another page on the Web is important—in other words, a social signal. Google's breakthrough was in recognizing that social signals can be a very powerful way of organizing the Web. It was the start of a $100 billion company.

By analyzing our social relationships in much more detail, Facebook is looking to do something even more revolutionary. Tell me what you think of the Facebook revolution—do you look forward to the social-networking future, or do you fear it? Is

Facebook here to stay, or do you think we'll move on to something else?

For Discussion and Writing

1. Some dismiss Facebook as a "fad," but Manjoo declares that the site "isn't going to go away anytime soon" (par. 4). How does he support his claim? What specific reasons does he give?
2. According to Manjoo, Web companies want to track and anticipate your online behavior: "That trail of Likes you're leaving around the Web forms a picture of your deepest desires" (par. 9)? Do you agree? Are you conscious of this process—whether on Facebook or other online activities—in your day-to-day use of the Web?
3. **connections** "Every technology is both a burden and a blessing; not either-or, but this-and-that" (par. 2), writes Neil Postman in "The Judgment of Thamus" (p. 200). How would you apply Postman's claim to social networking sites? Are they more of a blessing than a curse, or vice versa?
4. Manjoo wrote this essay partly as a response to readers of his other columns on technology: "I often hear from readers who suggest that Facebook might be a fad. Someday soon something new will come along, they argue, and we'll all switch over to that. The larger complaint is that social networking isn't an important tech trend. . . . These comments, it seems to me, reflect a deep concern about what all our friending, Liking, and sharing amount to" (par. 3). How would you respond to such claims? Do you agree with them, or with Manjoo? What do you think all our social networking amounts to?

SHERRY TURKLE

Can You Hear Me Now?

*Sherry Turkle (b. 1948) is the Abby Rockefeller Mauzé Professor of the
Social Studies of Science and Technology at the Massachusetts Institute of Technology. Much of her work examines the intersection of sociology, psychology, and technology, especially with regard to our increasing use of computers and other devices. Her books include* Life on the
Screen: Identity in the Age of the Internet *(1995),* The Inner History
of Devices *(2008), and* Alone Together: Why We Expect More from
Technology and Less from Each Other *(2011). She also writes for
publications such as* Wired, New Scientist, *and the* New York Times.

In the following essay, which appeared in Forbes *magazine, Turkle
discusses "five troubles" of our hyperlinked and electronically "tethered" culture. Although she claims these troubles try her own "tethered
soul," they are ultimately ours as much as hers. For Turkle, technologies such as the Internet and text messaging do not merely change the
way we conduct our relationships or do business; rather, they alter our
very conceptions of the self: "Our devices have become more closely
coupled to our sense of our bodies and increasingly feel like extensions
of our minds." As you read, consider the benefits and drawbacks of this
development.*

I have traveled 36 hours to a conference on robotic technology in
central Japan. The grand ballroom is Wi-Fi enabled, and the
speaker is using the Web for his presentation. Laptops are open,
fingers are flying. But the audience is not listening. Most seem to
be doing their e-mail, downloading files, surfing the Web or looking for a cartoon to illustrate an upcoming presentation. Every
once in a while audience members give the speaker some attention, lowering their laptop screens in a kind of digital curtsy.

In the hallway outside the plenary session attendees are on
their phones or using laptops and pdas to check their e-mail.

Clusters of people chat with each other, making dinner plans, "networking" in that old sense of the term—the sense that implies sharing a meal. But at this conference it is clear that what people mostly want from public space is to be alone with their personal networks. It is good to come together physically, but it is more important to stay tethered to the people who define one's virtual identity, the identity that counts. I think of how Freud believed in the power of communities to control and subvert us, and a psychoanalytic pun comes to mind: "virtuality and its discontents."

The phrase comes back to me months later as I interview business consultants who seem to have lost touch with their best instincts for how to maintain the bonds that make them most competitive. They are complaining about the BlackBerry revolution. They accept it as inevitable, decry it as corrosive. Consultants used to talk to one another as they waited to give presentations; now they spend that time doing e-mail. Those who once bonded during limousine rides to airports now spend this time on their BlackBerrys. Some say they are making better use of their "downtime," but they argue their point without conviction. This waiting time and going-to-the-airport time was never downtime; it was work time. It was precious time when far-flung global teams solidified relationships and refined ideas.

We live in techno-enthusiastic times, and we are most likely to celebrate our gadgets. Certainly the advertising that sells us our devices has us working from beautiful, remote locations that signal our status. We are connected, tethered, so important that our physical presence is no longer required. There is much talk of new efficiencies; we can work from anywhere and all the time. But tethered life is complex; it is helpful to measure our thrilling new networks against what they may be doing to us as people.

Here I offer five troubles that try my tethered soul.   5

THERE IS A NEW STATE OF THE SELF, ITSELF

By the 1990's the Internet provided spaces for the projection of self. Through online games known as Multi-User Domains, one was able to create avatars that could be deployed into virtual lives. Although the games often took the forms of medieval quests, players admitted that virtual environments owed their holding power to the opportunities they offered for exploring identity. The plain represented themselves as glamorous; the introverted could try out being bold. People built the dream houses in the virtual that they could not afford in the real. They took online jobs of responsibility. They often had relationships, partners and even "marriages" of significant emotional importance. They had lots of virtual sex.

These days it is easier for people without technical expertise to blend their real and virtual lives. In the world of Second Life, a virtual world produced by Linden Lab, you can make real money; you can run a real business. Indeed, for many who enjoy online life, it is easier to express intimacy in the virtual world than in rl, that being real life. For those who are lonely yet fearful of intimacy, online life provides environments where one can be a loner yet not alone, have the illusion of companionship without the demands of sustained, intimate friendship.

Since the late 1990s social computing has offered an opportunity to experiment with a virtual second self. Now this metaphor doesn't go far enough. Our new online intimacies create a world in which it makes sense to speak of a new state of the self, itself. "I am on my cell . . . online . . . instant messaging . . . on the Web" — these phrases suggest a new placement of the subject, wired into society through technology.

ARE WE LOSING THE TIME TO TAKE OUR TIME?

The self that grows up with multitasking and rapid response measures success by calls made, e-mails answered and messages responded to. Self-esteem is calibrated by what the technology proposes, by what it makes easy. We live a contradiction: Insisting that our world is increasingly complex, we nevertheless have created a communications culture that has decreased the time available for us to sit and think, uninterrupted. We are primed to receive a quick message to which we are expected to give a rapid response. Children growing up with this may never know another way. Their experience raises a question for us all: Are we leaving enough time to take our time on the things that matter?

We spend hours keeping up with our e-mails. One person tells 10 me, "I look at my watch to see the time. I look at my BlackBerry to get a sense of my life." Think of the BlackBerry user watching the BlackBerry movie of his life as someone watching a movie that takes on a life of its own. People become alienated from their own experience and anxious about watching a version of their lives scrolling along faster than they can handle. They are not able to keep up with the unedited version of their lives, but they are responsible for it. People speak of BlackBerry addiction. Yet in modern life we have been made into self-disciplined souls who mind the rules, the time, our tasks. Always-on/always-on-you technology takes the job of self-monitoring to a new level.

BlackBerry users describe that sense of encroachment of the device on their time. One says, "I don't have enough time alone with my mind"; another, "I artificially make time to think." Such formulations depend on an "I" separate from the technology, a self that can put the technology aside so as to function apart from its demands. But it's in conflict with a growing reality of lives lived in the presence of screens, whether on a laptop, palmtop, cell phone or BlackBerry. We are learning to see ourselves as cyborgs, at one with our devices. To put it most starkly: To make more time means turning off our devices, disengaging from the always-on culture. But this is not a simple proposition, since our devices have become more closely coupled to our sense of our bodies and increasingly feel like extensions of our minds.

Our tethering devices provide a social and psychological Global Positioning System, a form of navigation for tethered selves. One television producer, accustomed to being linked to the world via her cell and Palm handheld, revealed that for her, the Palm's inner spaces were where her self resides: "When my Palm crashed it was like a death. It was more than I could handle. I felt as though I had lost my mind."

THE TETHERED ADOLESCENT

Kids get cell phones from their parents. In return they are expected to answer their parents' calls. On the one hand this arrangement gives teenagers new freedoms. On the other they do not have the experience of being alone and having to count on themselves; there is always a parent on speed dial. This provides comfort in a dangerous world, yet there is a price to pay in the development of autonomy. There used to be a moment in the life of an urban child, usually between the ages of 12 and 14, when there was a first time to navigate the city alone. It was a rite of passage that communicated, "You are on your own and responsible. If you feel frightened, you have to experience these feelings." The cell phone tether buffers this moment; with the parents on tap, the children think differently about themselves.

Adolescents naturally want to check out ideas and attitudes with peers. But when technology brings us to the point where we're used to sharing thoughts and feelings instantaneously, it can lead to a new dependence. Emotional life can move from "I have a feeling, I want to call a friend," to "I want to feel something, I need to make a call." In either case it comes at the expense of cultivating the ability to be alone and to manage and contain one's emotions.

And what of adolescence as a time of self-reflection? We communicate with instant messages, "check-in" cell calls and emoticons. All of these are meant to quickly communicate a state. They are not intended to open a dialogue about complexity of feeling. (Technological determinism has its place here: Cell calls get poor reception, are easily dropped and are optimized for texting.) The culture that grows up around the cell phone is a communications culture, but it is not necessarily a culture of self-reflection— which depends on having an emotion, experiencing it, sometimes electing to share it with another person, thinking about it differently over time. When interchanges are reduced to the shorthand of emoticon emotions, questions such as "Who am I?" and "Who are you?" are reformatted for the small screen and flattened out in the process.

VIRTUALITY AND ITS DISCONTENTS

The virtual life of Facebook or MySpace is titillating, but our fragile planet needs our action in the real. We have to worry that we may be connecting globally but relating parochially.

We have become virtuosos of self-preservation, accustomed to living our lives in public. The idea that "we're all being observed all the time anyway, so who needs privacy?" has become a commonplace. Put another way, people say, "As long as I'm not doing anything wrong, who cares who's watching me?" This state of mind leaves us vulnerable to political abuse. Last June I attended the Webby Awards, an event to recognize the best and most influential Web sites. Thomas Friedman won for his argument that the Web had created a "flat" world of economic and political opportunity, a world in which a high school junior in Brooklyn competes with a peer in Bangalore. MySpace won a special commendation as the year's most pathbreaking site.

The awards took place just as the government wiretapping scandal was dominating the press. When the question of illegal eavesdropping came up, a common reaction among the gathered Weberati was to turn the issue into a nonissue. We heard, "All information is good information" and "Information wants to be free" and "If you have nothing to hide, you have nothing to fear." At a pre-awards cocktail party one Web luminary spoke animatedly about Michel Foucault's[1] idea of the panopticon, an architectural structure of spokes of a wheel built out from a hub, used as a metaphor for how the modern state disciplines its citizens. When the panopticon serves as a model for a prison, a guard stands at its center. Since each prisoner (citizen) knows that the guard might be looking at him or her at any moment, the question of whether the guard is actually looking—or if there is a guard at all—ceases to matter. The structure itself has created its disciplined citizen. By analogy, said my conversation partner at the cocktail hour, on the Internet someone might always be watching; it doesn't matter if from time to time someone is. Foucault's discussion of the panopticon has been a critical take on disciplinary society. Here it has become a justification for the U.S. government to spy on its citizens. All around me there were nods of assent.

High school and college students give up their privacy on MySpace about everything from musical preferences to sexual hang-ups. They are not likely to be troubled by an anonymous government agency knowing whom they call or what Web sites they frequent. People become gratified by a certain public exposure; it is more validation than violation.

[1]Michel Foucault (1926–1984): French philosopher and social theorist. [Editor's note.]

SPLIT ATTENTION

Contemporary professional life is rich in examples of people 20 ignoring those they are meeting with to give priority to online others whom they consider a more relevant audience. Students do e-mail during classes; faculty members do e-mail during meetings; parents do e-mail while talking with their children; people do e-mail as they walk down the street, drive cars or have dinner with their families. Indeed, people talk on the phone, hold a face-to-face meeting and do their e-mail at the same time. Once done surreptitiously, the habit of self-splitting in different worlds is becoming normalized. Your dinner partner looks down with a quick glance and you know he is checking his BlackBerry.

"Being put on pause" is how one of my students describes the feeling of walking down the street with a friend who has just taken a call on his cell. "I mean I can't go anywhere; I can't just pull out some work. I've just been stopped in midsentence and am expected to remember, to hold the thread of the conversation until he wants to pick it up again."

Traditional telephones tied us to friends, family, colleagues from school and work and, most recently, to commercial, political and philanthropic solicitations. Things are no longer so simple. These days our devices link us to humans and to objects that represent them: answering machines, Web sites and personal pages on social networking sites. Sometimes we engage with avatars who anonymously stand in for others, enabling us to express ourselves in intimate ways to strangers, in part because we and they are able to veil who we really are. Sometimes we engage with synthetic voice-recognition protocols that simulate real people as they try to assist us with technical and administrative issues. We order food, clothes and airline tickets this way. On the Internet we interact with bots, anthropomorphic programs that converse with us about a variety of matters, from routine to romantic. In online games we are partnered with "nonplayer characters," artificial intelligences that are not linked to human players. The games require that we put our trust in these characters that can save our fictional lives in the game. It is a small jump from trusting nonplayer characters—computer programs, that is—to putting one's trust in a robotic companion.

When my daughter, Rebecca, was 14, we went to the Darwin exhibition at the American Museum of Natural History, which documents his life and thought and somewhat defensively presents the theory of evolution as the central truth that underpins contemporary biology. At the entrance are two Galápagos tortoises. One is hidden from view; the other rests in its cage, utterly still. "They could have used a robot," Rebecca remarks, thinking it a shame to bring the turtle all this way when it's just going to sit there. She is concerned for the imprisoned turtle and unmoved by its authenticity. It is Thanksgiving weekend. The line is long, the crowd frozen in place and my question, "Do you care that the turtle is alive?" is a welcome diversion. Most of the votes for the robots echo Rebecca's sentiment that, in this setting, aliveness doesn't seem worth the trouble. A 12-year-old girl is adamant: "For what the turtles do, you didn't have to have the live ones." Her father looks at her, uncomprehending: "But the point is that they are real."

When Animal Kingdom opened in Orlando, populated by breathing animals, its first visitors complained they were not as "realistic" as the animatronic creatures in other parts of Disney World. The robotic crocodiles slapped their tails and rolled their eyes; the biological ones, like the Galápagos tortoises, pretty much kept to themselves.

I ask another question of the museumgoers: "If you put in a 25 robot instead of the live turtle, do you think people should be told that the turtle is not alive?" Not really, say several of the children. Data on "aliveness" can be shared on a "need to know" basis, for a purpose. But what are the purposes of living things?

Twenty-five years ago the Japanese realized that demography was working against them and there would never be enough young people to take care of their aging population. Instead of having foreigners take care of the elderly, they decided to build robots and put them in nursing homes. Doctors and nurses like them; so do family members of the elderly, because it is easier to leave your mom playing with a robot than to leave her staring at a wall or a TV. Very often the elderly like them, I think, mostly because they sense there are no other options. Said one woman about Aibo, Sony's household-entertainment robot, "It is better than a real dog. . . . It won't do dangerous things, and it won't betray you. . . . Also, it won't die suddenly and make you feel very sad."

Might such robotic arrangements even benefit the elderly and their children in the short run in a feel-good sense but be bad for us in our lives as moral beings? The answer does not depend on what computers can do today or what they are likely to be able to do in the future. It hangs on the question of what we will be like, what kind of people we are becoming as we develop very intimate relationships with our machines.

For Discussion and Writing

1. Turkle identifies a "rite of passage" (par. 13) for urban children that has vanished. What was this experience? Why was it important?
2. Near the end of her essay, the writer includes a personal anecdote about visiting the American Museum of Natural History with her daughter. What is the point of this story? How does it fit into Turkle's larger argument?
3. **connections** Both Turkle and Clay Shirky in "Gin, Television, and Social Surplus" (p. 236) explore how technologies affect the way we use our time. Compare and contrast their attitudes toward this topic. Is one writer more optimistic than the other? Which point of view do you find more persuasive, and why?
4. Turkle writes: "Contemporary professional life is rich in examples of people ignoring those they are meeting with to give priority to online others whom they consider a more relevant audience" (par. 20). Choose an example from your own life and write about it. How would you compare online or electronically mediated relationships to face-to-face relationships? Which are more "real"? Do you think that contemporary communications limit your capacity for solitude and self-reflection? Why or why not?

CLAY SHIRKY

Gin, Television, and Social Surplus

Clay Shirky, born in Columbia, Missouri, in 1964, is a writer, social critic, and consultant. Shirky also teaches at New York University, where he is a Distinguished Writer in Residence at the Arthur L. Carter Journalism Institute, as well as an assistant arts professor in the Interactive Telecommunications Program. *He has written for the* New York Times, *the* Wall Street Journal, Wired, *and other publications. He is also the author of several books, including* Here Comes Everybody: The Power of Organizing Without Organizations *(2008) and* Cognitive Surplus: Creativity and Generosity in a Connected Age *(2010).*

As its style indicates, Shirky's "Gin, Television, and Social Surplus" originated as a speech; the talk was given at the 2008 Web 2.0 conference, an annual event featuring discussions of the World Wide Web. This selection touches on several key themes for Shirky, including the collaborative nature of the Internet and the idea of a "cognitive surplus." As you read, think about the writer's use of analogy. What analogies underlie his main point? Do they seem like valid connections and comparisons?

I was recently reminded of some reading I did in college, way back in the last century, by a British historian arguing that the critical technology, for the early phase of the industrial revolution, was gin.

The transformation from rural to urban life was so sudden, and so wrenching, that the only thing society could do to manage was to drink itself into a stupor for a generation. The stories from that era are amazing—there were gin pushcarts working their way through the streets of London.

And it wasn't until society woke up from that collective bender that we actually started to get the institutional structures that we associate with the industrial revolution today. Things like public libraries and museums, increasingly broad education for children, elected leaders—a lot of things we like—didn't happen until having all of those people together stopped seeming like a crisis and started seeming like an asset.

It wasn't until people started thinking of this as a vast civic surplus, one they could design for rather than just dissipate, that we started to get what we think of now as an industrial society.

If I had to pick the critical technology for the twentieth century, the bit of social lubricant without which the wheels would've come off the whole enterprise, I'd say it was the sitcom. Starting with the Second World War, a whole series of things happened— rising GDP per capita, rising educational attainment, rising life expectancy and, critically, a rising number of people who were working five-day work weeks. For the first time, society forced onto an enormous number of its citizens the requirement to manage something they had never had to manage before—free time.

And what did we do with that free time? Well, mostly we spent it watching TV.

We did that for decades. We watched *I Love Lucy*. We watched *Gilligan's Island*. We watch *Malcolm in the Middle*. We watch *Desperate Housewives*. *Desperate Housewives* essentially functioned as a kind of cognitive heat sink, dissipating thinking that might otherwise have built up and caused society to overheat.

And it's only now, as we're waking up from that collective bender, that we're starting to see the cognitive surplus as an asset rather than as a crisis. We're seeing things being designed to take advantage of that surplus, to deploy it in ways more engaging than just having a TV in everybody's basement.

This hit me in a conversation I had about two months ago. . . . I've finished a book called *Here Comes Everybody*, which has recently come out, and this recognition came out of a conversation I had about the book. I was being interviewed by a TV producer to see whether I should be on her show, and she asked me, "What are you seeing out there that's interesting?"

I started telling her about the *Wikipedia* article on Pluto. You may remember that Pluto got kicked out of the planet club a couple of years ago, so all of a sudden there was all of this activity on *Wikipedia*. The talk pages light up, people are editing the article like mad, and the whole community is in a ruckus—"How should we characterize this change in Pluto's status?" And a little bit at a time they move the article—fighting offstage all the while—from "Pluto is the ninth planet" to "Pluto is an odd-shaped rock with an odd-shaped orbit at the edge of the solar system."

So I tell her all this stuff, and I think, "Okay, we're going to have a conversation about authority or social construction or whatever." That wasn't her question. She heard this story, and shook her head and said, "Where do people find the time?" That was her question. And I just kind of snapped. And I said, "No one who works in TV gets to ask that question. You know where the time comes from. It comes from the cognitive surplus you've been masking for fifty years."

So how big is that surplus? So if you take *Wikipedia* as a kind of unit, all of *Wikipedia*, the whole project—every page, every edit, every talk page, every line of code, in every language that *Wikipedia* exists in—that represents something like the cumulation of 100 million hours of human thought. I worked this out with Martin Wattenberg at IBM; it's a back-of-the-envelope calculation, but it's the right order of magnitude, about 100 million hours of thought.

And television watching? Two hundred billion hours, in the U.S. alone, every year. Put another way, now that we have a unit, that's 2,000 *Wikipedia* projects a year spent watching television. Or put still another way, in the U.S., we spend 100 million hours every weekend, just watching the ads. This is a pretty big surplus. People asking, "Where do they find the time?" when they're looking at things like *Wikipedia* don't understand how tiny that entire project is, as a carve-out of this asset that's finally being dragged into what Tim calls an architecture of participation.

Now, the interesting thing about a surplus like that is that society doesn't know what to do with it at first—hence the gin, hence the sitcoms. Because if people knew what to do with a surplus with reference to the existing social institutions, then it wouldn't be a surplus, would it? It's precisely when no one has any idea how to deploy something that people have to start experimenting with it, in order for the surplus to get integrated, and the course of that integration can transform society.

The early phase for taking advantage of this cognitive surplus, the phase I think we're still in, is all special cases. The physics of participation is much more like the physics of weather than it is like the physics of gravity. We know all the forces that combine to

make these kinds of things work: there's an interesting community over here, there's an interesting sharing model over there,
those people are collaborating on open source software. But
despite knowing the inputs, we can't predict the outputs yet
because there's so much complexity.

The way you explore complex ecosystems is you just try lots
and lots and lots of things, and you hope that everybody who fails
fails informatively so that you can at least find a skull on a pike-
staff near where you're going. That's the phase we're in now.

Just to pick one example, one I'm in love with, but it's tiny. A
couple of weeks ago one of my students at ITP forwarded me a
project started by a professor in Brazil, in Fortaleza, named Vasco
Furtado. It's a Wiki Map for crime in Brazil. If there's an assault,
if there's a burglary, if there's a mugging, a robbery, a rape, a murder, you can go and put a push-pin on a Google Map, and you can
characterize the assault, and you start to see a map of where these
crimes are occurring.

Now, this already exists as tacit information. Anybody who
knows a town has some sense of "Don't go there. That street corner is dangerous. Don't go in this neighborhood. Be careful there
after dark." But it's something society knows without society
really knowing it, which is to say there's no public source where
you can take advantage of it. And the cops, if they have that information, they're certainly not sharing. In fact, one of the things
Furtado says in starting the Wiki crime map was, "This information may or may not exist some place in society, but it's actually
easier for me to try to rebuild it from scratch than to try and get
it from the authorities who might have it now."

Maybe this will succeed or maybe it will fail. The normal case
of social software is still failure; most of these experiments don't
pan out. But the ones that do are quite incredible, and I hope that
this one succeeds, obviously. But even if it doesn't, it's illustrated
the point already, which is that someone working alone, with
really cheap tools, has a reasonable hope of carving out enough of
the cognitive surplus, enough of the desire to participate, enough
of the collective goodwill of the citizens, to create a resource you
couldn't have imagined existing even five years ago.

So that's the answer to the question, "Where do they find the
time?" Or, rather, that's the numerical answer. But beneath that
question was another thought, this one not a question but an

observation. In this same conversation with the TV producer, I was talking about *World of Warcraft* guilds, and as I was talking, I could sort of see what she was thinking: "Losers. Grown men sitting in their basement pretending to be elves."

At least they're doing something.

Did you ever see that episode of *Gilligan's Island* where they almost get off the island and then Gilligan messes up and then they don't? I saw that one. I saw that one a lot when I was growing up. And every half-hour that I watched that was a half an hour I wasn't posting at my blog or editing *Wikipedia* or contributing to a mailing list. Now, I had an ironclad excuse for not doing those things, which is none of those things existed then. I was forced into the channel of media the way it was because it was the only option. Now it's not, and that's the big surprise. However lousy it is to sit in your basement and pretend to be an elf, I can tell you from personal experience it's worse to sit in your basement and try to figure if Ginger or Mary Ann is cuter.

And I'm willing to raise that to a general principle. It's better to do something than to do nothing. Even lolcats, even cute pictures of kittens made even cuter with the addition of cute captions, hold out an invitation to participation. When you see a lolcat, one of the things it says to the viewer is, "If you have some sans-serif fonts on your computer, you can play this game, too." And that message—I can do that, too—is a big change.

This is something that people in the media world don't understand. Media in the twentieth century was run as a single race—consumption. How much can we produce? How much can you consume? Can we produce more and you'll consume more? And the answer to that question has generally been yes. But media is actually a triathlon, it's three different events. People like to consume, but they also like to produce, and they like to share.

And what's astonished people who were committed to the structure of the previous society, prior to trying to take this surplus and do something interesting, is that they're discovering that when you offer people the opportunity to produce and to share, they'll take you up on that offer. It doesn't mean that we'll never sit around mindlessly watching *Scrubs* on the couch. It just means we'll do it less.

And this is the other thing about the size of the cognitive surplus we're talking about. It's so large that even a small change could have huge ramifications. Let's say that everything stays 99 percent the same, that people watch 99 percent as much television as they used to, but 1 percent of that is carved out for producing and for sharing. The Internet-connected population watches roughly a trillion hours of TV a year. That's about five times the size of the annual U.S. consumption. One percent of that is 100 *Wikipedia* projects per year worth of participation.

I think that's going to be a big deal. Don't you?

Well, the TV producer did not think this was going to be a big deal; she was not digging this line of thought. And her final question to me was essentially, "Isn't this all just a fad?" You know, sort of the flag-pole-sitting of the early twenty-first century? It's fun to go out and produce and share a little bit, but then people are going to eventually realize, "This isn't as good as doing what I was doing before," and settle down. And I made a spirited argument that no, this wasn't the case, that this was in fact a big one-time shift, more analogous to the industrial revolution than to flagpole-sitting.

I was arguing that this isn't the sort of thing society grows out of. It's the sort of thing that society grows into. But I'm not sure she believed me, in part because she didn't want to believe me, but also in part because I didn't have the right story yet. And now I do.

I was having dinner with a group of friends about a month ago, 30 and one of them was talking about sitting with his four-year-old daughter watching a DVD. And in the middle of the movie, apropos of nothing, she jumps up off the couch and runs around behind the screen. That seems like a cute moment. Maybe she's going back there to see if Dora is really back there or whatever. But that wasn't what she was doing. She started rooting around in the cables. And her dad said, "What you doing?" And she stuck her head out from behind the screen and said, "Looking for the mouse."

Here's something four-year-olds know: A screen that ships without a mouse ships broken. Here's something four-year-olds know: Media that's targeted at you but doesn't include you may not be worth sitting still for. Those are things that make me believe that this is a one-way change. Because four-year-olds, the people who are soaking most deeply in the current environment, who won't have to go through the trauma that I have to go through of trying to unlearn a childhood spent watching *Gilligan's Island*, they just assume that media includes consuming, producing, and sharing.

It's also become my motto, when people ask me what we're doing—and when I say "we," I mean the larger society trying to figure out how to deploy this cognitive surplus, but I also mean we, especially, the people in this room, the people who are working hammer and tongs at figuring out the next good idea. From now on, that's what I'm going to tell them: We're looking for the mouse. We're going to look at every place that a reader or a listener or a viewer or a user has been locked out, has been served up passive or a fixed or a canned experience, and ask ourselves, "If we carve out a little bit of the cognitive surplus and deploy it here, could we make a good thing happen?" And I'm betting the answer is yes.

For Discussion and Writing

1. Shirky sees the Internet functioning similarly to other manifestations of cognitive surplus, such as gin and television. At the same time, the Internet is distinct in a crucial way. What makes the Internet so different from television, according to the writer?

2. How does Shirky incorporate numbers and statistics into his argument? Do you find these calculations and claims credible and easy to understand? Are they sufficiently rigorous for his purpose? Do they help his argument? Why or why not?

3. **connections** Shirky tells a story about talking to a television producer. As he describes "guilds" for the video game *World of Warcraft*, he notes: "I could sort of see what she was thinking: 'Losers. Grown men sitting in their basement pretending to be elves'" (par. 20). In contrast, Shirky sees this phenomenon in a positive light: "At least they're doing something" (par. 21). How might Sherry Turkle interpret the image of these men differently than both the TV producer and Shirky? What might they represent or illustrate for her argument in "Can You Hear Me Now?" (p. 227)?

4. Shirky incorporates several personal anecdotes to illustrate different points throughout the essay. In paragraph 29, he even refers to finding the "right story" to make a particular argument. Choose a specific anecdote or experience from your life; then use it to illustrate a point about your own—or our society's—relationship to technology. What does your story reveal?

CHAPTER 5

Television

Over the last sixty years, no pop culture medium has done more to shape American life than television. To take just one facet of society, consider its effects on U.S. politics, from Joseph McCarthy's televised congressional hearings, the first televised presidential debate between John Kennedy and Richard Nixon, and news images from the Vietnam War, to today's cable news channel shoutfests. Indeed, TV provides the space and occasion for national public discourse. But the medium's social and cultural influence goes much deeper. In "Gin, Television, and Social Surplus," Clay Shirky sees twentieth-century American TV as a "cognitive heat sink, dissipating thinking that might otherwise have built up and caused society to overheat." Yet we should consider what Americans have been thinking about while watching all that television: national greatness and human progress with the 1969 moon landing; bigotry and intergenerational struggle on *All In the Family*; concerns about nuclear war in *The Day After*; idyllic family lives on *The Waltons* and *Happy Days*; a new image of the affluent African-American family on *The Cosby Show*; criminal lives on *The Sopranos* and *The Wire*. To talk about American popular culture is, almost axiomatically, to talk about television. And television programming over the years provides capsule summaries of American concerns, hopes, and enthusiasms: American history by way of *TV Guide*.

Although experimental television had existed since the late 1920s, the RCA corporation introduced the new medium to the American public at the 1939 World's Fair. A writer for the *New York Times* responded dubiously: "The problem with television is that people must sit and keep their eyes glued on a screen; the average American family hasn't time for it." But the average

243

family made time: Within two decades, over forty million American families owned television sets. TV has always had its idealistic boosters and skeptical critics, of course. Newton Minow, chairman of the Federal Communications Commission, embodied both sides of this debate in a famous 1961 speech: "When television is good, nothing — not the theater, not the magazines or newspapers — nothing is better. But when television is bad, nothing is worse. I invite each of you to sit down in front of your own television set when your station goes on the air and stay there, for a day, without a book, without a magazine, without a newspaper, without a profit and loss sheet or a rating book to distract you. Keep your eyes glued to that set until the station signs off. I can assure you that what you will observe is a vast wasteland."

All of the following essays engage this dichotomy in one way or another. In "Television Addiction Is No Mere Metaphor," Robert Kubey and Mihaly Csikszentmihalyi examine the term "TV addiction" and discover that it "captures the essence of a very real phenomenon." Marie Winn looks at the profound effects of television on children and family life in "Television: The Plug-In Drug." In "Mary Tyler More," Erica Lies performs a deft close reading of the show *30 Rock*; she also places it in a tradition with other workplace comedies about smart single women. Steven Johnson ("Watching Television Makes You Smarter") surveys contemporary television and finds, not a wasteland, but sophisticated, challenging, and cognitively demanding shows that subvert conventional wisdom about our supposedly debased popular culture. In the paired readings, columnist George F. Will and Mark Greif weigh the merits—and explore the cultural consequences—of "reality television."

ROBERT KUBEY AND MIHALY
CSIKSZENTMIHALYI

Television Addiction Is No Mere Metaphor

Robert Kubey (b. 1952) is the director of the Center for Media Studies and professor of journalism and media studies at Rutgers University. He is the author of several books, including Television and the Quality of Life: How Viewing Shapes Everyday Experience *(1990) and* Creating Television: Conversations With the People Behind 50 Years of American TV *(2004). Kubey has written for the* New York Times, Scientific American, *and other publications. Mihaly Csikszentmihalyi (b. 1934) is the C. S. and D. J. Davidson Professor of Psychology and Management at Claremont Graduate University's Drucker School of Management. Csikszentmihalyi is best known for his theory of "flow": a state of intense concentration associated with productivity and satisfaction. His books include* Flow: The Psychology of Optimal Experience *(1990) and* Good Business: Leadership, Flow, and the Making of Meaning *(2003).*

People often use the term addiction *metaphorically to describe the appeal of pleasures, habits, and leisure activities in their day-to-day lives. In the following article from* Scientific American, *Kubey and Csikszentmihalyi argue that television can be addictive in a clinical sense, causing physiological responses commonly associated with drugs like alcohol and cigarettes. As you read, note how Kubey and Csikszentmihalyi try to distinguish healthy, harmless television viewing from television addiction. How do you make such distinctions in your own life, whether about television or any other activity?*

Perhaps the most ironic aspect of the struggle for survival is how easily organisms can be harmed by that which they desire. The trout is caught by the fisherman's lure, the mouse by cheese. But at least those creatures have the excuse that bait and cheese look

245

like sustenance. Humans seldom have that consolation. The temptations that can disrupt their lives are often pure indulgences. No one has to drink alcohol, for example. Realizing when a diversion has gotten out of control is one of the great challenges of life. Excessive cravings do not necessarily involve physical substances. Gambling can become compulsive; sex can become obsessive. One activity, however, stands out for its prominence and ubiquity—the world's most popular leisure pastime, television. Most people admit to having a love–hate relationship with it. They complain about the "boob tube" and "couch potatoes," then they settle into their sofas and grab the remote control. Parents commonly fret about their children's viewing (if not their own). Even researchers who study TV for a living marvel at the medium's hold on them personally. Percy Tannenbaum of the University of California at Berkeley has written: "Among life's more embarrassing moments have been countless occasions when I am engaged in conversation in a room while a TV set is on, and I cannot for the life of me stop from periodically glancing over to the screen. This occurs not only during dull conversations but during reasonably interesting ones just as well."

Scientists have been studying the effects of television for decades, generally focusing on whether watching violence on TV correlates with being violent in real life (see "The Effects of Observing Violence," by Leonard Berkowitz; *Scientific American*, February 1964; and "Communication and Social Environment," by George Gerber, September 1972). Less attention has been paid to the basic allure of the small screen—the medium, as opposed to the message.

The term "TV addiction" is imprecise and laden with value judgments, but it captures the essence of a very real phenomenon. Psychologists and psychiatrists formally define substance dependence as a disorder characterized by criteria that include spending a great deal of time using the substance; using it more often than one intends; thinking about reducing use or making repeated unsuccessful efforts to reduce use; giving up important social, family, or occupational activities to use it; and reporting withdrawal symptoms when one stops using it.

All these criteria can apply to people who watch a lot of television. That does not mean that watching television, per se, is problematic. Television can teach and amuse; it can reach aesthetic 5 heights; it can provide much needed distraction and escape. The difficulty arises when people strongly sense that they ought not to watch as much as they do and yet find themselves strangely unable to reduce their viewing. Some knowledge of how the medium exerts its pull may help heavy viewers gain better control over their lives.

A BODY AT REST TENDS TO STAY AT REST

The amount of time people spend watching television is astonishing. On average, individuals in the industrialized world devote three hours a day to the pursuit—fully half of their leisure time, and more than on any single activity save work and sleep. At this rate, someone who lives to seventy-five would spend nine years in front of the tube. To some commentators, this devotion means simply that people enjoy TV and make a conscious decision to watch it. But if that is the whole story, why do so many people experience misgivings about how much they view? In Gallup polls in 1992 and 1999, two out of five adult respondents and seven out of ten teenagers said they spent too much time watching TV. Other surveys have consistently shown that roughly 10 percent of adults call themselves TV addicts.

To study people's reactions to TV, researchers have undertaken laboratory experiments in which they have monitored the brain waves (using an electroencephalograph, or EEG), skin resistance or heart rate of people watching television. To track behavior and emotion in the normal course of life, as opposed to the artificial conditions of the lab, we have used the Experience Sampling Method (ESM). Participants carried a beeper, and we signaled them six to eight times a day, at random, over the period of a week; whenever they heard the beep, they wrote down what they were doing and how they were feeling using a standardized scorecard.

As one might expect, people who were watching TV when we beeped them reported feeling relaxed and passive. The EEG studies similarly show less mental stimulation, as measured by alpha brain-wave production, during viewing than during reading.

What is more surprising is that the sense of relaxation ends when the set is turned off, but the feelings of passivity and lowered alertness continue. Survey participants commonly reflect that television has somehow absorbed or sucked out their energy, leaving them depleted. They say they have more difficulty concentrating after viewing than before. In contrast, they rarely indicate such difficulty after reading. After playing sports or engaging in hobbies, people report improvements in mood. After watching TV, people's moods are about the same or worse than before.

Within moments of sitting or lying down and pushing the 10 "power" button, viewers report feeling more relaxed. Because the relaxation occurs quickly, people are conditioned to associate viewing with rest and lack of tension. The association is positively reinforced because viewers remain relaxed throughout viewing, and it is negatively reinforced via the stress and dysphoric rumination that occurs once the screen goes blank again.

Habit-forming drugs work in similar ways. A tranquilizer that leaves the body rapidly is much more likely to cause dependence than one that leaves the body slowly, precisely because the user is more aware that the drug's effects are wearing off. Similarly, viewers' vague learned sense that they will feel less relaxed if they stop viewing may be a significant factor in not turning the set off. Viewing begets more viewing.

Thus, the irony of TV: people watch a great deal longer than they plan to, even though prolonged viewing is less rewarding. In our ESM studies the longer people sat in front of the set, the less satisfaction they said they derived from it. When signaled, heavy viewers (those who consistently watch more than four hours a day) tended to report on their ESM sheets that they enjoy TV less than light viewers did (less than two hours a day). For some, a twinge of unease or guilt that they aren't doing something more productive may also accompany and depreciate the enjoyment of prolonged viewing. Researchers in Japan, the U.K. and the U.S. have found that this guilt occurs much more among middle-class viewers than among less affluent ones.

GRABBING YOUR ATTENTION

What is it about TV that has such a hold on us? In part, the attraction seems to spring from our biological "orienting response." First described by Ivan Pavlov in 1927, the orienting response is our instinctive visual or auditory reaction to any sudden or novel stimulus. It is part of our evolutionary heritage, a built-in

"The irony of TV: people watch a great deal longer than they plan to, even though prolonged viewing is less rewarding."

sensitivity to movement and potential predatory threats. Typical orienting reactions include dilation of the blood vessels to the brain, slowing of the heart, and constriction of blood vessels to major muscle groups. Alpha waves are blocked for a few seconds before returning to their baseline level, which is determined by the general level of mental arousal. The brain focuses its attention on gathering more information while the rest of the body quiets.

In 1986, Byron Reeves of Stanford University, Esther Thorson of the University of Missouri and their colleagues began to study whether the simple formal features of television—cuts, edits, zooms, pans, sudden noises—activate the orienting response, thereby keeping attention on the screen. By watching how brain waves were affected by formal features, the researchers concluded that these stylistic tricks can indeed trigger involuntary responses and "derive their attentional value through the evolutionary significance of detecting movement. . . . It is the form, not the content, of television that is unique."

The orienting response may partly explain common viewer 15 remarks such as: "If a television is on, I just can't keep my eyes off it," "I don't want to watch as much as I do, but I can't help it," and "I feel hypnotized when I watch television." In the years since Reeves and Thorson published their pioneering work, researchers have delved deeper. Annie Lang's research team at Indiana University has shown that heart rate decreases for four to six seconds after an orienting stimulus. In ads, action sequences, and music videos, formal features frequently come at a rate of one per second, thus activating the orienting response continuously.

Lang and her colleagues have also investigated whether formal features affect people's memory of what they have seen. In one of their studies, participants watched a program and then filled out a score sheet. Increasing the frequency of edits—defined here as a change from one camera angle to another in the same visual scene—improved memory recognition, presumably because it focused attention on the screen. Increasing the frequency of cuts—changes to a new visual scene—had a similar effect but only up to a point. If the number of cuts exceeded ten in two minutes, recognition dropped off sharply.

Producers of educational television for children have found that formal features can help learning. But increasing the rate of cuts and edits eventually overloads the brain. Music videos and commercials that use rapid intercutting of unrelated scenes are designed to hold attention more than they are to convey information. People may remember the name of the product or band, but the details of the ad itself float in one ear and out the other. The orienting response is overworked. Viewers still attend to the screen, but they feel tired and worn out, with little compensating psychological reward. Our ESM findings show much the same thing.

Sometimes the memory of the product is very subtle. Many ads today are deliberately oblique: they have an engaging story line, but it is hard to tell what they are trying to sell. Afterward you may not remember the product consciously. Yet advertisers believe that if they have gotten your attention, when you later go to the store you will feel better or more comfortable with a given product because you have a vague recollection of having heard of it.

The natural attraction to television's sound and light starts very early in life. Dafna Lemish of Tel Aviv University has described babies at six to eight weeks attending to television. We have observed slightly older infants who, when lying on their backs on the floor, crane their necks around 180 degrees to catch what light through yonder window breaks. This inclination suggests how deeply rooted the orienting response is.

"TV IS PART OF THEM"

That said, we need to be careful about overreacting. Little evi-   20
dence suggests that adults or children should stop watching TV altogether. The problems come from heavy or prolonged viewing.

The Experience Sampling Method permitted us to look closely at most every domain of everyday life: working, eating, reading, talking to friends, playing a sport, and so on. We wondered whether heavy viewers might experience life differently than light viewers do. Do they dislike being with people more? Are they more alienated from work? What we found nearly leaped off the page at us. Heavy viewers report feeling significantly more anxious and less happy than light viewers do in unstructured situations, such as doing nothing, daydreaming, or waiting in line. The difference widens when the viewer is alone.

Subsequently, Robert D. McIlwraith of the University of Manitoba extensively studied those who called themselves TV addicts on surveys. On a measure called the Short Imaginal Processes Inventory (SIPI), he found that the self-described addicts are more easily bored and distracted and have poorer attentional control than the nonaddicts. The addicts said they used TV to distract themselves from unpleasant thoughts and to fill time. Other studies over the years have shown that heavy viewers are less likely to participate in community activities and sports and are more likely to be obese than moderate viewers or nonviewers.

The question that naturally arises is: In which direction does the correlation go? Do people turn to TV because of boredom and loneliness, or does TV viewing make people more susceptible to boredom and loneliness? We and most other researchers argue that the former is generally the case, but it is not a simple case of either/or. Jerome L. and Dorothy Singer of Yale University, among others, have suggested that more viewing may contribute to a shorter attention span, diminished self-restraint, and less patience with the normal delays of daily life. More than twenty-five years ago, psychologist Tannis M. MacBeth Williams of the University of British Columbia studied a mountain community that had no television until cable finally arrived. Over time, both adults and children in the town became less creative in problem solving, less able to persevere at tasks, and less tolerant of unstructured time.

To some researchers, the most convincing parallel between TV and addictive drugs is that people experience withdrawal symptoms when they cut back on viewing. Nearly forty years ago, Gary A. Steiner of the University of Chicago collected fascinating individual accounts of families whose set had broken—this back in the days when households generally had only one set: "The family walked around like a chicken without a head." "It was terrible. We did nothing—my husband and I talked." "Screamed constantly. Children bothered me, and my nerves were on edge. Tried to interest them in games, but impossible. TV is part of them."

In experiments, families have volunteered or been paid to stop   25
viewing, typically for a week or a month. Many could not complete the period of abstinence. Some fought, verbally and physically. Anecdotal reports from some families that have tried the annual "TV turn-off" week in the U.S. tell a similar story.

If a family has been spending the lion's share of its free time watching television, reconfiguring itself around a new set of activities is no easy task. Of course, that does not mean it cannot be done or that all families implode when deprived of their set. In a review of these cold-turkey studies, Charles Winick of the City University of New York concluded: "The first three or four days for most persons were the worst, even in many homes where viewing was minimal and where there were other ongoing activities. In over half of all the households, during these first few days of loss, the regular routines were disrupted, family members had difficulties in dealing with the newly available time, anxiety and aggressions were expressed. . . . People living alone tended to be bored and irritated. . . . By the second week, a move toward adaptation to the situation was common." Unfortunately, researchers have yet to flesh out these anecdotes; no one has systematically gathered statistics on the prevalence of these withdrawal symptoms.

Even though TV does seem to meet the criteria for substance dependence, not all researchers would go so far as to call TV addictive. McIlwraith said in 1998 that "displacement of other activities by television may be socially significant but still fall short of the clinical requirement of significant impairment." He argued that a new category of "TV addiction" may not be necessary if heavy viewing stems from conditions such as depression and social phobia. Nevertheless, whether or not we formally diagnose someone as TV-dependent, millions of people sense that they cannot readily control the amount of television they watch.

SLAVE TO THE COMPUTER SCREEN

Although much less research has been done on video games and computer use, the same principles often apply. The games offer escape and distraction; players quickly learn that they feel better when playing; and so a kind of reinforcement loop develops. The obvious difference from television, however, is the interactivity. Many video and computer games minutely increase in difficulty along with the increasing ability of the player. One can search for months to find another tennis or chess player of comparable ability, but programmed games can immediately provide a near-perfect match of challenge to skill. They offer the psychic pleasure—what one of us (Csikszentmihalyi) has called "flow"— that accompanies increased mastery of most any human endeavor. On the other hand, prolonged activation of the orienting response can wear players out. Kids report feeling tired, dizzy and nauseated after long sessions.

In 1997, in the most extreme medium-effects case on record, 700 Japanese children were rushed to the hospital, many suffering from "optically stimulated epileptic seizures" caused by viewing bright flashing lights in a Pokemon video game broadcast on Japanese TV. Seizures and other untoward effects of video games are significant enough that software companies and platform manufacturers now routinely include warnings in their instruction booklets. Parents have reported to us that rapid movement on the screen has caused motion sickness in their young children after just fifteen minutes of play. Many youngsters, lacking self-control and experience (and often supervision), continue to play despite these symptoms.

Lang and Shyam Sundar of Pennsylvania State University have 30 been studying how people respond to Web sites. Sundar has shown people multiple versions of the same Web page, identical except for the number of links. Users reported that more links conferred a greater sense of control and engagement. At some point, however, the number of links reached saturation, and adding more of them simply turned people off. As with video games, the ability of Web sites to hold the user's attention seems to depend less on formal features than on interactivity.

For growing numbers of people, the life they lead online may often seem more important, more immediate, and more intense than the life they lead face-to-face. Maintaining control over one's media habits is more of a challenge today than it has ever been. TV sets and computers are everywhere. But the small screen and the Internet need not interfere with the quality of the rest of one's life. In its easy provision of relaxation and escape, television can be beneficial in limited doses. Yet when the habit interferes with the ability to grow, to learn new things, to lead an active life, then it does constitute a kind of dependence and should be taken seriously.

For Discussion and Writing

1. What is the "orienting response" (par. 13)? How is it related to television viewing and addiction?
2. What kinds of evidence do Kubey and Csikszentmihalyi use to support their argument? Is it clearly presented and effective? How do they integrate it into their essay?
3. **connections**   While Kubey and Csikszentmihalyi concede that television can be a harmless pleasure, their main point is that TV viewing can be physiologically addictive. Studies show that it can also make viewers passive and lethargic: "Survey participants commonly reflect that television has somehow absorbed or sucked out their energy, leaving them depleted. . . . In contrast, they rarely indicate such difficulty after reading" (par. 9). How do you think Steven Johnson in "Watching TV Makes You Smarter" (p. 275) would respond to this evidence? Is Johnson's claim that the "most debased forms of mass diversion . . . turn out to be nutritional after all" (par. 3) incompatible with Kubey and Csikszentmihalyi's argument? Why or why not?

4. The authors write, "Maintaining control over one's media habits is more of a challenge today than it has ever been" (par. 31). Do you have any misgivings over your television viewing, online activity, video game playing, or any other similar activities? How do you maintain control over your "media habits"?

MARIE WINN

Television: The Plug-In Drug

Author, ornithologist, and wildlife advocate Marie Winn was born in Czechoslovakia in 1936. In 1939, her family moved to the United States, where she attended Radcliffe College and Columbia University. Winn is best known for her classic study of television and families, The Plug-In Drug: Television, Children, and Family *(1977; updated in 2002). She has also written about wildlife in works such as* Central Park in the Dark *(2008) and produced several children's books. Winn's writing has appeared in the* Wall Street Journal, *the* New York Times, *and* Smithsonian *magazine.*

In the following essay, excerpted from The Plug-In Drug: Television, Children, and Family, *Winn writes about television's effect on families: "Television is not merely one of a number of important influences upon today's child. Through the changes it has made in family life, television emerges as* the *important influence in children's lives today." The first edition of Winn's book came out in 1977. How well does her argument hold up in hindsight? Does television still play such a large role in the lives of children and families? How are her criticisms similar to the ones leveled at the Internet and other technologies today?*

Not much more than fifty years after the introduction of television into American society, the medium has become so deeply ingrained in daily life that in many states the TV set has attained the rank of a legal necessity, safe from repossession in case of debt along with clothes and cooking utensils. Only in the early years after television's introduction did writers and commentators have sufficient perspective to separate the activity of watching television from the actual content it offers the viewer. In those days writers frequently discussed the effects of television on family life. However, a curious myopia afflicted those first observers:

almost without exception they regarded television as a favorable, beneficial, indeed, wondrous influence upon the family.

"Television is going to be a real asset in every home where there are children," predicted a writer in 1949.

"Television will take over your way of living and change your children's habits, but this change can be a wonderful improvement," claimed another commentator.

"No survey's needed, of course, to establish that television has brought the family together in one room," wrote the *New York Times*'s television critic in 1949.

The early articles about television were almost invariably accompanied by a photograph or illustration showing a family cozily sitting together before the television set, Sis on Mom's lap, Buddy perched on the arm of Dad's chair, Dad with his arm around Mom's shoulder. Who could have guessed that twenty or so years later Mom would be watching a drama in the kitchen, the kids would be looking at cartoons in their room, while Dad would be taking in the ball game in the living room? 5

Of course television sets were enormously expensive when they first came on the market. The idea that by the year 2000 more than three quarters of all American families would own two or more sets would have seemed preposterous. The splintering of the multiple-set family was something the early writers did not foresee. Nor did anyone imagine the number of hours children would eventually devote to television, the changes television would effect upon child-rearing methods, the increasing domination of family schedules by children's viewing requirements — in short, the power of television to dominate family life.

As children's consumption of the new medium increased together with parental concern about the possible effects of so much television viewing, a steady refrain helped soothe and reassure anxious parents. "Television always enters a pattern of influences that already exist: the home, the peer group, the school, the church and culture generally," wrote the authors of an early and influential study of television's effects on children. In other words, if the child's home life is all right, parents need not worry about the effects of too much television watching.

But television did not merely influence the child; it deeply influenced that "pattern of influences" everyone hoped would ameliorate the new medium's effects. Home and family life have changed in important ways since the advent of television. The peer group has become television-oriented, and much of the time children spend together is occupied by television viewing. Culture generally has been transformed by television. Participation in church and community activities has diminished, with television a primary cause of this change. Therefore it is improper to assign to television the subsidiary role its many apologists insist it plays. Television is not merely one of a number of important influences upon today's child. Through the changes it has made in family life, television emerges as *the* important influence in children's lives today.

THE QUALITY OF LIFE

Television's contribution to family life has been an equivocal one. For while it has, indeed, kept the members of the family from dispersing, it has not served to bring them together. By its domination of the time families spend together, it destroys the special quality that distinguishes one family from another, a quality that depends to a great extent on what a family does, what special rituals, games, recurrent jokes, familiar songs, and shared activities it accumulates.

Yet parents have accepted a television-dominated family life so completely that they cannot see how the medium is involved in whatever problems they might be having. A first-grade teacher reports: 10

> I have one child in the group who's an only child. I wanted to find out more about her family life because this little girl was quite isolated from the group, didn't make friends, so I talked to her mother. Well, they don't have time to do anything in the evening, the mother said. The parents come home after picking up the child at the baby-sitter's. Then the mother fixes dinner while the child watches TV. Then they have dinner and the child goes to bed. I said to this mother, "Well, couldn't she help you fix dinner? That would be a nice time for the two of you to talk," and the mother said, "Oh, but I'd hate to have her miss *Zoom*. It's such a good program!"

Several decades ago a writer and mother of two boys aged three and seven described her family's television schedule in a newspaper article. Though some of the programs her kids watched then have changed, the situation she describes remains the same for great numbers of families today:

> We were in the midst of a full-scale War. Every day was a new battle and every program was a major skirmish. We agreed it was a bad scene all around and were ready to enter diplomatic negotiations. . . . In principle we have agreed on 2½ hours of TV a day, *Sesame Street, Electric Company* (with dinner gobbled up in between) and two half-hour shows between 7 and 8:30, which enables the grown-ups to eat in peace and prevents the two boys from destroying one another. Their pre-bedtime choice is dreadful, because, as Josh recently admitted, "There's nothing much I really like." So . . . it's *What's My Line* or *To Tell the Truth*. . . . Clearly there is a need for first-rate children's shows at this time. . . .

Consider the "family life" described here: Presumably the father comes home from work during the *Sesame Street–Electric Company* stint. The children are either watching television, gobbling their dinner, or both. While the parents eat their dinner in peaceful privacy, the children watch another hour of television. Then there is only a half-hour left before bedtime, just enough time for baths, getting pajamas on, brushing teeth, and so on. The children's evening is regimented with an almost military precision. They watch their favorite programs, and when there is "nothing much on I really like," they watch whatever else is on — because *watching* is the important thing. Their mother does not see anything amiss with watching programs just for the sake of watching; she only wishes there were some first-rate children's shows on at those times.

Without conjuring up fantasies of bygone eras with family games and long, leisurely meals, the question arises: isn't there a better family life available than this dismal, mechanized arrangement of children watching television for however long is allowed them, evening after evening?

Of course, families today still do things together at times: go camping in the summer, go to the zoo on a nice Sunday, take various trips and expeditions. But their ordinary daily life together is diminished — those hours of sitting around at the dinner table, the spontaneous taking up of an activity, the little games invented by children on the spur of the moment when there is nothing else to do, the scribbling, the chatting, and even the quarreling, all the things that form the fabric of a family, that define a childhood. Instead, the children have their regular schedule of television programs and bedtime, and the parents have their peaceful dinner together.

The author of the quoted newspaper article notes that "keeping 15 a family sane means mediating between the needs of both children and adults." But surely the needs of the adults in that family were being better met than the needs of the children. The kids were effectively shunted away and rendered untroublesome, while their parents enjoyed a life as undemanding as that of any childless couple. In reality, it is those very demands that young children make upon a family that lead to growth, and it is the way parents respond to those demands that builds the relationships upon which the future of the family depends. If the family does not accumulate its backlog of shared experiences, shared everyday experiences that occur and recur and change and develop, then it is not likely to survive as anything other than a caretaking institution.

FAMILY RITUALS

Ritual is defined by sociologists as "that part of family life that the family likes about itself, is proud of and wants formally to continue." Another text notes that "the development of a ritual by a family is an index of the common interest of its members in the family as a group."

What has happened to family rituals, those regular, dependable, recurrent happenings that gave members of a family a feeling of belonging to a home rather than living in it merely for the sake of convenience, those experiences that act as the adhesive of family unity far more than any material advantages?

Mealtime rituals, going-to-bed rituals, illness rituals, holiday rituals—how many of these have survived the inroads of the television set?

A young woman who grew up near Chicago reminisces about her childhood and gives an idea of the effects of television upon family rituals:

> As a child I had millions of relatives around—my parents both came
> from relatively large families. My father had nine brothers and sisters.

And so every holiday there was this great swoop-down of aunts, uncles, and millions of cousins. I just remember how wonderful it used to be. These thousands of cousins would come and everyone would play and ultimately, after dinner, all the women would be in the front of the house, drinking coffee and talking, all the men would be in the back of the house, drinking and smoking, and all the kids would be all over the place, playing hide and seek. Christmas time was particularly nice because everyone always brought all their toys and games. Our house had a couple of rooms with go-through closets, so there were always kids running in a great circle route. I remember it was just wonderful.

And then all of a sudden one year I remember becoming suddenly aware of how different everything had become. The kids were no longer playing Monopoly or Clue or the other games we used to play together. It was because we had a television set which had been turned on for a football game. All of that socializing that had gone on previously had ended. Now everyone was sitting in front of the television set, on a holiday, at a family party! I remember being stunned by how awful that was. Somehow the television had become more attractive.

As families have come to spend more and more of their time together engaged in the single activity of television watching, those rituals and pastimes that once gave family life its special quality have become more and more uncommon. Not since prehistoric times, when cave families hunted, gathered, ate, and slept, with little time remaining to accumulate a culture of any significance, have families been reduced to such a sameness.

REAL PEOPLE

The relationships of family members to each other are affected by television's powerful competition in both obvious and subtle ways. For surely the hours that children spend in a one-way relationship with television people, an involvement that allows for no communication or interaction, must have some effect on their relationships with real-life people.

Studies show the importance of eye-to-eye contact, for instance, in real-life relationships, and indicate that the nature of one's eye-contact patterns, whether one looks another squarely in the eye or looks to the side or shifts one's gaze from side to side, may play a significant role in one's success or failure in human relationships. But no eye contact is possible in the child-television relationship, although in certain children's programs people purport to speak directly to the child and the camera fosters this illusion by focusing directly upon the person being filmed. How might such a distortion affect a child's development of trust, of openness, of an ability to relate well to *real* people? Bruno Bettelheim suggested an answer:

> Children who have been taught, or conditioned, to listen passively most of the day to the warm verbal communications coming from the TV screen, to the deep emotional appeal of the so-called TV personality, are often unable to respond to real persons because they arouse so much less feeling than the skilled actor. Worse, they lose the ability to learn from reality because life experiences are much more complicated than the ones they see on the screen. . . .

A teacher makes a similar observation about her personal viewing experiences:

> I have trouble mobilizing myself and dealing with real people after watching a few hours of television. It's just hard to make that transition from watching television to a real relationship. I suppose it's because there was no effort necessary while I was watching, and dealing with real people always requires a bit of effort. Imagine, then, how much harder it might be to do the same thing for a small child, particularly one who watches a lot of television every day.

But more obviously damaging to family relationships is the   25 elimination of opportunities to talk and converse, or to argue, to air grievances between parents and children and brothers and sisters. Families frequently use television to avoid confronting their problems, problems that will not go away if they are ignored but will only fester and become less easily resolvable as time goes on.

A mother reports:

> I find myself, with three children, wanting to turn on the TV set when they're fighting. I really have to struggle not to do it because I feel that's telling them this is the solution to the quarrel—but it's so tempting that I often do it.

A family therapist discusses the use of television as an avoidance mechanism:

> In a family I know the father comes home from work and turns on the television set. The children come and watch with him and the wife serves

them their meal in front of the set. He then goes and takes a shower, or works on the car or something. She then goes and has her own dinner in front of the television set. It's a symptom of a deeper-rooted problem, sure. But it would help them all to get rid of the set. It would be far easier to work on what the symptom really means without the television. The television simply encourages a double avoidance of each other. They'd find out more quickly what was going on if they weren't able to hide behind the TV. Things wouldn't necessarily be better, of course, but they wouldn't be anesthetized.

A number of research studies done when television was a relatively new medium demonstrated that television interfered with family activities and the formation of family relationships. One survey showed that 78 percent of the respondents indicated no conversation taking place during viewing except at specified times such as commercials. The study noted: "The television atmosphere in most households is one of quiet absorption on the part of family members who are present. The nature of the family social life during a program could be described as 'parallel' rather than interactive, and the set does seem to dominate family life when it is on." Thirty-six percent of the respondents in another study indicated that television viewing was the only family activity participated in during the week.

The situation has only worsened during the intervening decades. When the studies were made, the great majority of American families had only one television set. Though the family may have spent more time watching TV in those early days, at least they were all together while they watched. Today the vast majority of all families have two or more sets, and nearly a third of all children live in homes with four or more TVs. The most telling statistic: almost 60 percent of all families watch television during meals, and not necessarily at the same TV set. When do they talk about what they did that day? When do they make plans, exchange views, share jokes, tell about their triumphs or little disasters? When do they get to be a real family?

UNDERMINING THE FAMILY

Of course television has not been the only factor in the decline of family life in America. The steadily rising divorce rate, the increase in the number of working mothers, the trends towards people

30

moving far away from home, the breakdown of neighborhoods and communities—all these have seriously affected the family. Obviously the sources of family breakdown do not necessarily come from the family itself, but from the circumstances in which the family finds itself and the way of life imposed upon it by those circumstances. As Urie Bronfenbrenner has suggested:

> When those circumstances and the way of life they generate undermine relationships of trust and emotional security between family members, when they make it difficult for parents to care for, educate, and enjoy their children, when there is no support or recognition from the outside world for one's role as a parent, and when time spent with one's family means frustration of career, personal fulfillment, and peace of mind, then the development of the child is adversely affected.

Certainly television is not the single destroyer of American family life. But the medium's dominant role in the family serves to anesthetize parents into accepting their family's diminished state and prevents them from struggling to regain some of the richness the family once possessed.

One research study alone seems to contradict the idea that television has a negative impact on family life. In their important book *Television and the Quality of Life*, sociologists Robert Kubey and Mihaly Csikszentmihalyi observe that the heaviest viewers of TV among their subjects were "no less likely to spend time with their families" than the lightest viewers. Moreover, those heavy viewers reported feeling happier, more relaxed, and satisfied when watching TV with their families than light viewers did. Based on these reports, the researchers reached the conclusion that "television viewing harmonizes with family life."

Using the same data, however, the researchers made another observation about the heavy and light viewers: ". . . families that spend substantial portions of their time together watching television are likely to experience greater percentages of their family time feeling relatively passive and unchallenged compared with families who spend small proportions of their time watching TV."

At first glance the two observations seem at odds: the heavier 35 viewers feel happy and satisfied, yet their family time is more passive and unchallenging—less satisfying in reality. But when one considers the nature of the television experience, the contradiction vanishes. Surely it stands to reason that the television experience is instrumental in preventing viewers from recognizing its dulling effects, much as a mind-altering drug might do.

In spite of everything, the American family muddles on, dimly aware that something is amiss but distracted from an understanding of its plight by an endless stream of television images. As family ties grow weaker and vaguer, as children's lives become more separate from their parents', as parents' educational role in their children's lives is taken over by the media, the school, and the peer group, family life becomes increasingly more unsatisfying for both parents and children. All that seems to be left is love, an abstraction that family members know is necessary but find great difficulty giving to each other since the traditional opportunities for expressing it within the family have been reduced or eliminated.

For Discussion and Writing

1. Early media accounts of television emphasized its benefits to family life. What did these writers fail to foresee, according to Winn?

2. While Winn focuses on the negative effects of television, she also includes some research suggesting that television makes people more satisfied, happy, and relaxed. How does she respond to this evidence? Do you find her explanation persuasive? Why or why not?

3. **connections**   Writing in the 1970s, Winn sees television as the dominant influence on children. Writing in 2008, Clay Shirky, in "Gin, Television, and Social Surplus" (p. 236), claims that television and the television situation comedy, in particular, was the "critical technology for the twentieth century." The two writers essentially agree about television's dominance, but they come to different conclusions about the meaning of that dominance. How might Shirky respond to Winn's argument?

4. Winn makes broad and perhaps questionable generalizations about families and family rituals: "Not since prehistoric times, when cave families hunted, gathered, ate, and slept, with little time remaining to accumulate a culture of any significance, have families been reduced to such a sameness" (par. 20). Respond to one or more of her claims. For example, write about your own family rituals and "culture." Do Winn's assertions in this essay correspond to your experience? How does technology (television or otherwise) affect — or even mediate — your family relationships? Does it diversify and enrich them, or "reduce them" to sameness? Do you find that opportunities for "expressing [love] within the family have been reduced or eliminated" (par. 36)?

ERICA LIES

Mary Tyler More

Erica Lies is a freelance arts writer and comedian based in Austin, Texas. She received a Master's degree in Performance as Public Practice from The University of Texas at Austin in 2008. She has written for bitch *magazine,* Sidesplitter, *and other Web publications. In this essay from* bitch, *Lies places* 30 Rock *in the context of other workplace television comedies about single working women. She demonstrates that sitcoms can be closely read and analyzed formally, like literary texts. But she also illustrates how television shows can tell us much about a culture's attitudes, preoccupations, and anxieties. Lies focuses primarily on images of women and gender roles, but she also touches on subjects like race, class, and comedy itself. As you read, consider a question asked by Tina Fey's character, Liz Lemon: "What does [being sexy] have to do with comedy?"*

In a memorable episode of *30 Rock*, an awkward Liz Lemon stands with a lingerie-clad Jenna Maroney at a photo shoot, exclaiming unconvincingly, "Wow, this is . . . an honor. I'm friends with No. 4 on *Maxim's* list of the sexiest women in comedy!" Maroney, the star performer in *The Girlie Show*, the TV sketch-comedy program for which Lemon is the chief writer, clutches a rubber chicken and just as unconvincingly insists that posing for *Maxim* will be a smart career move—even as she comically fails to achieve "sexy" when her grease-slathered legs slide off a leather chaise in the shoot.

It's a funny scene, and not just because it takes the just-out-of-the-pool imitation sex appeal of *Maxim's* buxom babes to its laughable extreme. In fact, the scene's humor is hilariously meta, considering that Jenna's fictional appearance in *Maxim* was no coincidence, but part of a product-placement deal among Verizon, *Maxim*, and *30 Rock*. And it's rooted in offscreen history, too:

Fey herself was number 80 on *Maxim*'s "Hot 100 of 2002," taking her place on the list alongside usual suspects Tara Reid and Elisha Cuthbert—although Fey didn't pose for the list. When asked about her selection as a lad-mag hottie, Fey told *Believer* in 2004, "The *Maxim* thing was a little weird. It's probably a career move, but not one I care to be a part of."

The career moves Fey has chosen have been much smarter—creating and starring in the self-referential *30 Rock* has provided ample opportunity to influence the culture she loves to mock. The first season of *30 Rock* introduced us to Lemon, whose primary problems take the form of her insecure, egotistical staff of writers and performers, a nonexistent personal life, and a slimy corporate boss, Jack Donaghy, who is forever offering her advice. A comedy about making a comedy, *30 Rock* borrows material from Fey's own experiences as *Saturday Night Live* head writer, forming a meta-commentary that gestures outside the show to satirize gender relations as well as politics, race, and the increasingly corporate media. While awkwardness in a lead character is nothing new in prime-time comedy, it's generally reserved for a universally relatable male character. Lemon stands out because she's a woman—and, specifically, a nerdy one. To top it off, she's played by an actual comedy writer, not a starlet.

Like Fey herself, Lemon is a professional comedy geek who wears glasses and makes crass jokes. Lemon pairs blazers with jeans and Converse shoes, and though she's successful in the cutthroat comedy world, she gets lettuce stuck in her hair. Her name suggests imminent disaster—the sour fruit, the letdown car, the Liz Lemon. A self-described square ("I don't drink. Don't do any drugs—except for my allergy medication"), Lemon is a bumbling manager with a history of awkwardly truncated romantic relationships and a boundless knack for *Star Wars* references. But in Lemon—the supposedly unfeminine, socially awkward, lonely-though-successful woman—Fey has created a brainy female character rarely seen at the center of a comedy.

While few are interested in challenging Fey's critical acclaim   5 and comic chops, some folks have balked at *30 Rock*'s self-deprecating humor. Writing in the pages of this very publication, Sarah Seltzer lamented that Lemon's character perpetuates stereotypes attached to powerful women, citing the punch lines aimed at Lemon that highlight her status as "woefully single" and

"Mary Richards turned the world on with her smile."

"allegedly unattractive" ("Sour Lemon," no. 36). Of course, half of the joke is that Fey is attractive, but Seltzer raises an important question: How exactly do audiences interpret humor that mocks a female character? And how does that self-deprecating humor function? The series aims many a punch line at Lemon's perceived lack of femininity ("She thought you looked like Jennifer Jason Leigh. I made her repeat it. I was sure she meant Jason Lee."), but who exactly is the butt of the joke? Is it Lemon, for falling short of society's feminine ideal, or is it the society that emphasizes that ideal? Recent male television characters have had the luxury of being aggressively antisocial (*Curb Your Enthusiasm*'s Larry David), or unhappily single (*Arrested Development*'s

MARY TYLER MORE   269

Michael Bluth). Yet their unflattering qualities aren't attributed to their gender. Fey herself suggests it's unfair to ask individual female characters to represent their entire sex. In a 2004 *New Yorker* profile on Fey, Virginia Hefferman quoted Fey's response to a male colleague who asked if she thought her *SNL* sketches were antiwoman. Fey asserted that *SNL*'s job is "to make fun of people," adding, "If we don't make fun of women, the female performers don't have any parts."

Few successful recent sitcoms have revolved around a smart, independent woman, so it's no surprise that television critics relate *30 Rock*'s premise to venerable 1970s TV touchstone *The Mary Tyler Moore Show*. The comparison is not off the mark; Fey told the *New York Times* that she and her writers used *MTM* as a structural model when writing *30 Rock*'s early episodes. But in critics' nostalgia for the smart and independent Mary Richards, they forget that the show revealed its own set of anxieties surrounding independent women.

Alternately asserting her power and then retreating immediately, Mary could live alone at age 30, but her overaccommodating nature and inability to say no to both superiors and colleagues continually reassured viewers that she hadn't abandoned traditional femininity. Mary was portrayed as consistently smart and consistently pleasant. She never raised her voice, and for six seasons she called her boss "Mr. Grant" when everyone else simply called him "Lou." As the smartest character in the room, Mary had punch lines, but she was never the object of a joke, and she never had so much as a hair out of place. Mary Richards turned the world on with her smile, and—save for a stumble here and there—remained on her pedestal of perfection for the span of the show.

Liz Lemon, on the other hand, has Mary's central position but Rhoda Morgenstern's personality. Like Rhoda, Liz can say no—and be mean and inflexible when she does. *30 Rock*'s pilot episode opens with Lemon at a New York hot-dog stand, angrily protesting when a man cuts in front of her in line. To punish him, she buys all the vendor's hot dogs and refuses to give one to the linecutter. A parody of the *MTM* theme song begins to play as Lemon walks away, teetering under the oversized box of hot dogs; she hands one to a homeless man, who responds by throwing it back at her in the next shot. When questioned by a coworker about the

Who says women aren't funny? Tina Fey and Alec Baldwin on *30 Rock*.

box, Lemon's grouchy response—"You know how I hate it when people cheat or break rules?"—busts through the *MTM* illusion: New York is not Minneapolis, and Liz Lemon is no Mary Richards.

In the years between *MTM* and *30 Rock*, several other workplace comedies have centered on a single professional woman, and each has played on the gender anxieties of its decade. In the late '80s, the title character of *Murphy Brown* did Mary Richards one better: A brilliant, hard-talking, self-centered TV journalist, Murphy was over 40 and utterly uninterested in the institution of marriage. (She's now best remembered for incurring Dan Quayle's public criticism when she became a single mother.) Murphy came very close to assuming the privileges of being a man at the time, but the show's plotlines often served to tame her fierce ego by the conclusion—in one episode, her much younger male boss ordered her out of work for two weeks for walking out on an interview. If working women like Murphy frightened the status quo with their dangerous financial independence, the late-'90s debut of young, insecure, and kittenish Ally McBeal tamed the working-woman shrew by conveniently co-opting the fearsome F-word. Ally was a Harvard-educated lawyer who critics also likened to Mary Richards (single, white, non-blond professionals seem to call up the comparison). She brazenly wore short skirts, dared to sue a sexual harasser, and was determined to find the right man. Like Mary, men precipitated Ally's professional and geographic moves—even her career was the result of following a boyfriend's dreams. Ally scolded herself for displaying wit on a date ("I hate myself when funny"), and her dancing-baby hallucinations are firmly implanted in public memory. Ally bemoaned inequality, but though she talked revolution, she was never a real threat: "If women want to change society, they could do it. I plan to do it. I just want to get married first."

Breakout female characters of the Mary Richards variety seem 10
to come along at the rate of about once a decade (and are most often middle-class and white), but *30 Rock*'s Lemon debuted in the same season as another single brunet—Betty Suarez of ABC's *telenovela* sendup *Ugly Betty*. A young, up-for-any challenge striver from working-class Queens, Betty lucks into a job at *Mode*, a fashion magazine where her coworkers mock her geeky, unsophisticated clothes, her untweezed eyebrows, and her mouth full of metal. But her competence makes her indispensable to her playboy boss, who can barely get dressed without Betty's input, much less keep his job. Collectively, *30 Rock* and *Ugly Betty* have dominated comedy-award categories since their premieres in 2006, and *30 Rock* simultaneously acknowledges and distinguishes itself from its counterpart: In a meta moment when Lemon is caught literally crawling out of Jack Donaghy's office, she addresses the

camera directly, sighing, "This would have worked on *Ugly Betty*." And therein lies the difference—while *30 Rock* traffics in gender satire, *Ugly Betty* primarily intersects with class. Situated comfortably within the white managerial rungs, Lemon alone has the privilege of screwing up. Betty is smart and honest, with rock-solid moral character and a personality that outshines her over-plucked foils, but as an underling at her job, she is robbed of the opportunity to be mean. Betty has to ignore her shallow coworkers when they crack the wit whips, but Lemon can crack back.

Apparently prime-time television can now handle two lady-geek stars in the same decade, but it seems that two in the same show is still a no-go. Despite *30 Rock's* on-screen criticisms of gender relations, the show itself is not exempt from the gender politicking that it lampoons. Rachel Dratch, Fey's fellow Second City and *SNL* alumna, was originally slated to play the lead actress on *30 Rock's* fictional sketch show. Though a pilot had been shot with Dratch as Jenna, she was pulled at the last minute; separate interviews with Dratch and Fey in *New York* magazine and *Entertainment Weekly* claimed that *30 Rock's* producers felt Dratch was better suited to sketch-style character roles. Was it Donaghy's favorite market-research tool, the focus group, that precipitated the change? Jane Krakowski (of *Ally McBeal* fame) stepped into the role of Jenna; the character was rewritten and the pilot reshot. Though Dratch has recurring cameos (most memorably as a lesbian cat wrangler with a crush on Liz), one wonders how the surely unavoidable tension filtered into the show—a common theme in Lemon's interactions with Donaghy has Fey repeating some version of the line, "But these are my friends; you can't just fire them!"

Of course, without Fey in a primary power role behind the scenes, it's hard to imagine that a character like Liz Lemon would even get written. Where Mary Richards laughed at jokes, Lemon writes them for a living—and makes them at other people's expense. After Liz takes a crack at a male junior writer in "The C-word," she overhears him call her that special derogatory word reserved for women in power, and spends the rest of the episode struggling between her desire to be liked and her need to be an effective—if not always popular—manager. Because the audience is aware of Fey's offscreen status as *30 Rock's* showrunner, the episode delivers a satiric punch. Fey similarly drew on this double consciousness when she hosted the first post-strike episode of *SNL*, mocking the gendered criticisms of Hillary Clinton's campaign in a now-notorious statement — "People say Hillary is a bitch. Let me say something about that: Yeah, she is. So am I. . . . Bitches get stuff done."

Significantly, *30 Rock* uses Fey's experiences (and those of the female writers on her staff) to ridicule the contradictory expectations placed on single American women: Be professionally successful and independent, but also sexy, contained, and accommodating. A deleted scene from "The C-Word" exemplifies the inconsistent messages bubbling beneath *30 Rock*, when Jenna consoles Liz in her characteristically vapid manner: "The difficult part of being a modern woman, Liz, is learning to protect your strength while maintaining your femininity." Jenna then reveals the back of her dress, which plunges southward in parodic excess, and adds, "Is this too much butt cleavage?"

As a performer who wrote her way to the screen, Fey's ordinary-girl persona chips away at a toweringly unrealistic physical expectation for female performers. In another episode, when Liz admits she secretly wanted part of her friend's spotlight, Jenna's shocked response is strategically inappropriate: "Liz, you couldn't have been serious about acting for a living — you have brown hair!" The joke lands on Lemon, but audiences can't look at her without seeing Fey, whose very career disproves the statement. The April 2008 issue of *Vanity Fair* featured Fey on its cover, while Alessandra Stanley's accompanying story on self-scripting female comedians (titled "Who Says Women Aren't Funny?" — a direct retort to pundit Christopher Hitchens' now-infamous January 2007 *VF* essay that said just that) praised Fey as a leader. Unfortunately, Stanley focused more on female comedians' desirability than on their material; while Fey is attractive, her primary goal is to be funny. (Dratch was excluded from the piece entirely, which didn't help unpack the story's equation of hot + funny = truly funny.)

Perhaps audiences love Fey-as-Lemon because of Fey's embrace of her brain and her relative disinterest in her sex appeal. Of course, *30 Rock* is aware of its male viewership (Fey's neckline seems to drop with every episode), but Lemon isn't simply eye candy in service of male titillation. Where *The Mary Tyler Moore Show* and *Murphy Brown* drew on societal concerns surrounding single, working women, Lemon taps into women's apprehensions directly. She's ambivalent about marriage ("Slow down. I'm not ready to move my humidifiers yet.") and slings feminist barbs that manage to be funny ("How come men can be heavy and still be respected, like James Gandolfini — or Fat Albert?"). On *30 Rock*, Fey has the confidence to make fun of herself while delivering potshots at the crusty Hitchens-esque status quo. As Lemon says to Jenna in the *Maxim* scene, "What does [being sexy] have to do with comedy?"

Apparently, I'm not the only one who's noticed her disinterest in being a pleaser — in the fall of 2007, Liz Lemon graced *Maxim*'s list of "TV's Least Attractive Ladies," alongside Betty Suarez and Jerri Blank. Guess the boys at *Maxim* just can't take a joke.

For Discussion and Writing

1. Lies compares Liz Lemon to several other female television characters, including Betty Suarez of the show *Ugly Betty*. What is the key difference between Lemon and Suarez, in Lies's view?

2. Lies claims that a particular scene from a *30 Rock* episode is "hilariously meta" (par. 2). What does the term "meta" mean? What qualities does it suggest? Can you point to other examples of a show, a story, a film, a play, or a song being "meta"?

3. **connections** Lies quotes Tina Fey, who hosted *Saturday Night Live* and mocked the "gendered" criticism of Hillary Clinton during the 2008 presidential campaign: "People say Hillary is a bitch. Let me say something about that: Yeah, she is. So am I. . . . Bitches get stuff done" (par. 12). How do you think Ariel Levy, in "Women and the Rise of Raunch Culture" (p. 158), would interpret this statement? How might she respond to *30 Rock* and Lies's article? Does Liz Lemon seem emblematic of "raunch culture," or a reaction against it?

4. In this essay, the writer uses *30 Rock* and Liz Lemon to reflect on issues of women, gender, comedy, sex, work, and power. Choose another character from contemporary popular culture that you find representative or revealing in similar ways. What larger issues or problems does the character raise or embody? How is he or she representative of a particular time and place?

STEVEN JOHNSON

Watching TV Makes You Smarter

Born in 1968, Steven Johnson is a journalist and critic who writes about science, technology, and popular culture. Johnson has taught at Columbia University and New York University. He also advises Internet media companies such as Betaworks and Nerve.com and contributes regularly to publications such as the New York Times, *the* Wall Street Journal, *and* Wired *magazine, where he is a contributing editor. His books include* Mind Wide Open: Your Brain and the Neuroscience of Everyday Life *(2004),* Everything Bad is Good for You: How Today's Popular Culture Is Actually Making Us Smarter *(2005), and* Where Good Ideas Come From: The Natural History of Innovation *(2010).*

"Watching TV Makes You Smarter," adapted from Everything Bad Is Good for You, *originally appeared in the* New York Times Magazine. *In the essay, Johnson argues against common presumptions regarding the "dumbing down" of American culture. He also offers sensitive and revealing readings of television shows—their formal elements, narrative structures, and technical devices. As you read, try to define the "Sleeper Curve" in your own words. Does it seem like a valid explanation for changes in television programming? Does it apply to your own media preferences and habits?*

SCIENTIST A: *Has he asked for anything special?*
SCIENTIST B: *Yes, this morning for breakfast . . . he requested something called "wheat germ, organic honey and tiger's milk."*
SCIENTIST A: *Oh, yes. Those were the charmed substances that some years ago were felt to contain life-preserving properties.*
SCIENTIST B: *You mean there was no deep fat? No steak or cream pies or . . . hot fudge?*
SCIENTIST A: *Those were thought to be unhealthy.*
        —From Woody Allen's *Sleeper*

On Jan. 24, the Fox network showed an episode of its hit drama *24*, the real-time thriller known for its cliffhanger tension and often-gruesome violence. Over the preceding weeks, a number of public controversies had erupted around *24*, mostly focused on its portrait of Muslim terrorists and its penchant for torture scenes. The episode that was shown on the 24th only fanned the flames higher: in one scene, a terrorist enlists a hit man to kill his child for not fully supporting the jihadist cause; in another scene, the secretary of defense authorizes the torture of his son to uncover evidence of a terrorist plot.

But the explicit violence and the post-9/11 terrorist anxiety are not the only elements of *24* that would have been unthinkable on prime-time network television 20 years ago. Alongside the notable change in content lies an equally notable change in form. During its 44 minutes—a real-time hour, minus 16 minutes for commercials—the episode connects the lives of 21 distinct characters, each with a clearly defined "story arc," as the Hollywood jargon has it: a defined personality with motivations and obstacles and specific relationships with other characters. Nine primary narrative threads wind their way through those 44 minutes, each drawing extensively upon events and information revealed in earlier episodes. Draw a map of all those intersecting plots and personalities, and you get structure that—where formal complexity is concerned—more closely resembles *Middlemarch*[1] than a hit TV drama of years past like *Bonanza*.

For decades, we've worked under the assumption that mass culture follows a path declining steadily toward lowest-common-denominator standards, presumably because the "masses" want dumb, simple pleasures and big media companies try to give the masses what they want. But as that *24* episode suggests, the exact opposite is happening: the culture is getting more cognitively demanding, not less. To make sense of an episode of *24*, you have to integrate far more information than you would have a few decades ago watching a comparable show. Beneath the violence and the ethnic stereotypes, another trend appears: to keep up with entertainment like *24*, you have to pay attention, make inferences,

---

[1]*Middlemarch:* A serialized novel by British author George Eliot (the pen name of Mary Ann Evans; 1819–1880), known for its large cast of characters and multiple plots, first published as a single volume in 1874. [Editor's note.]

track shifting social relationships. This is what I call the Sleeper Curve: the most debased forms of mass diversion—video games and violent television dramas and juvenile sitcoms—turn out to be nutritional after all.

I believe that the Sleeper Curve is the single most important new force altering the mental development of young people today, and I believe it is largely a force for good: enhancing our cognitive faculties, not dumbing them down. And yet you almost never hear this story in popular accounts of today's media. Instead, you hear dire tales of addiction, violence, mindless escapism. It's assumed that shows that promote smoking or gratuitous violence are bad for us, while those that thunder against teen pregnancy or intolerance have a positive role in society. Judged by that morality-play standard, the story of popular culture over the past 50 years—if not 500—is a story of decline: the morals of the stories have grown darker and more ambiguous, and the antiheroes have multiplied.

The usual counterargument here is that what media have lost in moral clarity, they have gained in realism. The real world doesn't come in nicely packaged public-service announcements, and we're better off with entertainment like *The Sopranos* that reflects our fallen state with all its ethical ambiguity. I happen to be sympathetic to that argument, but it's not the one I want to make here. I think there is another way to assess the social virtue of pop culture, one that looks at media as a kind of cognitive workout, not as a series of life lessons. There may indeed be more "negative messages" in the mediasphere today. But that's not the only way to evaluate whether our television shows or video games are having a positive impact. Just as important—if not more important—is the kind of thinking you have to do to make sense of a cultural experience. That is where the Sleeper Curve becomes visible.

TELEVISED INTELLIGENCE

Consider the cognitive demands that televised narratives place on their viewers. With many shows that we associate with "quality" entertainment—*The Mary Tyler Moore Show, Murphy Brown, Frasier*—the intelligence arrives fully formed in the words and actions of the characters on-screen. They say witty things to one another and avoid lapsing into tired sitcom clichés, and we smile along in our living rooms, enjoying the company of these smart people. But assuming we're bright enough to understand the sentences they're saying, there's no intellectual labor involved in enjoying the show as a viewer. You no more challenge your mind by watching these intelligent shows than you challenge your body watching *Monday Night Football*. The intellectual work is happening on-screen, not off.

But another kind of televised intelligence is on the rise. Think of the cognitive benefits conventionally ascribed to reading: attention, patience, retention, the parsing of narrative threads. Over the last half-century, programming on TV has increased the demands it places on precisely these mental faculties. This growing complexity involves three primary elements: multiple threading, flashing arrows and social networks.

According to television lore, the age of multiple threads began with the arrival in 1981 of *Hill Street Blues*, the Steven Bochco police drama invariably praised for its "gritty realism." Watch an episode of *Hill Street Blues* side by side with any major drama from the preceding decades—*Starsky and Hutch*, for instance, or *Dragnet*—and the structural transformation will jump out at you. The earlier shows follow one or two lead characters, adhere to a single dominant plot and reach a decisive conclusion at the end of the episode. Draw an outline of the narrative threads in almost every *Dragnet* episode, and it will be a single line: from the initial crime scene, through the investigation, to the eventual cracking of the case. A typical *Starsky and Hutch* episode offers only the slightest variation on this linear formula: the introduction of a comic subplot that usually appears only at the tail end of the episode.

A *Hill Street Blues* episode complicates the picture in a number of profound ways. The narrative weaves together a collection of distinct strands—sometimes as many as 10, though at least half of the threads involve only a few quick scenes scattered through the episode. The number of primary characters—and not just bit parts—swells significantly. And the episode has fuzzy borders: picking up one or two threads from previous episodes at the outset and leaving one or two threads open at the end.

Critics generally cite *Hill Street Blues* as the beginning of   10 "serious drama" native in the television medium—differentiating the series from the single-episode dramatic programs from the 50's, which were Broadway plays performed in front of a camera. But the *Hill Street* innovations weren't all that original; they'd long played a defining role in popular television, just not during the evening hours. The structure of a *Hill Street* episode—and indeed of all the critically acclaimed dramas that followed, from *thirtysomething* to *Six Feet Under*—is the structure of a soap opera. *Hill Street Blues* might have sparked a new golden age of television drama during its seven-year run, but it did so by using a few crucial tricks that *Guiding Light* and *General Hospital* mastered long before.

Bochco's genius with *Hill Street* was to marry complex narrative structure with complex subject matter. *Dallas* had already shown that the extended, interwoven threads of the soap-opera genre could survive the weeklong interruptions of a prime-time show, but the actual content of *Dallas* was fluff. (The most probing issue it addressed was the question, now folkloric, of who shot J.R.) *All in the Family* and *Rhoda* showed that you could tackle complex social issues, but they did their tackling in the comfort of the sitcom living room. *Hill Street* had richly drawn characters confronting difficult social issues and a narrative structure to match.

Since *Hill Street* appeared, the multi-threaded drama has become the most widespread fictional genre on prime time: *St. Elsewhere, L.A. Law, thirtysomething, Twin Peaks, N.Y.P.D. Blue, E.R., The West Wing, Alias, Lost.* (The only prominent holdouts in drama are shows like *Law and Order* that have essentially updated the venerable *Dragnet* format and thus remained anchored to a single narrative line.) Since the early 80's, however, there has been a noticeable increase in narrative complexity in these dramas. The most ambitious show on TV to date, *The Sopranos*, routinely follows up to a dozen distinct threads over the course of an episode, with more than 20 recurring characters.

The total number of active threads equals the multiple plots of *Hill Street*, but on *The Sopranos* each thread is more substantial. The show doesn't offer a clear distinction between dominant and minor plots; each story line carries its weight in the mix. Episodes also display a chordal mode of storytelling entirely absent from *Hill Street*: a single scene in *The Sopranos* will often connect

"The Sopranos routinely follow[ed] up to a dozen distinct threads over the course of an episode, with more than 20 recurring characters."

to three different threads at the same time, layering one plot atop another. And every single thread in many *Sopranos* episodes builds on events from previous episodes and continues on through the rest of the season and beyond.

Taken together, these programs show the Sleeper Curve rising over the past 30 years of popular television. In a sense, this is as much a map of cognitive changes in the popular mind as it is a map of on-screen developments, as if the media titans decided to condition our brains to follow ever-larger numbers of simultaneous threads. Before *Hill Street*, the conventional wisdom among television execs was that audiences wouldn't be comfortable following more than three plots in a single episode, and indeed, the *Hill Street* pilot, which was shown in January 1981, brought complaints from viewers that the show was too complicated. Fast-forward two decades, and shows like *The Sopranos* engage their audiences with narratives that make *Hill Street* look like *Three's Company*. Audiences happily embrace that complexity because they've been trained by two decades of multi-threaded dramas.

Multi-threading is the most celebrated structural feature of the [15] modern television drama, and it certainly deserves some of the honor that has been doled out to it. And yet multi-threading is only part of the story.

THE CASE FOR CONFUSION

Shortly after the arrival of the first-generation slasher movies—*Halloween, Friday the 13th*—Paramount released a mock-slasher flick called *Student Bodies*, parodying the genre just as the *Scream* series would do 15 years later. In one scene, the obligatory nubile teenage babysitter hears a noise outside a suburban house; she opens the door to investigate, finds nothing and then goes back inside. As the door shuts behind her, the camera swoops in on the doorknob, and we see that she has left the door unlocked. The camera pulls back and then swoops down again for emphasis. And then a flashing arrow appears on the screen, with text that helpfully explains: *Unlocked!*

That flashing arrow is parody, of course, but it's merely an exaggerated version of a device popular stories use all the time. When a sci-fi script inserts into some advanced lab a nonscientist who keeps asking the science geeks to explain what they're doing with that particle accelerator, that's a flashing arrow that gives the audience precisely the information it needs in order to make sense of the ensuing plot. ("Whatever you do, don't spill water on it, or you'll set off a massive explosion!") These hints serve as a kind of narrative hand-holding. Implicitly, they say to the audience, "We realize you have no idea what a particle accelerator is, but here's the deal: all you need to know is that it's a big fancy thing that explodes when wet." They focus the mind on relevant details: "Don't worry about whether the babysitter is going to break up with her boyfriend. Worry about that guy lurking in the bushes." They reduce the amount of analytic work you need to do to make sense of a story. All you have to do is follow the arrows.

By this standard, popular television has never been harder to follow. If narrative threads have experienced a population explosion over the past 20 years, flashing arrows have grown correspondingly scarce. Watching our pinnacle of early 80's TV drama, *Hill Street Blues*, we find there's an informational wholeness to each scene that differs markedly from what you see on shows like *The West Wing* or *The Sopranos* or *Alias* or *E.R.*

Hill Street has ambiguities about future events: will a convicted killer be executed? Will Furillo marry Joyce Davenport? Will Renko find it in himself to bust a favorite singer for cocaine possession? But the present-tense of each scene explains itself to the viewer with little ambiguity. There's an open question or a mystery driving each of these stories—how will it all turn out?—but there's no mystery about the immediate activity on the screen. A contemporary drama like *The West Wing*, on the other hand, constantly embeds mysteries into the present-tense events: you see characters performing actions or discussing events about which crucial information has been deliberately withheld. Anyone who has watched more than a handful of *The West Wing* episodes closely will know the feeling: scene after scene refers to some clearly crucial but unexplained piece of information, and after the sixth reference, you'll find yourself wishing you could rewind the tape to figure out what they're talking about, assuming you've missed something. And then you realize that you're supposed to be confused. The open question posed by these sequences is not "How will this turn out in the end?" The question is "What's happening right now?"

The deliberate lack of hand-holding extends down to the micro- 20 level of dialogue as well. Popular entertainment that addresses technical issues—whether they are the intricacies of passing legislation, or of performing a heart bypass, or of operating a particle accelerator—conventionally switches between two modes of information in dialogue: texture and substance. Texture is all the arcane verbiage provided to convince the viewer that they're watching Actual Doctors at Work; substance is the material planted amid the background texture that the viewer needs to make sense of the plot.

Conventionally, narratives demarcate the line between texture and substance by inserting cues that flag or translate the important data. There's an unintentionally comical moment in the 2004 blockbuster *The Day After Tomorrow* in which the beleaguered climatologist (played by Dennis Quaid) announces his theory about the imminent arrival of a new ice age to a gathering of government officials. In his speech, he warns that "we have hit a critical desalinization point!" At this moment, the writer-director Roland Emmerich—a master of brazen arrow-flashing—has an official follow with the obliging remark: "It would explain what's driving this extreme weather." They might as well have had a flashing "Unlocked!" arrow on the screen.

The dialogue on shows like *The West Wing* and *E.R.*, on the other hand, doesn't talk down to its audiences. It rushes by, the words accelerating in sync with the high-speed tracking shots that glide through the corridors and operating rooms. The characters talk faster in these shows, but the truly remarkable thing about the dialogue is not purely a matter of speed; it's the willingness to immerse the audience in information that most viewers won't understand. Here's a typical scene from *E.R.*:

[*WEAVER AND WRIGHT push a gurney containing a 16-year-old girl. Her parents, JANNA AND FRANK MIKAMI, follow close behind. CARTER AND LUCY fall in.*]

WEAVER: 16-year-old, unconscious, history of biliary atresia.
CARTER: Hepatic coma?
WEAVER: Looks like it.
MR. MIKAMI: She was doing fine until six months ago.
CARTER: What medication is she on?
MRS. MIKAMI: Ampicillin, tobramycin, vitamins a, d and k.
LUCY: Skin's jaundiced.
WEAVER: Same with the sclera. Breath smells sweet.
CARTER: Fetor hepaticus?
WEAVER: Yep.
LUCY: What's that?
WEAVER: Her liver's shut down. Let's dip a urine. *[To CARTER]* Guys, it's getting a little crowded in here, why don't you deal with the parents? Start lactose, 30 cc's per NG.
CARTER: We're giving medicine to clean her blood.
WEAVER: Blood in the urine, two-plus.
CARTER: The liver failure is causing her blood not to clot.
MRS. MIKAMI: Oh, God. . . .
CARTER: Is she on the transplant list?
MR. MIKAMI: She's been Status 2a for six months, but they haven't been able to find her a match.
CARTER: Why? What's her blood type?
MR. MIKAMI: AB.

[*This hits CARTER like a lightning bolt. Lucy gets it, too. They share a look.*]

There are flashing arrows here, of course—"The liver failure is causing her blood not to clot"—but the ratio of medical jargon to layperson translation is remarkably high. From a purely narrative point of view, the decisive line arrives at the very end: "AB." The 16-year-old's blood type connects her to an earlier plot line, involving a cerebral hemorrhage victim who—after being dramatically revived in one of the opening scenes—ends up brain-dead. Far earlier, before the liver-failure scene above, Carter briefly discusses harvesting the hemorrhage victim's organs for transplants, and another doctor makes a passing reference to his blood type being the rare AB (thus making him an unlikely donor). The twist here revolves around a statistically unlikely event happening at the E.R.—an otherwise perfect liver donor showing up just in time to donate his liver to a recipient with the same rare blood type. But the show reveals this twist with remarkable subtlety. To make sense of that last "AB" line—and the look of disbelief on Carter's and Lucy's faces—you have to recall a passing remark uttered earlier regarding a character who belongs to a completely different thread. Shows like *E.R.* may have more blood and guts than popular TV had a generation ago, but when it comes to storytelling, they possess a quality that can only be described as subtlety and discretion.

EVEN BAD TV IS BETTER

Skeptics might argue that I have stacked the deck here by focusing on relatively high-brow titles like *The Sopranos* or *The West Wing*, when in fact the most significant change in the last five years of narrative entertainment involves reality TV. Does the contemporary pop cultural landscape look quite as promising if the representative show is *Joe Millionaire* instead of *The West Wing*?

I think it does, but to answer that question properly, you have 25 to avoid the tendency to sentimentalize the past. When people talk about the golden age of television in the early 70's—invoking shows like *The Mary Tyler Moor Show* and *All in the Family*—they forget to mention how awful most television programming was during much of that decade. If you're going to look at pop-culture trends, you have to compare apples to apples, or in this case, lemons to lemons. The relevant comparison is not between *Joe Millionaire* and *MASH*; it's between *Joe Millionaire* and *The Newlywed Game*, or between *Survivor* and *The Love Boat*.

What you see when you make these head-to-head comparisons is that a rising tide of complexity has been lifting programming at the bottom of the quality spectrum and at the top. *The Sopranos* is several times more demanding of its audiences than *Hill Street* was, and *Joe Millionaire* has made comparable advances over *Battle of the Network Stars*. This is the ultimate test of the Sleeper Curve theory: even the junk has improved.

If early television took its cues from the stage, today's reality programming is reliably structured like a video game: a series of competitive tests, growing more challenging over time. Many reality shows borrow a subtler device from gaming culture as well: the rules aren't fully established at the outset. You learn as you play.

On a show like *Survivor* or *The Apprentice*, the participants— and the audience—know the general objective of the series, but each episode involves new challenges that haven't been ordained in advance. The final round of the first season of *The Apprentice*, for instance, threw a monkey wrench into the strategy that governed the play up to that point, when Trump announced that the two remaining apprentices would have to assemble and manage a team of subordinates who had already been fired in earlier episodes of the show. All of a sudden the overarching objective of the game—do anything to avoid being fired—presented a potential conflict to the remaining two contenders: the structure of the final round favored the survivor who had maintained the best relationships with his comrades. Suddenly, it wasn't enough just to have clawed your way to the top; you had to have made friends while clawing. The original *Joe Millionaire* went so far as to undermine the most fundamental convention of all—that the show's creators don't openly lie to the contestants about the prizes—by inducing a construction worker to pose as man of means while 20 women competed for his attention.

Reality programming borrowed another key ingredient from games: the intellectual labor of probing the system's rules for weak spots and opportunities. As each show discloses its conventions, and each participant reveals his or her personality traits and background, the intrigue in watching comes from figuring out how the participants should best navigate the environment that has been created for them. The pleasure in these shows comes not from watching other people being humiliated on national television; it comes from depositing other people in a complex, high-pressure environment where no established strategies exist and watching them find their bearings. That's why the water-cooler conversation about these shows invariably tracks in on the strategy displayed on the previous night's episode: why did Kwame pick Omarosa in that final round? What devious strategy is Richard Hatch concocting now?

When we watch these shows, the part of our brain that moni- 30 tors the emotional lives of the people around us—the part that tracks subtle shifts in intonation and gesture and facial expression—scrutinizes the action on the screen, looking for clues. We trust certain characters implicitly and vote others off the island in a heartbeat. Traditional narrative shows also trigger emotional connections to the characters, but those connections don't have the same participatory effect, because traditional narratives aren't explicitly about strategy. The phrase "Monday-morning quarterbacking" describes the engaged feeling that spectators have in relation to games as opposed to stories. We absorb stories, but we second-guess games. Reality programming has brought that second-guessing to prime time, only the game in question revolves around social dexterity rather than the physical kind.

THE REWARDS OF SMART CULTURE

The quickest way to appreciate the Sleeper Curve's cognitive training is to sit down and watch a few hours of hit programming from the late 70's on Nick at Nite or the SOAPnet channel or on DVD. The modern viewer who watches a show like *Dallas* today will be bored by the content—not just because the show is less salacious than today's soap operas (which it is by a small margin) but also because the show contains far less information in each scene, despite the fact that its soap-opera structure made it one of the most complicated narratives on television in its prime. With *Dallas*, the modern viewer doesn't have to think to make sense of what's going on, and not having to think is very boring. Many recent hit shows—*24, Survivor, The Sopranos, Alias, Lost, The Simpsons, E.R.*—take the opposite approach, layering each scene with a thick network of affiliations. You have to focus to follow the plot, and in focusing you're exercising the parts of your brain that map social networks, that fill in missing information, that connect multiple narrative threads.

Of course, the entertainment industry isn't increasing the cognitive complexity of its products for charitable reasons. The

Sleeper Curve exists because there's money to be made by making culture smarter. The economics of television syndication and DVD sales mean that there's tremendous financial pressure to make programs that can be watched multiple times, revealing new nuances and shadings on the third viewing. Meanwhile, the Web has created a forum for annotation and commentary that allows more complicated shows to prosper, thanks to the fan sites where each episode of shows like *Lost* or *Alias* is dissected with an intensity usually reserved for Talmud scholars. Finally, interactive games have trained a new generation of media consumers to probe complex environments and to think on their feet, and that gamer audience has now come to expect the same challenges from their television shows. In the end, the Sleeper Curve tells us something about the human mind. It may be drawn toward the sensational where content is concerned—sex does sell, after all. But the mind also likes to be challenged; there's real pleasure to be found in solving puzzles, detecting patterns or unpacking a complex narrative system.

In pointing out some of the ways that popular culture has improved our minds, I am not arguing that parents should stop paying attention to the way their children amuse themselves. What I am arguing for is a change in the criteria we use to determine what really is cognitive junk food and what is genuinely nourishing . Instead of a show's violent or tawdry content, instead of wardrobe malfunctions or the F-word, the true test should be whether a given show engages or sedates the mind. Is it a single thread strung together with predictable punch lines every 30 seconds? Or does it map a complex social network? Is your on-screen character running around shooting everything in sight, or is she trying to solve problems and manage resources? If your kids want to watch reality TV, encourage them to watch *Survivor* over *Fear Factor*. If they want to watch a mystery show, encourage *24* over *Law and Order*. If they want to play a violent game, encourage Grand Theft Auto over Quake. Indeed, it might be just as helpful to have a rating system that used mental labor and not obscenity and violence as its classification scheme for the world of mass culture.

Kids and grown-ups each can learn from their increasingly shared obsessions. Too often we imagine the blurring of kid and grown-up cultures as a series of violations: the 9-year-olds who have to have nipple broaches explained to them thanks to Janet Jackson; the middle-aged guy who can't wait to get home to his Xbox. But this demographic blur has a commendable side that we don't acknowledge enough. The kids are forced to think like grown-ups: analyzing complex social networks, managing resources, tracking subtle narrative intertwinings, recognizing long-term patterns. The grown-ups, in turn, get to learn from the kids: decoding each new technological wave, parsing the interfaces and discovering the intellectual rewards of play. Parents should see this as an opportunity, not a crisis. Smart culture is no longer something you force your kids to ingest, like green vegetables. It's something you share.

For Discussion and Writing

1. Johnson discusses the practice of "multiple threading" (par. 7) in contemporary television shows. What does "multiple threading" mean? Why is it important to his argument?

2. In evaluating the quality of television today, Johnson uses comparison and contrast. Choose a particularly revealing example of comparison and contrast in the essay. What specific elements make it effective? How does it further Johnson's main point?

3. **connections** While Johnson focuses primarily on television drama, he also analyzes—and ultimately praises—reality shows such as *Survivor* and *The Apprentice*. How would you compare and contrast Johnson's view of reality television with that of George F. Will in "Reality Television: Oxymoron" (p. 289)?

4. According to Johnson, we have mistakenly accepted the assumption that "mass culture follows a path declining steadily toward lowest-common denominator standards, presumably because the 'masses' want dumb, simple pleasures and big media companies try to give the masses what they want" (par. 3). He supports that argument by using examples of sophisticated contemporary television shows which have changed viewer expectations: "not having to think is boring" (par. 31). How does this apply to your own television viewing and your consumption of entertainment, generally? Do you agree that "not having to think is boring"?

GEORGE F. WILL

Reality Television: Oxymoron

Pulitzer Prize–winning political columnist George F. Will (b. 1941) has been one of the most distinctive and enduring conservative voices of the last four decades. After earning a Ph.D. in political science from Princeton University, Will was a professor and Capitol Hill staffer before turning to journalism at the National Review *magazine. In the years since, he has written a regular column for the* Washington Post *and* Newsweek *magazine, and appeared regularly on ABC news as an analyst. His books include* Men at Work: The Craft of Baseball *(1990);* Restoration: Congress, Term Limits and the Recovery of Deliberative Democracy *(1992); and* One Man's America: The Pleasures and Provocations of Our Singular Nation *(2008).*

In this Washington Post *column, Will expresses contempt for reality television. But his argument goes beyond evaluating the artistic merit of shows like* Surivor *to questions of taste, choice, and public morality. According to Will, we live in an "increasingly infantilized" and "unshockable" society. Do you agree with him?*

Fred Allen, a mordantly sophisticated radio performer, died (mercifully, if not causally) just as television was permeating America, in 1956. He warned us: "Imitation is the sincerest form of television." So there will be limitations of "Fear Factor." That NBC program, in its first episode last week, attracted nearly 12 million voyeurs to watch simpletons confront their fears, for a fee. In that episode, confronters were covered by a swarm of biting rats. This week the program featured a willingness to eat worms and sit in a tub of them. "Fear Factor" is an imitation of an MTV program, "Jackass," named, perhaps, for its target viewer.

But American television is being imitative. ABC's "Nightline" reports that French, Spanish and Japanese television have similar programming, although none has—yet—matched the Peruvian show that pays poor people to eat maggots and be splattered with frog excrement. Last spring NBC concocted XFL football, promising more violence on the field and more cheerleaders' breasts on the sidelines than the NFL provides. The league drew a big audience for the first telecast, but the ratings began to plunge by the third quarter, and the league died after one season.

Optimists concluded that NBC had underestimated the viewing public. The optimists were, as usual, wrong. NBC understood that it had underestimated only the perversity required to rivet the attention of millions in an era when graphic violence and sexual puerilities are quotidian television. So NBC sank to the challenge of thinking lower. But it had better not rest on its laurels because its competitors in the race to the bottom will not rest, and the bottom is not yet in sight. The possible permutations of perversity programming—the proper name for what is called, oxymoronically, "reality television"—are as limitless as, apparently, is the supply of despicably greedy or spectacularly stupid people willing to degrade themselves for money. (A philosophical puzzle: *Can* such people be degraded?)

But perhaps the monetary incentive is superfluous, given today's endemic exhibitionism that makes many people feel unrecognized, unauthenticated—or something—unless they are presented, graphically, to an audience. Ours is an age besotted with graphic entertainments. And in an increasingly infantilized society, whose moral philosophy is reducible to a celebration of "choice," adults are decreasingly distinguishable from children in their absorption in entertainments and the kinds of entertainments they are absorbed in—video games, computer games, hand-held games, movies on their computers and so on. This is progress: more sophisticated delivery of stupidity. An optimistic premise of our society, in which "choice" is the ideal that trumps all others, is that competition improves things, burning away the dross and leaving the gold. This often works with commodities like cars but not with mass culture. There competition corrupts.

America, determined to amuse itself into inanition, is becoming increasingly desensitized. So entertainment seeking a mass audience is ratcheting up the violence, sexuality and degradation, becoming increasingly coarse and trying to be—its largest challenge—shocking in an unshockable society. The primitive cosmopolitans among us invariably say: Relax. Chaucer's Wife of 5

Bath,[1] the Impressionists and James Joyce's *Ulysses* have been considered scandalous. As the Supreme Court has said, "One man's vulgarity is another man's lyric." All right, then: One man's bearbaiting is another's opera. That British pastime involved pitting a chained bear against a pack of dogs, who fought, and usually killed, the bear. The historian Macaulay famously said that the Puritans opposed bearbaiting not because it gave pain to the bears but because it gave pleasure to the spectators.

The Puritans were right: Some pleasures are contemptible because they are coarsening. They are not merely private vices, they have public consequences in driving the culture's downward spiral. A mass audience is its own justification to purveyors of perversity television, who say: We are only supplying a market. As though there was a strong spontaneous demand for televised degradation. The argument that the existence of customers justifies the product distinguishes the purveyors of "Fear Factor" not at all from heroin pushers, who are not the purveyors' moral inferiors. How will a "pro-choice" society object to a program—let's call it "Who *Really* Wants to be a Millionaire?"—on which consenting contestants will be offered $1 million to play Russian roulette with a revolver loaded with a real bullet? Imagine the audience for the chance to see violent death in living color in prime time in the comfort of one's living room.

That's entertainment.

For Discussion and Writing

1. According to Will's column, why did the English Puritans oppose the practice of bearbaiting? How is this example related to his overall argument?

2. Will writes: "The argument that the existence of customers justifies the product distinguishes the purveyors of 'Fear Factor' not at all from heroin pushers, who are not the purveyors' moral inferiors" (par. 6). How effective is this analogy? Do you agree with Will's moral equivalence argument? Why or why not, specifically?

3. **connections**   Will's essay was originally published as a column, syndicated in many daily newspapers. Mark Greif's "The Reality of Reality Television" (p. 293) originally appeared in the literary journal *n+1*, which is published three times a year. How do the demands of

[1]Chaucer's Wife of Bath: The highly sexed narrator of one of the bawdier stories in Geoffrey Chaucer's *The Canterbury Tales* (1490). [Editor's note.]

their respective publications and formats shape the authors' essays? For example, how is Will's audience different from Greif's? How can you tell, specifically? What effects do length requirements have on their respective arguments? What are the advantages and disadvantages of each format?

4. According to Will, the assumption that "choice" and "competition" improve things "works with commodities like cars but not with mass culture"; when applied to mass culture, "competition corrupts" (par. 4). Do you agree or disagree with this distinction and this negative view of individual choice? How would you extend Will's argument, or (alternatively) argue against his position?

MARK GREIF

The Reality of Reality Television

Mark Greif (b. 1975) cofounded and coedits n+1, *a literary magazine devoted to cultural criticism, political commentary, poetry, and fiction; "The Reality of Reality Television" originally appeared in* n+1. *Like much of Greif's work, the essay is dense, leisurely, and informed by his wide breadth of knowledge: Reference points run from the eighteenth-century Swiss philosopher Jean Jacques Rousseau to* Extreme Makeover: Home Edition. *Alongside his work for* n+1, *Greif has written for* Harper's, *the* American Prospect, *the* New York Times, *and other publications. He teaches literary studies at Eugene Lang College, New School University in New York City.*

In this essay, Greif examines the role of reality television—its meaning, implications, and social consequences—in a republic. According to Greif, the "reality of reality television is that it is the one place that, first, shows us our fellow citizens to us and, then, shows that they have been changed by television." As you read, consider the connections between our mass entertainment and our sense of ourselves as "citizens." How might reality television shape our sense of community—and our politics?

There is a persistent dream that television will be more than it is: that it will not only sit in every home, but make a conduit for those homes to reach back to a shared fund of life.

The utopia of television nearly came within reach in 1992, on the day cable providers announced that cable boxes would expand to 500 channels. Back then, our utopian idea rested on assumptions both right and wrong. We assumed network-sized broadcasters could never afford new programming for so many active channels. That was right. We also assumed TV subscribers wouldn't stand for 500 channels of identical fluff, network reruns, syndicated programs, second-run movies, infomercials, and home shopping. That was wrong.

We were sure the abundance of channels would bring on stations of pure environmental happiness, carrying into our homes the comforts everyone craves: the 24-hour Puppy Channel, the Sky Channel, the Ocean Channel, the Baby Channel—showing nothing but frolicsome puppies, placid sky, tumultuous ocean, and big-headed babies. It never happened. And yet cable TV did indeed get cut up for small pleasures, in the advertisement of more utilitarian interests, on the Food Network, the InStyle Network, and Home and Garden Television (HGTV). (Natural beauty took hold on cable only in the pious slideshows of the Christian channels, where Yosemite is subtitled by 1st Corinthians.)

The meaningful history of technology turns out to be a history of its fantasized uses as much as of the shapes it actually takes. Our cable-box dreams finally rested on one beautiful notion: the participatory broadcasting of real life. With such a ludicrous number of channels, companies would just *have* to give some of the dial over to the rest of us, the viewers—wouldn't they? And we millions would flow into the vacuum of content. We'd manifest our nature on channels 401 to 499 as surely as do puppies, ocean, and sky. We'd do it marrying, arguing, staring at the wall, dining, studying our feet, holding contests, singing, sneezing. Hundreds of thousands of us had cameras. Well, we'd plug them in and leave the tape running for our real life.

In this underlying dream, we were neither exactly wrong nor right. The promise of the 500 channels went to waste. The techno-utopians' fantasies shifted to the internet. Nothing like the paradise we hoped for came to fruition on TV, that's for sure. Instead we got reality TV. 5

The assessment of reality television depends first on your notion of television; second, on your idea of political community.

Here is a standard misconception: since the noblest forms of artistic endeavor are fictional and dramatic (the novel, film, painting, plays), it can be assumed that the major, proper products of television will be its dramatic entertainments, the sitcom and the hour-long drama. I think this is wrong, and very possibly wrong for a whole number of reasons. Drama has a different meaning in a commercial medium where "programming" came into being as bacon to wrap the real morsels of steak, the 90-second advertisements. It means something different when it exists in a medium we switch on to see "what's on TV" rather than to find a given single work; when the goal is more often to watch television than to watch a particular drama and then turn it off.

From its beginnings in the early 1950s, TV has been blamed for encouraging overindividualism, for hastening consumer sucker-dom, for spurring passivity and couch-potatoness, and for making up the sensational bread-and-circuses of mass-culture tyranny. That pretty much covers it. And yet when opponents tried to divide the wretched things flickering inside the idiot-box into categories, they made excuses for quite unnecessary forms that they felt they recognized (highbrow TV dramas) while deriding unique and far more important items that didn't suit their vision of dramatic art (game shoes, local news, now reality shows).

The real principled problem *ought* to be with drama. The modern form of the long-standing Western philosophical argument placing drama at the center of a republic was articulated twenty years before the American Revolution. Rousseau[1] insisted in his *Letter to M. D'Alembert* that a republic (in his case Geneva, circa 1758) was correct to keep a theater out of its public life. To Rousseau, a republic is a political community in which each person is equal and sovereign—as it should be to us, today, living in the American republic. The citizen is not sovereign alone, but sovereign through his activity in a community of peers. The drama, when it was given too much power, crowded out the true entertainments of any republican political community—entertainments whose delights must be rooted in that self-regard and free judgment in daily activity which strengthens the bonds of citizen to citizen. (Bear in mind that Rousseau, in ancien régime Paris, loved the theater: "Racine charms me and I have never willingly missed a performance of Molière." A corrupt order, of nobility and monarchy, could hardly be made worse by drama and might be made better. But the philosopher loved a republic more.)

Rousseau expected that a republic's civic entertainments would   10 be displays of what people already do. Singing, building, decorating, beauty, athletics, and dancing gave pleasure and "entertainment" because the participants not only accomplished the acts but became spectacles to themselves—and to others, their equals and fellow-citizens, who had done just the same activities. Republican entertainments might often take the form of the contest or

---

[1]Jean Jacques Rousseau (1712–1778): Swiss philosopher and Enlightenment figure. [Editor's note.]

the demonstration. But they might also be the special celebration of ordinary living itself—the "festival":

Plant a stake crowned with flowers in the middle of a square; gather the people together there, and you will have a festival. Do better yet; let the spectators become an entertainment to themselves; let them become actors themselves; do it so each sees and loves himself in the others so that all will be better united.

"Let the spectators become an entertainment to themselves": a part of TV has always done this. It has meant, at different times, local programming, Huntley and Brinkley, the national news at 6 and local news at 11, talk shows and talent shows, *This is Your Life* and the regional tours of *Wheel of Fortune*. Accept, though, that television's most important function might always have been to let citizens *see* each other and *be seen* in their representatives— in our only truly national universal medium—and you're left to ask what will accomplish it best today. Reality television may furnish its dark apotheosis—a form for an era in which local TV has been consolidated out of existence, regional differences are said to be diminishing (or anyway are less frequently represented), and news, increasingly at the service of sales departments, has forfeited its authority to represent the polity.

We need myths, not only of our ideal, and our average, but of our fallen extreme. Since the establishment of informed-consent rules in the 1970s, the golden age of social psychology is gone. No more Stanley Milgram's[2] proof that ordinary citizens will push the voltage to the red zone while the electrocuted actor screams— so long as a lab-coated tester is there to give the orders. No more Philip Zimbardo's[3] proof that fake guards will brutalize fake prisoners if you arbitrarily split Stanford students into two groups, lock them in a basement, and leave them to their own devices. No more Harold Garfinkel's[4] demonstrations that testers can drive

---

[2]Stanley Milgram (1933–1984): American social psychologist who conducted controversial experiments on obedience and authority. [Editor's note.]

[3]Philip Zimbardo (b. 1933): An American psychologist known for his infamous "prison study," in which college students were assigned to be "prisoners" or "guards" in a mock prison. [Editor's note.]

[4]Harold Garfinkel (1917–2011): A sociologist and pioneer of ethnomethodology, which researches the ways in which members of a society make sense of the world and their place within it. [Editor's note.]

strangers berserk if they stare at other riders on the elevator or if children refuse to recognize their parents. Today we are reliant on *Elimidate, Punk'd,* and *Survivor.* Watching reality television is like walking one long hallway of an unscrupulous and peculiarly indefatigable psychology department.

The first ideal-type of reality TV is the show of the pure event. *Cops* represents one end of its spectrum, the low-budget dating shows (*Blind Date, Elimidate, Fifth Wheel, Xtreme Dating*) the other. You discern patterns in each—the effect on the watchful viewer is of a patterned repetition of wholly singular encounters. In the endless scenes of arrests, traffic stops, drive-by warnings ("OK, you ain't going to do it again"), domestic disturbances, and interviews with complainants ("Calm down, ma'am, just tell me what happened"), it becomes clear that justice, at the level of the arrest, has less to do than you might have thought with the code of law. Between cop and civilian, everything is determined by personality; each word is a step in a negotiation; the tools each side possesses seem arbitrary and confused, in the wheedling or vagueness of the suspect, the mock-authoritativeness and lack of information of the cop. So you make notes to your criminal self: never voluntarily submit to a search. But it doesn't take long to realize that, in the situation, you wouldn't remember all you'd learned watching *Cops*; politeness and hustling would take over. In the immediate interaction between two people, each staring into the other's eyes and trying to persuade him toward escape or incrimination, drugged by fear when not hazy with narcotics, you see the hidden face-to-face interactions of your countrymen.

And on *Blind Date* and *Xtreme Dating* and *Fifth Wheel,* with 15 wary daters eyeing each other over pasta dinners, leglessly drunk in a hundred indistinguishable neon dives and, afterwards, on the best dates, mumbling vulgar blandishments in hot tubs, you see that romance is not angelic recognition nor simple animal lust but a negotiation—the same as in the *Cops* arrest. The blind date and the traffic stop become on late-night TV the two paradigmatic experiences of American encounters between strangers. Homogenous America is instantly disproved by bizarre America. It is reassuring to watch this openness and fumbling. Finally you see without intermediary dramatization the landscape of tanning salons and restaurants and aikido studios in every corner of the country, the still-distinct accents but universalized, television-influenced behaviors, the dilemma of what to say and which personality to project, as if the social relation were being rebuilt, in a cutaway scale model of our society—a great televised Ark of a changing civilization—two by two.

So even though evidently all women look for "sense of humor" and all men want someone "I can have fun with," even though all good girls say they are "wild" and all good boys avow that they are "players," this has only an equivocal effect on individuals' relentlessly erroneous attempts to approximate trends and manners learned from TV, which seems to be what's really going on. Yoyoing modesty and immodesty ("I'm a bad girl. I mean, I'm mostly bad in bed"); frank talk about penis size and boob jobs but wildly variable estimates on the morality of kissing on a first date; shy clumsiness masked under pornographic aspirations ("Have you ever had a threesome?" "No, that's more like, a goal of mine")— *this*, the cameras prove, is the current American performing-reality. Everyone tries to play someone else on TV, but still feels so many tethering strings from the prosaic, deficient, and plain polite that conformity becomes chaotic and imitation idiosyncratic.

"Voyeurism" was never the right word for what it means to watch these shows. You feel some identification with the participants, and even more sympathy with the situation. "And if I were pulled over—and if I were set up on a blind date—how would I fare?" But primarily, and this is the more important thing to say about reality TV, there is always *judgment*. You can't know the deeds your countrymen will do until you see them; and once these deeds are seen, you won't fail to judge and retell them. Reality TV is related in this respect to the demimonde of *The People's Court, Divorce Court, Judge Hatchett*, and *Judge Judy*. Classy critics hate these shows too, or claim to. I think that's a mistake. The way in which all reality TV—and much of daytime TV—can be "real" across social classes is in its capacity for judgment. The "friends" on *Friends* were an ideological group, propagandists for a bland class of the rich in a sibling-incest sitcom. The show didn't allow you to take their idiocy to task, nor ever to question the details of how they paid their rent or their hairdresser's bill, or how they acted on the "outside." If only Judge Judy could sit in judgment of them, once! If only *Cops* would break down their door and throw

them against the wall! Monica, you ignorant Skeletor, eat a sandwich! Ross, you vainglorious paleontologist, read a book! *You
mortuary creep!* Truly, the judge shows have a vengeful appeal:
they gather every inept, chiseling, weaseling, self-focused sort of
person you meet in your daily life and, counting on each one's
stupidity and vanity to get him up into the dock, they yell at him.
   This is one way to come to terms with your fellow citizens.
Much reality TV, by contrast, communicates a relative openness
of judgment, though judgment is its one constant—and does so
also by its wider identity of situation between the viewer and
those before the cameras. (Nearly everybody has dated, and, from
rich to poor, nearly everybody fears the police when driving and
will call on them when threatened.) Reality TV's judgment falls on
"another oneself," however much one retains the right to disown
and ridicule this nitwitted fellow-citizen. Nowadays, at every level
of our society, there is a hunger for judgment. Often this becomes
summary judgment—not so much the wish to know the truth,
but the brutal decisionism that would rather be wrong than stay
in suspension. This is the will not to deliberate but to sentence. In
the political realm, it has influenced the shape of the current
disaster. Its soft manifestations own the therapeutic talk shows,
in the sniffling and nose wiping of a *Dr. Phil*, where the expert is
never at a loss. He will not say: "No, your situation is too messed
up for me to advise you; I have a similar problem; think for yourself." Whereas the cheapest and rawest reality TV offers you a
chance to judge people like you, people who do lots of the same
things you do. It is cheap, it is amoral, it has no veneer of virtue,
it is widely censured and a guilty pleasure, and it can be more
educational and truthful and American than most anything else,
very suitable for our great republic.

Until, that is, one began to see what the capital-rich networks
would make of it. For they got into the act, like dinosaurs in an
inland sea, and they made the waters heave. They developed the
grandiose second ideal-type of filmed reality, courtesy of bigger
budgets and serial episodes: the show of the group microcosm.
   The microcosms were large-scale endeavors, financed by FOX,   20
MTV, NBC, ABC, CBS, and the WB. (The other shows had been
cheaply made and served up to UHF and low-budget cable stations by syndication, or, like *Cops*, run in the early barebones

Survivor: Redemption Island (2011): Tribal council or reality TV republic?

years of FOX and retained.) MTV's *The Real World*, which put teens in a group house with cameras, was the earliest and most incomplete example. The pun in its "real world" title meant both that you would see how non-actors interacted (initially fascinating) and that this was, for many of the children of the show, their first foray away from home (pretty boring, after the umpteenth homesick phone call). MTV's goal was to make up a "generation," not a society, as MTV is the most aggressive promoter of one version of youth as a wholesale replacement of adult life.

Subsequently the broadcast networks converted the dating "event" show into sagas of thirty suitors, peeling them away one by one until only the chosen bride or groom remained. *Big Brother* turned the house show, too, into a competition. An even more triumphant microcosm was *Survivor*—followed, in time, by *The Amazing Race*. The newer shows that defined the microcosmic reality and blended it with competition adopted the same basic forms of social discovery that had animated the birth of the English novel: the desert-island Robinsonade of *Survivor*, the at-the-ends-of-the-earth-bedragons imperialist travelogue and quest romance of *The Amazing Race*, even, perhaps, the sentimental seductions of *The Bachelor*, where so many willing Clarissas[5] rode

---

[5]Clarissas: Clarissa Harlowe, title character of Samuel Richardson's 1748 English novel *Clarissa*, who is pursued by the villainous Robert Lovelace. [Editor's note.]

in limousines squealing to a manor house to hand their hearts to Lovelace.

Yet *Survivor* never took up the society-from-nothing isolation of the desert island, which had motivated the original *Robinson Crusoe*. *The Amazing Race* didn't care about the Englishman-in-Lilliput foreignness of Swift or the chance meetings of picaresque or even the travelers' tall tales in Hakluyt. The shows had no interest in starting civilization from scratch. Nor for that matter were they much interested in travel—on *The Amazing Race*, you glimpse the blurred locals out the windows of speeding cars. These shows were about the spectacularization of a microcosmic America—about the reduction of society to a cross-section of our countrymen—still so very American, never "going native."

The shows put together sociable Americans, so they would have nothing left but their group interactions, their social negotiations, to keep them going. Nobody let them starve, nothing endangered them. Nominally structured as a contest of skill, skill mattered little and "alliances" much on *Survivor*. The sniping and soothing in couples and trios—forming and reforming, betraying and sticking together—were the main things of interest on that show and on *The Amazing Race*, where it was hard to tell if we were supposed to care, really, that one pair ran faster than another. How do Americans talk and how do they arrange things, in a completely minimal setting, a little like the office and a little like the home but not totally unlike a sequestered jury? So many of the contestants brought the workplace with them, and they were meant to, since they were identified at every subtitle of their names with their stateside jobs: Actor/Model, Computer Programmer, Fireman. This was our festival. Let's see if the alliance can hold between the Stock Trader, the Carpenter, and the Actress. Who will emerge as the "Survivor"? Let's race the Midget and her Cousin, so lovable, against the Bad Couple Who Should Not Marry. Let's see who our true representatives are.

The structure of each of the shows that "voted people off the island," requiring the microcosm to draw itself down each week, echoed, with static, the old idea of a republic of political equals, who despite unequal skills and endowments one by one would recuse themselves from activity to leave a single best representative behind to speak in public for their interests. If we truly all are equals in America, this would be a picture, in ideal form, of how we choose aldermen and selectmen and Congressmen—using

our sovereignty to withdraw our sovereignty, that is to say, to
focus it in the hands, for two or four years, of individuals who act
for us. By this means the microcosm programs resembled political allegories.

And yet many of the reality shows of the microcosmic commu-   25
nity were quite deliberately, self-consciously implanted, sometimes by the rules, sometimes by the informal instructions given
to players, with an original sin. That sin was the will to power by
trickery, the will to deception, which puts the power-mad ahead
of the natural leader. And the players did not rebel—they accepted
this, knowing it too well from home, from what they would call
their "real life." "That's how you play the game," each aspiring
survivor explained, with the resignation of a trapped bear chewing off its leg, "you have to fool people, you can only be loyal to
yourself." They had the republican ideal in their hands, and didn't
use it. It got confused with the economic or Darwinian model of
competition, in which anti-representative stratagems are justified
because one wins in the defeat and eradication of all others to
gain a single jackpot. This, too, was an aspect of the realness of
"reality" for Americans: we knew we were witnessing republics of
voting or shared excellence competing, or perhaps blending, with
another force in our lives.

As deception and power-hunger are the sins built into the microcosm, so the *fixed norm* is the flaw introduced into shows of pure
judgment. It produces the third ideal type of reality TV: the show
of the industry standard.

It was latent in the grand-scale dating shows, these contests
that brought in the single judge and red roses and arbitrary rules
and an image of romantic love from somewhere in the minds
of Hallmark: but who knows, maybe this was close enough to
the values of dreamy romance to form some people's preexisting
reality. In *American Idol*, though, you see the strong beginning of
the reality show of the third type. *American Idol* was the best, and
the most insinuating, of the industry shows because it took one
of the basic categories of common endeavor, that Rousseau loved
well—a singing contest, the commonplace sibling of a beauty or
dancing or athletic contest. Everyone sings, if only in the shower—
and the footage of the worst contestants made clear that the
contest *did* include all of us, that the equivalent of singing in the

shower was being considered, too, on the way to the final idol. The show had "America" judge, by casting the final votes, *en masse*. Yet it used professional judges in the meantime, a panel of allegorical experts, Simon Cowell (rhymes with "scowl"; the Stern Judge; George III), Paula Abdul (the Universal Sexy Mommy; Betsy Ross), and Randy Jackson (the Spirit of Diversity). Allegorically, America would free itself from the tyranny of the English King, having learned his wisdom, pay due homage to its own diversity, and enjoy the independence to make its own choice — which the hands-tied Englishman's production company would have to live with, and distribute to record stores. Poor George III! What one really learned was that, unlike a singing contest in the high school gym, the concern of the recording industry was not just, or no longer, whether someone could sing. It was whether a contestant was fitted to the industry, malleable enough to meet the norms of music marketing. The curtain was pulled away from the Great Oz, and the public invited to examine his cockpit and vote which lever or switch to pull next. As it turns out, it is really no less pleasant to choose a winner to suit the norms of music marketing, than to choose on individual talent. One was still choosing, and the idol would still be ours. An idol of the marketplace, to be sure, but still our representative American idol.

The major new successes of the past few years have taught (or pretended to teach) the norms of other industries. *The Apprentice*, a show in which one tries to learn skill in business, teaches the arbitrariness of contemporary success in relation to skill. The winners are conditioned to meet a certain kind of norm, not really familiar from anywhere else in life, which corresponds to "the values of business" as interpreted by Trump. *America's Next Top Model* shows how a beauty contest ceases to be about beauty. The real fascination of the show is learning, first, how the norms of the fashion industry don't correspond to ordinary ideas of beauty (you knew it abstractly, here's proof!), but to requirements of the display of clothes and shilling for cosmetics; second, how the show will, in the name of these norms, seek something quite different in its contestants — a psychological adhesiveness, a willingness to be remade and obey. *The Starlet* suggests the distance between the norms of TV acting and the craft of acting — and yet again, in the name of "how it's done in the industry," which provides one kind of interest, the contestants are recast psychologically, which provides the other. And on it goes, with "how to become a chef" (*Hell's Kitchen*) and "how to be a clothing designer's minion" (*The Cut*), et cetera.

All this is interesting and revealing in its way. But the final stage is all too familiar: that is, the flow back of norms justified by industry into norms for inner spaces—first the mind, which accepts insane instructions and modifications, then the spaces that have nothing to do with either public life or work, and should offer safety from their demands. I am thinking of the home and the integral body, underneath the skin.

For a final, baroque range of reality shows has emerged in the 30 last two years: *The Swan, Extreme Makeover*, and, when these turned out to be slightly more than viewers could bear, *Extreme Makeover: Home Edition* and its copycat shows. *The Swan* and *Extreme Makeover* also drew on the most basic of all spectacles-of-excellence, the beauty contest or "pageant"—which once formed a way of seeing or understanding the country, as in the Miss America contests (when you would root for your state while admiring the flowers of the other forty-nine). And the new shows advanced a new kind of norm by recreating it surgically, by literally rebuilding people's faces and bodies to suit, not beauty, but a kind of televisual glamour. Ordinary unattractive people, given nose jobs, boob jobs, liposuction, lip collagen, tummy tucks, and chin pulls—plus fifty minutes of therapy—looked like wax mannequins when, alone and imprisoned in a Gothic mansion, the naturally lovely host pulled the velvet drapes back from the mirror, and the rebuilt women, inevitably, began to weep, shocked. Then the host spoke: "You're crying because you've never seen yourself so beautiful. You're crying because you've been transformed," intoning these words until the weeping speechless victim nodded. If this looked like brainwashing, you hardly knew the horror of it until the camera cut to a boardroom of the delighted surgical experts who had done the work—each one of them equally off-kilter and monstrous because of surgical modifications made to his own face or teeth or eyes or hair. (Flashback to one of the famous Rod Serling-written *Twilight Zone* episodes, this one from 1960: an ordinary woman is called "ugly" and pressured into damaging facial surgery that we can't understand—until the camera pulls back to show us that everyone in her world is hideously disfigured! Yee-ikes!)

The point of these shows was not just how people would be altered, but that they *could* be altered. As the *Six Million Dollar Man* introduction used to say, "We have the technology . . ." but what was needed was the rationale. When this transdermal insertion of the norm into average people came to seem suspect, the networks increasingly devoted episodes to already hideously ugly and disfigured people, so that the norm could be disguised as charity or medical necessity. But the greater success proved to be the subtle turn, with charitable aspect intact, to demolishing and rebuilding people's homes rather than their faces, in the adjunct called *Extreme Makeover: Home Edition*, which supersized existing home-decorating reality shows like *Trading Spaces* (on which two neighbors agree to redecorate one room in each other's home). *Extreme Makeover* would get at privacy in one way or another; if not through the body then through the private space that shelters it. A team of experts came in to wreck your shabby domicile and rebuild it. The dwellings that resulted were no longer homes, but theme houses; instead of luxuries, the designers filled rooms with stage sets keyed to their ten-minute assessments of the residents' personalities: "Little Timmy wants to be a fireman, so we made his room look like it's on fire!" As long as the homeowners were poor or handicapped enough, anything was a step up. The show has been an enormous hit.

Whatever can be done in the name of charity or medicine or health will allow the reinsertion of the norm into further spheres of privacy. Fox is said to be planning *Who Wants to Live Forever?*, a "program that predicts when participants will die and then helps them extend their lifespan through dieting, exercise, [and] breaking bad habits." The circle is closed, and "reality" here no longer lets us observe our real life, but its modifications in the name of a statistical life to come. The private matters we can't, or shouldn't, see flow in to replace our public witnessing of each other. And the festival is no longer of ourselves, but of phantasms projected by industries of health, beauty, home, all industries requiring our obedience; worse than the monsters of drama, because they don't admit their degree of fiction.

The reality of reality television is that it is the one place that, first, shows our fellow citizens to us and, then, shows *that they have been changed by television*. This reality is the unacknowledged

truth that drama cannot, and will not, show you. A problem of
dramatic television, separate from what the corrupt characters
say and do, is that it shows people who live as if they were *not*
being shaped by television. On this point it profoundly fails to
capture our reality. (The novel, in contrast, was always obsessed
with the way consciousness was shaped and ruined by reading
novels.) And this is consistent with the way in which television,
more than other media, has a willingness to do the work of shaping life, and subservience to advertising and industry, even when
its creators do not understand what they're up to. Drama says:
this is harmless, fictional. In fact it pushes certain ways of life.
But wherever industrial norms repenetrate the televised rendition of reality, they can *directly* push certain ways of life, no longer even needing to use the mediation of "harmless" fiction and
drama.

One can sometimes fight corruption with corruption: *Blind
Date* to counter *Friends*. So what in our television experience,
against *Extreme Makeover*, will show the ways in which homes
and faces cannot be remade? Who will make the reality to counter "reality"?

For Discussion and Writing

1. While many critics of reality television emphasize its voyeurism,
   Greif does not. What is the "more important thing to say about
   reality TV" (par. 17) according to him? What do such shows allow
   viewers to do "always"?

2. In his analysis of the show *Survivor*, Greif writes: "They had the
   republican ideal in their hands, and didn't use it. It got confused
   with the economic or Darwinian model of competition, in which
   anti-representative stratagems are justified because one wins in the
   defeat and eradication of all others to gain a single jackpot" (par. 25).
   What does this mean, exactly? Why is it important to Greif's argument? How does it imply a relationship between our entertainment
   and our politics? Do you find it persuasive to "read" a television
   show in this way?

3. **connections**   In "Reality Television: Oxymoron" (p. 289), George F.
   Will argues that competition in the realm of mass culture "corrupts" (par. 4) because it forces shows to "ratche[t] up the violence,
   sexuality and degradation" (par. 5). Does Greif's essay support this
   view? For example, Greif begins by citing the "utopian idea" of 500
   competing cable channels (par. 2). Does he take the same attitude

toward the proliferation of reality television and mass culture, generally, that Will does?

4. Greif writes: "We need myths, not only of our ideal, and our average, but of our fallen extreme" (par. 13). Greif finds examples of the fallen extreme in reality television shows such as *Cops*. First, consider how he's using the word *myth*: What does it mean in this context? Second, supply examples of each of these three myths from your own reading, viewing, or observations of culture. Where do we find these myths? What purpose do they serve? Why, for example, would we need a myth for "our average"?

CHAPTER 6

Movies

In his essay "Why Hollywood Hates Capitalism," included here, Rick Groen refers to Hollywood as a "dream factory." The anthropologist Hortense Powdermaker coined that term in *Hollywood, The Dream Factory*, her 1950 anthropological study of the movie business. As she pointed out, Hollywood is "not an exact geographical area," but rather a "state of mind." We all live within that state of mind, to some degree. Hollywood dreams inform our own dreams—our visions of romantic love, our images of glamour and success, our ideas about American history, even our sense that Hollywood itself is a "mythic" place. That place extends well beyond America's borders: Hollywood entertainment remains one of the U.S.'s largest and most enduring exports.

Of course, moviemaking is as much a matter of making money as it is a matter of making myths. Stories about the corrupting effects of the film industry or the struggles of individuals to carve meaningful art out of mass entertainment have long been fodder for Hollywood films from *Sunset Boulevard* (1950) to *Barton Fink* (1991) and *Mulholland Drive* (2001). When we consider some of the most well-known filmmakers of the last forty years, like Steven Spielberg, George Lucas, and James Cameron, we see that they manufacture big profits by manufacturing big myths, uniting the two main functions of the dream factory. But the cultural influence and significance of the movie industry transcends the work of blockbuster producers, independent art-film auteurs, or any individual or corporation. Perhaps even more than they do with television, Americans look to the big screen to work through their dreams and their nightmares, their ideals and their fears, and their collective sense of a cultural moment—past, present, and future.

That principle applies as much to a popular, frivolous-seeming comedy as it does to the most somber Oscar contender.

The essays in this section give diverse perspectives on movies, the film industry, and the role of Hollywood in American culture. In "Mystical Black Characters Play Complex Cinematic Role," Rita Kempley examines the film archetype of the "magic negro," a stock figure in movies dating back to the 1940s and 1950s. Susan Sontag unpacks the formal elements and themes of science fiction and disaster films in "The Imagination of Disaster." In the process, she shows how these movies meet certain cultural and psychological needs. Linda Seger's classic "Creating the Myth" reveals the archetypal characters and mythical narratives that structure many popular films. In "Why Are So Many Films for Latinos Bad?" Alonso Duralde considers Hollywood's tendency to make "dreadful movies for Latino audiences," especially at a time when the Latino population is growing as both an economic and cultural force. The paired readings explore the film industry's relationship to capitalism, labor, and social class. Rick Groen's "Why Hollywood Hates Capitalism" investigates the irony of a "big business that, on the screen at least, loathes and despises big business." In "Remembering Norma Rae," Robert Nathan and Jo-Ann Mort argue that the film industry largely ignores stories about "working people fighting to better their lives."

RITA KEMPLEY

Mystical Black Characters Play Complex Cinematic Role

Rita Kempley (b. 1945) was a longtime film critic for the Washington
Post. *In this essay from the* Post, *she highlights the figure of the "magic
negro," a stereotypical film image of African Americans. As Kempley
illustrates, this character endures in a variety of forms, from Morgan
Freeman playing God in* Bruce Almighty *to Michael Clark Duncan's
portrayal of the wrongly convicted black healer John Coffey in* The
Green Mile. *Kempley also shows that this character is nothing new.
What does its history and persistence suggest about race in America?*

Morgan Freeman plays God in "Bruce Almighty"; Laurence
Fishburne a demigod in "The Matrix Reloaded"; and Queen
Latifah a ghetto goddess in "Bringing Down the House."

What's the deal with the holy roles?

Every one of the actors has to help a white guy find his soul or
there won't be a happy ending. Bruce (Jim Carrey) won't get the
girl. Neo (Keanu Reeves) won't become the next Messiah. And
klutzy guy Peter (Steve Martin) won't get his groove on.

In movie circles, this figure is known as a "magic Negro," a
term that dates to the late 1950s, around the time Sidney Poitier
sacrifices himself to save Tony Curtis in "The Defiant Ones." Spike
Lee, who satirizes the stereotype in 2000's "Bamboozled," goes
even further and denounces the stereotype as the "super-duper
magical Negro."

"[Filmmakers] give the black character special powers and   5
underlying mysticism," says Todd Boyd, author of "Am I Black
Enough for You?" and co-writer of the 1999 film "The Wood."
"This goes all the way back to 'Gone with the Wind.' Hattie
McDaniel is the emotional center, but she is just a pawn. Pawns

310

help white people figure out what's going wrong and fix it, like Whoopi Goldberg's psychic in 'Ghost.'"

It isn't that the actors or the roles aren't likeable, valuable or redemptive, but they are without interior lives. For the most part, they materialize only to rescue the better-drawn white characters. Sometimes they walk out of the mists like Will Smith's angelic caddy in "The Legend of Bagger Vance." Thanks to Vance, the pride of Savannah (Matt Damon) gets his "authentic swing" back.

A case of the yips hardly seems to call for divine intervention, but then neither does Carrey's crisis in "Bruce Almighty." He's a TV funny guy who wants to be a news anchor. After he loses out to another contender, he verbally lambastes the Lord (played by Freeman with as much dignity as he can muster), and the Lord takes an interest.

Freeman's God can walk on water. But when He first appears, God is mopping the floors. Yes, He humbles Himself to teach the title character, Bruce, about humility. He then hands his powers over to him, popping in from time to time to save the world from Bruce's bumbling.

In "The Family Man," a 2000 version of "It's a Wonderful Life," Don Cheadle turns up as Cash, a meddlesome guardian angel disguised as a street tough. Cash shows Wall Street wheeler-dealer Jack Campbell (Nicolas Cage) how things would have been if he hadn't ditched his college sweetheart to pursue his career. When the fantasy ends, Jack must choose between love or money. Thanks to Cash, Jack has a chance to make amends for his capitalistic piggishness. Cue the heavenly chorus.

"Historically, if a black person is thrust into a white universe, it is inevitable that the white people will become a better person," says Thomas Cripps, author of "Making Movies Black: The Hollywood Message Movie from World War II to the Civil Rights Era" and other books on African-American cinema. "Sidney Poitier spent his whole career in this position. Sidney actually carried the cross for Jesus in 'The Greatest Story Ever Told.'"

In 1943 alone, black men became the moral conscience of white characters in four World War II movies: "Sahara," "Bataan," "Crash Dive" and "Lifeboat." Cripps is especially fond of the example set by actor Rex Ingram in "Sahara," the tale of a tank full of men lost in the desert. "When they decide to get rid of

In *The Legend of Bagger Vance*, starring Will Smith and Matt Damon, a game of golf calls for divine intervention.

somebody so the rest can survive, who stands up and says, 'We either all live or we all die together'? Ingram. The black man becomes the spokesman for Western democracy."

Like Ingram's soldier and Queen Latifah's salty soul sister, many black exemplars don't have halos, but they still work miracles. Her Highness' performance "is especially unusual because most of these characters are male," says Jacqueline Bobo, chair of women's studies at the University of California at Santa Barbara. "When women do show up, they end up in exoticized roles like Halle Berry's in 'Monster's Ball.'"

Bobo's colleague Cedric Robinson, author of "Black Marxism," says: "Males, more problematic in the American imagination, have become ghostly. The black male simply orbits above the history of white supremacy. He has no roots, no grounding. In that context, black anger has no legitimacy, no real justification. The only real characters are white. Blacks are kind of like Tonto, whose name meant fool."

Audiences, black and white, seem to be accepting of these one-note roles, judging by the financial success of "Bringing Down the House," which brought in about $130 million, and "Bruce

Almighty," which has raked in $149 million and was ranked No. 2 at the box office last week.

And yet other viewers and most critics were appalled by the extreme odd-couple comedy "Bringing Down the House," in which Charlene (Latifah), an obnoxious escaped con, invades the staid bourgeois universe of Peter (Martin), the uptight suburbanite.

Charlene not only shows Peter how to jump, jive and pleasure a woman, but teaches his son to read (a nudie magazine piques the tyke's interest), saves his daughter from a date-rapist and then reunites him with his estranged wife. And she does it all while pretending to be Peter's maid.

"If you were to say to the average person playing God was representative of a stereotype, you would get a curious look," Boyd says. "People are uninformed. They see a black man playing God and that's a good thing. The same principle is at work when it comes to 'Bringing Down the House.' People know she had a hand in creating the movie, so everything must be OK. White people and black people are getting along and having fun. Isn't that great?"

Aaron McGruder, creator of "The Boondocks" comic strip, didn't think so. He upbraided Latifah for her "less-than-dignified and racially demeaning performance." His character Huey e-mailed Latifah, informing her that the "Almighty Council of Blackness has unanimously voted to revoke your 'Queen' status."

Michael Clarke Duncan of "The Green Mile" received an Oscar nomination for the role of gentle giant John Coffey, a black healer wrongly convicted of murdering two children. Coffey cures the jaded prison guard of corrosive cynicism and a kidney infection. He also saves the lives of the warden's wife and the prison mouse.

Ariel Dorfman sees sinister forces in such portrayals. "The magic Negro is an easy way of making the characters and the audiences happy. And I am for happiness, but the real joy of art is to reveal certain intractable ways in which humans interact. This phenomenon may be a way of avoiding confrontation," says Dorfman, a playwright, poet and cultural critic.

"The black character helps the white character, which demonstrates that (the former) feels this incredible interest in maintaining the existing society. Since there is no cultural interchange, the character is put there to give the illusion that there is cultural crossover to satisfy that need without actually addressing the issue," Dorfman says.

"As a Chilean, however, I sense that maybe deep inside, mainstream Americans somehow expect those who come from the margins will save them emotionally and intellectually."

Damon Lee, producer of the hard-hitting satire "Undercover Brother," has come up with a similarly intriguing hypothesis drawn from personal experience. "The white community has been taught not to listen to black people. I truly feel that white people are more comfortable with black people telling them what to do when they are cast in a magical role. They can't seem to process the information in any other way," he says.

"Whoever is king of the jungle is only going to listen to someone perceived as an equal. That is always going to be the case. The bigger point is that no minority can be in today's structure. Somehow the industry picked up on that."

Robert McKee, who has taught screenwriting to about 40,000 25 writers, actors and producers, says: "You can't expect writers to think like sociologists. They aren't out there trying to change the world; they are just trying to tell a good story."

In "The Matrix," Morpheus (Fishburne) has an interesting mission, to ensure the rise of the messiah, Neo (Reeves). But Morpheus is the ultimate outsider. He and 100,000 or so others have been enslaved by the Matrix.

Morpheus, a captain in the war against the Matrix, is both a freethinking renegade and a religious zealot. In other words, he is more complex than similar characters. But his powers are in the service of the chosen one.

Such a worthy cause is no consolation for those who would prefer a fulfilling life of their own, rather than the power to change someone else's. Especially if the souls being saved aren't really in dire straits.

For Discussion and Writing

1. Kempley suggests that "magic negroes" are "likable, valuable or redemptive" (par. 6). Often, they are powerful characters, too. What is the problem with the stereotype?
2. How does Kempley use exemplification? Choose one of Kempley's specific examples and then explain how it supports a general point. Can you think of your own examples that would further her argument?

Can you think of any counterexamples that would challenge her thesis?

3. **connections** The "magic negro" is a mythic character. How does it fit into the scheme of Linda Seger's "Creating the Myth" (p. 334)? Can Seger's essay help us understand the role of the "magic negro" within movie plots and archetypal story lines?

4. Kempley takes a dim view of the "magic negro" stereotype. She cites critics who see "sinister forces in such portrayals" (par. 20). Yet she also quotes a screenwriting teacher who claims: "You can't expect writers to think like sociologists. They aren't out there trying to change the world; they are just trying to tell a good story" (par. 25). How do you view the causes and consequences of this film archetype? Do you think such images are significant in shaping—or reflecting—cultural attitudes? Is it useful to judge movies in this way, or should critics focus on entertainment value and whether films tell a "good story"?

SUSAN SONTAG

The Imagination of Disaster

A prolific fiction writer, critic, and political activist, Susan Sontag
(1933–2004) was a prominent, if often controversial, public intellec-
tual—both in the United States and abroad—for nearly forty years.
Her interests ranged widely, from art, philosophy, photography, litera-
ture, film, and drama, to war, illness, morality, and aesthetics. She was
also notable for her engagement with popular culture, evident in "The
Imagination of Disaster," which appeared in her celebrated 1966 book
Against Interpretation. *Her books include* Death Kit *(1967),* Styles of
Radical Will *(1966),* On Photography *(1973), and* The Volcano Lover
(1992). She wrote for the New York Times, *the* New Yorker, *the* Nation,
Art in America, *and many other publications.*

In the following essay, Sontag unpacks the components of science
fiction and disaster films, revealing the devices that give movies their
shape, their meaning, and their cultural resonance. "The Imagination
of Disaster" was first published in the mid-1960s. As you read, note
how many of the writer's claims and conclusions are still applicable
now. Do films contain the same elements? Do movies still work out
similar problems, desires, and fears?

Ours is indeed an age of extremity. For we live under continual threat of two equally fearful, but seemingly opposed, desti-
nies: unremitting banality and inconceivable terror. It is fantasy,
served out in large rations by the popular arts, which allows most
people to cope with these twin specters. For one job that fantasy can do is to lift us out of the unbearably humdrum and to
distract us from terrors, real or anticipated—by an escape into
exotic dangerous situations which have last-minute happy endings. But another one of the things that fantasy can do is to normalize what is psychologically unbearable, thereby inuring us to

it. In the one case, fantasy beautifies the world. In the other, it neutralizes it.

The fantasy to be discovered in science fiction films does both jobs. These films reflect world-wide anxieties, and they serve to allay them. They inculcate a strange apathy concerning the processes of radiation, contamination, and destruction that I for one find haunting and depressing. The naïve level of the films neatly tempers the sense of otherness, of alien-ness, with the grossly familiar. In particular, the dialogue of most science fiction films, which is generally of a monumental but often touching banality, makes them wonderfully, unintentionally funny. Lines like: "Come quickly, there's a monster in my bathtub"; "We must do something about this"; "Wait, Professor. There's someone on the telephone"; "But that's incredible"; and the old American stand-by (accompanied by brow-wiping), "I hope it works!"—are hilarious in the context of picturesque and deafening holocaust. Yet the films also contain something which is painful and in deadly earnest.

Science fiction films are one of the most accomplished of the popular art forms, and can give a great deal of pleasure to sophisticated film addicts. Part of the pleasure, indeed, comes from the sense in which these movies are in complicity with the abhorrent. It is no more, perhaps, than the way all art draws its audience into a circle of complicity with the thing represented. But in science fiction films we have to do things which are (quite literally) unthinkable. Here, "thinking about the unthinkable"—not in the way of Herman Kahn,[1] as a subject for calculation, but as a subject for fantasy—becomes, however inadvertently, itself a somewhat questionable act from a moral point of view. The films perpetuate clichés about identity, volition, power, knowledge, happiness, social consensus, guilt, responsibility which are, to say the least, not serviceable in our present extremity. But collective nightmares cannot be banished by demonstrating that they are, intellectually and morally, fallacious. This nightmare—the one reflected in various registers in the science fiction films—is too close to our reality.

A typical science fiction film has a form as predictable as a

[1]Herman Kahn (1922–1983): Military strategist and systems theorist known for studying the possible effects of nuclear war and recommending ways of surviving such a disaster. [Editor's note.]

Western, and is made up of elements which are as classic as the saloon brawl, the blonde schoolteacher from the East, and the gun duel on the deserted main street.

One model scenario proceeds through five phases: 5

1. The arrival of the thing. (Emergence of the monsters, landing of the alien spaceship, etc.) This is usually witnessed, or suspected, by just one person, who is a young scientist on a field trip. Nobody, neither his neighbors nor his colleagues, will believe him for some time. The hero is not married, but has a sympathetic though also incredulous girlfriend.
2. Confirmation of the hero's report by a host of witnesses to a great act of destruction. (If the invaders are beings from another planet, a fruitless attempt to parley with them and get them to leave peacefully.) The local police are summoned to deal with the situation and massacred.
3. In the capital of the country, conferences between scientists and the military take place, with the hero lecturing before a chart, map, or blackboard. A national emergency is declared. Reports of further atrocities. Authorities from other countries arrive in black limousines. All international tensions are suspended in view of the planetary emergency. This stage often includes a rapid montage of news broadcasts in various languages, a meeting at the UN, and more conferences between the military and the scientists. Plans are made for destroying the enemy.
4. Further atrocities. At some point the hero's girlfriend is in grave danger. Massive counterattacks by international forces, with brilliant displays of rocketry, rays, and other advanced weapons, are all unsuccessful. Enormous military casualties, usually by incineration. Cities are destroyed and/or evacuated. There is an obligatory scene here of panicked crowds stampeding along a highway or a big bridge, being waved on by numerous policemen who, if the film is Japanese, are immaculately white-gloved, preternaturally calm, and call out in dubbed English, "Keep moving. There is no need to be alarmed."
5. More conferences, whose motif is: "They must be vulnerable to   10 something." Throughout, the hero has been experimenting in his lab on this. The final strategy, upon which all hopes depend, is drawn up; the ultimate weapon—often a super-powerful, as yet untested, nuclear device—is mounted. Countdown. Final repulse of the monster or invaders. Mutual congratulations, while the hero and girlfriend embrace cheek to cheek and scan the skies sturdily. "But have we seen the last of them?"

The film I have just described should be in technicolor and on a wide screen. Another typical scenario is simpler and suited to black-and-white films with a lower budget. It has four phases:

1. The hero (usually, but not always, a scientist) and his girlfriend, or his wife and children, are disporting themselves in some innocent ultra-normal middle-class house in a small town, or on vacation (camping, boating). Suddenly, someone starts behaving strangely or some innocent form of vegetation becomes monstrously enlarged and ambulatory. If a character is pictured driving an automobile, something gruesome looms up in the middle of the road. If it is night, strange lights hurtle across the sky.
2. After following the thing's tracks, or determining that It is radioactive, or poking around a huge crater—in short, conducting some sort of crude investigation—the hero tries to warn the local authorities, without effect; nobody believes anything is amiss. The hero knows better. If the thing is tangible, the house is elaborately barricaded. If the invading alien is an invisible parasite, a doctor or friend is called in, who is himself rather quickly killed or "taken possession of" by the thing.
3. The advice of anyone else who is consulted proves useless. Meanwhile, It continues to claim other victims in the town, which remains implausibly isolated from the rest of the world. General helplessness.
4. One of two possibilities. Either the hero prepares to do battle alone, accidentally discovers the thing's one vulnerable point, and destroys it. Or, he somehow manages to get out of town and succeeds in laying his case before competent authorities. They, along the lines of the first script but abridged, deploy a complex technology which (after initial setbacks) finally prevails against the invaders.

15

Another version of the second script opens with the scientist-hero in his laboratory, which is located in the basement or on the grounds of his tasteful, prosperous house. Through his experiments, he unwittingly causes a frightful metamorphosis in some class of plants or animals, which turn carnivorous and go on a rampage. Or else, his experiments have caused him to be injured (sometimes irrevocably) or "invaded" himself. Perhaps he has been experimenting with radiation, or has built a machine to communicate with beings from other planets or to transport him to other places or times.
Another version of the first script involves the discovery of

some fundamental alteration in the conditions of existence of our planet, brought about by nuclear testing, which will lead to the extinction in a few months of all human life. For example: the temperature of the earth is becoming too high or too low to support life, or the earth is cracking in two, or it is gradually being blanketed by lethal fallout.

A third script, somewhat but not altogether different from the first two, concerns a journey through space—to the moon, or some other planet. What the space-voyagers commonly discover is that the alien terrain is in a state of dire emergency, itself threatened by extra-planetary invaders or nearing extinction through the practice of nuclear warfare. The terminal dramas of the first and second scripts are played out there, to which is added a final problem of getting away from the doomed and/or hostile planet and back to Earth.

I am aware, of course, that there are thousands of science fiction novels (their heyday was the late 1940's), not to mention the transcriptions of science fiction themes which, more and more, provide the principal subject matter of comic books. But I propose to discuss science fiction films (the present period began in 1950 and continues, considerably abated, to this day) as an independent sub-genre, without reference to the novels from which, in many cases, they were adapted. For while novel and film may share the same plot, the fundamental difference between the resources of the novel and the film makes them quite dissimilar. Anyway, the best science fiction movies are on a far higher level, as examples of the art of the film, than the science fiction books are, as examples of the art of the novel or romance. That the films might be better than the books is an old story. Good novels rarely make good films, but excellent films are often made from poor or trivial novels.

Certainly, compared with the science fiction novels, their film 20 counterparts have unique strengths, one of which is the immediate representation of the extraordinary: physical deformity and mutation, missile and rocket combat, toppling skyscrapers. The movies are, naturally, weak just where the science fiction novels (some of them) are strong—on science. But in place of an intellectual workout, they can supply something the novels can never provide—sensuous elaboration. In the films it is by means of images and sounds, not words that have to be translated by the

"And it is in the imagery of destruction that the core of a good science fiction film lies."

imagination, that one can participate in the fantasy of living through one's own death and more, the death of cities, the destruction of humanity itself.

Science fiction films are not about science. They are about disaster, which is one of the oldest subjects of art. In science fiction films, disaster is rarely viewed intensively; it is always extensive. It is a matter of quantity and ingenuity. If you will, it is a question of scale. But the scale, particularly in the wide-screen Technicolor films (of which the ones by the Japanese director, Inoshiro Honda, and the American director, George Pal, are technically the most brilliant and convincing, and visually the most exciting), does raise the matter to another level.

Thus, the science fiction film (like a very different contemporary genre, the Happening) is concerned with the aesthetics of destruction, with the peculiar beauties to be found in wreaking havoc, making a mess. And it is in the imagery of destruction that the core of a good science fiction film lies. This is the disadvantage of the cheap film—in which the monster appears or the rocket lands in a small dull-looking town. (Hollywood budget needs usually dictate that the town be in the Arizona or California desert. In *The Thing from Another World* [1951], the rather sleazy and confined set is supposed to be an encampment near the North Pole.) Still, good black-and-white science fiction films have been made. But a bigger budget, which usually means Technicolor, allows a much greater play back and forth among several model environments. There is the populous city. There is the lavish but ascetic interior of the space ship—either the invaders' or ours—replete with streamlined chromium fixtures and dials, and machines whose complexity is indicated by the number of colored lights they flash and strange noises they emit. There is the laboratory crowded with formidable machines and scientific apparatus. There is a comparatively old-fashioned looking conference room, where the scientist brings charts to explain the desperate state of things to the military. And each of these standard locales or backgrounds is subject to two modalities—intact and destroyed. We may, if we are lucky, be treated to a panorama of melting tanks, flying bodies, crashing walls, awesome craters and fissures in the earth, plummeting spacecraft, colorful deadly rays; and to a symphony of screams, weird electronic signals, the noisiest military hardware going, and the leaden tones of the laconic denizens of alien planets and their subjugated earthlings.

Certain of the primitive gratifications of science fiction films—for instance, the depiction of urban disaster on a colossally magnified scale—are shared with other types of films. Visually there is little difference between mass havoc as represented in the old horror and monster films and what we find in science fiction films, except (again) scale. In the old monster films, the monster always headed for the great city where he had to do a fair bit of rampaging, hurling buses off bridges, crumpling trains in his bare hands, toppling buildings, and so forth. The archetype is King Kong, in Schoedsack's great film of 1933, running amok, first in the African village (trampling babies, a bit of footage excised from most prints), then in New York. This is really not any different from Inoshiro Honda's *Rodan* (1957), where two giant reptiles—with a wingspan of five-hundred feet and supersonic speeds—by flapping their wings whip up a cyclone that blows most of Tokyo to smithereens. Or, the tremendous scenes of rampage by the giant robot who destroys half of Japan with the great incinerating ray which shoots forth from his eyes, at the beginning of Honda's *The Mysterians* (1959). Or, the destruction, by the rays from a fleet of flying saucers of New York, Paris, and

Tokyo, in *Battle in Outer Space* (1960). Or, the inundation of New York in *When Worlds Collide* (1951). Or, the end of London in 1968 depicted in George Pal's *The Time Machine* (1960). Neither do these sequences differ in aesthetic intention from the destruction scenes in the big sword, sandal, and orgy color spectaculars set in Biblical and Roman times—the end of Sodom in Aldrich's *Sodom and Gomorrah*, of Gaza in de Mille's *Samson and Delilah*, of Rhodes in *The Colossus of Rhodes*, and of Rome in a dozen Nero movies. D. W. Griffith began it with the Babylon sequence in *Intolerance*, and to this day there is nothing like the thrill of watching all those expensive sets come tumbling down.

In other respects as well, the science fiction films of the 1950's take up familiar themes. The famous movie serials and comics of the 1930's of the adventures of Flash Gordon and Buck Rogers, as well as the more recent spate of comic book super-heroes with extraterrestrial origins (the most famous is Superman, a foundling from the planet, Krypton, currently described as having been exploded by a nuclear blast) share motifs with more recent science fiction movies. But there is an important difference. The old science fiction films, and most of the comics, still have an essentially innocent relation to disaster. Mainly they offer new versions of the oldest romance of all—of the strong invulnerable hero with the mysterious lineage come to do battle on behalf of good and against evil. Recent science fiction films have a decided grimness, bolstered by their much greater degree of visual credibility, which contrasts strongly with the older films. Modern historical reality has greatly enlarged the imagination of disaster, and the protagonists—perhaps by the very nature of what is visited upon them—no longer seem wholly innocent.

The lure of such generalized disaster as a fantasy is that it releases 25 one from normal obligations. The trump card of the end-of-the-world movies—like *The Day the Earth Caught Fire* (1962)—is that great scene with New York or London or Tokyo discovered empty, its entire population annihilated. Or, as in *The World, the Flesh, and the Devil* (1959), the whole movie can be devoted to the fantasy of occupying the deserted city and starting all over again—Robinson Crusoe on a world-wide scale.
  Another kind of satisfaction these films supply is extreme

moral simplification—that is to say, a morally acceptable fantasy where one can give outlet to cruel or at least amoral feelings. In this respect, science fiction films partly overlap with horror films. This is the undeniable pleasure we derive from looking at freaks, at beings excluded from the category of the human. The sense of superiority over the freak conjoined in varying proportions with the titillation of fear and aversion makes it possible for moral scruples to be lifted, for cruelty to be enjoyed. The same thing happens in science fiction films. In the figure of the monster from outer space, the freakish, the ugly, and the predatory all converge—and provide a fantasy target for righteous bellicosity to discharge itself, and for the aesthetic enjoyment of suffering and disaster. Science fiction films are one of the purest forms of spectacle; that is, we are rarely inside anyone's feelings. (An exception to this is Jack Arnold's *The Incredible Shrinking Man* [1957].) We are merely spectators; we watch.

But in science fiction films, unlike horror films, there is not much horror. Suspense, shocks, surprises are mostly abjured in favor of a steady inexorable plot. Science fiction films invite a dispassionate, aesthetic view of destruction and violence—a *technological* view. Things, objects, machinery play a major role in these films. A greater range of ethical values is embodied in the décor of these films than in the people. Things, rather than the helpless humans, are the locus of values because we experience them, rather than people, as the sources of power. According to science fiction films, man is naked without his artifacts. *They* stand for different values, they are potent, they are what gets destroyed, and they are the indispensable tools for the repulse of the alien invaders or the repair of the damaged environment.

The science fiction films are strongly moralistic. The standard message is the one about the proper, or humane, uses of science, versus the mad, obsessional use of science. This message the science fiction films share in common with the classic horror films of the 1930's, like *Frankenstein, The Mummy, The Island of Doctor Moreau, Dr. Jekyll and Mr. Hyde.* (Georges Franju's brilliant *Les Yeux Sans Visage* [1959], called here *The Horror Chamber of Doctor Faustus*, is a more recent example.) In the horror films, we have the mad or obsessed or misguided scientist who pursues his experiments against good advice to the contrary, creates a monster or monsters, and is himself destroyed—often recognizing his folly himself, and dying in the successful effort to destroy his own creation. One science fiction equivalent of this is the scientist, usually a member of a team, who defects to the planetary invaders because "their" science is more advanced than "ours." This is the case in *The Mysterians*, and, true to form, the renegade sees his error in the end, and from within the Mysterian space ship destroys it and himself. In *This Island Earth* (1955), the inhabitants of the beleaguered planet Metaluna propose to conquer Earth, but their project is foiled by a Metalunan scientist named Exeter who, having lived on Earth a while and learned to love Mozart, cannot abide such viciousness. Exeter plunges his space ship into the ocean after returning a glamorous pair (male and female) of American physicists to Earth. Metaluna dies. In *The Fly* (1958), the hero, engrossed in his basement-laboratory experiments on a matter-transmitting machine, uses himself as a subject, accidentally exchanges head and one arm with a housefly which had gotten into the machine, becomes a monster, and with his last shred of human will destroys his laboratory and orders his wife to kill him. His discovery, for the good of mankind, is lost.

Being a clearly labeled species of intellectual, the scientists in science fiction films are always liable to crack up or go off the deep end. In *Conquest of Space* (1955), the scientist-commander of an international expedition to Mars suddenly acquires scruples about the blasphemy involved in the undertaking, and begins reading the Bible mid-journey instead of attending to his duties. The commander's son, who is his junior officer and always addresses his father as "General," is forced to kill the old man when he tries to prevent the ship from landing on Mars. In this film, both sides of the ambivalence toward scientists are given voice. Generally, for a scientific enterprise to be treated entirely sympathetically in these films, it needs the certificate of utility. Science, viewed without ambivalence, means an efficacious response to danger. Disinterested intellectual curiosity rarely appears in any form other than caricature, as a maniacal dementia that cuts one off from normal human relations. But this suspicion is usually directed at the scientist rather than his work. The creative scientist may become a martyr to his own discovery, through an accident or by pushing things too far. The implication remains that other men, less imaginative—in short, technicians—would administer the same scientific discovery better and more safely. The most ingrained contemporary mistrust of the intellect is visited, in these movies, upon the scientist-as-intellectual. The message that the scientist is one who releases forces which, if not controlled for good, could destroy man himself seems innocuous enough. One of the oldest images of the scientist is Shakespeare's Prospero,[2] the over-detached scholar forcibly retired from society to a desert island, only partly in control of the magic forces in which he dabbles. Equally classic is the figure of the scientist as satanist (Dr. Faustus, stories of Poe and Hawthorne). Science is magic, and man has always known that there is black magic as well as white. But it is not enough to remark that contemporary attitudes—as reflected in science fiction films— remain ambivalent, that the scientist is treated both as satanist and savior. The proportions have changed, because of the new context in which the old admiration and fear of the scientist is located. For his sphere of influence is no longer local, himself or his immediate community. It is planetary, cosmic.

One gets the feeling, particularly in the Japanese films, but not only there, that mass trauma exists over the use of nuclear weapons and the possibility of future nuclear wars. Most of the science fiction films bear witness to this trauma, and in a way, attempt to exorcise it.

The accidental awakening of the super-destructive monster who has slept in the earth since pre-history is, often, an obvious metaphor for the Bomb. But there are many explicit references as well. In *The Mysterians*, a probe ship from the planet Mysteroid has landed on earth, near Tokyo. Nuclear warfare having been practiced on Mysteroid for centuries (their civilization is "more advanced than ours"), 90 per cent of those now born on the planet have to be destroyed at birth, because of defects caused by the huge amounts of Strontium 90 in their diet. The Mysterians have come to earth to marry earth women and possibly to take over our relatively uncontaminated planet. . . . In *The Incredible Shrinking Man*, the John Doe hero is the victim of a gust of radiation which blows over the water, while he is out boating with his wife; the radiation causes him to grow smaller and smaller, until at the end of the movie he steps through the fine mesh of a window screen to become "the infinitely small. . . ." In *Rodan*, a horde

---

[2]*Prospero*: Character in Shakespeare's *The Tempest*. [Editor's note.]

of monstrous carnivorous prehistoric insects, and finally a pair of giant flying reptiles (the prehistoric Archeopteryx), are hatched from dormant eggs in the depths of a mine shaft by the impact of nuclear test explosions, and go on to destroy a good part of the world before they are felled by the molten lava of a volcanic eruption. . . . In the English film, *The Day the Earth Caught Fire*, two simultaneous hydrogen bomb tests by the U.S. and Russia change by eleven degrees the tilt of the earth on its axis and alter the earth's orbit so that it begins to approach the sun.

Radiation casualties—ultimately, the conception of the whole world as a casualty of nuclear testing and nuclear warfare—is the most ominous of all the notions with which science fiction films deal. Universes become expendable. Worlds become contaminated, burnt out, exhausted, obsolete. In *Rocketship X-M* (1950), explorers from Earth land on Mars, where they learn that atomic warfare has destroyed Martian civilization. In George Pal's *The War of the Worlds* (1953), reddish spindly alligator-skinned creatures from Mars invade Earth because their planet is becoming too cold to be habitable. In *This Island Earth*, also American, the planet Metaluna, whose population has long ago been driven underground by warfare, is dying under the missile attacks of an enemy planet. Stocks of uranium, which power the force-shield shielding Metaluna, have been used up; and an unsuccessful expedition is sent to Earth to enlist earth scientists to devise new sources of power.

There is a vast amount of wishful thinking in science fiction films, 35 some of it touching, some of it depressing. Again and again, one detects the hunger for a "good war," which poses no moral problems, admits of no moral qualifications. The imagery of science fiction films will satisfy the most bellicose addict of war films, for a lot of the satisfactions of war films pass, untransformed, into science fiction films. Examples: the dogfights between earth "fighter rockets" and alien spacecraft in the *Battle of Outer Space* (1959); the escalating firepower in the successive assaults upon the invaders in *The Mysterians*, which Dan Talbot correctly described as a nonstop holocaust; the spectacular bombardment of the underground fortress in *This Island Earth*.

Yet at the same time the bellicosity of science fiction films is neatly channeled into the yearning for peace, or for at least peaceful coexistence. Some scientist generally takes sententious note of the fact that it took the planetary invasion or cosmic disaster to make the warring nations of the earth come to their senses, and suspend their own conflicts. One of the main themes of many science fiction films—the color ones usually, because they have the budget and resources to develop the military spectacle—is this UN fantasy, a fantasy of united warfare. (The same wishful UN theme cropped up in a recent spectacular which is not science fiction, *Fifty-Five Days at Peking* [1963]. There, topically enough, the Chinese, the Boxers, play the role of Martian invaders who united the earthmen, in this case the United States, Russia, England, France, Germany, Italy, and Japan.) A great enough disaster cancels all enmities, and calls upon the utmost concentration of the earth's resources.

Science—technology—is conceived of as the great unifier. Thus the science fiction films also project a utopian fantasy. In the classic models of utopian thinking—Plato's Republic, Campanella's City of the Sun, More's Utopia, Swift's land of the Houyhnhnms, Voltaire's Eldorado—society had worked out a perfect consensus. In these societies reasonableness had achieved an unbreakable supremacy over the emotions. Since no disagreement or social conflict was intellectually plausible, none was possible. As in Melville's *Typee*, "they all think the same." The universal rule of reason meant universal agreement. It is interesting, too, that societies in which reason was pictured as totally ascendant were also traditionally pictured as having an ascetic and/or materially frugal and economically simple mode of life. But in the utopian world community projected by science fiction films, totally pacified and ruled by scientific concensus, the demand for simplicity of material existence would be absurd.

But alongside the hopeful fantasy of moral simplification and international unity embodied in the science fiction films, lurk the deepest anxieties about contemporary existence. I don't mean only the very real trauma of the Bomb—that it has been used, that there are enough now to kill everyone on earth many times over, that those new bombs may very well be used. Besides these new anxieties about physical disaster, the prospect of universal mutilation and even annihilation, the science fiction films reflect powerful anxieties about the condition of the individual psyche.

For science fiction films may also be described as a popular mythology for the contemporary *negative* imagination about the impersonal. The other-world creatures which seek to take "us" over, are an "it," not a "they." The planetary invaders are usually zombie-like. Their movements are either cool, mechanical, or lumbering, blobby. But it amounts to the same thing. If they are nonhuman in form, they proceed with an absolutely regular, unalterable movement (unalterable save by destruction). If they are human in form—dressed in space suits, etc.—then they obey the most rigid military discipline, and display no personal characteristics whatsoever. And it is this regime of emotionlessness, of impersonality, of regimentation, which they will impose on the earth if they are successful. "No more love, no more beauty, no more pain," boasts a converted earthling in *The Invasion of the Body Snatchers* (1956). The half earthling-half alien children in *The Children of the Damned* (1960) are absolutely emotionless, move as a group and understand each others' thoughts, and are all prodigious intellects. They are the wave of the future, man in his next stage of development.

These alien invaders practice a crime which is worse than murder. They do not simply kill the person. They obliterate him. In *The War of the Worlds*, the ray which issues from the rocket ship disintegrates all persons and objects in its path, leaving no trace of them but a light ash. In Honda's *The H-Men* (1959), the creeping blob melts all flesh with which it comes in contact. If the blob, which looks like a huge hunk of red jello, and can crawl across floors and up and down walls, so much as touches your bare boot, all that is left of you is a heap of clothes on the floor. (A more articulated, size-multiplying blob is the villain in the English film *The Creeping Unknown* [1956].) In another version of this fantasy, the body is preserved but the person is entirely reconstituted as the automatized servant or agent of the alien powers. This is, of course, the vampire fantasy in new dress. The person is really dead, but he doesn't know it. He's "undead," he has become an "unperson." It happens to a whole California town in *The Invasion of the Body Snatchers*, to several earth scientists in *This Island Earth*, and to assorted innocents in *It Came from Outer Space, Attack of the Puppet People* (1961), and *The Brain Eaters* (1961). As the victim always backs away from the vampire's horrifying embrace, so in science fiction films the person always fights being "taken over"; he wants to retain his humanity. But once the deed has been done, the victim is eminently satisfied with his condition. He has not been converted from human amiability to monstrous "animal" bloodlust (a metaphoric exaggeration of sexual desire), as in the old vampire fantasy. No, he has simply become far more efficient—the very model of technocratic man, purged of emotions, volitionless, tranquil, obedient to all orders. The dark secret behind human nature used to be the upsurge of the animal—as in *King Kong*. The threat to man, his availability to dehumanization, lay in his own animality. Now the danger is understood as residing in man's ability to be turned into a machine.

The rule, of course, is that this horrible and irremediable form of 40 murder can strike anyone in the film except the hero. The hero and his family, while grossly menaced, always escape this fact and by the end of the film the invaders have been repulsed or destroyed. I know of only one exception, *The Day That Mars Invaded Earth* (1963), in which, after all the standard struggles, the scientist-hero, his wife, and their two children are "taken over" by the alien invaders—and that's that. (The last minutes of the film show them being incinerated by the Martians' rays and their ash silhouettes flushed down their empty swimming pool, while their simulacra drive off in the family car.) Another variant but upbeat switch on the rule occurs in *The Creation of the Humanoids* (1964), where the hero discovers at the end of the film that he, too, has been turned into a metal robot, complete with highly efficient and virtually indestructible mechanical insides, although he didn't know it and detected no difference in himself. He learns, however, that he will shortly be upgraded into a "humanoid" having all the properties of a real man.

Of all the standard motifs of science fiction films, this theme of dehumanization is perhaps the most fascinating. For, as I have indicated, it is scarcely a black-and-white situation, as in the vampire films. The attitude of the science fiction films toward depersonalization is mixed. On the one hand, they deplore it as the ultimate horror. On the other hand, certain characteristics of the dehumanized invaders, modulated and disguised—such as the ascendancy of reason over feelings, the idealization of teamwork and the consensus-creating activities of science, a marked degree of moral simplification—are precisely traits of the savior-scientists. For it is interesting that when the scientist in these films is treated negatively, it is usually done through the portrayal of an individual scientist who holes up in his laboratory and neglects his fiancée or his loving wife and children, obsessed by his daring and dangerous experiments. The scientist as a loyal member of a team, and therefore considerably less individualized, is treated quite respectfully.

There is absolutely no social criticism, of even the most implicit kind, in science fiction films. No criticism, for example, of the conditions of our society which create the impersonality and dehumanization which science fiction fantasies displace onto the influence of an alien It. Also, the notion of science as a social activity, interlocking with social and political interests, is unacknowledged. Science is simply either adventure (for good or evil) or a technical response to danger. And, typically, when the fear of science is paramount—when science is conceived of as black magic rather than white—the evil has no attribution beyond that of the perverse will of an individual scientist. In science fiction films the antithesis of black magic and white is drawn as a split between technology, which is beneficent, and the errant individual will of a lone intellectual.

Thus, science fiction films can be looked at as thematically central allegory, replete with standard modern attitudes. The theme of depersonalization (being "taken over") which I have been talking about is a new allegory reflecting the age-old awareness of man that, sane, he is always perilously close to insanity and unreason. But there is something more there than just a recent, popular image which expresses man's perennial, but largely unconscious, anxiety about his sanity. The image derives most of its power from a supplementary and historical anxiety, also not experienced *consciously* by most people, about the depersonalizing conditions of modern urban society. Similarly, it is not enough to note that science fiction allegories are one of the new myths about—that is, ways of accommodating to and negating—the perennial human anxiety about death. (Myths of heaven and hell, and of ghosts, had the same function.) Again, there is a historically specifiable twist which intensifies the anxiety, or better, the trauma suffered by everyone in the middle of the 20th century when it became clear that from now on to the end of human history, every person would spend his individual life not only under the threat of individual death, which is certain, but of something almost unsupportable psychologically—collective incineration and extinction which could come any time, virtually without warning.

From a psychological point of view, the imagination of disaster does not greatly differ from one period in history to another. But from a political and moral point of view, it does. The expectation of the apocalypse may be the occasion for a radical disaffiliation from society, as when thousands of Eastern European Jews in the 17th century gave up their homes and businesses and began to trek to Palestine upon hearing that Shabbethai Zevi had been proclaimed Messiah and that the end of the world was imminent. But peoples learn the news of their own end in diverse ways. It is reported that in 1945 the populace of Berlin received without great agitation the news that Hitler had decided to kill them all, before the Allies arrived, because they had not been worthy enough to win the war. We are, alas, more in the position of the Berliners than of the Jews of 17th-century Eastern Europe; and our response is closer to theirs, too. What I am suggesting is that the imagery of disaster in science fiction films is above all the emblem of an *inadequate response*. I do not mean to bear down on the films for this. They themselves are only a sampling, stripped of sophistication, of the inadequacy of most people's response to the unassimilable terrors that infect their consciousness. The interest of the films, aside from their considerable amount of cinematic charm, consists in this intersection between a naïvely and largely debased commercial art product and the most pro-found dilemmas of the contemporary situation.

For Discussion and Writing

1. Sontag writes, "Science fiction films are not about science" (par. 21). What are they about, according to her? Why is this important to her argument?

2. Sontag is well known for her writing about "high" art and culture. What is her attitude toward popular science fiction? How does this attitude come across in her style? Do the structure and tone of the essay suggest her relationship with her subject?

3. **connections** According to Sontag, vicarious film fantasies serve two purposes: "For one job that fantasy can do is to lift us out of the unbearably humdrum and to distract us from terrors, real or

anticipated—by an escape into exotic dangerous situations which have last-minute happy endings. But another one of the things that fantasy can do is to normalize what is psychologically unbearable, thereby inuring us to it. In the one case, fantasy beautifies the world. In the other, it neutralizes it" (par. 1). These fantasies offer promise of "moral simplification" and allow us a space where we can "give outlet to cruel or at least amoral feelings" (par. 26). How would you apply these claims to Gerard Jones's "Violent Media Is Good for Kids" (p. 372)? Do Sontag and Jones share the same attitude toward vicarious violence? How do their arguments differ? How are they similar?

4. Although Sontag provides close readings of specific films in her essay, she also proposes more general, theoretical strategies for interpreting science fiction, disaster, and horror films: their common themes, structural elements, moral values, and other patterns. Choose a contemporary science fiction, disaster, or horror film, and analyze it using Sontag's critical approach. You may also want to show how your choice subverts or challenges Sontag's argument.

LINDA SEGER

Creating the Myth

Linda Seger is a script consultant, screenwriting coach, author, and *speaker. She has consulted on many movies and television shows. Her* *books include* Creating Unforgettable Characters *(1990),* The Art of Adaptation: Turning Fact and Fiction into Film *(1992), and* When Women Called the Shots: The Developing Power and Influence of Women in Television and Film *(1996). In the following excerpt from* Making a Good Script Great *(1987), Seger reveals the archetypal characters and mythic narratives that underlie popular movies such as* Star Wars. *According to the writer, "Many of the most successful films are based on these universal stories." Why do these plots endure despite their familiarity?*

All of us have similar experiences. We share in the life journey of growth, development, and transformation. We live the same stories, whether they involve the search for a perfect mate, coming home, the search for fulfillment, going after an ideal, achieving the dream, or hunting for a precious treasure. Whatever our culture, there are universal stories that form the basis for all our particular stories. The trappings might be different, the twists and turns that create suspense might change from culture to culture, the particular characters may take different forms, but underneath it all, it's the same story, drawn from the same experiences.

Many of the most successful films are based on these universal stories. They deal with the basic journey we take in life. We identify with the heroes because we were once heroic (descriptive) or because we wish we could do what the hero does (prescriptive). When Joan Wilder finds the jewel and saves her sister, or James Bond saves the world, or Shane saves the family from the evil ranchers, we identify with the character, and subconsciously recognize the story as having some connection with our own lives.

It's the same story as the fairy tales about getting the three golden hairs from the devil, or finding the treasure and winning the princess. And it's not all that different a story from the caveman killing the woolly beast or the Roman slave gaining his freedom through skill and courage. These are our stories—personally and collectively—and the most successful films contain these universal experiences.

Some of these stories are "search" stories. They address our desire to find some kind of rare and wonderful treasure. This might include the search for outer values such as job, relationship, or success; or for inner values such as respect, security, self-expression, love, or home. But it's all a similar search.

Some of these stories are "hero" stories. They come from our own experiences of overcoming adversity, as well as our desire to do great and special acts. We root for the hero and celebrate when he or she achieves the goal because we know that the hero's journey is in many ways similar to our own.

We call these stories *myths*. Myths are the common stories at the root of our universal existence. They're found in all cultures and in all literature, ranging from the Greek myths to fairy tales, legends, and stories drawn from all of the world's religions.

A myth is a story that is "more than true." Many stories are true because one person, somewhere, at some time, lived it. It is based on fact. But a myth is more than true because it is lived by all of us, at some level. It's a story that connects and speaks to us all.

Some myths are true stories that attain mythic significance because the people involved seem larger than life, and seem to live their lives more intensely than common folk. Martin Luther King, Jr., Gandhi, Sir Edmund Hillary, and Lord Mountbattan personify the types of journeys we identify with, because we've taken similar journeys—even if only in a very small way.

Other myths revolve around make-believe characters who might capsulize for us the sum total of many of our journeys. Some of these make-believe characters might seem similar to the characters we meet in our dreams. Or they might be a composite of types of characters we've met.

In both cases, the myth is the "story beneath the story." It's the universal pattern that shows us that Gandhi's journey toward independence and Sir Edmund Hillary's journey to the top of Mount Everest contain many of the same dramatic beats. And these beats are the same beats that Rambo takes to set free the MIAs, that Indiana Jones takes to find the Lost Ark, and that Luke Skywalker takes to defeat the Evil Empire.

In *Hero with a Thousand Faces*, Joseph Campbell traces the 10 elements that form the hero myth. "In their own work with myth, writer Chris Vogler and seminar leader Thomas Schlesinger have applied this criteria to *Star Wars*. The myth within the story helps explain why millions went to see this film again and again.

The hero myth has specific story beats that occur in all hero stories. They show who the hero is, what the hero needs, and how the story and character interact in order to create a transformation. The journey toward heroism is a process. This universal process forms the spine of all the particular stories, such as the *Star Wars* trilogy.

THE HERO MYTH

1. In most hero stories, the hero is introduced in ordinary surroundings, in a mundane world, doing mundane things. Generally, the hero begins as a nonhero: innocent, young, simple, or humble. In *Star Wars*, the first time we see Luke Skywalker, he's unhappy about having to do his chores, which consist of picking out some new droids for work. He wants to go out and have fun. He wants to leave his planet and go to the Academy, but he's stuck. This is the setup of most myths. This is how we meet the hero before the call to adventure.

2. Then something new enters the hero's life. It's a catalyst that sets the story in motion. It might be a telephone call, as in *Romancing the Stone*, or the German attack in *The African Queen*, or the holograph of Princess Leia in *Star Wars*. Whatever form it takes, it's a new ingredient that pushes the hero into an extraordinary adventure. With this call, the stakes are established, and a problem is introduced that demands a solution.

3. Many times, however, the hero doesn't want to leave. He or she is a reluctant hero, afraid of the unknown, uncertain, perhaps, if he or she is up to the challenge. In *Star Wars*, Luke receives a double call to adventure. First, from Princess Leia in the holograph, and then through Obi-Wan Kenobi, who says he needs Luke's help. But Luke is not ready to go. He returns home, only to find that the Imperial Stormtroopers

In *Star Wars*, Obi-Wan Kenobi is a perfect example of the "helper" character.

have burned his farmhouse and slaughtered his family.
Now he is personally motivated, ready to enter into the
adventure.

4. In any journey, the hero usually receives help, and the help   15
   often comes from unusual sources. In many fairy tales, an
   old woman, a dwarf, a witch, or a wizard helps the hero.
   The hero achieves the goal because of this help, and because
   the hero is receptive to what this person has to give.

There are a number of fairy tales where the first and second
son are sent to complete a task, but they ignore the helpers,
often scorning them. Many times they are severely punished
for their lack of humility and unwillingness to accept help.
Then the third son, the hero, comes along. He receives the
help, accomplishes the task, and often wins the princess.

In *Star Wars*, Obi-Wan Kenobi is a perfect example of the
"helper" character. He is a kind of mentor to Luke, one who
teaches him the Way of the Force and whose teachings
continue even after his death. This mentor character appears
in most hero stories. He is the person who has special
knowledge, special information, and special skills. This
might be the prospector in *The Treasure of the Sierra Madre*,
or the psychiatrist in *Ordinary People*, or Quint in *Jaws*, who

knows all about sharks, or the Good Witch of the North who gives Dorothy the ruby slippers in *The Wizard of Oz*. In *Star Wars*, Obi-Wan gives Luke the light saber that was the special weapon of the Jedi Knight. With this, Luke is ready to move forward to do his training and meet adventure.

5. The hero is now ready to move into the special world where he or she will change from the ordinary into the extraordinary. This starts the hero's transformation, and sets up the obstacles that must be surmounted to reach the goal. Usually, this happens at the first Turning Point of the story, and leads into Act Two development. In *Star Wars*, Obi-Wan and Luke search for a pilot to take them to the planet of Alderaan, so that Obi-Wan can deliver the plans to Princess Leia's father. These plans are essential to the survival of the Rebel Forces. With this action, the adventure is ready to begin.

6. Now begin all the tests and obstacles necessary to overcome the enemy and accomplish the hero's goals. In fairy tales, this often means getting past witches, outwitting the devil, avoiding robbers, or confronting evil. In Homer's *Odyssey*, it means blinding the Cyclops, escaping from the island of the Lotus-Eaters, resisting the temptation of the singing Sirens, and surviving a shipwreck. In *Star Wars*, innumerable adventures confront Luke. He and his cohorts must run to the *Millennium Falcon*, narrowly escaping the Stormtroopers before jumping into hyperspace. They must make it through the meteor shower after Alderaan has been destroyed. They must evade capture on the Death Star, rescue the Princess, and even survive a garbage crusher.

7. At some point in the story, the hero often hits rock bottom. He often has a "death experience," leading to a type of rebirth. In *Star Wars*, Luke seems to have died when the serpent in the garbage-masher pulls him under, but he's saved just in time to ask R2D2 to stop the masher before they're crushed. This is often the "black moment" at the second turning point, the point when the worst is confronted, and the action now moves toward the exciting conclusion.

8. Now, the hero seizes the sword and takes possession of the treasure. He is now in charge, but he still has not completed the journey. Here Luke has the Princess and the plans, but the final confrontation is yet to begin. This starts the third-act escape scene, leading to the final climax.

9. The road back is often the chase scene. In many fairy tales, this is the point where the devil chases the hero and the hero has the last obstacles to overcome before really being free and safe. His challenge is to take what he has learned and integrate it into his daily life. He *must* return to renew the mundane world. In *Star Wars*, Darth Vader is in hot pursuit, planning to blow up the Rebel Planet.

10. Since every hero story is essential a transformation story, we need to see the hero changed at the end, resurrected into a new type of life. He must face the final ordeal before being "reborn" as the hero, proving his courage and becoming transformed. This is the point, in many fairy tales, where the Miller's Son becomes the Prince or the King and marries the Princess. In *Star Wars*, Luke has survived, becoming quite a different person from the innocent young man he was in Act One.

At this point, the hero returns and is reintegrated into his society. In *Star Wars*, Luke has destroyed the Death Star, and he receives his great reward.

This is the classic "Hero Story." We might call this example a *mission* or *task myth*, where the person has to complete a task, but the task itself is not the real treasure. The real reward for Luke is the love of the Princess and the safe, new world he had helped create. 25

A myth can have many variations. We see variations on this myth in James Bond films (although they lack much of the depth because the hero is not transformed), and in *The African Queen*, where Rose and Allnutt must blow up the *Louisa*, or in *Places in the Heart*, where Edna overcomes obstacles to achieve family stability.

The *treasure myth* is another variation on this theme, as seen in *Romancing the Stone*. In this story, Joan receives a map and a phone call which forces her into the adventure. She is helped by an American birdcatcher and a Mexican pickup truck driver. She overcomes the obstacles of snakes, the jungle, waterfalls, shootouts, and finally receives the treasure, along with the "prince."

Whether the hero's journey is for a treasure or to complete a task, the elements remain the same. The humble, reluctant hero is called to an adventure. The hero is helped by a variety of unique characters. S/he must overcome a series of obstacles that transform him or her in the process, and then faces the final challenge that draws on inner and outer resources.

THE HEALING MYTH

Although the hero myth is the most popular story, many myths involve healing. In these stories, some character is "broken" and must leave home to become whole again.

The universal experience behind these healing stories is our psychological need for rejuvenation, for balance. The journey of the hero into exile is not all that different from the weekend in Palm Springs, or the trip to Hawaii to get away from it all, or lying still in a hospital bed for some weeks to heal. In all cases, something is out of balance and the mythic journey moves toward wholeness. 30

Being broken can take several forms. It can be physical, emotional, or psychological. Unusually, it's all three. In the process of being exiled or hiding out in the forest, the desert, or even the Amish farm in *Witness*, the person becomes whole, balanced, and receptive to love. Love in these stories is both a healing force and a reward.

Think of John Book in *Witness*. In Act One, we see a frenetic, insensitive man, afraid of commitment, critical and unreceptive to the feminine influences in his life. John is suffering from an "inner wound" which he doesn't know about. When he receives an "outer wound" from a gunshot, it forces him into exile, which begins his process of transformation.

At the beginning of Act Two, we see John delirious and close to death. This is a movement into the unconscious, a movement from the rational, active police life of Act One into a mysterious, feminine, more intuitive world. Since John's "inner problem" is the lack of balance with his feminine side, this delirium begins the process of transformation.

Later in Act Two, we see John beginning to change. He moves from his highly independent life-style toward the collective, communal life of his Amish hosts. John now gets up early to milk the cows and to assist with the chores. He uses his carpentry skills to help with the barn building and to complete the birdhouse. Gradually, he begins to develop relationships with Rachel and her son, Samuel. John's life slows down and he becomes more receptive, learning important lessons about love. In Act Three, John finally sees that the feminine is worth saving, and throws down his gun to save Rachel's life. A few beats later, when he has the opportunity to kill Paul, he chooses a nonviolent response instead. Although John doesn't "win" the Princess, he has nevertheless "won" love and wholeness. By the end of the film, we can see that the John Book of Act Three is a different kind of person from the John Book of Act One. He has a different kind of comradeship with his fellow police officers, he's more relaxed, and we can sense that somehow, this experience has formed a more integrated John Book.

COMBINATION MYTHS

Many stories are combinations of several different myths. Think 35 of *Ghostbusters*, a simple and rather outrageous comedy about three men saving the city of New York from ghosts. Now think of the story of "Pandora's Box." It's about the woman who let loose all manner of evil upon the earth by opening a box she was told not to touch. In *Ghostbusters*, the EPA man is a Pandora figure. By shutting off the power to the containment center, he inadvertently unleashes all the ghosts upon New York City. Combine the story of "Pandora's Box" with a hero story, and notice that we have our three heroes battling the Marshmallow Man. One of them also "gets the Princess" when Dr. Peter Venkman finally receives the affections of Dana Barrett. By looking at these combinations, it is apparent that even *Ghostbusters* is more than "just a comedy."

Tootsie is a type of reworking of many Shakespearean stories where a woman has to dress as a man in order to accomplish a certain task. These Shakespearean stories are reminiscent of many fairy tales where the hero becomes invisible or takes on another persona, or wears a specific disguise to hide his or her real qualities. In the stories of "The Twelve Dancing Princesses" or "The Man in the Bearskin," disguise is necessary to achieve a goal. Combine these elements with the transformation themes of the hero myth where a hero (such as Michael) must overcome many obstacles to his success as an actor and a human being. It's not difficult to understand why the *Tootsie* story hooks us.

ARCHETYPES

A myth includes certain characters that we see in many stories. These characters are called *archetypes*. They can be thought of as the original "pattern" or "character type" that will be found on the hero's journey. Archetypes take many forms, but they tend to fall within specific categories.

Earlier, we discussed some of the helpers who give advice to help the hero—such as the *wise old man* who possesses special knowledge and often serves as a mentor for the hero.

The female counterpart of the wise old man is the *good mother*. Whereas the wise old man has superior knowledge, the good mother is known for her nurturing qualities, and for her intuition. This figure often gives the hero particular objects to help on the journey. It might be a protective amulet, or the ruby slippers that Dorothy receives in *The Wizard of Oz* from the Good Witch of the North. Sometimes in fairy tales it's a cloak to make the person invisible, or ordinary objects that become extraordinary, as in "The Girl of Courage," an Afghan fairy tale about a maiden who receives a comb, a whetstone, and a mirror to help defeat the devil.

Many myths contain a *shadow figure*. This is a character who is 40 the opposite of the hero. Sometimes this figure helps the hero on the journey; other times this figure opposes the hero. The shadow figure can be the negative side of the hero which could be the dark and hostile brother in "Cain and Abel," the stepsisters in "Cinderella," or the Robber Girl in "The Snow Queen." The shadow figure can also help the hero, as the whore with the heart of gold who saves the hero's life, or provides balance to his idealization of woman.

Many myths contain *animal archetypes* that can be positive or negative figures. In "St. George and the Dragon," the dragon is the negative force which is a violent and ravaging animal, not unlike the shark in *Jaws*. But in many stories, animals help the hero. Sometimes there are talking donkeys, or a dolphin which saves the hero, or magical horses or dogs.

The *trickster* is a mischievous archetypical figure who is always causing chaos, disturbing the peace, and generally being an anarchist. The trickster uses wit and cunning to achieve his or her ends. Sometimes the trickster is a harmless prankster or a "bad boy" who is funny and enjoyable. More often, the trickster is a con man, as in *The Sting*, or the devil, as in *The Exorcist*, who demanded all the skills of the priest to outwit him. The "Till Eulenspigel" stories revolve around the trickster, as do the Spanish picaresque novels. Even the tales of Tom Sawyer have a trickster motif. In all countries, there are stories that revolve around this figure, whose job it is to outwit.

"MYTHIC" PROBLEMS AND SOLUTIONS

We all grew up with myths. Most of us heard or read fairy tales when we were young. Some of us may have read Bible stories, or stories from other religions or other cultures. These stories are part of us. And the best way to work with them is to let them come out naturally as you write the script.

Of course, some filmmakers are better at this than others. George Lucas and Steven Spielberg have a strong sense of myth and incorporate it into their films. They both have spoken about their love of the stories from childhood, and of their desire to bring these types of stories to audiences. Their stories create some of the same sense of wonder and excitement as myths. Many of the necessary psychological beats are part of their stories, deepening the story beyond the ordinary action-adventure.

Myths bring depth to a hero story. If a filmmaker is thinking only about the action and excitement of a story, audiences might fail to connect with the hero's journey. But if the basic beats of the hero's journey are evident, a film will often inexplicably draw audiences, in spite of critics' responses to the film.

Take *Rambo*, for instance. Why was this violent, simple story so popular with audiences? I don't think it was because everyone agreed with its politics. I do think Sylvester Stallone is a master at incorporating the American myth into his filmmaking. That doesn't mean it's done consciously. Somehow he is naturally in sync with the myth, and the myth becomes integrated into his stories.

Clint Eastwood also does hero stories, and gives us the adventure of the myth and the transformation of the myth. . . . Eastwood's films have given more attention to the transformation of the hero, and have been receiving more serious critical attention as a result.

All of these filmmakers—Lucas, Spielberg, Stallone, and Eastwood—dramatize the hero myth in their own particular ways. And all of them prove that myths are marketable.

APPLICATION

It is an important part of the writer's or producer's work to continually find opportunities for deepening the themes within a script. Finding the myth beneath the modern story is part of that process.

To find these myths, it's not a bad idea to reread some of 50 Grimm's fairy tales or fairy tales from around the world to begin to get acquainted with various myths. You'll start to see patterns and elements that connect with our own human experience.

Also, read Joseph Campbell and Greek mythology. If you're interested in Jungian psychology, you'll find many rich resources within a number of books on the subject. Since Jungian psychology deals with archetypes, you'll find many new characters to draw on for your own work.

With all of these resources to incorporate, it's important to remember that the myth is not a story to force upon a script. It's more a pattern which you can bring out in your stories when they seem to be heading in the direction of a myth.

As you work ask yourself:

Do I have a myth working in my script? If so, what beats am I using of the hero's journey? Which ones seem to be missing?

Am I missing characters? Do I need a mentor type? A wise old man? A wizard? Would one of these characters help dimensionalize the hero's journey?

Could I create new emotional dimensions to the myth by starting my character as reluctant, naive, simple, or decidedly "unheroic"?

Does my character get transformed in the process of the journey?

Have I used a strong three-act structure to support the myth, using the first turning point to move into the adventure and the second turning point to create a dark moment, or a reversal, or even a "near-death" experience?

Don't be afraid to create variations on the myth, but don't start with the myth itself. Let the myth grow naturally from your story. Developing myths are part of the rewriting process. If you begin with the myth, you'll find your writing becomes rigid, uncreative, and predictable. Working with the myth in the rewriting process will deepen your script, giving it new life as you find the story within the story.

For Discussion and Writing

1. Seger writes that both Luke Skywalker and James Bond are examples of the hero myth. What is the significant difference between the two characters, according to the writer?

2. Seger claims: "A myth is a story that is 'more than true.' Many stories are true because one person, somewhere, at some time, lived it. It is based on fact. But a myth is more than true because it is lived by all of us, at some level. It's a story that connects and speaks to us all" (par. 6). For the writer, these myths are useful. What is the relationship between "myth" and "fact"? How might "more than true" myths become problematic, or have negative consequences outside the realm of screenwriting?

3. **connections**   Seger writes in the context of popular movies, where myths reflect shared stories and universal ideals. Mark Greif focuses on the conventions of "reality" television, as well as the role of such programming in our society, in "The Reality of Reality Television" (p. 293). As he writes, "We need myths, not only of our ideal, and our average, but of our fallen extreme" (par. 13). Is he using the term "myth" in the same sense that Seger does? Does myth perform the same function in shows like *Survivor* and *American Idol* as it does in *Star Wars* or *Harry Potter*?

4. View a contemporary film and analyze the myths behind the storyline and characters. You may also choose to write more generally about a group of films, and how they use myths—or even work against conventional archetypes and plots.

ALONSO DURALDE

Why Are So Many Films
for Latinos Bad?

*Alonso Duralde (b. 1967) is a writer, film critic, and former artistic
director at the USA Film Festival. His work has appeared in the* Advocate *(where he was arts and entertainment editor), the* Village Voice,
Movieline, *and* Detour. *Duralde is also the author of* 101 Must-See
Movies for Gay Men *(2005) and* Have Yourself a Movie Little Christmas *(2010). In this essay, Duralde examines Hollywood's tendency to
make "dreadful movies for Latino audiences," even as the Latino population in the United States is growing as an economic and cultural
force. Ultimately, he concedes that we cannot blame the film industry
for "aiming at the lowest common denominator." Do you agree? "Why
Are So Many Films for Latinos Bad?" originally appeared on* Salon.com.

While it's ostensibly based on Jane Austen's "Sense and Sensibility," the new movie "From Prada to Nada" sells itself as a traditional Hollywood riches-to-rags comedy—overdressed brat gets
taken down a peg, falls in love with a hunky prole, and learns
that love is more important than shoes. But this is a movie
aimed squarely at Latino audiences, so the trailer throws in lots
of the usual window dressing: Lowriders! Scary chola girls who
look like they wandered in from "Mi Vida Loca"! Tequila shots!
Mantillas!

Statistics keep telling us that Latinos are coming into their
own in the United States, growing as both an economic force and
a cultural one. Spanish-speaking countries are giving Hollywood
bankable and critically acclaimed actors like Javier Bardem,
Salma Hayek, Gael García Bernal, and Penélope Cruz. So why is
Hollywood returning the favor by making such dreadful movies
for Latino audiences?

One of the more painful moviegoing experiences of recent

years would have to be "Our Family Wedding," about a Mexican-American woman (America Ferrera) and the African-American man (Lance Gross) she plans to marry. Not only do the characters in this movie act like a nuptial union of black and brown is the most shocking event of 2010, but the movie scrapes bottom in the laughs department, relying on food fights, a Viagra-addled goat, and Carlos Mencia as sources of comedy.

Or take the case of the rom-com "Chasing Papi," another clunker from Steven Antin, who co-wrote this dud several stops on the road to perdition before "Burlesque." The film's Rotten Tomatoes page comes loaded with raves like "Chiquita Banana and the Frito Bandito were subtle compared to the caricatures of Latino culture in this movie."

As a gay film critic, it's an issue with which I'm rather familiar.   5
I periodically get interviewed for pieces asking questions like "Why are queer films so bad?" or "Why are queer films getting better?" The answer to both questions is a simple one: Somebody—either Plato or Ben Franklin—once observed that "85 percent of everything is crap." It's all a matter, then, of expanding the playing field; in other words, the more gay movies that get made, the more likely we are to get ones that don't suck. And that's a formula that applies itself to all niche films: For every 10 or so Tyler Perry melodramas, African-Americans get a sophisticated romantic comedy like "Something New" or a thoughtful drama like "Night Catches Us." After enough terrible Nora Ephron or Penny Marshall movies, Kathryn Bigelow gets to make "The Hurt Locker." It's a numbers game.

And until now, the effort to reach Latin audiences has been feeble. According to USA Today film critic Claudia Puig, "It's different and much less robust than the effort to reach African-American audiences. Where is the Mexican-American Tyler Perry? Or the Cuban-American Tyler Perry or the Puerto Rican Tyler Perry?" Putting aside the occasional Latino-themed art-house hit that found an audience—"Real Women Have Curves," "Y Tú Mamá También," "Maria Full of Grace"—and the wonderfully loony oeuvre of Robert Rodriguez, much of what gets aimed at Latino moviegoers feels lazy and stereotypical.

Sometimes it's a matter of the Latin flavor feeling tacked on, like a discount piñata bought at the last minute, as in the case of "Tortilla Soup," a rather by-the-numbers, Mexican-American

A toast to better movies for Latinos? Raquel Welch and Hector Elizondo in *Tortilla Soup.*

reworking of Ang Lee's "Eat Drink Man Woman." And while the Christmas movie "Nothing Like the Holidays," set in the Puerto Rican Humboldt Park neighborhood of Chicago, gets the ethnic details right, it's saddled with one of those plots where everything could be settled by one five-minute conversation that none of the characters are having.

There are a series of tropes you can find in most Latino movies, even in many of the good ones—closed-minded and tradition-bound fathers, dialogue about how we people from [insert specific Spanish-speaking country here] like to talk loud and get in each other's business, a boisterous dancing-in-a-nightclub scene, and at least one rebellious child who wants to either go to college, marry outside of *la raza*, or come out of the closet.

Not that you can blame these filmmakers for aiming at the lowest common denominator; after all, that's how most power brokers in Hollywood made their fortune. And when discussing niche audiences, it's easy for white commentators to moan about the fact that, say, African-American filmgoers shunned Sundance hits like "Love and Basketball" in favor of something dopey like Ice Cube's "Are We There Yet?"

Just one problem with that complaint, says Latin magazine 10 associate entertainment editor Lee Hernandez: "If you take something like [African-American director Theodore Witcher's 1997

Sundance hit] 'Love Jones,' which did well on the festival circuit, there are equivalencies for that in terms of whiter movies that do well at film festivals but didn't make a boatload of money. That's not a minority thing." In other words, don't blame black and Latino audiences for not turning out to see arthouse movies aimed at them unless you also blame white audiences for not making "Synecdoche, New York" a hit. "We watch movies and TV shows all the time to look for Latinos that are in them, but even if they make a movie that's, say, set in Central Los Angeles, and a bunch of Latinos are in it, and the movie sucks? It's not going to do well. I think the quality of the product is the most important thing."

Gay and lesbian moviegoers have gone through similar hunger to see themselves portrayed on film, even in movies that were insulting or badly made. I still remember dutifully trooping out to see any remotely queer movie until that magic moment in 1995, when I walked out of a dreadful comedy called "Lie Down With Dogs" midway through. By that point in history, there were enough gay movies getting made that I could choose to see just the ones that weren't "Clockwork Orange"[1]-style eyeball torture. A few disappointments here and there would seem more par for the course if audiences got a steady stream of Latino-themed movies. But when there's just one or two a year, it's harder for those films to avoid the 85-percent-of-everything rule.

But "From Prada to Nada" is a sign that those numbers are about to get better. It's the debut feature of Pantelion Films, a new venture announced last year by the powerhouses Lionsgate Films (home of Perry and, perhaps more important, Madea) and Mexican media giant Televisa. "From Prada to Nada," opens in limited release (250 screens) today, and represents the opening salvo of Pantelion's ambitious efforts—with a proposed production and release slate of eight to ten films per year—to aggressively target the Latino audience with mainstream movies. According to AMC Theatres, Latino audiences currently represent about one quarter of ticket-buyers, and current population figures projecting that by 2050 the Hispanic population will grow to 24 percent (from 14 percent today).

---

[1]*Clockwork Orange*: Anthony Burgess's 1962 dystopian novel (later made into a movie) in which the protagonist is forced to watch violent films. [Editor's note.]

That said, it doesn't mean Latino movies are necessarily going to more critical accolades. The company's business plan focuses specifically on making mainstream movies for mainstream audiences that happen to be Latino. "We've done a bunch of focus groups," says Pantelion CEO Paul Presburger, and those surveys of Latino viewers tell him that they "don't want to be hit over the head with the Latino issues of the day—border wars and things that are happening with drugs and violence, or problems with gangs. They're going to Hollywood movies. They want to be entertained."

Jim McNamara, the chairman of Pantelion and former CEO of Telemundo adds, "With 'From Prada to Nada,' we want to do a broad comedy that just happens to be set in the Latino world. And most of these [previous Latino] movies, since they are not made independently, they are works of art, labors of love by auteurs. And very often what happens is that they are not conceived of as commercial titles but as works of art. Because the struggle to get a movie made is so hard that the only thing that keeps them going is that passion and personal story. And so what we are trying to do is turn it around and say, 'Wait a minute, the main purpose here is not to tell an intense personal story.' There's nothing wrong with that, but what we are really trying to do is to entertain the broadest number of people."

It's not like Latinos aren't making slow progress in the enter-   15
tainment industry. Hernandez notes that the most recent Oscar wins of Spanish actors Penélope Cruz and Javier Bardem represent a breakthrough, but they're still the exception and not the rule. And the success of the aforementioned Latino actors in Hollywood doesn't always give a boost to niche cinema. When the ethnicity of Gael García Bernal's character in "Letters to Juliet" is never discussed—and when Cameron Diaz can be one of the biggest Latina stars in the world without ever playing a Latina role—that's a giant step for assimilation, but not even a small step toward a vibrant American cinema that's aimed at Latino audiences.

But still, it's better than nada.

For Discussion and Writing

1. According to the writer, Latino movies usually contain a "series of tropes" (par. 8). What does "trope" mean? What are the standard tropes found in these films?

2. Where in the essay does Duralde use comparison and contrast? How does it support his main point?

3. **connections**   Duralde and Rita Kempley in "Mystical Black Characters Play Complex Cinematic Role" (p. 310) write about images of race and ethnicity in mainstream films. How are their approaches to the topic and their conclusions similar? How are they different? Do the essays reflect the relative significance of Latinos and African Americans in American popular culture?

4. Duralde writes: "Gay and lesbian moviegoers have gone through a similar hunger to see themselves portrayed on film, even in movies that were insulting or badly made" (par. 11). Why do you think particular groups or individuals would have this hunger? Why would it be important? Do you think such representations influence culture and society? Why or why not?

RICK GROEN

Why Hollywood Hates Capitalism

Rick Groen is a film critic for the Globe and Mail, *a Canadian newspaper where this essay first appeared. In "Why Hollywood Hates Capitalism," he explores a persistent pop-culture paradox: "Of all the ironies in Tinseltown, none is richer than this: Hollywood is a big business that, on screen at least, loathes and despises big business." As you read, compare Groen's examples and analysis with your own experiences watching—and thinking about—movies. Does he provide enough evidence to prove that "Hollywood Hates Capitalism"?*

Of all the ironies in Tinseltown, none is richer than this: Hollywood is a big business that, on screen at least, loathes and despises big business.

A trio of recent and upcoming films—the reprise of Gordon Gekko in the *Wall Street* sequel, the plight of laid-off execs in *The Company Men*, a documentary account of systemic greed in next week's *Inside Job*—merely continue a business-bashing trend whose roots stretch all the way back to the silent era. As James Surowiecki has pointed out in a *New Yorker* piece, even ol' D.W. Griffith himself, in 1909's *A Corner in Wheat*, was wagging a righteous finger at the big bad money-men.

That piece goes on to catalogue a whole litany of pictures that, ever since, have extended and broadened the condemnation of capitalism's evil ways. But what it doesn't do is address the question that cries out: Why?

Yes, why does Hollywood hate what it essentially is?

Well, the answer is that Hollywood is really two businesses in 5 one: It's a profit-obsessed industry but it's also a dream factory. What the factory manufactures is myths, and, typically, there's no dissonance between the industry and the product, between (to use today's parlance) the "core values" of the manufacturer and those inherent in the myths it creates. But the whole issue of capitalism is a huge exception. Capitalism throws a spanner in the factory's works, for the simple reason that its values are often directly at odds with Hollywood's dominant myth—the Great American Dream.

Of course, the Dream is all about freedom, mainly the freedom of the rugged individual to climb the ladder of success and, thus, get rich. But capitalism is about free enterprise which emphasizes a different sort of gain, not the growth of the individual but the growth from the individual to the corporation, from small to big, from rugged David to mighty Goliath.

Already, you can see the tension brewing. Capitalism fits into the Dream, but only up to a point, when it gets inflated and messy. In that sense, capitalism is to American movies what marriage is to Shakespeare's plays. The Bard ends his comedies with the wedding and never ventures into the murky marriage beyond— otherwise, he'd have a tragedy on his hands.

Accordingly, in the battles between the "isms"—capitalism versus communism or fascism or terrorism—Hollywood (not to mention the politicians who either hail from Hollywood or emulate it) likes to frame the conflict as a war between freedom and tyranny. Alas, back on the home front, capitalism has a slippery habit of morphing from friend to foe, of changing from democracy's smiling cousin into an anti-democratic, hierarchical, non-egalitarian behemoth. There, these corporate Goliaths aren't tyranny's enemy by tyranny itself—in Depression-era films, for instance, they're the assembly line that crushes souls in Chaplin's *Modern Times*, or they're every faceless bank that forecloses on yet another poor homeowner.

Naturally, since no one roots for Goliath, the movies trooped out a continuing parade of Davids fighting the good fight against the evil giant. David comes in many guises—the plucky union activist (*Norma Rae*), the brave whistle-blower (*The China Syndrome, Silkwood, The Insider*), the emboldened justice-seeker (*Erin Brockovich, Michael Clayton*), the cheated inventor (*Flash of Genius*), the political crusader (*The Constant Gardener*), the little entrepreneur (*Other People's Money*). As for Goliath, whether Big Auto or Big Energy or Big Tobacco or Big Pharmacy, he's always the same polluting, penny-pinching, deceitful, destructive, even murdering titan.

Michael Douglas and Shia LaBeouf in *Wall Street: Money Never Sleeps*.

That way, both the necessities of drama, and the rugged indi- 10 vidualism inherent to the American myth, are better served. And, generally, the audience delights in the typecasting. Sure, many of us work for and owe our livelihoods to those same corporate giants, but who on occasion doesn't see their employer less as benefactor than oppressor? Here, Hollywood is everybody's loyal accomplice in the time-honored practice of biting the hand that feeds them.

Not that the hand doesn't deserve its teeth-marks. It took a Canadian documentary, *The Corporation*, to give historical weight to the evil corporate stereotype. The doc explained how a corporation is legally "a person," but a person who, over time, has developed a psychopathic character devoid of conscience and amoral in the singular pursuit of filthy lucre. Remind you of someone? Yep, none other than Hollywood's favourite bundle of sex and violence: the gangster. Sometimes, of course the gangster is the anti-hero waving his gun at the cruel business establishment (*Bonnie and Clyde*); often, though, he and his mob are just the metaphoric embodiment of the establishment itself (*The Godfather* saga).

In that latter case, then, the notion that the corporation has a gangster's personality blends with the idea that the gangster has corporate ambitions. Nowhere is that fusion more complete than in Paul Thomas Anderson's aptly titled *There Will Be Blood*, focused on a rising devil in the oil biz. As for the actual captains of industry, Hollywood tends to stay away from them, unless they can be portrayed as eccentrically rugged individuals themselves, like Howard Hughes in *The Aviator*, or the barely fictionalized William Randolph Hearst in *Citizen Kane*, or, currently, Mark Zuckerberg in *The Social Network*. There, the corporation is reduced to its lone owner, who is then pushed off his lofty perch and slapped down to a tragic victim, if only of his own peculiar nature. In this iteration, it's not the story of David and Goliath but of Achilles and his heel.

Still, these corporate portraits are relatively rare, an absence that James Surowiecki laments in his piece, citing Henry Ford as an obvious example. But Ford is the perfect illustration of why capitalists get stuck in Hollywood's myth-making machine. Initially, he would seem the personification of the American Dream—humble beginnings, self-made man, founds a company that pays generous wages to workers and provides affordable transportation for millions. Oops, then comes the spanner—he's the damned inventor of the soul-crushing assembly line; he viciously fights off all attempts to unionize his shop; he publishes anti-Semitic tracts and displays an appalling fondness for that other ism, nazism.

There's definitely a great film to be made about Henry Ford, but Hollywood wouldn't know how to cast him: Is he the lead hand in the dream factory or the boss-man of the corporate nightmare? Either way, Nazi sympathies can't be written off as wacky eccentricities.

Ford, like many such captains, is a hard guy to pin down dra- 15 matically. Just ask Michael Moore. In his classic *Roger & Me*, Moore sets out to find and interrogate the CEO of General Motors, the honcho behind massive layoffs leading to plant closures and urban blight. But the failed quest speaks volumes about the movies' century-long treatment of capitalism: The elusive money-man is nowhere to be found, and so settles into his customary role as the faceless villain.

To its credit, Hollywood the big business is ready and willing to cast itself in the role of the corporate heavy. In pics like *The Player* or *Barton Fink*, flawed but artsy Davids can be seen sling-shotting volleys at the Philistine studios. And the studios are delighted to fund any attacks on themselves, albeit with a tiny proviso: They had better make money. That's because Tinseltown's objections to capitalism aren't moral or political, but merely practical. It's just that Hollywood is an industry that manufactures entertaining myths and, on screen, business must be bad so that, off screen, business can be good.

For Discussion and Writing

1. According to Groen, the Hollywood film industry is willing to cast itself as a movie villain, with one requirement. What is this requirement?

2. For the most part, the writer argues by using a series of analogies. Note each analogy in the essay. How are they related to his premise that Hollywood is a "dream factory" that manufactures "myths" (par. 5)? How do the analogies support his overall thesis?

3. **connections** Do Groen's thesis and his examples contradict Robert Nathan and Jo-Ann Mort's argument in "Remembering *Norma Rae*" (p. 357)? How might Groen respond to Nathan and Mort's summary of *Norma Rae*'s political message: "The little guy may have a prayer of getting social justice, but he'll have to fight desperately to get it" (par. 6)? Is there any common ground between the essays? Can both be true?

4. Groen gives many examples showing how Hollywood films represent capitalism and business. In some cases, those representations are literal (*Erin Brockovich*); in others, the image is metaphorical (*The Godfather*). In every case, filmmakers make capitalists and their industries conform, somehow, to the dramatic, narrative, and commercial demands of "Hollywood's myth-making machine" (par. 13). Choose your own example of a film that shows images of corporations or capitalists. Does the portrayal conform to Groen's argument? Does it counter his argument? What point or message does your example suggest?

ROBERT NATHAN AND JO-ANN MORT

Remembering *Norma Rae*

Robert Nathan (b. 1948) is a writer and television producer who has worked on shows such as Law and Order *and E.R. Jo-Ann Mort (b. 1956) is CEO of ChangeCommunications, a New York-based media messaging consultancy. For thirteen years, she was director of communications for Unite and the Amalgamated Clothing and Textile Workers Union. She is also the author of* Our Hearts Invented a Place: Can Kibbutzim Survive in Today's Israel? *(2003). Her writing has appeared in the* Chicago Tribune, *the* American Prospect, *and other publications.*

In the following 2007 essay from the Nation *magazine, Nathan and Mort consider the fate of the 1979 film* Norma Rae—*a movie that has "essentially disappeared" from our cultural memory, despite its Oscar-winning acting, its "elegant and gritty" writing, and its powerful message about organized labor. For the authors, this disappearance suggests larger shifts in our society's attitude toward labor and working people, generally. As you read, think about the relationship between films and politics. Do you expect movies to have social or political messages?*

Here are some words you are unlikely to hear in any of the movie clips shown during the Academy Awards this year:

Ladies and gentlemen, the textile industry, in which you are spending your lives and your substance . . . is the only industry in the whole length and breadth of these United States of America that is not unionized. Therefore, they are free to exploit you, to lie to you, to cheat you and to take away from you what is rightfully yours—your health, a decent wage, a fit place to work.

"Unionized" isn't a word you hear in many American movies. "A decent wage," now there's a phrase that doesn't crop up too often. As for the evocative "your lives and your substance," poetic descriptions of the human condition aren't generally found in contemporary entertainment.

This speech is from Martin Ritt's classic 1979 film *Norma Rae*, delivered in an impassioned sermon by Ron Leibman in the role of an organizer for the Textile Workers Union of America, a real union at the time and a predecessor to the current trade union UNITE HERE. *Norma Rae* is an aberration in recent Hollywood history. The movie portrays a realistic union-organizing campaign and the fierce corporate response at the fictional O. P. Henley textile mill in the fictional town of Henleyville. As everyone knew at the time, the mill and the town were unambiguous stand-ins for J. P. Stevens and its sixteen-year war against union organizers in Roanoke Rapids, North Carolina, and the movie accurately depicted the state of American labor in 1979.

The situation has not improved much since. The only remaining Stevens factory in the United States (owned by its successor company, Westpoint Home) is a unionized blanket mill in Maine. In other industries, union organizers are battling adversaries as unyielding as any in the days of *Norma Rae*. According to the labor advocacy group American Rights at Work, last year more than 23,000 Americans were fired or penalized for legal union activity.

On a human level, *Norma Rae* is the story of one woman, played by Sally Field, who finds redemption risking her life for economic justice, and of factory workers demanding to be treated as more than slaves. In the realm of the political, it is virtually the only American movie of the modern era to deal substantially with any of these subjects. Even today it remains iconic—a major studio movie about the lives of working people with a profound and, for its time, disturbing political message: The little guy may have a prayer of getting social justice, but he'll have to fight desperately to get it. Try to think of a contemporary American film with a similar message or a political statement anywhere near that blunt. The closest thing to a message in this year's crop of Oscar nominees for Best Picture can be found in *Babel*, which poses the rather mild question, Why can't we all just get along?

European filmmakers, like England's Ken Loach and Mike Leigh, don't shy from the subject of class. Loach's *Bread and Roses* dramatized the 1990 Service Employees International Union's Justice for Janitors campaign in Los Angeles, and Leigh's entire career is virtually a paean to the working class. This is not to say that American studios don't make topical mainstream films. A

Sally Field in *Norma Rae.*

kind of renaissance seemed to be blossoming in 2005, with material as varied as *Good Night, and Good Luck* and *The Constant Gardener.* But *Blood Diamond*—about the 1990s civil war in Sierra Leone partly sparked by international diamond speculators—was perhaps this season's only major studio picture that could be called politically daring, and it was a box-office disappointment. In the end, of course, financially successful or not, such movies don't fundamentally threaten the established order. They're well-crafted stories delivering conventional wisdom with considerable artistic skill.

Norma Rae was different. Its subject matter, never mind its politics, was enough to make a studio executive cringe: a movie about a union. On top of that, it was a story of platonic love between a Jewish intellectual and a factory worker; in Hollywood love stories, the audience wants the heroes to end up in bed. Even with a trio of creative giants—Ritt and his writers, Irving Ravetch and Harriet Frank Jr.—this was no easy sell. Casting could have helped; stars get movies made. But several leading actresses, among them Jane Fonda and Jill Clayburgh, turned down the title role. Creative issues aside, there was the problem of location.

Where would you shoot the movie? Because of J. P. Stevens's influence, taking the production to most Southern towns would be impossible, and building your own textile mill, prohibitively costly. (With help from the union, Ritt found a unionized mill in Opelika, Alabama, where management agreed to let him shoot, with mill workers as extras playing themselves.) Finally, after overcoming all the odds, when released the movie was anything but an instant hit, and only after Sally Field won Best Actress at Cannes did it gradually go from dud to box-office success.

Since then, the entertainment community has kept its distance from the film. One indication of Hollywood's indifference came six years later, at the 1985 Academy Awards, when Field accepted her Oscar as Best Actress for *Places in the Heart*. "You like me," she said effusively, "right now, you like me." The audience response was nervous laughter, as if Sally Field were so needy as to consider an Academy Award a sign that she was "liked." This was, of course, not the case. Field had assumed, incorrectly, that most of her colleagues had seen her astonishing performance in *Norma Rae*. But in fact, many in the audience had no idea that she was referencing one of the picture's most memorable pieces of dialogue—her character's realization that her union organizer not merely respected her but liked her as a human being.

In the ensuing twenty years, the movie essentially disappeared. 10 Otherwise movie-literate folks only vaguely remember Norma's quest. Alas, they don't know what they're missing. With Leibman and Field, the movie has two of the toughest and most generous performances in the history of American film. The film's language is simultaneously elegant and gritty. Of powerful moments, there is no end. When Norma commits herself to the organizing campaign, she asks the local minister to lend his church for a union meeting. "That's blacks and whites sitting together," Norma says. The minister, horrified, tells her, "We're going to miss your voice in the choir, Norma." She replies, "You're going to hear it raised up somewhere else."

In an unusual twist, the movie's story played itself out in reality the year following its release. Sixteen years after a successful union election at the Roanoke Rapids mill, union members finally forced J. P. Stevens to the bargaining table. The film was a key factor in a nationwide boycott against Stevens—a campaign that became a model for coalitions of union supporters and union members. The Rev. David Dyson, who helped spearhead the Stevens boycott when he was on the union's staff, recalls: "The movie came along at the two-year point in the boycott, which hadn't picked up any steam. We found Crystal Lee Jordan [now Crystal Lee Sutton, the worker who inspired the Norma Rae character]. . . . We put on a tour, including a great event in Los Angeles with Sally Field and Crystal Lee. The lights would come up and there would be the real Norma Rae and people would leap to their feet."

It's nearly impossible to imagine a similar movie that would bring them to their feet today. Television, a broader medium, is different, with an audience more fractionated and therefore, theoretically, more open to content that some might label controversial. Not so long ago there was *Roseanne*, which addressed head-on the darkness of power and social class and the tribulations of working life. Last year's Emmy winner *The Office* included a story line mocking a nasty anti-union campaign; the hugely popular *Grey's Anatomy* followed a nurses' strike with obvious sympathy for the nurses—even management, in the person of doctor George O'Malley, joined the picket line as the story revealed his upbringing in a pro-union home. One could argue that the brilliantly corrosive *Rescue Me*, about Denis Leary as a New York City firefighter and the personal lives of his colleagues, is a bold step into the interior world of the working class; but firefighters are unmistakably post-9/11 heroes. What's ultimately most telling about these examples is how unusual they are, far from television's norm, at a time when most Americans are losing economic ground. One new show this season, the polished and artful *Brothers & Sisters*, is about a wealthy family in Pasadena who own a business in which workers are nearly invisible; the primary stories involve the characters' tortured love lives. Ironically, the family matriarch—albeit a liberal ACLU-ish matriarch—is played by none other than Sally Field.

It would be easy to blame the entertainment industry for the invisibility of working people fighting to better their lives. Ask writers in show business and they'll say, "Nobody cares about seeing those people on a screen" and "If audiences wanted to see that, the studios would make it" and, finally, the answer to nearly every question about the current condition of American filmmaking, "The studios have a mega-hit mentality; they don't want to make small pictures." But maybe there's another reason. Making *Norma Rae* in 1979 was hard enough; now it would probably be impossible. The country has changed. It's more difficult to build a mass movement for social and economic change, to find large numbers of Americans who care about social solidarity. If popular entertainment is, by definition, mass entertainment, what happens when no mass exists, when an insufficient number of people occupy cultural common ground? In that case, for whom would you make *Norma Rae*?

"You live there, and you become one of them," Sally Field said in a documentary issued with the DVD of *Norma Rae*, "and you try to stand at their machine and thread it and run it, and . . . you learn to appreciate how difficult their lives are, and chances are you're never getting out." Which, for the most part, is how things remain. The American labor movement is arguably in more trouble now than it was then. Where is the next movie that might hope to change the course of history?

Of movies about ideas and social justice, Sam Goldwyn 15 famously said, "If you want to send a message, call Western Union." In other words, moviemakers are in the movie business, not the social change business. And so tomorrow we won't go to the tenplex and find movies about Wal-Mart workers fighting for health and pension benefits, or turn on the television and find a working-class hero struggling to pay the electric bill. (Isn't it odd that people on TV hardly ever seem to worry about gas prices?) If we are to find a *Roseanne* or a *Norma Rae* again in popular entertainment, if we are to make movies that can affect the course of history, we need to find something else first, something difficult to see on the horizon. We need to find a belief in an ideal disappearing not only from our movies but also from our lives—the notion that we do, in fact, share common ground, and that if we ignore the lives of the least fortunate in our society we may well be ignoring the future of our society itself.

For Discussion and Writing

1. What's the difference between American filmmakers and European filmmakers, according to Nathan and Mort?
2. Nathan and Mort concede that American studios make "topical mainstream films," but the writers argue that these movies "don't

fundamentally threaten the established order" (par. 7). What does that mean, exactly? Do you agree? Do you generally want films to "threaten the established order"? Should we expect them to "affect the course of history" (par. 15)? Why or why not?

3. **connections**   Which essay is more persuasive? "Remembering *Norma Rae*" or Rick Groen's "Why Hollywood Hates Capitalism" (p. 352)? Why? What, specifically, about the essay (either regarding its style or its substance) makes it more effective?

4. The writers refer to the "invisibility of working people fighting to better their lives" in popular entertainment (par. 13). Do you agree that television and film provide few images of poor and working people? Should writers and producers focus more on these characters and their stories? Should viewers care more about them? Address these questions in an essay using your own examples.

CHAPTER 7

Media Dreams

From the earliest spoken tales and poems to the most recent blockbuster movie, we have always craved fictions and vicarious experiences. And for almost as long, we have tried to explain that hunger. The Greek philosopher Aristotle argued that tragedies allow spectators to purge themselves of excessive pity and fear through the vicarious experience of watching a play. For writers in the Romantic tradition, imaginative works reveal glimpses of transcendent truth and beauty: a glimmer of hope that the "world imagined is the ultimate good," in the words of poet Wallace Stevens. For thinkers like Sigmund Freud, fictional works function like dreams, allowing space for unconscious fears and wish fulfillment. These works perform more mundane tasks, too. They allow us to escape from the ordinariness of our daily lives and selves—or even escape from sorrow, pain, and unpleasant realities. In this context, our love of vicarious distraction contradicts the value we ascribe to "authenticity" and "truth." But as T. S. Eliot wrote, "human kind / Cannot bear very much reality." Or, as Jack Nicholson's character Colonel Jessep yells in *A Few Good Men*: "You can't handle the truth!"

If our love of imaginative escape has aroused the curiosity of philosophers and critics, it has also aroused their fear and loathing. A strong distrust of imaginative fictions and entertainments runs through the history of Western literature and culture. In *The Republic*, Plato famously banishes poets from his ideal society because fiction-makers mislead and debase people with their falsehoods. After the 1642 Puritan Revolution in England, all English theaters were closed to stop the corrupting influence of theatrical performances. "To indulge the power of fiction and send imagination out upon the wing is often the sport of those who delight too much in silent speculation," wrote the critic Samuel Johnson in his 1759 work *Rasselas* (itself, a work of fiction). In these centuries-old concerns about the dangers of imaginative and vicarious experiences, we can see early versions of contemporary debates about whether the graphic imagery of video games desensitizes children or causes violent behavior.

All of the selections in this section address the value of vicarious experience and take the measure of imaginative flights in popular culture. In "The Art of Immersion: Fear of Fiction," Frank Rose explores the history of such fears, from the early years of the novel to films like *Avatar*, as every new technological medium "increases the transporting power of narrative." Gerard Jones ("Violent Media Is Good for Kids") argues that violent media allows children to participate in "creative violence." Through imaginative identification and vicarious experience, children learn to manage their emotions. Guillermo del Toro and Chuck Hogan's "Why Vampires Never Die" and Chuck Klosterman's "My Zombie, Myself: Why Modern Life Feels Rather Undead" reveal how our monsters reflect—and embody—cultural fears and preoccupations, past and present. In the paired readings, Lane Wallace ("Can Video Games Teach Us How to Succeed in the Real World?") and Kyle Chayka ("Why Video Games Are Works of Art") investigate the value of video games as educational tools and as works of art, respectively.

FRANK ROSE

The Art of Immersion: Fear of Fiction

Frank Rose began his journalism career at the Village Voice, *writing about the bourgeoning 1970s punk rock scene in New York City. Since then he has been a contributing editor at* Travel + Leisure *and* Esquire *magazines, as well as a contributing writer at* Premiere. *He is currently a contributing editor at* Wired *magazine. Rose's work has also appeared in the* New York Times Magazine, Vanity Fair, Rolling Stone, *and other publications. His most recent book is* The Art of Immersion: How the Digital Generation Is Remaking Hollywood, Madison Avenue, and the Way We Tell Stories *(2011).*

In this essay, adapted from his book of the same title, Rose explores the history of "weirdly immersive" technologies, as well as cultural responses to them. He also questions the conventional wisdom that people desire "authenticity." As you read, think about your own experiences with—and reactions to—the "transporting power of narrative." Do you believe that power can be dangerous?

Two years ago this month, as editors worldwide were beginning to debate whether anyone would actually go see *Avatar*, the $200 million-plus, 3-D movie extravaganza that James Cameron was making, Josh Quittner wrote in *Time* about getting an advance look. "I couldn't tell what was real and what was animated," he gushed. "The following morning, I had the peculiar sensation of wanting to return there, as if Pandora were real."

It was not the first time someone found an entertainment experience to be weirdly immersive. For all the cutting-edge technology that went into the making of *Avatar*, in that sense there was nothing new about it all.

Some four centuries earlier, Miguel de Cervantes reported in

366

his satirical novel that Don Quixote went tilting at windmills because he'd lost his mind from too much reading:

> He read all night from sundown to dawn, and all day from sunup to dusk, until with virtually no sleep and so much reading he dried out his brain and lost his sanity. . . . He decided to turn himself into a knight errant, traveling all over the world with his horse and his weapons, seeking adventures and doing everything that, according to his books, earlier knights had done.

As Janet Murray of Georgia Tech observed in her 1997 book *Hamlet on the Holodeck*, every new medium that's been invented, from print to film to television to cyberspace, has increased the transporting power of narrative. And every new medium has aroused fear and even hostility as a result.

Ray Bradbury wrote *Fahrenheit 451* in the early '50s—the   5 dawn of the television era. It's about a man whose job is burning books, a medium that by this time had long since ceased to cause alarm.

The man's wife, like her friends, is mesmerized by the video transmissions on the giant "televisors" on her living room walls. "My wife says books aren't 'real,' " he tells Faber, the former English professor who gradually transforms him into a savior of books.

"Thank God for that," Faber replies. "You can shut them and say, 'Hold on a moment!' But who has ever torn himself from . . . a TV parlor? . . . It is an environment as real as the world. It becomes and is the truth."

That was Bradbury's beef with television—it was just too immersive. Logical, linear thought was no match for its seductively phosphorescent glow. It became and was the truth.

Before television, the same danger could be found in the movies. In Aldous Huxley's *Brave New World*—published in 1932, five years after the birth of talkies—young John the Savage is taken to the "feelies," where he is revolted by the sensation of phantom lips grazing his own as the actors kiss.

"Suddenly, dazzling and incomparably more solid-looking   10 than they would have seemed in actual flesh and blood, far more real than reality, there stood the stereoscopic images, locked in one another's arms. . . . The Savage started. That sensation on his lips!"

From *Don Quixote* to *Avatar*, we have always feared immersive fictions.

Too real. Dangerously, immersively, more-real-than-reality real. Better to curl up with a good book.

Oh, right.

For all the cutting-edge technology that went into the making of *Avatar*, in that sense there was nothing new about it all.

But even after books gained acceptance, novels could still seem dangerously immersive in other formats.

A century before talkies, there was serialization. England in 15 the 1830s was being radically transformed by technology. Industrialization was drawing people to the cities in unimaginable numbers, crowding them together in appalling conditions but also producing a dramatic rise in literacy.

At the same time, improvements in paper, printing, and transportation were making it possible to print and distribute periodicals on a much greater scale. Book publishers, being young and scrappy, saw a market for serial fiction—books released a few chapters at a time in flimsy paperback editions that sold for pennies.

Many authors were published in this manner, but one became identified with it above all. As a young boy, Charles Dickens had imbibed *Don Quixote* and *Robinson Crusoe*; at 25 he was writing *Oliver Twist* in monthly installments for a new library journal he'd been hired to edit.

The tale of an indigent boy forced into the miasma of crime and despair that was contemporary London, *Oliver Twist* spoke directly to the new audience that cheap serials had created. The same technological upheaval that gave rise to the workhouses Dickens described also created a readership for his story, and a way of reaching them that was cheap enough to be practicable.

From our perspective, Dickens is a literary master, an icon of a now-threatened culture. But at the time, he represented the threat of what was coming. Novels themselves were only beginning to find acceptance in polite society; for upper-class commentators, serialization was entirely too much.

In 1845, a critic for the patrician *North British Review* railed 20 against the multiplying effects of serialization on the already hallucinatory powers of the novel:

> Useful as a certain amount of novel reading may be, this is not the right way to indulge in it. It is not a mere healthy recreation like a match at

cricket, a lively conversation, or a game at backgammon. It throws us into a state of unreal excitement, a trance, a dream, which we should be allowed to dream out, and then be sent back to the atmosphere of reality again, cured . . . of the desire to indulge again soon in the same delirium of feverish interest. But now our dreams are mingled with our daily business.

Novels, in other words, were not yet on a par with more acceptable pursuits, like games and social networking. But if you had to indulge in them, best to get it over with as quickly as possible.

Now it's the Internet that seems new and dangerously immersive. Three decades after William Gibson introduced the concept of cyberspace ("A consensual hallucination experienced daily by billions. . . . Clusters and constellations of data. Like city lights, receding"), the Internet has redefined our expectations from stories.

It's no coincidence that we are beset by questions of authenticity. Value is a function of scarcity, and in a time of scripted reality TV and Photoshop everywhere, authenticity is a scarce commodity.

But though we live in a world in which identity is always in question, we also have the media savvy to sniff out fakery and the tools to spread the word. Technology makes authenticity suspect, and technology gives us the wherewithal to demand it—if that's what we really want.

Except that it's not what we want. It's what we think we want.   25 What we really want is to go back to Pandora, even though we've never been there in the first place. We want to be sucked inside the computer like Jeff Bridges in *Tron*. We want to be immersed in something that's not real at all.

Just like Don Quixote.

For Discussion and Writing

1. Besides 3-D film technology, list other narrative technologies and examples of "immersion" in this essay. What point does Rose make by using them?

2. According to Rose, we are "beset by questions of authenticity," which is a "scarce commodity" (par. 23). What does he mean? Do you agree with his assessment?

3. **connections** How does Rose's rhetorical strategy in the "Art of Immersion" parallel Neil Postman's in "The Judgment of Thamus"

(p. 200)? Do the writers have similar attitudes toward their subjects? Do they come to similar conclusions?

4. The writer makes a bold claim in his concluding paragraphs, namely, that we do not want "authenticity": "It's what we think we want. What we really want is to go back to Pandora, even though we've never been there in the first place" (par. 25). Respond to this assertion. How would you further Rose's argument, or refute it? He uses examples from film and literature in this essay. Incorporate your own examples—whether from popular culture or real life—into your response.

GERARD JONES

Violent Media Is Good for Kids

An author, critic, and comic book writer, Gerard Jones (b. 1957) spent fourteen years writing for Marvel Comics, DC Comics, and other publishers. His books include Killing Monsters: Why Children Need Fantasy, Super Heroes, and Make-Believe Violence *(2002),* Men of Tomorrow: Geeks, Gangsters, and the Birth of the Comic Book *(2004), and* The Undressing of America: How a Bodybuilder, a Swimming Queen and a Magician Created Reality Media *(in progress). In this provocative essay from* Mother Jones *magazine, the writer argues that "every aspect of even the trashiest pop-culture story can have its own developmental function." As you read, consider your own relationship to violent media and entertainment. Were they "good" for you?*

At 13 I was alone and afraid. Taught by my well-meaning, progressive, English-teacher parents that violence was wrong, that rage was something to be overcome and cooperation was always better than conflict, I suffocated my deepest fears and desires under a nice-boy persona. Placed in a small, experimental school that was wrong for me, afraid to join my peers in their bumptious rush into adolescent boyhood, I withdrew into passivity and loneliness. My parents, not trusting the violent world of the late 1960s, built a wall between me and the crudest elements of American pop culture.

Then the Incredible Hulk smashed through it.

One of my mother's students convinced her that Marvel Comics, despite their apparent juvenility and violence, were in fact devoted to lofty messages of pacifism and tolerance. My mother borrowed some, thinking they'd be good for me. And so they were. But not because they preached lofty messages of benevolence. They were good for me because they were juvenile. And violent.

372

The character who caught me, and freed me, was the Hulk: overgendered and undersocialized, half-naked and half-witted, raging against a frightened world that misunderstood and persecuted him. Suddenly I had a fantasy self to carry my stifled rage and buried desire for power. I had a fantasy self who was a self: unafraid of his desires and the world's disapproval, unhesitating and effective in action. "Puny boy follow Hulk!" roared my fantasy self, and I followed.

I followed him to new friends—other sensitive geeks chasing their own inner brutes—and I followed him to the arrogant, self-exposing, self-assertive, superheroic decision to become a writer. Eventually, I left him behind, followed more sophisticated heroes, and finally my own lead along a twisting path to a career and an identity. In my 30s, I found myself writing action movies and comic books. I wrote some Hulk stories, and met the geek-geniuses who created him. I saw my own creations turned into action figures, cartoons, and computer games. I talked to the kids who read my stories. Across generations, genders, and ethnicities I kept seeing the same story: people pulling themselves out of emotional traps by immersing themselves in violent stories. People integrating the scariest, most fervently denied fragments of their psyches into fuller senses of selfhood through fantasies of superhuman combat and destruction.

I have watched my son living the same story—transforming himself into a bloodthirsty dinosaur to embolden himself for the plunge into preschool, a Power Ranger to muscle through a social competition in kindergarten. In the first grade, his friends started climbing a tree at school. But he was afraid: of falling, of the centipedes crawling on the trunk, of sharp branches, of his friends' derision. I took my cue from his own fantasies and read him old Tarzan comics, rich in combat and bright with flashing knives. For two weeks he lived in them. Then he put them aside. And he climbed the tree.

But all the while, especially in the wake of the recent burst of school shootings, I heard pop psychologists insisting that violent stories are harmful to kids, heard teachers begging parents to keep their kids away from "junk culture," heard a guilt-stricken friend with a son who loved Pokémon lament, "I've turned into the bad mom who lets her kid eat sugary cereal and watch cartoons!" That's when I started the research.

"Fear, greed, power-hunger, rage: these are aspects of our selves that we try not to experience in our lives but often want, even need, to experience vicariously through stories of others," writes Melanie Moore, Ph.D., a psychologist who works with urban teens. "Children need violent entertainment in order to explore the inescapable feelings that they've been taught to deny, and to reintegrate those feelings into a more whole, more complex, more resilient selfhood."

Moore consults to public schools and local governments, and is also raising a daughter. For the past three years she and I have been studying the ways in which children use violent stories to meet their emotional and developmental needs—and the ways in which adults can help them use those stories healthily. With her help I developed Power Play, a program for helping young people improve their self-knowledge and sense of potency through heroic, combative storytelling.

We've found that every aspect of even the trashiest pop-culture story can have its own developmental function. Pretending to have superhuman powers helps children conquer the feelings of powerlessness that inevitably come with being so young and small. The dual-identity concept at the heart of many superhero stories helps kids negotiate the conflicts between the inner self and the public self as they work through the early stages of socialization. Identification with a rebellious, even destructive, hero helps children learn to push back against a modern culture that cultivates fear and teaches dependency.

At its most fundamental level, what we call "creative violence"—head-bonking cartoons, bloody videogames, playground karate, toy guns—gives children a tool to master their rage. Children will feel rage. Even the sweetest and most civilized of them, even those whose parents read the better class of literary magazines, will feel rage. The world is uncontrollable and incomprehensible; mastering it is a terrifying, enraging task. Rage can be an energizing emotion, a shot of courage to push us to resist greater threats, take more control, than we ever thought we could. But rage is also the emotion our culture distrusts the most. Most of us are taught early on to fear our own. Through immersion in imaginary combat and identification with a violent protagonist, children engage the rage they've stifled, come to fear it less, and become more capable of utilizing it against life's challenges.

I knew one little girl who went around exploding with fantasies so violent that other moms would draw her mother aside to whisper, "I think you should know something about Emily. . . ." Her parents were separating, and she was small, an only child, a tomboy at an age when her classmates were dividing sharply along gender lines. On the playground she acted out *"Sailor Moon"* fights, and in the classroom she wrote stories about people being stabbed with knives. The more adults tried to control her stories, the more she acted out the roles of her angry heroes: breaking rules, testing limits, roaring threats.

Then her mother and I started helping her tell her stories. She wrote them, performed them, drew them like comics: sometimes bloody, sometimes tender, always blending the images of pop culture with her own most private fantasies. She came out of it just as fiery and strong, but more self-controlled and socially competent: a leader among her peers, the one student in her class who could truly pull boys and girls together.

I worked with an older girl, a middle-class "nice girl," who held 15 herself together through a chaotic family situation and a tumultuous adolescence with gangsta rap. In the mythologized street violence of Ice T, the rage and strutting of his music and lyrics, she found a theater of the mind in which she could be powerful, ruthless, invulnerable. She avoided the heavy drug use that sank many of her peers, and flowered in college as a writer and political activist.

I'm not going to argue that violent entertainment is harmless. I think it has helped inspire some people to real-life violence. I am going to argue that it's helped hundreds of people for every one it's hurt, and that it can help far more if we learn to use it well. I am going to argue that our fear of "youth violence" isn't well-founded on reality, and that the fear can do more harm than the reality. We act as though our highest priority is to prevent our children from growing up into murderous thugs—but modern kids are far more likely to grow up too passive, too distrustful of themselves, too easily manipulated.

We send the message to our children in a hundred ways that their craving for imaginary gun battles and symbolic killings is wrong, or at least dangerous. Even when we don't call for censorship or forbid *"Mortal Kombat,"* we moan to other parents within our kids' earshot about the "awful violence" in the entertainment

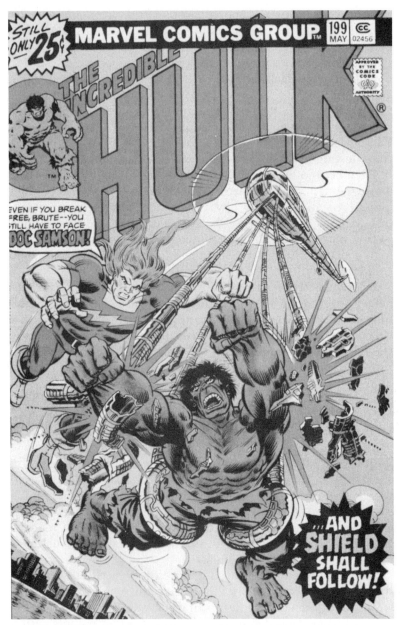

"'Creative violence' . . . gives children a tool to master their rage."

they love. We tell our kids that it isn't nice to playfight, or we steer them from some monstrous action figure to a *pro-social doll*. Even in the most progressive households, where we make such a point of letting children feel what they feel, we rush to substitute an enlightened discussion for the raw material of rageful fantasy. In the process, we risk confusing them about their natural aggression in the same way the Victorians confused their children about their sexuality. When we try to protect our children from their own feelings and fantasies, we shelter them not against violence but against power and selfhood.

For Discussion and Writing

1. How, specifically, did Jones help his son overcome his fears? What point does this anecdote illustrate?

2. How does Jones include and address counterarguments in his essay? Point out specific moments where he engages an opposing point of view. Is his response effective?

3. **connections**   How would you compare Jones's argument with Guillermo del Toro and Chuck Hogan's in "Why Vampires Never Die" (p. 378)? Jones focuses on children and their need for fantasies of aggression and fear. Do classic monsters perform similar functions? For example, how might vampires allow people to (in the words of psychologist Melanie Moore, whom Jones quotes) "explore the inescapable feelings that they've been taught to deny" (par. 9)? Would del Toro and Hogan agree with "Violent Media Is Good for Kids"? Why or why not?

4. Jones writes about the need—especially in childhood—for a "fantasy self" (par. 4): "The dual-identity concept at the heart of many superhero stories helps kids negotiate the conflicts between the inner self and the public self as they work through the early stages of socialization. Identification with a rebellious, even destructive, hero helps children learn to push back against a modern culture that cultivates fear and teaches dependency" (par. 11). How do you respond to this claim? Do you agree? What experiences do you have with vicarious "identification," whether from comic book heroes or other sources?

GUILLERMO DEL TORO AND CHUCK HOGAN

Why Vampires Never Die

*Born in Guadalajara, Mexico, Guillermo del Toro (b. 1964) is a writer
and filmmaker known for films such as* Pan's Labyrinth *(2006) and the*
Hellboy *series. In 2009, he published his first novel,* The Strain, *cowritten with Chuck Hogan. The book is the first in a vampire trilogy by
the two authors. Chuck Hogan is a crime fiction and horror novelist
whose books include* The Blood Artists *(1999),* Prince of Thieves
(2004), and The Killing Moon *(2007). In this column from the New
York Times, the writers discuss the origins and perennial appeal of
vampire stories. They suggest that vampires—figures imagined and
reinvented by different cultures at different times—often reflect society's anxieties and preoccupations. According to del Toro and Hogan,
the Dracula myth may speak to us on a more primal level, as well. As
you read, think about the ways that imaginary monsters can be metaphors for real-life problems and fears.*

Tonight, you or someone you love will likely be visited by a vampire—on cable television or the big screen, or in the bookstore.
Our own novel describes a modern-day epidemic that spreads
across New York City.

It all started nearly 200 years ago. It was the "Year Without a
Summer" of 1816, when ash from volcanic eruptions lowered
temperatures around the globe, giving rise to widespread famine.
A few friends gathered at the Villa Diodati on Lake Geneva and
decided to engage in a small competition to see who could come
up with the most terrifying tale—and the two great monsters of
the modern age were born.

One was created by Mary Godwin, soon to become Mary
Shelley, whose Dr. Frankenstein gave life to a desolate creature.
The other monster was less created than fused. John William
Polidori stitched together folklore, personal resentment, and erotic

378

anxieties into "The Vampyre," a story that is the basis for vampires as they are understood today.

With "The Vampyre," Polidori gave birth to the two main branches of vampiric fiction: the vampire as romantic hero, and the vampire as undead monster. This ambivalence may reflect Polidori's own, as it is widely accepted that Lord Ruthven, the titular creature, was based upon Lord Byron—literary superstar of the era and another resident of the lakeside villa that fateful summer. Polidori tended to Byron day and night, both as his doctor and most devoted groupie. But Polidori resented him as well: Byron was dashing and brilliant, while the poor doctor had a rather drab talent and unremarkable physique.

But this was just a new twist to a very old idea. The myth, 5 established well before the invention of the word "vampire," seems to cross every culture, language and era. The Indian Baital, the Ch'ing Shih in China, and the Romanian Strigoi are but a few of its names. The creature seems to be as old as Babylonia and Sumer. Or even older.

The vampire may originate from a repressed memory we had as primates. Perhaps at some point we were—out of necessity— cannibalistic. As soon as we became sedentary, agricultural tribes with social boundaries, one seminal myth might have featured our ancestors as primitive beasts who slept in the cold loam of the earth and fed off the salty blood of the living.

Monsters, like angels, are invoked by our individual and collective needs. Today, much as during that gloomy summer in 1816, we feel the need to seek their cold embrace.

Herein lies an important clue: in contrast to timeless creatures like the dragon, the vampire does not seek to obliterate us, but instead offers a peculiar brand of blood alchemy. For as his contagion bestows its nocturnal gift, the vampire transforms our vile, mortal selves into the gold of eternal youth, and instills in us something that every social construct seeks to quash: primal lust. If youth is desire married with unending possibility, then vampire lust creates within us a delicious void, one we long to fulfill.

In other words, whereas other monsters emphasize what is mortal in us, the vampire emphasizes the eternal in us. Through the panacea of its blood it turns the lead of our toxic flesh into golden matter.

In a society that moves as fast as ours, where every week a new 10

"In the vampire we find Eros and Thanatos fused together in archetypal embrace. . . ."

"blockbuster" must be enthroned at the box office, or where idols are fabricated by consensus every new television season, the promise of something everlasting, something truly eternal, holds a special allure. As a seductive figure, the vampire is as flexible and polyvalent as ever. Witness its slow mutation from the pansexual, decadent Anne Rice creatures to the current permutations—promising anything from chaste eternal love to wild nocturnal escapades—and there you will find the true essence of immortality: adaptability.

Vampires find their niche and mutate at an accelerated rate now—in the past one would see, for decades, the same variety of fiend, repeated in multiple storylines. Now, vampires simultaneously occur in all forms and tap into our every need: soap opera storylines, sexual liberation, noir detective fiction, etc. The myth seems to be twittering promiscuously to serve all avenues of life, from cereal boxes to romantic fiction. The fast pace of technology accelerates its viral dispersion in our culture.

But if Polidori remains the roots in the genealogy of our creature, the most widely known vampire was birthed by Bram Stoker in 1897.

Part of the reason for the great success of his "Dracula" is generally acknowledged to be its appearance at a time of great technological revolution. The narrative is full of new gadgets (telegraphs, typing machines), various forms of communication (diaries, ship logs), and cutting-edge science (blood transfusions)—a mash-up of ancient myth in conflict with the world of the present.

Today as well, we stand at the rich uncertain dawn of a new level of scientific innovation. The wireless technology we carry in our pockets today was the stuff of the science fiction in our youth. Our technological arrogance mirrors more and more the Wellsian[1] dystopia of dissatisfaction, while allowing us to feel safe and connected at all times. We can call, see or hear almost anything and anyone no matter where we are. For most people then, the only remote place remains within. "Know thyself" we do not.

Despite our obsessive harnessing of information, we are still 15
ultimately vulnerable to our fates and our nightmares. We enthrone the deadly virus in the very same way that "Dracula" allowed the British public to believe in monsters: through science. Science becomes the modern man's superstition. It allows him to experience fear and awe again, and to believe in the things he cannot see.

[1]Wellsian: Refers to British writer H. G. Wells (1866–1946), best known for his science fiction. [Editor's note.]

Robert Pattinson and Kristen Stewart in *The Twilight Saga: New Moon.*

And through awe, we once again regain spiritual humility. The current vampire pandemic serves to remind us that we have no true jurisdiction over our bodies, our climate or our very souls. Monsters will always provide the possibility of mystery in our mundane "reality show" lives, hinting at a larger spiritual world; for if there are demons in our midst, there surely must be angels lurking nearby as well. In the vampire we find Eros and Thanatos fused together in archetypal embrace, spiraling through the ages, undying.

Forever.

For Discussion and Writing

1. What are the two great monsters of the modern age, according to del Toro and Hogan? When were they created?

2. How do del Toro and Hogan use comparison and contrast to make their argument? Where do they use historical analogies? Point to specific examples in the essay and explain how they are related to the writers' main point.

3. **connections**   The writers see technology as one paradoxical source of our fears and our enduring fascination with monsters: "Our

technological arrogance mirrors more and more the Wellsian dystopia of dissatisfaction, while allowing us to feel safe and connected at all times. We can call, see or hear almost anything and anyone no matter where we are. For most people then, the only remote place remains within. 'Know thyself' we do not" (par. 14). How might Sherry Turkle respond to this claim and explain its paradox in "Can You Hear Me Now?" (p. 227)? Would she agree that technology prevents us from knowing ourselves?

4. Del Toro and Hogan write: "Despite our obsessive harnessing of information, we are still ultimately vulnerable to our fates and our nightmares" (par. 15). What other cultural manifestations of our "nightmares" can you identify? What monsters or imaginative horrors do you find compelling, alluring, or fascinating?

CHUCK KLOSTERMAN

My Zombie, Myself: Why Modern Life Feels Rather Undead

A prolific author, essayist, and pop culture critic, Chuck Klosterman (b. 1972) has written for Esquire, the New York Times Magazine, Spin, the Washington Post, *and many other publications. His books include* Fargo Rock City: A Heavy Metal Odyssey in Rural North Dakota *(2001) and* Sex, Drugs, and Cocoa Puffs: A Low Culture Manifesto *(2003), as well as a novel* The Visible Man *(2011). In this* New York Times *column, Klosterman argues that zombies are the representative monsters of our age: "Zombies are like the Internet and the media and every conversation we don't want to have." Is Klosterman suggesting that we fight zombies every day, or is he proposing that we have become zombies?*

Zombies are a value stock. They are wordless and oozing and brain dead, but they're an ever-expanding market with no glass ceiling. Zombies are a target-rich environment, literally and figuratively. The more you fill them with bullets, the more interesting they become. Roughly 5.3 million people watched the first episode of "The Walking Dead" on AMC, a stunning 83 percent more than the 2.9 million who watched the Season 4 premiere of "Mad Men." This means there are at least 2.4 million cable-ready Americans who might prefer watching Christina Hendricks if she were an animated corpse.

Statistically and aesthetically that dissonance seems perverse. But it probably shouldn't. Mainstream interest in zombies has steadily risen over the past 40 years. Zombies are a commodity that has advanced slowly and without major evolution, much like the staggering creatures George Romero popularized in the 1968 film "Night of the Living Dead." What makes that measured amplification curious is the inherent limitations of the zombie itself: You can't add much depth to a creature who can't talk, doesn't think and whose only motive is the consumption of flesh. You can't humanize a zombie, unless you make it less zombie-esque. There are slow zombies, and there are fast zombies—that's pretty much the spectrum of zombie diversity. It's not that zombies are changing to fit the world's condition; it's that the condition of the world seems more like a zombie offensive. Something about zombies is becoming more intriguing to us. And I think I know what that something is.

Zombies are just so easy to kill.

When we think critically about monsters, we tend to classify them as personifications of what we fear. Frankenstein's monster illustrated our trepidation about untethered science; Godzilla was spawned from the fear of the atomic age; werewolves feed into an instinctual panic over predation and man's detachment from nature. Vampires and zombies share an imbedded anxiety about disease. It's easy to project a symbolic relationship between vampirism and AIDS (or vampirism and the loss of purity). From a creative standpoint these fear projections are narrative linch-pins; they turn creatures into ideas, and that's the point.

But what if the audience infers an entirely different metaphor?   5

What if contemporary people are less interested in seeing depictions of their unconscious fears and more attracted to allegories of how their day-to-day existence feels? That would explain why so many people watched the first episode of "The Walking Dead": They knew they would be able to relate to it.

A lot of modern life is exactly like slaughtering zombies.

If there's one thing we all understand about zombie killing, it's that the act is uncomplicated: you blast one in the brain from point-blank range (preferably with a shotgun). That's Step 1. Step 2 is doing the same thing to the next zombie that takes its place. Step 3 is identical to Step 2, and Step 4 isn't any different from Step 3. Repeat this process until (a) you perish, or (b) you run out of zombies. That's really the only viable strategy.

Every zombie war is a war of attrition. It's always a numbers game. And it's more repetitive than complex. In other words, zombie killing is philosophically similar to reading and deleting 400 work e-mails on a Monday morning or filling out paperwork that only generates more paperwork, or following Twitter gossip out of obligation, or performing tedious tasks in which the only

"Zombie killing is philosophically similar to reading and deleting 400 work e-mails on a Monday morning or filling out paperwork that only generates more paperwork."

true risk is being consumed by avalanche. The principal down-side to any zombie attack is that the zombies will never stop com-ing; the principal downside to life is that you will never be fin-ished with whatever it is you do.

The Internet reminds us of this every day. 10

Here's a passage from a youngish writer named Alice Gregory, taken from a recent essay on Gary Shteyngart's dystopic novel "Super Sad True Love Story" in the literary journal *n+1*: "It's hard not to think 'death drive' every time I go on the Internet," she writes. "Opening Safari is an actively destructive decision. I am asking that consciousness be taken away from me."

Ms. Gregory's self-directed fear is thematically similar to how the zombie brain is described by Max Brooks, author of the fic-tional oral history "World War Z" and its accompanying self-help manual, "The Zombie Survival Guide": "Imagine a computer pro-grammed to execute one function. This function cannot be paused, modified or erased. No new data can be stored. No new com-mands can be installed. This computer will perform that one func-tion, over and over, until its power source eventually shuts down."

This is our collective fear projection: that we will be consumed. Zombies are like the Internet and the media and every conversation we don't want to have. All of it comes at us endlessly (and thoughtlessly), and—if we surrender—we will be overtaken and absorbed. Yet this war is manageable, if not necessarily winnable. As long we keep deleting whatever's directly in front of us, we survive. We live to eliminate the zombies of tomorrow. We are able to remain human, at least for the time being. Our enemy is relentless and colossal, but also uncreative and stupid.

Battling zombies is like battling anything . . . or everything.

Because of the "Twilight" series it's easy to manufacture an argument in which zombies are merely replacing vampires as the monster of the moment, a designation that is supposed to matter for metaphorical, nonmonstrous reasons. But that kind of thinking is deceptive. The recent five-year spike in vampire interest is only about the multiplatform success of "Twilight," a brand that isn't about vampirism anyway. It's mostly about nostalgia for teenage chastity, the attractiveness of its film cast and the fact that contemporary fiction consumers tend to prefer long serialized novels that can be read rapidly. But this has still created a domino effect. The 2008 Swedish vampire film "Let the Right One In" was fantastic, but it probably wouldn't have been remade in the United States if "Twilight" had never existed. "The Gates" was an overt attempt by ABC to tap into the housebound, preteen "Twilight" audience; HBO's "True Blood" is a camp reaction to Robert Pattinson's flat earnestness.

The difference with zombies, of course, is that it's possible to like a specific vampire temporarily, which isn't really an option with the undead. Characters like Mr. Pattison's Edward Cullen in "Twilight" and Anne Rice's Lestat de Lioncourt, and even boring old Count Dracula can be multidimensional and erotic; it's possible to learn why they are and who they once were. Vampire love can be singular. Zombie love, however, is always communal. If you dig zombies, you dig the entire zombie concept. It's never personal. You're interested in what zombies signify, you like the way they move, and you understand what's required to stop them. And this is a reassuring attraction, because those aspects don't really shift. They've become shared archetypal knowledge.

A few days before Halloween I was in upstate New York with three other people, and we somehow ended up at the Barn of

Terror, outside a town call Lake Katrine. Entering the barn was mildly disturbing, although probably not as scary as going into an actual abandoned barn that didn't charge $20 and doesn't own its own domain name. Regardless, the best part was when we exited the terror barn and were promptly herded onto a school bus, which took us to a cornfield about a quarter of a mile away. The field was filled with amateur actors, some playing military personnel and others what they called the infected. We were told to run through the moonlit corn maze if we wanted to live; as we ran, armed soldiers yelled contradictory instructions while hissing zombies emerged from the corny darkness. It was designed to be fun, and it was. But just before we immersed ourselves in the corn, one of my companions sardonically critiqued the reality of our predicament.

"I know this is supposed to be scary," he said. "But I'm pretty confident about my ability to deal with a zombie apocalypse. I feel strangely informed about what to do in this kind of scenario."

I could not disagree. At this point who isn't? We all know how this goes: If you awake from a coma, and you don't immediately see a member of the hospital staff, assume a zombie takeover has transpired during your incapacitation. Don't travel at night and keep your drapes closed. Don't let zombies spit on you. If you knock a zombie down, direct a second bullet into its brain stem. But above all, do not assume that the war is over, because it never is. The zombies you kill today will merely be replaced by the zombies of tomorrow. But you can do this, my friend. It's disenchanting, but it's not difficult. Keep your finger on the trigger. Continue the termination. Don't stop believing. Don't stop deleting. Return your voice mails and nod your agreements. This is the zombies' world, and we just live in it. But we can live better.

For Discussion and Writing

1. How are zombies different from vampires, according to Klosterman? Why are these distinctions important to his argument?

2. Where in the essay does the writer use classification and division? Locate an example and explain how it furthers his main point.

3. **connections**   Like Klosterman, Guillermo del Toro and Chuck Hogan, in "Why Vampires Never Die" (p. 378), argue that our culture's monsters can illustrate or speak to our anxieties and fears. For Klosterman, zombies are the emblematic figure of our cultural

moment; for del Toro and Hogan, however, vampires are more representative. Which essay seems the most persuasive? How would you compare the authors' approaches to their topics? Do you agree with Klosterman's assessment of vampires? Would del Toro and Hogan agree with it?

4. Klosterman writes: "This is our collective fear projection: that we will be consumed" (par. 13). What do you think he means by this? Do you agree that this is a "collective fear"? Do you share it? What are other cultural manifestations of that fear?

LANE WALLACE

Can Video Games Teach Us How to Succeed in the Real World?

Lane Wallace is a writer, editor, speaker, pilot, and founder of the multi-author travel blog No Map. No Guide. No Limits. *She is also a correspondent for the* Atlantic *magazine, a columnist for* Flying *magazine, and the author of* Unforgettable: My 10 Best Flights *(2009). Her work has appeared in the* New York Times, ForbesLife, *the* Dallas Morning News, *and other publications. In this essay from the* Atlantic, *Wallace discusses the applicability of video game skills to life, work, and education—especially for teenagers who will spend "an average of 10,000 hours playing video games" by the time they are twenty years old. Do you think educators should use gaming as a "framework for teaching," as in the case of the experimental school Wallace describes below? Could a similar approach make adults more productive and efficient, as well?*

As the holiday sales season reaches its peak this week, video games are proving themselves, as always, as some of the biggest winners. When the new video game *World of Warcraft: Cataclysm* was released last week, it sold 3.3 million copies in the first 24 hours it was on the market. That feat comes only a week after Activision Blizzard (the company that produces the *World of Warcraft* game) set a five-day sales record of $650 million with its newest version of the popular *Call of Duty* first-person shooter video game. Not that game popularity is limited to the holiday season. A silly application game called Angry Birds (in which players catapult cartoon birds at fortresses built by pigs who've stolen the birds' eggs) has been downloaded by over 50 million people over the past year.

What's more, the time people spend playing all those games is increasing. The 12 million subscribers to *World of Warcraft* spend an accumulated 200 million hours, or so, a week engrossed in the game. And according to the Kaiser Family Foundation, the amount of time children spend playing video games has almost doubled in the past 10 years. By the time teenagers today reach the age of 20, they will have spent an average of 10,000 hours playing video games—or the equivalent of five working years. All of which is to say: Video games are huge. Very huge. And getting bigger. Exactly what one thinks about this development depends partly on how one views the possibilities or evils of technology. But a growing number of people are trying to figure out if or how other parts of life, from school to exercise to work to household chores, could be structured to capture the same kind of attention, energy focus, and potential addiction that video games inspire.

On one level, the results reveal some fascinating—if slightly embarrassing—facts about human responses and behaviors. For all of our advanced mental capacity, it appears we respond to stimuli very much like lab rats.

In an article in last week's *Science Times* John Tierney said a crucial element to the appeal of video games was the fact that they provided "instantaneous feedback and continual encouragement . . . while also providing occasional unexpected rewards." That assessment mirrors the research results of Dr. Paul Howard-Jones, a British neuroscientist who has found that (as a *Times* article reported earlier this fall), "children's engagement levels are higher when they are anticipating a reward but cannot predict whether they will get it."

As anyone who's ever taken college psychology knows, lab rats too will continue to hit a lever if they keep getting rewarded, but will stick with the task far more persistently if the rewards are unpredictable. I'd love to be able to argue that human motivations are more complicated than that (and, indeed, in some or many areas of behavior, they are), but the evidence for how easily we get transfixed by little bells, lights, and other sensory reward pellets is hard to ignore.

> There is no task on a video game—not even repetitive zapping of evil gnomes—that is anywhere near as unpleasant as cleaning a toilet.

In addition to video games, there is, for example, the increasing number and popularity of individual activity tracking devices

"By the time teenagers today reach the age of 20, they will have spent an average of 10,000 hours playing video games—or the equivalent of five working years."

and websites that allow people to record, upload and share (and in some cases get rewarded with charity donations for) their exercise during the day: FitBit, Nike Plus, Run Keeper, the Garmin FR 60, FitDay, FitWatch, MapMyRun, FitTracker . . . the list goes on and on, even though the phenomenon puzzles me just a bit.

Really? We're more motivated to exercise if a little gizmo lets us track each step, and we can see cool little trend lines or achieve new levels on a computer screen? Apparently. Come to think of it, running on a treadmill in pursuit of those disappearing dot-lines of hills and distance conquered doesn't, on the surface, differ all that much from the hamsters who run on an exercise wheel in pursuit of . . . well, whatever it is they're in pursuit of.

Not that our connection with rodents in the behavior/motivation category is all that surprising. There's a reason, after all, that researchers watch rat behavior in an effort to understand humans. But the comparisons have their limits. Even if it's true that we respond to immediate feedback, constant encouragement, and unexpected rewards, how transferable, really, is the video game framework to real life?

A *New York Times Magazine* article this fall profiled "Quest to 10 Learn," an experimental school in New York City that uses a video game format as a primary framework for teaching. Instead of grades, students achieve levels of experience. Assignments are gaming problems, or "quests" that often require the application of multi-disciplinary skills (English, history and math, for example) to complete. In some cases, the assignment involves the design of a video game, itself.

On some levels, using a video game approach to learning a subject makes a lot of sense, and might work well with kids. One of the big complaints kids have about school is that they can't see how or why what they're learning applies to their lives. Creating a game task that requires an algorithm to solve it, or English skills to describe a story line, or enough history knowledge to make a game realistic, provides context and illustrates the relevance for individual skills. And changing the emphasis from grades to knowledge is far more appropriate, in the big scheme of things. After all, it's not your grades that matter. It's the knowledge, skills, and understanding you acquire and retain after the test is over.

But what about adults? Can employers make working for a defense contractor a larger-scale version of *Star Wars: The Old Republic*? And can a website that offers video game rewards for doing real-world tasks like cleaning the toilets really motivate adults to do unpleasant tasks they otherwise would avoid? (Seriously—there's a website called ChoreWars that offers this service. Some testimonials on the site swear it helps, even though one reviewer called it one of the "Dumbest Start-Ups of 2007" when it was released.)

For all the appeal of gaming, I'm skeptical. Even if we respond well to silly little rewards or birds smashing against castle walls, video games do not operate like life. On several levels. For one thing, there is no task on a video game—not even repetitive zapping of evil gnomes, forging sword after sword after sword to earn cash credits, or even the endless running, running, running to get from point A to all other points—that is anywhere near as unpleasant as cleaning a toilet. Video games are, relatively speaking, all fun. Life is not always all fun.

Second, video games are linear. Your character proceeds along a task, then a sub-task, and perhaps spends some time on a diversionary point or resource-improving side story line. But each task requires singular focus, and is a fairly straightforward challenge. Real life is multi-dimensional, multi-task, and, in most cases, hugely complex. The problem of defeating a virtual wizard or conquering a town in a game is a tough, but straightforward, task. The problem of figuring out how to win over a big client who's unhappy about your team, while your factory is experiencing technical problems and delays, the competition is releasing a similar product and one of your executives is revealed as skimming from the expense till . . . is a problem less geared toward immediate feedback and constant encouragement, or easy-to-assess level achievements.

Third, there is no such thing as dismal failure in a video game. 15 Educators at Quest to Learn are trying to replace the sense of failure in kids with a more aspirational "haven't succeeded yet." It works in video games—you get killed 20 times, and finally defeat the opponent when you figure the game out well enough or develop better playing skills. It might also work in school. And even, on a large, philosophical level, life. But in a job, where you are paid a certain amount to perform a certain task, the "oh, well, you failed for six months, keep trying" approach is not realistic. In the real world, you are expected to perform at a certain level. It's not about learning. It's about doing. And both the possibility of real failure, and real consequences for that failure, is well . . . *real*.

We may love video games because they appeal to our craving for entertainment, reward and the possibility of achieving control over *some* world, even if it's not the real one. And we may be closer to rats than we'd like to admit, in terms of how easily we're motivated to perform repetitive activities in pursuit of small "pellet" rewards. Especially when they come in electronic form.

But there's still a difference between virtual reality and reality itself, and limits to how far the game analogy goes. That may be unfortunate, from the perspective of employers wishing to better motivate their employees. But on the other hand, no virtual reward is as sweet as those that come from real experience, real risk and real achievement. And those achievements are generally driven not by artificial frameworks, but by someone caring deeply about accomplishing the challenge at hand. Explaining a goal in terms of the compelling mission or quest it is furthering can certainly help create that motivation in employees or team members. The military relies on it, in fact. But engendering that kind of motivation often comes from a team's sense that their task is anything *but* a game. And that takes more than bells and whistles to sustain.

For Discussion and Writing

1. What are the three main differences between life and video games, according to Wallace?

2. Wallace includes a variety of statistics in her first two paragraphs. Why does she do this? How are they related to her overall point?

3. **connections** Compare Wallace's view of video games with Kyle Chayka's in "Why Video Games are Works of Art" (p. 396). Do you think Chayka would agree with Wallace about the practical uses of video games and their applications to "reality"? Why or why not?

4. According to the writer, a "growing number of people are trying to figure out if or how other parts of life, from school to exercise to work to household chores, could be structured to capture the same kind of attention, energy focus, and potential addiction that video games inspire" (par. 3). Do you think this is a good idea? How applicable are video games and the skills they require to school, work, and life, generally? You may want to structure your essay as a response to Wallace's article.

KYLE CHAYKA

Why Video Games Are Works of Art

Kyle Chayka (b. 1988) is an assistant editor at Artinfo.com, a visual art and culture site. His work has been published in the Atlantic, ART- news, LEAP, *and* Hyperallergic.com. *In the following piece from the* Atlantic, *Chayka responds to a blog post by longtime film critic Roger Ebert. For Ebert, video games cannot be works of art: "No one . . . has ever been able to cite a game worthy of comparison with the great poets, filmmakers, [and] novelists." Chayka strongly disagrees. In the process, he explores the nature and meaning of art, as well as our engagement with it: "A video game isn't just a game—it is a controlled passage through an overwhelming aesthetic experience." How do you define art? Where do you go to find "overwhelming aesthetic experience"?*

I've stood at the top of a grass-blown knoll overlooking the sea, a view that stretched to cover a land of sprawling islands traversed only by my sailboat and me. I have played a musical instrument that controls the wind. I've been a sword-wielding teenage adven- turer, a ghostbuster, and a short Italian plumber in search of his kidnapped love.

Robert Ebert would say that none of these experiences were real or meaningful because they happened through video games. In a recent post, simply entitled "Video games can never be art" published on his Chicago Sun-Times blog, the famed movie critic shoots down one of my favorite art forms as unable to fulfill his definition of 'art.' The critic reacts specifically to a TED talk[1] given by independent game developer Kellee Santiago of thatgame- company, a video game production firm known as a forerunner in a movement that takes for granted that video games are art.

[1]TED talk: Presentation at a Technology Entertainment and Design conference. [Editor's note.]

The trick, according to Santiago, is to make them great art. I agree.

But let's hear Ebert make his argument for himself. The critic first dismisses video games as art on the grounds that they are foremost games, and games, having rules and objectives, can be "won." Traditional art forms, "a story, a novel, a play," he writes, "are things you cannot win; you can only experience them." He measures video games against the Platonic definition of art as an imitation of nature and reality. Ebert writes, "[art] grows better the more it improves or alters nature through a passage through what we might call the artist's soul, or vision." He concedes that he thinks art is "usually the creation of one artist," and does not believe video games, the products of large teams, are capable of having a singular artistic "vision" behind them.

But video games are nothing if not experiential. They are visuals and music and poetry all wrapped up into a single package. A video game isn't just a game—it is a controlled passage through an overwhelming aesthetic experience. This is also the basis for my own definition of art as any sensory aesthetic experience that provokes an emotional response in its audience, be it wonder, anger, love, frustration or joy.

Yoshi's Island fills me with the same awe as a full-bloom   5
Matisse[2] canvas. Super Mario 64 is as much of a world to me as that created in *The Godfather*, with as much directorial vision as Coppola. And I can even explore it at my own free will! Video games are art because they inspire us and make us feel and give us experiences unreachable within the realm of the real. It doesn't matter if it's the fantasy of Pokémon and taking pride in caring for something as it grows or Ta-Nehisi Coates' escapist immersion in World of Warcraft as a place with politics and race and social conflicts all its own. These emotions and experiences are gifts given to us by video games just as any other art form.

Ebert denies video games the status of art on a de-facto basis, having never played one himself; no video game yet has deserved his "attention long enough to play it." This is the biggest red flag in a series of holes in his argument. After all, aren't movies also produced by a team, led perhaps by a director? Video games likewise have their auteurs, directors whose overwhelming vision is

[2]Matisse: French painter and sculptor Henry Matisse (1869–1954). [Editor's note.]

the soul of their games. Nintendo's Shigeru Miyamoto, creator of the Super Mario, Legend of Zelda and Donkey Kong series of video games, is acclaimed as the greatest. Miyamoto's oeuvre, with its postmodern sense of play and worlds-within-worlds-within-worlds, is as defining a body of art as we can hope to have for the twenty-first century.

Sure, video games can be "won," but "winning" a video game isn't just earning the most points. Winning, in most single-player video games, involves completing the game's narrative arc, reaching the end of the plot in a way very similar to a movie's climax and denouement. Video games don't just stop at the narrative resolution, though. "Winning" often gains the player the ability to explore and wander at will through the game, an experience driven by aesthetics alone. Beat Super Mario World and you'll go back and play through levels simply because they're as beautiful as Kandinsky's[3] Blaue Reiter paintings. Finish the Legend of Zelda: Ocarina of Time and head back to the mountains to look out over the world, to feel the virtual wind. Video games are, if anything, more experiential than films.

To conclude his post, Ebert writes, "No one in or out of the field has ever been able to cite a game worthy of comparison with the great poets, filmmakers, [and] novelists." Here's my shot: the sailing sequences in The Legend of Zelda: Wind Waker are worthy of comparison to Coleridge's Mariner.[4] Pokémon is a coming of age story that doesn't pander or condescend to its young audience, a self-guided Catcher in the Rye.[5] Miyamoto has said that he came up with the original Zelda game as a "miniature garden that [gamers] can put inside their drawer." Likewise, the endless castle of Super Mario 64 is certainly a "world in a grain of sand."

Video games allow us, as William Blake[6] says, as children do, as Miyamoto does, to "hold infinity in the palms of your hand and eternity in an hour." The question is not if video games qualify as art, or if video games can stand up to the art of the past, rather, it

---

[3]Kandinsky: Russian artist Wassily Wassilyevich Kandinsky (1866–1944). [Editor's note.]

[4]Mariner: "Rime of the Ancient Mariner," poem by English Romantic poet Samuel Taylor Coleridge (1772–1834). [Editor's note.]

[5]*Catcher in the Rye*: 1951 novel by American writer J. D. Salinger (1919–2010). [Editor's note.]

[6]William Blake (1757–1827): English poet and painter. [Editor's note.]

is how to find a new language to speak of video games as art. In this Ebert fails entirely.

For Discussion and Writing

1. What primary distinction does Roger Ebert draw between "art" and "games," according to Chayka?
2. Chayka refers to many different works of art, literature, and film. How do these specific references support his argument? Why are they important to his main point?
3. **connections**   For Chayka, video games provide profound, powerful, and multilayered aesthetic experiences. How does his account of gaming's attractions and effects differ from Lane Wallace's in "Can Video Games Teach Us How to Succeed in the Real World?" (p. 390)? Whose view seems more persuasive, Chayka's or Wallace's? Are the two accounts mutually exclusive?
4. Chayka's argument with Ebert is, in part, a matter of definition: "A video game isn't just a game—it is a controlled passage through an overwhelming aesthetic experience. This is also the basis for my own definition of art as any sensory aesthetic experience that provokes an emotional response in its audience, be it wonder, anger, love, frustration or joy" (par. 4). Do you agree with Chayka about the meaning of art? How would you define it? What specific examples would you cite to support your definition? Would video games count as "art"?

Acknowledgments (continued from p. ii)

Benjamin R. Barber. "Overselling Capitalism with Consumerism." Published originally in the *Los Angeles Times*, April 4, 2007. Copyright © 2007 by Benjamin Barber. Reprinted with the permission of the author.

Roland Barthes. "Toys." From *Mythologies* by Roland Barthes, translated by Annette Lavers and published by Vintage Books. Translation copyright © 1972 by Jonathan Cape Ltd. Reprinted by permission of Hill and Wang, a division of Farrar, Straus and Giroux, LLC, and in Canada by permission of the Random House Group Limited.

Bill Bryson. "The Hard Sell: Advertising in America." Chapter 14 from *Made in America* by Bill Bryson, pp. 235–47. Copyright © 1994 by Bill Bryson. Reprinted by permission of HarperCollins Publishers.

Raquel Cepeda. "The N-Word Is Flourishing Among Generation Hip-Hop Latinos: Why Should We Care Now?" *Village Voice*, October 22, 2008. Copyright © 2008 by Raquel Cepeda. Reprinted by permission of the author.

Kyle Chayka. "Why Video Games Are Works of Art." *Atlantic*, May 5, 2010. Copyright © 2010, The Atlantic Media Company as published in the *Atlantic*. Distributed by Tribune Media Services.

Aymar Jean Christian. "The Problem of YouTube." *Flow*, February 11, 2011, http://flowtv.org/2011/02/the-problem-of-youtube/. Copyright © 2011 by Aymar Jean Christian. Reprinted by permission of the author.

Donna Woolfolk Cross. "Propaganda: How Not To Be Bamboozled." From *Speaking of Words: A Language Reader*, edited by James MacKillop and Donna Woolfolk Cross. Copyright © 1977 by Donna Woolfolk Cross. Reprinted by permission of the author.

Guillermo del Toro and Chuck Hogan. "Why Vampires Never Die." From the *New York Times*, July 31, 2009. Copyright © 2009 The New York Times. All rights reserved. Used by permission and protected by the copyright laws of the United States. The printing, copying, redistribution, or retransmission of this content without express written permission is prohibited.

Alonso Duralde. "Why Are So Many Films for Latinos Bad?" *Salon*, January 28, 2011, http://www.salon.com/2011/01/28/from_prada_to_nada_latino_film/. This article first appeared in Salon.com, at http://www.Salon.com. An online version remains in the *Salon* archives. Reprinted with permission.

The Economist. "The Ultimate Marketing Machine." July 6, 2006. Copyright © 2006 by The Economist Magazine. Reproduced with permission of the *Economist* via Copyright Clearance Center.

Barbara Ehrenreich. "Selling in Minnesota." From *Nickel and Dimed: On (Not) Getting By in America* by Barbara Ehrenreich. Copyright © 2001 by Barbara Ehrenreich. Reprinted by permission of Henry Holt and Company, LLC.

Winston Fletcher. "Art or Puffery? A Defence of Advertising." *New Humanist*, June 2008, http://newhumanist.org.uk/1804/art-or-puffery-a-defence-of-advertising. Copyright © 2008. Reprinted by permission of the Rationalist Association.

Malcolm Gladwell. "The Sports Taboo." Copyright © 1997 by Malcolm Gladwell. Originally published in the *New Yorker*. Reprinted by permission of the author.

Mark Greif. "The Reality of Reality Television." *n+1* no. 3, "Reality Principle" (Fall 2005); http://nplusonemag.com/reality-reality-television. Copyright © 2005 by Mark Greif. Reprinted by permission.

Robert Nathan and Jo-Ann Mort. "Remembering *Norma Rae*." Reprinted with permission from the March 12, 2007, issue of the *Nation*. For subscription information, call 1-800-333-8536. Portions of each week's *Nation* magazine can be accessed at http://www.thenation.com.

Neil Postman. "The Judgment of Thamus." From *Technopoly* by Neil Postman. Copyright © 1992 by Neil Postman. Used by permission of Alfred A. Knopf, a division of Random House, Inc.

Virginia Postrel. "In Praise of Chain Stores." *Atlantic Monthly*, December 2006. Copyright © 2006 by Virginia Postrel. Reprinted by permission of the author.

Frank Rose. "The Art of Immersion: Fear of Fiction." From *The Art of Immersion: How the Digital Generation Is Remaking Hollywood, Madison Avenue, and the Way We Tell Stories* by Frank Rose. Copyright © 2011 by Frank Rose. Used by permission of W. W. Norton & Company, Inc. This excerpt originally appeared in the March 10, 2011, issue of *Wired* magazine.

Rob Ruck. "Where Have African-American Baseball Players Gone?" *Salon*, March 5, 2011; http://www.salon.com/2011/03/05/race_in_baseball/singleton/. This article first appeared in Salon.com, at http://www.Salon.com. An online version remains in the *Salon* archives. Reprinted with permission.

Nikil Saval. "Wall of Sound: The iPod Has Changed the Way We Listen to Music." *Slate*, March 28, 2011, http://www.slate.com/articles/arts/culturebox/2011/03/wall_of_sound.html. Excerpted from "Wall of Sound," *n+1* no. 11, "Dual Power" (Spring 2011). Copyright © 2011 by Nikil Saval. Reprinted by permission of the n+1 Foundation.

Eric Schlosser. "Behind the Counter." Excerpt from *Fast Food Nation: The Dark Side of the All-American Meal* by Eric Schlosser. Copyright © 2001 by Eric Schlosser. Reprinted by permission of Houghton Mifflin Harcourt Publishing Company. All rights reserved.

Linda Seger. "Creating the Myth." From *Making a Good Script Great* by Linda Seger. Copyright © 1987 by Linda Seger. Reprinted by permission of the author.

Clay Shirky. "Gin, Television, and Social Surplus." http://www.herecomes everybody.org/2008/04/looking-for-the-mouse.html. Available under a Creative Commons Attribution-Noncommercial-Share Alike 3.0 United States License: http://creativecommons.org/licenses/by-sa/3.0/.

Susan Sontag. "The Imagination of Disaster." As published in *Commentary* magazine, October 1965. Copyright © 1965 by Susan Sontag. Used by permission of the Wylie Agency LLC.

Jason Tanz. "Selling Down: The Marketing of the Hip-Hop Nation." From *Other People's Property: A Shadowy History of Hip-Hop in White America* by Jason Tanz. Copyright © 2007 by Jason Tanz. Reprinted by permission of Bloomsbury Publishing Plc.

Sherry Turkle. "Can You Hear Me Now?" *Forbes Magazine*, May 7, 2007, http://www.forbes.com/forbes/2007/0507/176.html. Reprinted by permission of Forbes Media LLC © 2011.

Lane Wallace. "Can Video Games Teach Us How to Succeed in the Real World?" This essay first appeared on theatlantic.com in December 2010. Copyright © 2010 by Lane Wallace. Reprinted by permission of the author. All rights reserved.

George Will. "Reality Television: Oxymoron." From the *Washington Post*, June 21, 2001. Copyright © 2001 The Washington Post. All rights reserved. Used by permission and protected by the copyright laws of the United States. The printing, copying, redistribution, or retransmission of the material without express written permission is prohibited.

Marie Winn. "Television: The Plug-In Drug." "Family Life" from *The Plug-In Drug: Television, Children and Family, Revised and Updated—25th Anniversary Edition* by Marie Winn. Copyright © 1977, 1985, 2002 by Marie Winn Miller. Used by permission of Viking Penguin, a division of Penguin Group (USA) Inc.

PHOTO CREDITS

Page 16: Woman with shopping bags. © Floresco Productions/Getty Images.

Page 20: Spam. © Sang An/FoodPix/Getty Images.

Page 26: Boy with model train. © Simon Battensby/Photographers Choice/Getty Images.

Page 32: Olive Garden. © Bloomberg via Getty Images.

Page 37: Credit card trap. © Peter Scholey/Photographers Choice/Getty Images.

Page 46: Wal-Mart greeter. © J.D. Pooley/Getty Images.

Page 51: McDonald's worker. © Justin Sullivan/Getty Images.

Page 63: Weasel. © Keven Law/Flickr/Getty Images.

Page 75: Mitt Romney in Iowa. © Chip Somodevilla/Getty Images.

Page 76: Barack Obama bowling. © Stan Honda/AFP/Getty Images.

Page 90: Youth rapper. © Aaron Cobbett/Stone/Getty Images.

Page 108: Free Rice poster. © World Food Programme, 2011.

Page 109: Marines poster. Courtesy of The United States Marine Corps and the advertising agency of record, JWT.

Page 110: Kinky-Curly advertisement. Courtesy of Kinky-Curly.

Page 111: M&M's advertisement. © Mars Chocolate, North America.

Page 112: Dress Barn advertisement. Courtesy of Dress Barn.

Page 123: Kodak advertisement. © Hulton Archive/Getty Images.

Page 149: Sean Combs hosts white party. © Mat Szwajkos/Getty Images.

Page 164: Soulja Boy. © Isaac Brekken/WireImage/Getty Images.

Page 170: Jackie Robinson. © Kidwiler Collection/Diamond Images/Getty Images.

Page 191: Father and toddler son with MP3 player. © PhotoAlto/Sandro Di Carlo Darsa/Getty Images.

Page 205: Technicians in computer lab. © SuperStock, Inc./Getty Images.

Page 249: Teens on sofa watching television. © Howard Kingsnorth/Getty Images.

Page 268: *Mary Tyler Moore Show* still. © CBS Photo Archive/Getty Images.

Page 270: *30 Rock* still. © WireImage/Getty Images.

Page 280: *Sopranos* still. © HBO/Photofest.

Page 300: *Survivor: Redemption Island* still. © CBS Photo Archive/Getty Images.

Page 312: *The Legend of Bagger Vance* still. © Getty Images.

Page 321: *War of the Worlds* still. © Paramount/Photofest.

Page 337: *Star Wars* still. © Twentieth Century-Fox Film Corporation/Photofest.

Page 348: *Tortilla Soup* still. © The Samuel Goldwyn Company/Photofest.

Page 354: *Wall Street* (2010) still. © Twentieth Century-Fox Film Corporation/ Photofest.

Page 359: *Norma Rae* still. © Twentieth Century-Fox Film Corporation/Photofest.

Page 368: *Avatar* poster. © Twentieth Century-Fox Film Corporation/Photofest.

Page 376: *The Incredible Hulk* comic book cover. © Photofest.

Page 380: Bela Lugosi as Dracula. © Michael Ochs Archives/Getty Images.

Page 382: *Twilight New Moon* still. © Summit Entertainment/Photofest.

Page 386: *Walking Dead* still. © AMC/Photofest.

Page 392: Boy playing computer game. © Nigel Treblin/AFP/Getty Images).

Index of Authors and Titles

Art of Immersion: Fear of Fiction, The (Rose), 366
Art or Puffery? A Defense of Advertising (Fletcher), 114
Atwood, Margaret
  Debtor's Prism, 36

Barber, Benjamin
  Overselling Capitalism with Consumerism, 15
Barthes, Roland
  Toys, 25
Behind the Counter (Schlosser), 49
Bryson, Bill
  The Hard Sell: Advertising in America, 120

Can Video Games Teach Us How to Succeed in the Real World? (Wallace), 390
Can You Hear Me Now? (Turkle), 227
Cepeda, Raquel
  The N-Word Is Flourishing Among Generation Hip-Hop Latinos: Why Should We Care Now?, 138
Chayka, Kyle
  Why Video Games Are Works of Art, 396
Christian, Aymar Jean
  The Problem of YouTube, 216
Creating the Myth (Seger), 334

Debtor's Prism (Atwood), 36
del Toro, Guillermo, and Chuck Hogan
  Why Vampires Never Die, 378
Duralde, Alonso
  Why Are So Many Films for Latinos Bad?, 346

Economist, The
  The Ultimate Marketing Machine, 97
Ehrenreich, Barbara
  Selling in Minnesota, 44
End of Spam Shame: On Class, Colonialism, and Canned Meat, The (Kim), 19
End of White America?, The (Hsu), 144

Fletcher, Winston
  Art or Puffery? A Defense of Advertising, 114

Gin, Television, and Social Surplus (Shirky), 236
Gladwell, Malcolm
  The Sports Taboo, 174
Greif, Mark
  The Reality of Reality Television, 293
Groen, Rick
  Why Hollywood Hates Capitalism, 352

Hard Sell: Advertising in America, The (Bryson), 120
Hip-Hop Is No Longer Cooler Than Me (Kix), 162
Hsu, Hua
  The End of White America?, 144

Imagination of Disaster, The (Sontag), 316
In Praise of Chain Stores (Postrel), 30
Is Facebook a Fad? (Manjoo), 222

Johnson, Steven
  Watching TV Makes You Smarter, 275

Jones, Gerard
Violent Media Is Good for Kids,
372
Judgment of Thamus, The (Postman),
200

Kempley, Rita
*Mystical Black Characters Play
Complex Cinematic Role*, 310
Kim, Sylvie
*The End of Spam Shame: On Class,
Colonialism, and Canned Meat*, 19
Kix, Paul
*Hip-Hop Is No Longer Cooler Than
Me*, 162
Klosterman, Chuck
*My Zombie, My Self: Why Modern
Life Feels Rather Undead*, 384
Kubey, Robert, and Mihaly
Csikszentmihalyi
*Television Addiction Is No Mere
Metaphor*, 245

Levy, Ariel
*Women and the Rise of Raunch
Culture*, 158
Lies, Erica
Mary Tyler More, 266
Lutz, William
*With These Words, I Can Sell You
Anything*, 62

Manjoo, Farhad
Is Facebook a Fad?, 222
Mary Tyler More (Lies), 266
*My Zombie, Myself: Why Modern Life
Feels Rather Undead* (Klosterman),
384
*Mystical Black Characters Play
Complex Cinematic Role*
(Kempley), 310

Nathan, Robert, and Jo-Ann Mort
Remembering Norma Rae, 357
*N-Word Is Flourishing Among
Generation Hip-Hop Latinos: Why
Should We Care Now?, The*
(Cepeda), 138

*Overselling Capitalism with
Consumerism* (Barber), 15

Postman, Neil
The Judgment of Thamus, 200
Postrel, Virginia
In Praise of Chain Stores, 30
Problem of YouTube, The (Christian),
216
*Propaganda: How Not To Be
Bamboozled* (Woolfolk Cross), 71

Reality of Reality Television, The
(Greif), 293
Reality Television: Oxymoron (Will),
289
Remembering Norma Rae (Nathan/
Mort), 357
Rose, Frank
*The Art of Immersion: Fear of
Fiction*, 366
Ruck, Rob
*Where Have African-American
Baseball Players Gone?*, 168

Saval, Nikil
*Wall of Sound: The iPod has Changed
the Way We Listen to Music*, 188
Schlosser, Eric
Behind the Counter, 49
Seger, Linda
Creating the Myth, 334
*Selling Down: The Marketing of the
Hip-Hop Nation* (Tanz), 87
Selling in Minnesota (Ehrenreich), 44
Shirky, Clay
Gin, Television, and Social Surplus,
236
Sontag, Susan
The Imagination of Disaster, 316
Sports Taboo, The (Gladwell), 174

Tanz, Jason
*Selling Down: The Marketing of the
Hip-Hop Nation*, 87
*Television Addiction Is No Mere
Metaphor* (Kubey/
Csikszentmihalyi), 245

Television: The Plug-In Drug (Winn), 256
Toys (Barthes), 25
Turkle, Sherry
  Can You Hear Me Now?, 227

Ultimate Marketing Machine, The (*The Economist*), 97

Violent Media Is Good for Kids (Jones), 372

Wall of Sound: The iPod Has Changed the Way We Listen to Music (Saval), 188
Wallace, Lane
  Can Video Games Teach Us How to Succeed in the Real World?, 390
Watching TV Makes You Smarter (Johnson), 275

Where Have African-American Baseball Players Gone? (Ruck), 168
Why Are So Many Films for Latinos Bad? (Duralde), 346
Why Hollywood Hates Capitalism (Groen), 352
Why Vampires Never Die (del Toro/ Hogan), 378
Why Video Games Are Works of Art (Chayka), 396
Will, George F.
  Reality Television: Oxymoron, 289
Winn, Marie
  Television: The Plug-In Drug, 256
With These Words, I Can Sell You Anything (Lutz), 62
Women and the Rise of Raunch Culture (Levy), 158
Woolfolk Cross, Donna
  Propaganda: How Not To Be Bamboozled, 71